Shades of Gray in the Changing Religious Markets of China

Religion and the Social Order

AN OFFICIAL PUBLICATION OF THE ASSOCIATION
FOR THE SOCIOLOGY OF RELIGION

General Editor

Inger Furseth (University of Oslo, Norway)

Editorial Committee

Lori Beaman (University of Ottawa, Canada)
Michele Dillon (University of New Hampshire, USA)
David Herbert (Kingston University London, UK)
Juan Marco Vaggione (Universidad Nacional de Córdoba, Argentina)
Rhys Williams (Loyola University, Chicago, USA)
Melissa M. Wilcox (University of California at Riverside, USA)

VOLUME 28

The titles published in this series are listed at *brill.com/reso*

Shades of Gray in the Changing Religious Markets of China

Edited by

Fenggang Yang, Jonathan E. E. Pettit and Chris White

BRILL

LEIDEN | BOSTON

Library of Congress Cataloging-in-Publication Data

Names: Yang, Fenggang, editor. | Pettit, Jonathan E. E., editor. | White,
 Christopher M., editor. | Religious Groups in a Rapidly Changing Society:
 East Asia (Conference) (2016 : Seoul, Korea)
Title: Shades of gray in the changing religious markets of China / edited by
 Fenggang Yang, Jonathan E.E. Pettit, and Chris White.
Description: Leiden ; Boston : Brill, [2021] | Series: Religion and the social order,
 1061-5210 ; volume 28 | Includes bibliographical references and index. |
 Summary: "This volume is a collection of studies of various religious groups
 in the changing religious markets of China: registered Christian congregations,
 unregistered house churches, Daoist masters, and folk-religious temples.
 The contributing authors are emerging Chinese scholars who apply and
 respond to Fenggang Yang's tricolor market theory of religion in China: the red,
 black, and gray markets for legal, illegal, and ambiguous religious groups,
 respectively. These ethnographic studies demonstrate a great variety within
 the gray market, and fluidity across different markets. The volume concludes
 with Fenggang Yang reviewing the introduction of the religious market theories
 to China and formally responding to major criticisms of these theories.
 Conributors are HE Ling, HU Mengyin, Ke-hsien HUANG, JIANG Shen,
 KONG Deji, LI Hui, LIN Weizhi, Yan LIU, Jonathan E. E. Pettit, WANG Ling,
 Chris White, XIAO Yunze, YAN Jun, Fenggang Yang, YUAN Hao, ZHANG
 Zhipeng, ZHAO Cuicui, ZHAO Hao"– Provided by publisher.
Identifiers: LCCN 2021017452 (print) | LCCN 2021017453 (ebook) |
 ISBN 9789004456730 (hardback : acid-free paper) |
 ISBN 9789004456747 (ebook)
Subjects: LCSH: Religion and state–China–History–21st century–Congresses. |
 Religion and law–China–History–21st century–Congresses. | Religion and
 sociology–China–History–21st century–Congresses. | China–Religion–
 21st century–Congresses.
Classification: LCC BL65.S8 S53 2021 (print) | LCC BL65.S8 (ebook) |
 DDC 322/.10951–dc23
LC record available at https://lccn.loc.gov/2021017452
LC ebook record available at https://lccn.loc.gov/2021017453

Typeface for the Latin, Greek, and Cyrillic scripts: "Brill". See and download: brill.com/brill-typeface.

ISSN 1061-5210
ISBN 978-90-04-45673-0 (hardback)
ISBN 978-90-04-45674-7 (e-book)

Copyright 2021 by Fenggang Yang, Jonathan E. E. Pettit, and Chris White. Published by Koninklijke Brill NV, Leiden, The Netherlands.
Koninklijke Brill NV incorporates the imprints Brill, Brill Hes & De Graaf, Brill Nijhoff, Brill Rodopi, Brill Sense, Hotei Publishing, mentis Verlag, Verlag Ferdinand Schöningh and Wilhelm Fink Verlag.
Koninklijke Brill NV reserves the right to protect this publication against unauthorized use. Requests for re-use and/or translations must be addressed to Koninklijke Brill NV via brill.com or copyright.com.

This book is printed on acid-free paper and produced in a sustainable manner.

Contents

Note to the Reader   IX
Abbreviations   X
List of Figures and Tables   XI
Notes on Contributors   XII

Introduction   1
   Fenggang YANG, Jonathan E. E. PETTIT, and Chris WHITE

PART 1
Between Red and Black

1   Becoming "Patriotic" for God
    Why Churches Join State-Sanctioned Protestant Organizations   17
      Ke-hsien HUANG

2   The Transformation of Mentuhui (Society of Disciples)
    Constructing Legitimacy and Adapting to a Changing Religious Economy   35
      YUAN Hao

3   Between Interests and Politics
    The Changing Status of Two Protestant Churches in China's Tricolor Religious Market   60
      LI Hui

4   State Appropriation of Society
    Refashioning the Miao through a Public Display of Christianity   80
      KONG Deji

5   Worship of the God of Wealth and a Portrait of Rural Public Life   99
      ZHAO Hao

PART 2
Group Competition

6   Competing Interests and Conflicting Beliefs
    A Case Study of a Seaside Church in Zhejiang   119
        ZHAO Cuicui

7   House Churches in Northern Jiangsu
    Patterns of Transformation and the State Effect   138
        XIAO Yunze

8   Demands for Faith, Institutional Constraints, and Niche Choices of an Urban Church in China   164
        ZHANG Zhipeng

9   The Tricolor Market in Yunnan
    The Christian Life of the Hani   183
        JIANG Shen and HE Ling

PART 3
Beyond Religious Regulation

10 Between the Sacred and the Secular
    Zhanjiang Daoshi and the Religious Economy   207
        YAN Jun and LIN Weizhi

11 Urbanization and the Transformation of Migrant Worker Churches
    A Case Study of Mount of Olives Church in Beijing   238
        YUAN Hao

12 Modern Individuals in Imagined Communities
    An Anthropological Examination of Artist Churches in Songzhuang, Beijing   260
        HU Mengyin

13 Choosing between God's Will and the Law
    A Study of Chinese Christians' Dilemma over Fertility Desires and Behaviors   280
        WANG Ling

14 Online Religious Communities in a WeChat Age
    From Public Accounts to Megagroups   299
       Yan LIU

    Conclusion: Whence and Whither Religious Markets in China   322
       Fenggang YANG

    Bibliography   355
    Index   375

Note to the Reader

Chinese characters are given for names of individuals, places, and important terms under discussion. Characters are not provided for pseudonyms or names of well-known places. In general, footnoted references do not include Chinese characters; see the bibliography for full Chinese citations for articles, chapters, or books in Chinese. When a pseudonym is used for a person, place, or organization, it is retained in the bibliography.

The names of contributors to this volume are given with the surname in capital letters. When Chinese names are referenced in the text, typically they are given in the normal Chinese order of surname, given name. When Chinese scholars who publish in English are referenced, however, the name under which they publish will typically be used (which often may be written in the order given name, surname). For example, Fenggang Yang (given name, surname) will be used in the text when referring to publications in English, but Yang Fenggang also appears when there is discussion of his works in Chinese.

When Chinese translations of English scholarship are referenced, both the English and Chinese (pinyin) titles are given in the first instance in each chapter. Subsequent footnotes only include the original English citation. To make this more useful to an English-reading audience, all page citations refer to the English editions, as do all quotations.

The rate of 1 USD = 6.5 RMB is used to convert monetary amounts in all chapters. This is based on the average conversion rate in 2015. In some instances, an approximate USD amount is given.

All biblical citations follow the New International Version (NIV).

Abbreviations

AG	Assemblies of God
CCC	China Christian Council
CCP	Chinese Communist Party
CFPS	China Family Panel Studies
CGSS	Chinese General Social Survey
CIM	China Inland Mission
CMA	Christian and Missionary Alliance
CNNIC	Chinese Internet Network Information Center
CRCS	Center on Religion and Chinese Society
PRC	People's Republic of China
RAB	Religious Affairs Bureau
SARA	State Administration of Religious Affairs
TJC	True Jesus Church
TSPM	Three-Self Patriotic Movement
UFWD	United Front Work Department

Figures and Tables

Figures

3.1   Transformations in the Tricolor Market   75
4.1   The choir as the primary source in refashioning the Miao public image   95
8.1   Conditions for maintaining a healthy cycle of growth in a house church   172
10.1 The secular–sacred continuum of religious consumers, an expansion of Stark and Finke's category of "believers" in their model of religious markets   215
10.2 The secular–sacred continuum of religious providers, an expansion of Stark and Finke's category of "suppliers" in their model of religious economies/markets   217
10.3 Personal connections among three generations of Daoshi in Zhanjiang   221
15.1 Number of articles and theses in CNKI with the keywords "Tricolor Market & Yang Fenggang," "Religious Market & Yang Fenggang," and "Stark & Yang Fenggang"   331

Tables

2.1   Comparison of characteristics of religious organizations: Three-Self Patriotic Movement (TSPM), Mentuhui, and the Church of Almighty God (CAG)   56
4.1   Performance schedule for the Fumin Xiaoshuijing Chorus, 2003–2008. Source: Zhao Dianhua, "Miaozhai feichu jinfenghuang—ji Fuminxian Xiaoshuijing miaozu nongmin hechang tuan," *Jinri minzu*, 2008.5: 21–24   92
14.1 Responses to the top three articles released on "Ijingjie" in November 2016 as of December 5, 2016, with average responses to all articles released by the account in November 2016   306
14.2 Responses to the top three articles released on "Wang Yi's Microphone" in November 2016 as of December 5, 2016, with average responses to all articles released by the account in November 2016   307

Notes on Contributors

He Ling 何玲
is a graduate student in Religion at Yunnan Minzu University.

Hu Mengyin 胡梦茵
is a Ph.D. candidate in Anthropology at East China Normal University. She (along with Huang Jianbo) is the author of "Becoming Christians: Prayers and Subject Formation in an Urban Church in China" in *Approaching Religion*, and "Trends and Reflections: A Review of Empirical Studies of Christianity in Mainland China since 2000" in *Review of Religion and Chinese Society*.

Ke-hsien Huang 黃克先
is currently an Associate Professor of Sociology at National Taiwan University. He is the author of the book *Homeland, Host Country, and Heaven: A Large-Scale Religious Conversion to Christianity among Chinese Political Refugees in the 1950s* (in Chinese). He has published several articles on Chinese Pentecostalism in academic journals such as *Journal for the Scientific Study of Religion*, *Social Compass*, *Taiwanese Journal of Sociology*, and *Taiwanese Sociology*.

Jiang Shen 姜伸
a researcher at Yunnan Minzu University, is mainly engaged in the sociology of religion. He is the author of "Life Practice and Cultural Reconstruction: An Investigation of *mengsong aini* Traditional Culture" in *Mingri fengshang* (in Chinese).

Kong Deji 孔德继
is a doctoral student in Rural Development and Management at the China Agricultural University. He is the author of "Research on the Narrative and Communication of Homecoming Articles during Spring Festival" in the *Journal of Modern Communication* (in Chinese).

Li Hui 李辉
received a Ph.D. in Religious Studies at the Chinese University of Hong Kong and is an Assistant Researcher at the Institute of Religious Studies, Shanghai Academy of Social Science. His research interests are contemporary Chinese Christianity, church–state relations, and the Chinese Pentecostal-Charismatic movement. He is the author of "Spiritual Politics in China: A Comparative

Study of City Z in Zhejiang Province and City A in Henan Province" in *Sociology of Religion* (in Chinese).

LIN Weizhi 林伟挚
is a doctoral student at the School of Sociology and Political Science, Shanghai University. He is the author of "The Dynamic Equilibrium of Sacred Space and Belief Norms: A Case Study of the Changes of Xianghuo-house in Leizhou Peninsula" in the *Journal of Nanjing Agricultural University (Social Sciences Edition)* (in Chinese).

Yan LIU 刘焱
is a Ph.D. student majoring in Religion and Culture at the School of Theology and Religious Studies at the Catholic University of America.

Jonathan E. E. PETTIT 裴玄铮
is Assistant Professor of Chinese Religions at the University of Hawaiʻi. He received a dual Ph.D. in Religious Studies and Chinese Literature from the University of Indiana. He is the author of *Library of Clouds: A Bibliographic History of Daoist Scriptures* (Hawaiʻi, 2020).

WANG Ling 王羚
is a senior correspondent for *China Business News* (*Diyi caijing ribao* 第一财经日报) who specializes in Chinese demographic and birth control policies, fertility desires by age, changes in fertility behaviors, and the aging of the population.

Chris WHITE 白克瑞
received his Ph.D. in Modern Chinese History from Xiamen University. He has been a researcher at the Max Planck Institute for the Study of Religious and Ethnic Diversity and is currently the Assistant Director of the Center on Religion and the Global East at Purdue University. He is the author of *Sacred Webs: The Social Lives and Networks of Minnan Protestants, 1840s–1920s* (Brill, 2017) and the editor of *Protestantism in Xiamen, Then and Now* (Palgrave, 2019).

XIAO Yunze 肖云泽
received a Ph.D. degree in Sociology from East China Normal University and is currently a lecturer at the Zhejiang Center of Public Opinion and Research at Zhejiang University of Technology. He is the author of "Belief Patterns and Land Rules: A Case Study of Christianity Based on Land-Control Act in Province A" in *LOGOS & PNEUMA: Chinese Journal of Theology*.

Yan Jun 严俊

is a Lecturer at the School of Sociology and Political Science, Shanghai University. His research interests include economic sociology and the sociology of religion. He is the author of "What Makes Art Art?" in the *China Agricultural University Journal (Social Sciences Edition)* (in Chinese).

Fenggang Yang 杨凤岗

is Professor of Sociology at Purdue University and the founding director of the Center on Religion and the Global East. He is also the founding editor of *Review of Religion and Chinese Society*. He was elected as the President of the Society for the Scientific Study of Religion (2014–2015) and served as the first President of the East Asian Society for the Scientific Study of Religion (2018–2020). His most recent book is *Atlas of Religion in China: Social and Geographical Contexts* (Brill, 2018).

Yuan Hao 袁浩

is a postdoctoral fellow at the School of Philosophy, Beijing Normal University.

Zhang Zhipeng 张志鹏

is a Visiting Professor of Economics at Anhui University of Technology. His research interests include industrial economics, religious economics, and economic development theory. He has published several articles in Chinese academic journals, such as *Academia Bimestrie, Theory,* and *Dongyue Tribune*.

Zhao Cuicui 赵翠翠

holds a doctorate in Law and is an Associate Researcher at the Institute for Religius Studies at the Shanghai Academy of Social Science. Her specialization is religious sociology. She is the author of "Enlightenment Discourse and China's Faith Order" in the *Journal of East China Normal University (Philosophy and Social Sciences)* (in Chinese).

Zhao Hao 赵浩

is an Assistant Professor in the Department of Sociology, Southeast University. His areas of specialization include ethics, theoretical anthropology, and ethics and sociology. He has published several articles in academic journals, including *Journal of Southeast University, Journal of Philosophical Analysis,* and *Studies in Ethics*.

Introduction

Fenggang YANG, *Jonathan E. E.* PETTIT, *and Chris* WHITE

This collection presents fourteen case studies of religious communities in the changing religious markets in China. The groups are diverse in religion, location, ethnic composition, and sociocultural context. The case studies were undertaken by young Chinese scholars who conducted fieldwork over extended periods of time in the second decade of the twenty-first century. While each case was examined independently, all of the studies respond to the tricolor market theory of religion in China. The authors of these chapters participated in research and writing workshops organized by the Center on Religion and Chinese Society at Purdue University, presented their work at international conferences, and made at least two rounds of revisions. The workshops and conferences provided opportunities for these scholars to interact with each other and adjust the focus of each chapter. Together, these studies constitute a kaleidoscopic view of the changing market of religion in China.

In 2006, Fenggang Yang published "The Red, Black, and Gray Markets of Religion in China," in which he laid out an analytical framework for understanding religion in China under Communist rule.[1] Prior to the appearance of this article, scholarship on the religious economy had been growing, spurred by publications from scholars such as Rodney Stark, Roger Finke, and others.[2] However, most of the theoretical models employed were based on examples from the United States, where the religious market was largely unregulated. Yang adopted the religious economy approach but highlighted the political nature of the religious market in China, which is highly regulated. Yang argued that

> heavy regulation leads not to religious reduction, but to complication of the religious markets, resulting in a tripartite market with different dynamics. ... A red market comprises all legal (officially permitted) religious organizations, believers, and religious activities. ... A black market comprises all illegal (officially banned) religious organizations, believers, and religious activities. ... A gray market comprises all religious and

---

1 Fenggang Yang, "The Red, Black, and Gray Markets of Religion in China," *Sociological Quarterly* 47 (2006): 93–122.
2 Rodney Stark and Roger Finke, *Acts of Faith: Explaining the Human Side of Religion* (Berkeley: University of California Press, 2000).

spiritual organizations, practitioners, and activities with ambiguous legal status.[3]

After taking power in 1949, the Chinese Communist Party (CCP) began to suppress various religious groups. However, followers of Buddhism, Daoism, Islam, Catholicism, and Christianity (Protestantism) were too numerous to be eliminated immediately, and so these five major religions were allowed to operate but were controlled through the establishment of so-called patriotic associations. When the Cultural Revolution broke out in 1966, all religious venues were either closed or converted for secular use. Religion, however, persisted in the underground. Indeed, the number of Protestants even multiplied. Following the launch of economic reforms and China's opening up to the outside world at the end of the 1970s, the CCP adopted a more pragmatic religious policy, as decreed in the CCP's Document No. 19, promulgated in 1982, and in the revised Constitution of the People's Republic of China (PRC). Each of the five major religions was permitted to reopen a limited number of religious venues. Religious revivals soon swept over China, catching the party-state by surprise and prompting the control apparatus to enact formal administrative regulations in 1994. Soon after, various provinces developed their own local religious regulations, and a national code, the "Regulations on Religious Affairs," was enacted by the State Council in 2005. These regulations were difficult to implement due to a lack of clarity in wording and the active challenges lodged by some religious groups. The state's ineffective control left greater social space for various religions in all three kinds of markets. For example, red-market religious leaders found creative ways to enlarge social space for their various religious activities, Christian "house churches" flourished outside the patriotic Protestant association, and some banned religious sects managed to grow and expand across provincial boundaries. While there were periodical clampdown campaigns against house churches and similar groups in the 1980s and 1990s, most of these organizations were infrequently disturbed by the state's control apparatuses after the year 2000. Indeed, many house churches went aboveground, meeting rather publicly in rented hotel halls, office buildings, or apartment complexes. Their operations were known to the police and other control apparatuses. Some of these groups tried to register with the government without joining the "patriotic" association.

Responding to this change in the religious situation in the first decade of the twenty-first century, Yang modified his tricolor market theory to reflect the

---

3 Yang, "Red, Black, and Gray Markets," 97.

growth in the gray market. In his initial statement of the theory in 2006, the gray religious market included registered religious groups (in the red market) engaged in unsanctioned activities, as well as nonreligious groups (such as a *qigong* health group) engaged in religious or quasi-religious activities, while unregistered house churches were part of the black market. But in his 2012 book *Religion in China: Survival and Revival under Communist Rule*, Yang treated open and public religious groups, such as the new wave of house churches, as part of the gray market.[4] Although their lack of formal registration meant that they were not admitted into the red market, such groups were largely left unbothered by the authorities until recently.

In both the 2006 and 2012 formulations, Yang argues that under heavy regulation, the emergence of black and gray markets of religion is inevitable, and that "the more restrictive and suppressive the regulation, the larger the gray market."[5] Moreover, he writes,

> The concept of a gray market of religion is central to the triple-market model. The gray market is also the most difficult to demarcate because of its ambiguous and amorphous nature. Broadly speaking, it includes two types of practices: (1) illegal religious activities of legally existing religious groups, and (2) religious or spiritual practices that manifest in culture or science instead of religion.[6]

Indeed, not only have house churches vacillated among the three markets in response to regulation and social conditions, but some folk religious groups have also moved across the boundaries. Folk temples have emerged across China as a way to preserve traditional cultural heritage, and these sites have been encouraged by government agencies as a measure to counterbalance the fast growth of Christianity.

Therefore, there are many shades of gray in the constantly changing religious markets in China. Religious regulations have been adjusted, religious groups have evolved, and the interactive dynamics between religion and the state and among religions have changed. In the fluctuating religious markets, some religious leaders have positioned themselves to enter the gray or red market, but there are multiple factors that may either facilitate or block their entry to a particular market. Groups may move between the black and the gray

---

4   Fenggang Yang, *Religion in China: Survival and Revival under Communist Rule* (New York: Oxford University Press, 2012).
5   Ibid., 99.
6   Ibid., 97.

or the red and the gray depending on a number of factors: revisions in party-state regulations, the appointment of new officials of religious affairs, ethnic minority status and local ethnic relations, the social legitimacy of a religion in the minds of local residents, and competitions among various local religious groups. A shift in the political winds may lead to a formerly gray community registering with the state as an official (i.e., red) religious group. The personal experiences of an individual religious leader, on the other hand, may result in a red group choosing to leave its patriotic religious association and enter the black religious market. The legal Protestant organizations have reached out to some house churches in an effort to incorporate these communities into their legal (red) patriotic association. This shift from gray market to red market gives religious organizations legal status and other resources but also introduces intense government scrutiny and control. Sometimes, legally permitted groups shift from the red or gray market to the black market. In 1999, Falun Gong, a large *qigong* group spreading throughout the country, launched a sit-in surrounding the headquarters of the CCP. This event irritated the authorities, who subsequently suppressed Falun Gong and converted this formerly gray group into a black one.

Not only is there movement between the three colors of the religious market, but there is also movement within each of the markets. Instead of viewing the religious market model as comprising three distinct categories, it may be more helpful to think of it as a continuum. Religious groups within the red market are easiest to define because they are registered with the state. However, not all registered groups are equally red. A church may become a deeper red, for example, by proactively preaching content that accords with "Socialist core values"; a temple may underscore its redness by featuring the Chinese flag or plastering CCP slogans on walls. Likewise, there are many shades within the gray and black categories, and it is possible for religious groups to move up or down on this continuum. The Christian sect of the Local Church (*Zhaohui* 召会), known as the "Shouters" (*Huhan pai* 呼喊派) for their style of worship, is an example. In 1983, the Shouters were blacklisted and many members were arrested during a "strike hard" campaign. Over the years, however, Local Church members in and out of China have worked hard to rebrand their religious activities in the eyes of the Chinese state. While the group today is still not registered, and therefore officially in the black market, they have successfully moved much closer to the red market and are now rarely targeted in crackdowns on *xiejiao* 邪教, or evil cults.[7]

---

[7] Tereza Zimmerman-Liu and Teresa Wright, "What Is in a Name? A Comparison of Being Branded a Religious Cult in the United States and the People's Republic of China: Witness

The chapters in this book present studies that demonstrate the great variety within and fluidity among the red, gray, and black religious markets. These empirical studies are authored by junior scholars in China (all but Huang Ke-hsien are mainland China scholars), and all but two of the chapters were originally written in Chinese.[8] In 2015, the Center on Religion and Chinese Society (CRCS) at Purdue University, supported by a grant from the John Templeton Foundation, organized a paper competition for scholars on the topic of changes experienced by religious groups in contemporary China. Organizers selected twenty-nine papers to be presented at a conference held in Seoul, South Korea, in 2016. After significant revision, seventeen of these papers received prizes, and their authors were invited to present them at a conference at Hong Kong Baptist University the following year. Fourteen of these papers were then edited and translated into English for the present volume.

These case studies are particularly significant for the insider knowledge they demonstrate. Most of the chapters dialogue with existing scholarship in Chinese, but instead of focusing on theoretical discussions, authors were asked to provide "thick descriptions" of the particular cases under examination. These individual cases illustrate movements within and between religious markets. We have grouped these chapters into three sections, although many of the cases deal with religious groups or activities that transcend constructed boundaries.

The first section, "Between Red and Black," looks at religious groups that have positioned themselves in the red or gray market but have moved up or down the tricolor continuum due to multiple factors, despite the personal preferences of the religious leaders. Not all of the groups under discussion are registered with the state, and thus they may not officially be in the red market, but several have incorporated strategies that move them up the continuum, making them more palatable in the eyes of the state. The fieldwork behind the chapters in this section, as well as most of the chapters in this book, was largely conducted during an era of greater religious toleration due to open-mindedness among religious affairs officials or ineffective control measures. During periods of more lenient administration of religious affairs, it is not surprising to see religious groups willing to inch closer to entering the red market. However, some of the cases included here remind us that movement within or

---

Lee and the Local Churches," *Journal of Church and State* 60.2 (2018): 187–207; Jiayin Hu, "Spirituality and Spiritual Practice: Is the Local Church Pentecostal?," in *Global Chinese Pentecostal and Charismatic Christianity*, ed. Fenggang Yang, Joy K. C. Tong, and Allan H. Anderson (Leiden: Brill, 2017).

8 The papers by Huang and Yan Liu were written in English.

between religious markets may not be unidirectional, even during times of less restriction. For various reasons, some religious leaders may lead their groups to "deregister" with the state.

The first chapter, Ke-hsien Huang's "Becoming 'Patriotic' for God: How Churches Join the State-Sanctioned Protestant Organizations," tackles the empirical question of how and why many formerly unregistered churches became officially sanctioned religious sites by joining the Three-Self Patriotic Movement (TSPM) since the 1990s. By focusing on his fieldwork experience among the True Jesus Churches (TJC; *Zhen Yesu jiaohui* 真耶稣教会), a Chinese-initiated denomination with a long history, Huang illustrates the vulnerability of the dichotomous framework of Chinese Christianity, in which official groups are portrayed as secularized and politically oriented while unregistered ones are viewed as religious and nonpolitical. Huang's account portrays a new generation of church leaders who have been socialized according to the logic of bureaucracy and are adept at dealing with the state. They rely on previous experience as leaders in local affairs or industry and exhibit a level of comfort in interacting with the state that their predecessors rarely enjoyed. Nevertheless, Huang makes it clear that while many young TJC leaders are happy to negotiate with the state, they do so out of religious motivations and with the goal of benefiting the church.

The second chapter, by Yuan Hao, looks at a Christian sect as it analyzes Mentuhui 门徒会 (Society of Disciples). Mentuhui has been officially labeled a *xiejiao*, but unlike other groups classified as cults, its leadership and members have not adopted an antagonistic approach to the party-state. Instead, as Yuan shows, they have attempted to negotiate their position vis-à-vis the authorities, moving toward a lighter shade on the black/gray continuum. While Mentuhui is not accepted by most mainstream Christian groups in China, their tactics have worked insofar as they are not actively persecuted by the party-state like their rival, the Church of Almighty God (*Quanneng shen* 全能神, also known as Eastern Lightning).[9]

Li Hui's chapter compares Christian churches in two cities, Shanxi and Henan, and shows how religious groups may also move down the continuum. Li shows how church leaders in both cities have crossed the boundary of the red and gray markets by deregistering their congregations. The results of such transitions can at times be quite paradoxical, such as in one case discussed in this chapter in which a Three-Self church, home to the city's official patriotic

---

9 See Emily Dunn, *Lightning from the East: Heterodoxy and Christianity in Contemporary China* (Leiden: Brill, 2015).

association office, decided to leave the TSPM. In this instance, for a period of time, the city's TSPM/CCC (China Christian Council) office was housed in an unregistered church building.

Kong Deji's study of the Miao village built in the Yunnan Ethnic Theme Park presents a case of cultural appropriation of Christianity resulting from the complex interactions among the entrepreneur who founded the theme park, provincial officials, church leaders, and park employees of various ethnic backgrounds. Statistically, few of the Miao are Christian, but this park constructed a Christian church to serve as a representative symbol of the Miao people. Although not officially registered, the church has a full-time trained clergyperson and functions as a site of worship for workers at the ethnic minority theme park. Kong's study further details how Miao church choirs, which have gained fame by winning numerous choral competitions organized by governmental agencies, have led to the further merging of Miao ethnicity with Christianity in the popular imagination.

Zhao Hao's case study paints a vivid picture of the worship of the God of Wealth (Caishen 财神) in a rural Sichuan county. This chapter reveals the complex interplay among the local folk religion, its worshipers, and the government. Unlike other neighboring folk temples that have registered with the official Buddhist or Daoist associations, this temple to the God of Wealth is an unregistered religious site. Because of this, temple leaders have consciously adopted strategies to ensure noninterference from the state. By constructing civic associations, such as a senior citizen center, within the temple grounds, religious leaders have moved the temple from the black market, where "superstitious" groups are typically relegated, into the gray area of civic communities.

The second section in this volume, "Group Competition," examines rival religious groups in different sociocultural contexts. Different religions compete for legalization or for social legitimation in the minds of local residents, and different groups of the same religion compete for resources and followers. The competition between religious groups often leads to movement up or down the tricolor continuum and encourages fluctuations in the religious markets. These chapters highlight how movement between different markets does not happen in a unilateral fashion between a group and government agencies. Rather, the legality of a religious community is shaped by the needs of various local and regional interests.

In the first chapter of this section, Cuicui Zhao reports on a conflict between Christians and folk religion believers in a seaside community of Zhejiang. Here, local villagers opposed the Christian minority, claiming that a sudden fire in a local sacred tree was proof that the construction of a new church was inauspicious. While believers of folk religion garnered support from villagers by couching their opposition in religious terms, railing against the destruction of *fengshui* that the new church would bring, in their interaction with the state they inched toward the red market, relying on a legal discourse and claiming that the church had not followed proper procedures in gaining approval for construction.

The next chapter, by Xiao Yunze, examines the transformations within Christian house churches in the gray market as they transition from rural churches into urban institutions. The house churches in northern Jiangsu covered in this chapter shed light on the transformations of the church "order," the state's management of house churches, and the subsequent state effect. Churches that laid down roots of evangelism in the region are traditional, fundamentalist, and paternalistic, and have been troubled by internal division and decline. As the state increases its control and scrutiny over these churches, religious elites have responded with varying strategies. Some are passive and evasive, while others endeavor to reform church organization, especially the emerging urban churches that are the outgrowth of fundamentalist house churches.

Zhang Zhipeng's chapter on an intellectual house church in Nanjing argues that the individualism of educated urban Chinese encourages the creation of niche religious groups. His ethnographic account of a small unregistered congregation made up largely of university professors and cosmopolitan urbanites suggests that the vast amount of choices available to contemporary urban religious consumers makes it difficult for most Protestant groups to grow beyond a few dozen members. A change in a group's chosen niche may drive a member who no longer resonates with the group to leave it in search of a better fit.

The final chapter in this section is a case study of churches in a Hani minority region of Yunnan in southwestern China. Jiang Shen and He Ling study how some Hani churches have managed to register with the state and thus join the red market, while others have not been successful in their efforts to register and thus remain in the black market. The disorganized and irregular evangelizing efforts of Christian churches, church-state relationships, and the relationship between believers and nonbelievers, along with the tension between Christianity and traditional religious beliefs, all play a role in the suppression of the Christian faith.

The last section in this volume, "Beyond Religious Regulation," groups together studies that transcend the challenges of religious regulations. Indeed, some megatrends or grand transformations such as urbanization, globalization, individuality, modernity, fertility policy, and the Internet, are bigger challenges that religious groups have to confront. Indeed, these challenges are faced not only by religious believers, but also by other people and the party-state. Consequently, religious regulation is sometimes truncated by such megatrends, which often produce transitions within the religious market.

The first chapter in this section, by Yan Jun and Lin Weizhi, describes how the market for Daoist priests and the performance of ritual activities in Zhanjiang, Guangdong Province, has been commodified in recent years. This study highlights the benefits and limitations of market theory in trying to understand the complex interplay of religious practice and profit. Through the examination of theoretical frameworks as well as specific cases, Yan and Lin propose a new interpretive model for the religious market. Rather than simply regarding the behavior of both lay believers and religious specialists as driven by a singular and unchanging religious need, this study adopts a model that places religious behavior on a secular–sacred continuum. This framework helps illuminate the complexity, as well as the social consequences, of devotional practices in daily life.

The next chapter deals with a new kind of church popping up in China's large cities: migrant worker churches. As explained by Yuan Hao, these congregations gather in urban areas but consist of rural worshippers. They tend to be unregistered groups, but as Yuan shows in his study of migrant worker churches in Beijing, they often are connected together. Yuan analyzes migrant worker Christians by taking the organized church (i.e., the congregation) as the unit of analysis and approaches it from a sociological perspective. He observes a reciprocity between urbanization and the organizational transformation of migrant worker churches. On the one hand, urbanization leads to the rise of migrant worker churches and affects congregations in terms of their access to resources, organizing principles, and cultures; on the other hand, church leaders have actively pushed for reform and adapted their congregations to urban life.

Similar to the chapters by Zhang and Yuan that reveal specialized new Protestant congregations, Mengyin Hu's chapter presents a case study of churches composed of artists in an eastern suburb of Beijing. She analyzes ways in which these churches maintain their rural characteristics despite the quick urbanization of the city's suburbs. This chapter demonstrates the different ways in which "modernized" individuals construct imagined communities. These imaginations are instrumental for individuals to cope with life under the pressures of capitalism, life in a metropolis, and modernity itself.

Wang Ling's "Choosing between God's Will and the Law" examines a Christian community in the era of massive urbanization. As people began to move from rural to urban regions, the country introduced radical measures to control the absolute growth in national population. What became known in the West as the one-child policy affected citizens throughout China but was particularly enforced in the cities. Wang analyzes the predicament that Chinese Christians face with regard to government policies on childbirth. On the one hand, God orders people to "be fruitful and increase in number, fill the earth." On the other hand, the Chinese government strictly enforced limitations on births. Members of Grace Church, a house church congregation in the capital, have distinctively higher fertility desires than the average Beijing citizen. The actual fertility rate remains low, however, and in the face of the strict one-child policy, abortion was prevalent in Grace Church. After the universal two-child policy was implemented in China on January 1, 2016, fertility activities in Grace Church changed considerably. This chapter shows that adjustment to fertility policy has a greater impact on Christians than on non-Christians.

In the final case study of the volume, "Online Religious Communities in a WeChat Age," Yan Liu moves the discussion of Protestant communities to the virtual world. The market of online religious activities is gray not only because of the ambiguous legal identities of the participants but also because noninstitutionalized religious communities are harder to define and group together. This chapter features statistics from Chinese WeChat research reports and analyzes content from WeChat public accounts, WeChat groups, and WeChat individual conversations. The author finds that government control measures instigated heated discussion over religious issues both in private and public spaces as never before. New technologies of the Internet and cell phones enable religious resources to become more visible, accessible, and available, making it difficult for the government to block information exchange when multiple Internet platforms are linked together. The shutdown, rebuilding, and development of religious public accounts reveal the vitality of Christian communities under government restrictions. The functions of the WeChat platform enable new forms of knowledge transmission and creation; the forming of megagroups on WeChat reinforces fast transmission of shared knowledge and cultural awareness among group members. The mobile platform enables people from around the world to form communities with similar values and allows them to work together for the same cause and shared agenda.

This volume ends with an essay by Fenggang Yang detailing the development of the field since the initial publication of the tricolor market theory fifteen years ago. This chapter provides a behind-the-scenes look at what led to the development of the theory, as well as the various responses from scholars inside and outside of China. It is also the first time Yang has responded in writing to criticisms of the religious economy theory and the tricolor market theory. This concluding chapter attests to the staying power of the tricolor market theory, but it also suggests that further refinement of the theory is necessary. The case studies in this volume are one step in this process. Not only do they reveal the vibrancy of religious life found in contemporary China, but they also illustrate how religious communities move along the black, gray, and red continuum of the religious market. Scholars applying the religious economy approach to other cultures will benefit greatly from the empirical studies of Chinese religious life found in these chapters.

These case studies were carried out in the early 2010s, when religious regulations began to become increasingly restrictive. Much of the fieldwork for the chapters was completed during a more "open" time, but the general situation has clearly shifted since Xi Jinping began his rule in 2012. In 2018, for example, the authorities revised the "Regulations on Religious Affairs" to make them much more detailed and restrictive. In the past few years, the party-state has carried out fierce campaigns to tighten its control on legal, illegal, and ambiguous religious groups. It remains to be seen to what degree the new regulations will be effectively and comprehensively enforced.

Throughout this volume, the translator and editors have tried to express different scholarly voices by using translations closely reflecting the terminology of the original. Thus, some key terms are used in different ways by different authors. Take, for existence, "Christian" (*Jidujiao* 基督教), which is usually used to mean "Protestant," although other authors sometime refer to both Catholics and Protestants under this broader umbrella. Even when the term is restricted to Protestantism, it can be applied to extremely varied forms of religion. By law, Chinese authorities claim there is only one form of Christianity, since they banned all Protestant denominations in 1958. In practice, however, even aboveground red churches often preserve distinctive denominational traditions and forms of organization, such as the True Jesus Church analyzed by Huang. In the black or gray markets, some Christian sects are perceived by other Christians as borderline heretical, such as the Society of Disciples described by Yuan. The word "church" may be used by different authors in particular ways, including both well-organized congregations and informally formed groups meeting at someone's home (house or apartment), office, or some other temporary place.

The word "state" likewise appears in complicated ways throughout this volume. China is characterized by a parallel system of governance. At each level of government, there are agencies, such as the Religious Affairs Bureau, that oversee religious communities. All communities are subject to review by officials at the local, prefectural, and national levels. All of the bureaus are under the direction of the CCP, which maintains committees and branches at all corresponding levels of the government. Indeed, most government officials are members of the CCP. Therefore, when we talk about the state, it is always the inseparable party-state. In the 1980s, there were some attempts to separate the state from the party. However, that reform was interrupted by the 1989 democracy movement and the June Fourth Tiananmen Massacre. In recent years, under Xi Jinping's rule, the party has taken over the government, and the Religious Affairs Bureau of the government has been officially folded into the CCP United Front Work Department.

A majority of the chapters examine Christian groups or include a Christian group in interaction with folk religious groups. We speculate that this is in part due to the reality that Christian groups have a strong presence throughout many parts of China. At the same time, we recognize that the sighting of religious change in China presented in this book is that of a particular group of young scholars who came into our orbit. As noted above, these chapters were selected from submissions for a paper competition in 2015, and the scholars had been informed that they would be expected to make presentations at international conferences. Indeed, many of the young scholars participated in one or more of the Summer Institutes the CRCS organized and held in China between 2004 and 2013, during which we invited prominent North American and European scholars to lecture on theories and methods of the social scientific study of religion. During those ten years, the participants included those young scholars as well as graduate students whose primary research interests were in Buddhism, Daoism, Catholicism, and Islam.

Perhaps one of the most distinctive characteristics of this book is its foregrounding of empirical evidence about religions in China. Most studies of religion in China are text-centered and conducted in the tradition of the humanities. With few exceptions, scholars rarely present empirical research on religious groups and their activities. The Summer Institutes attracted young scholars and graduate students in sociology, anthropology, political science, and economics who are also interested in religious phenomena. For a variety of reasons, many scholars whose work is collected in this volume had an interest in Protestant Christianity and folk religion, both very active religions at the grassroots level in China today. We hope that this volume will reach and inspire a new generation of young scholars to do similar research in other parts of China.

Bibliography

Dunn, Emily. *Lightning from the East: Heterodoxy and Christianity in Contemporary China*. Leiden: Brill, 2015.

Hu, Jiayin. "Spirituality and Spiritual Practice: Is the Local Church Pentecostal?" In *Global Chinese Pentecostal and Charismatic Christianity*, edited by Fenggang Yang, Joy K. C. Tong, and Allan H. Anderson, 159–180. Leiden: Brill, 2017.

Stark, Rodney, and Roger Finke. *Acts of Faith: Explaining the Human Side of Religion*. Berkeley: University of California Press, 2000.

Yang, Fenggang. *Religion in China: Survival and Revival under Communist Rule*. New York: Oxford University Press, 2012.

Yang, Fenggang. "The Red, Black, and Gray Markets of Religion in China." *Sociological Quarterly* 47.1 (2006): 93–122.

Zimmerman-Liu, Tereza, and Teresa Wright. "What Is in a Name? A Comparison of Being Branded a Religious Cult in the United States and the People's Republic of China: Witness Lee and the Local Churches." *Journal of Church and State* 60.2 (2018): 187–207.

PART 1

Between Red and Black

CHAPTER 1

Becoming "Patriotic" for God

Why Churches Join State-Sanctioned Protestant Organizations

Ke-hsien HUANG

Scholars tend to analyze Christianity in China within the dichotomous framework of churches belonging to official, politically concerned groups versus underground, faith-centered groups. However, recent on-site observations reveal that the faiths of these two types of churches may have more in common than previously supposed.[1] Since the 1990s, more and more formerly unregistered churches have joined the Three-Self Patriotic Movement (TSPM). In a dichotomous framework, it is very easy to assume that the action of joining a government-sanctioned structure is a move toward the state and away from the faith. In this chapter, however, I argue that many of these moves were made out of religious, not political, motives. In other words, for many unregistered churches, making the shift from the gray to the red market was a strategy to foster the development of the church. To understand the motives for such decisions, we must situate the choice to accept or reject church registration in its specific historical context.

Here, I will focus on three factors that have led many churches to join the TSPM. First, a new generation of church leaders has emerged who are much more pragmatic and are equipped with "state-aiding" entrepreneurial skills. The political socialization process of these current leaders and their experiences in the reform era have provided the know-how to deal with the state in order to better develop their churches. Second, I will delineate the political opportunities for religious groups and leaders that were made available by the Chinese Communist party-state in the 1990s. In particular, I will show that the government maintained an active, inclusive strategy toward religious

---

1 Xie Xiaheng, "Religion and Modernity in China: Who is Joining the Three-Self Church and Why," *Journal of Church and State* 52.1 (2010): 74–93; Mark McLeister, "A Three-Self Protestant Church, the Local State and Religious Policy Implementation in a coastal Chinese City," in *Christianity in Contemporary China: Socio-Cultural Perspectives*, ed. Frances Khek Gee Lim (New York: Routledge, 2013), 234–246; Chris White, "The Haicang Voice: Modernity, Cultural Continuity and the Spirit World in a 1920s Chinese Church," in *Protestantism in Xiamen, Then and Now*, ed. Chris White (London: Palgrave, 2019), 103–139.

regulation. Third, I will closely analyze the situations in which these new-generation, pragmatic, church-development-minded church leaders made the decision to join the TSPM. The diversification of ideas, practices, and theology within churches has grown amid the rapid social change that has occurred in China, spurred in particular by age differences and denominational loyalty. After the appearance of division within existing religious communities, new resources provided by the state were sought or secured by certain parties seeking to either maintain the status quo or strike out on their own. Through this analysis, one may see how many Christian leaders joined the patriotic association and made connections with the state mainly for religious reasons.

1 Running Dogs of the State or Martyrs for the Church?

Over the last thirty years, state-religion relations in China have drawn a great deal of attention among scholars. Much analysis of this issue has relied on an antagonistic model whereby the state dominates religious groups, which are viewed as actively rebelling if they refuse to tender their loyalty to the state.[2] The appeal of the antagonistic model has continued for three decades. Focusing on the state as it expresses itself in official announcements and legal documents, the studies adhering to this model tend to detail religious policies, state-led religious administration, and the restricted concept of religious freedom in China.[3] According to this model, the state apparatus effectively exerts full control and implements regulations over religions in China, while

---

2 For example, see Jason Kindopp and Carol Lee Hamrin, eds., *God and Caesar in China: Policy Implications of Church-State Tensions* (Washington, DC: Brookings Institution Press, 2004); Jacqueline E. Wenger, "Official vs. Underground Protestant Churches in China: Challenges for Reconciliation and Social Influence," *Review of Religious Research* 46.2 (2004): 169–182; Zhao Tianen (Jonathan Chao) and Zhuang Wanfang (Rosanna Chong), *Dangdai zhongguo jidujiao fazhanshi, 1949–1997* (Taipei: Zhongguo fuyin hui, 1997). Recent works on the topic that go beyond the antagonistic model include Karrie J. Koesel, *Religion and Authoritarianism: Cooperation, Conflict, and the Consequences* (New York: Cambridge University Press, 2014); Carsten T. Vala, *The Politics of Protestant Churches and the Party-State in China: God above Party?* (Abingdon, Oxon: Routledge, 2018); Marie-Eve Reny, *Authoritarian Containment: Public Security Bureaus and Protestant House Churches in Urban China* (New York: Oxford University Press, 2018); Jifeng Liu and Chris White, "Old Pastor and Local Bureaucrats: Recasting Church-State Relations in Contemporary China," *Modern China* 45.5 (2019): 564–590.

3 Pitman B. Potter, "Belief in Control: Regulation of Religion in China," *China Quarterly* 174 (2003): 317–337; Hong Qu, "Religious Policy in the People's Republic of China: An Alternative Perspective," *Journal of Contemporary China* 20.70 (2011): 433–448.

also consolidating its stability, taking precautions against foreign infiltration, and fulfilling its atheist ideology.[4] Recent studies employing the antagonistic model find the historical inheritance of the current religio-political regulative regime not only in the imperial legacy of old China,[5] but also in the imported project of secularist modernity implemented since the late Qing dynasty and through the Republican era.[6] Others have applied an institutional lens to the reality of state control in analyzing state-led institutionalization and the key role of government-approved religious associations that connect religious people together under the auspices of state agencies.[7]

Amid the state-dominance discourse characteristic of the antagonistic model, there is little discussion about the role of religious groups, except for a few studies on rebellious sects, such as Eastern Lightning, fighting underground against the state.[8] Religious actors are mostly described as fearless martyrs insisting on the purity of their religious traditions at the risk of their own lives, thus refusing to compromise or cooperate with the government-approved religious associations.[9] Moreover, religious actors are also found to strategically employ religious traditions in their campaign against the state. For example, house church intellectuals appeal to neighborly love in the Bible to establish a new moral foundation for the design of Chinese democratic institutions;[10] Falun Gong elites restate the virtues of Buddhism and Confucianism in rebellious rhetoric against Chinese Communism trapped in an ideological vacuum;[11] and Tibetans use symbol-filled religious festivals to reveal that the

---

[4] Edmond Tang and Jean-Paul Wiest, eds., *The Catholic Church in Modern China* (New York: Orbis, 1993); Élisabeth Allès, Leïla Chérif-Chebbi, and Constance-Hélène Halfon, "Chinese Islam: Unity and Fragmentation," *Religion, State and Society* 31.1 (2003): 7–35.

[5] For example, Daniel Bays, "A Tradition of State Dominance," in *God and Caesar in China*, ed. Jason Kindopp and Carol Lee Hamrin (Washington, DC: Brookings Institution Press, 2004), 25–39; Qu, "Religious Policy in the People's Republic of China."

[6] Vincent Goossaert and David Palmer, *The Religious Question in Modern China* (Chicago: University of Chicago Press, 2011): 19–90.

[7] Fenggang Yang, *Religion in China: Survival and Revival under Communist Rule* (New York: Oxford University Press, 2012); Goossaert and Palmer, *Religious Question*, 315–358.

[8] Emily C. Dunn, "'Cult,' Church and the CCP: Introducing Eastern Lightning," *Modern China* 35.1 (2009): 96–119; Jason Kindopp, "Fragmented Yet Defiant: Protestant Resilience under Chinese Communist Party Rule," in *God and Caesar in China*, ed. Jason Kindopp and Carol Lee Hamrin (Washington, DC: Brookings Institution Press, 2004), 122–145.

[9] For example, see Christopher Marsh's *Religion and the State in Russia and China: Suppression, Survival, and Revival* (New York: Continuum, 2011), 183–210; Wenger, "Official vs. Underground."

[10] Gerda Wielander, "Protestant and Online: The Case of *Aiyan*," *China Quarterly* 197 (2009): 165–182.

[11] Cheris Shun-ching Chan, "The Falun Gong in China: A Sociological Perspective," *China Quarterly* 179 (2004): 665–683.

propaganda of religious freedom and liberation emitted by the Chinese state is empty rhetoric.[12] In contrast, official religions are seemingly assumed to be submissive to the state and to cooperate in attacking underground religions.[13] Furthermore, registered congregations, such as TSPM churches, are often marginalized or even invisible in the antagonistic model because of its focus on a dominant state and underground resistance groups.

Within the framework of the antagonistic model, it may be hard to understand why so many unregistered Christian churches joined the state-sanctioned, "patriotic" religious structure, particularly in the 1990s. These churches were not forced to make this decision, nor were they forced to abandon the faith after joining the TSPM. On the contrary, according to my experience in the field, these decisions were undertaken willingly and motivated by faith-related factors. How can we make sense of these churches' transformations in terms of navigating the state-religion relationship? In this chapter, I will answer this question in three ways. First, I will describe the uniqueness of the new emerging Christian leaders and contextualize this by comparing their experiences with those of their predecessors. Second, I will address the larger political context, from the 1980s to 2000, of the Chinese Communist Party's (CCP) policy on religious regulation, setting the stage for the actions of key Christian leaders. Finally, I will take a closer look at how church actors made the decision to join the patriotic structure. Overall, I argue that these religious leaders were much more influenced by religious motives than political ones when they chose to become "patriotic."

The qualitative data in this chapter was collected during eight months of fieldwork conducted intermittently in 2010 and 2012 for a project on the transformation of the True Jesus Church (TJC, *Zhen Yesu jiaohui* 真耶稣教会), one of the largest indigenous Chinese Protestant groups. Tracing the networks of the denomination, I traveled through seventeen provinces or provincial-level cities to understand the development of the TJC and visited more than 150 churches and meeting points. I also followed local leaders—typically, well-respected senior elders in the region—as they visited neighboring meeting points or remote churches and met with other church leaders or governmental officials. Along with this fieldwork, I conducted forty semi-structured interviews with local church leaders in order to understand their life history,

---

12   Robert Barnett, "Symbols and Protest: The Iconography of Demonstrations," in *Resistance and Reform in Tibet*, ed. Robert Barnett and Shirin Akiner (London: Hurst & Company, 1994), 238–258.
13   Tang and Wiest, *Catholic Church*; Kindopp, "Fragmented Yet Defiant," 122–145; Wenger, "Official vs. Underground," 169–182.

pathway to leadership, church development, and, in particular, their views on church-state relations. These leaders were asked to elaborate on how they interact with the two state-sanctioned Protestant associations—the Three-Self Patriotic Movement (TSPM) and the China Christian Council (CCC), often referred to as the "two associations"—and with three governmental units involving religious affairs: the Religious Affairs Bureau (RAB), the United Front Work Department, and the Public Security Bureau. These discussions with church leaders reveal how careful and thoughtful churches were in deciding to interact with the state or join the two associations.

2 New-Generation Christian Leaders: Pragmatism, Political Capacity, and State-Aiding Entrepreneurship

In the 1950s, the majority of Chinese Christian leaders were hesitant to interact with the CCP, an officially atheist regime that harshly condemned connections with the West. The leaders of the TJC, mostly peasants with limited education who knew little about politics or communism, tended to stay away from the state out of fear of the unknown and of being "polluted." However, since the 1970s the new emerging leadership has taken a totally different approach toward church-state relations, due to their experience of growing up with the development of this regime. In the late 1950s, China experienced a process of collectivization and then an era of hyper-politicization, including the creation of people's communes and the Great Leap Forward, and culminating with the Cultural Revolution. People's political consciousness and sensitivity were delicately cultivated while they were forced to take part in various new state-building organizations in everyday life, such as people's communes, production brigades, or *danwei* 单位 (work units). More than 80 percent of the Christian leaders I interviewed had served as leaders in these local organizations. They were semi-bureaucrats at the grassroots level (a captain in a production brigade, a commander in a commune, or a chief in a small *danwei* of a coal mine, for instance). Due to their careers, these new leaders accumulated lots of experience through constant interactions with the party-state apparatus. This political socialization prepared them very well to skillfully engage in their later negotiations of religious affairs with state officials.

In general, these new religious leaders, as opposed to their previous counterparts, are willing and able to develop amiable relationships with the state. First of all, they no longer perceive state officials in charge of religious affairs as irrelevant or, even worse, devil-like. A common sentiment among new leaders was bluntly expressed by a male church elder in his late forties from

Henan: "Without the state, what can you do [in running your church]?" In an interview, he compared church-state affairs to the mediation of disputes over benefits for coal workers on his team some years ago. Both required interaction with the state. Another leader, a local deaconess who used to be a production brigade commander, also attributed her success in managing a church to a principle she had learned in her *danwei*: "You must communicate first with your superior and get him to understand you." Most of the leaders I interviewed acknowledged that it was necessary for a church leader to build relationships with the state. Moreover, they learned how to effectively communicate with the state through their previous experiences of political socialization.

Unlike their counterparts in the previous generation, who were mostly peasants with little knowledge of how the political machine worked, these new leaders are good at navigating the complex bureaucratic system of the party-state. The same techniques they learned while leading local units in a hyper-politicized time include organizational skills that help them to cope with red tape in the government bureaucracy. Many in this generation of church leaders understand well that religious passion and loyalty to the church are insufficient to guarantee a church's legal rights or protect church interests. For such goals, interaction with the state is necessary.

Brother Lu became an important leader of a local church because his political experience facilitated the church's registration with the local government. This church successfully received approval with Lu's guidance, which included his advice to use a specific type of paper for an official document in the application package. The new-generation leaders also know well how to leverage different units within the local state in order to maximize the interest of their churches. For example, one leader who was unsuccessful in gaining approval from the RAB for a larger space for his church urged safety inspectors to pressure the RAB, claiming that the lack of space would be a safety problem if there was a fire. In addition, new TJC leaders skillfully display their political loyalty by giving lip service and using correct political rhetoric, whether in written or oral discourse. Couching a church's request in the correct politicized language may increase the odds of winning the trust of the party-state. Many of my interviewees are highly aware of the important documents, papers, and recent political announcements issued by the party-state, including Document No. 19 (1982), and references to religion in public speeches by top leaders of the CCP.

The political socialization process establishes in these Christian leaders a mindset to develop the church as a "state-aiding entrepreneurship." In the past, when talking about church development, it had been common to refer to Zechariah 4:6, a Bible verse which states: " 'Not by might nor by power, but by my Spirit,' says the Lord Almighty." Thus, the previous generation of church leaders usually prayed or fasted for hours when they were faced with difficult situations or had tough decisions to make. From the perspective of earlier church leaders, the only role the state played was as a barrier to church development. However, after the CCP's stable, successful political infiltration into everyday life over decades, the new generation of leaders regard the state as an indispensable piece in the picture of religious development. It is now unthinkable for these figures to plan the future of the church without considering the state. As one young pastor remarked when criticizing church elders of the previous generation, "[They] perceive the state as the devil and refused to interact with it … [but now] we don't fight against the state; otherwise, how could you live a peaceful life? God also wants us to be submissive." Another young church leader listening in on the conversation concurred, sarcastically stating, "What big thing can you achieve without the state?" (*Lile guojia, ni neng gao shenme dashi* 离了国家，你能搞什么大事). Some leaders even turned their successful interactions with the state into Christian testimonies, showing how God has blessed the church through such contacts. For example, a deaconess in northwestern China told me, "It was God's spirit that moved me in the 1990s, when the government had financial problems in constructing the People's Square in the city. I had the wisdom to take the initiative to collect donations from believers and gave the money to the government in the name of the church. … That opened doors for church development in our city."

The new generation of church leaders tends to have a positive impression of Deng Xiaoping, who initiated economic reform and oversaw the loosening of religious regulations. One young church elder in Fujian referred to Deng's famous mantra, "Developing is an unyielding principle" (*fazhan caishi ying daoli* 发展才是硬道理), when describing how he should lead the church with the aid of the state.[14] He went on to explain that "if you have a larger congregation, then the state will take you seriously." In his discussion, the state is a positive, honorable entity that a church must make an effort to win over, instead of a negative barrier to avoid. With such a mindset, when bureaucrats approach a church for cooperation, it is something to be proud of. An elder said, "We [i.e., the leader and the congregants] are highly cultured, have good *suzhi* 素质,[15] and are able to tackle things. The RAB can judge who are wise and who are not." State support is particularly important when these churches face harsh

---

14   This is one of the most famous quotations from Deng Xiaoping, who made this statement during his visit to southern China in early 1992.
15   *Suzhi* refers to an overall level of "culture." Someone with *suzhi* would be educated, rational, and easy to deal with. For more on this term, see Andrew Kipnis, "*Suzhi*: A Keyword Approach," *China Quarterly* 186 (2006): 295–313.

competition from other counterparts emerging within their neighboring areas. Leaders realize that if they want to get ahead of their competitors, the state is key for their development: "We must make use of them [state officials] in order to develop. We will not be used by them, as our predecessors wrongly feared."

This understanding of the church as a state-aided entrepreneurship is deeply rooted among the current generation of Christian leaders. As suggested in this chapter, this is related to the political socialization that occurred during the period of mass collectivization, as well as the new spirit of the reform era, when consciousness of state-sanctioned development spread from the economic sphere to other social arenas, including religion. New-generation Protestant leaders are pragmatic in their consideration of whether to join the TSPM. Joining is risky and costly, since the "atheist" Communists could then supervise and interfere in church affairs. Thus, church leaders would rather preserve the status quo and remain unregistered unless they anticipate specific returns or gains from registering with the state. In the following sections, I will discuss motivations behind decisions to join the TSPM. Remarkably, all are related to better developing their religion. In their accounts of why and how they joined the TSPM, church leaders, I argue, consider themselves as agents growing a church rather than as desparate patients grasping for a lifeline. Thus, when leaders perceived that the political situation was ripe for state-religion cooperation, they readily embraced the opportunity to better develop their churches.

3   Political Transformation and the Inclusive Institutionalization of Religion

The emergence of a new, pragmatic generation of Christian leaders was far from enough to facilitate large-scale waves of Christian groups joining the government-sanctioned structure. A new political opportunity within the state's apparatus for regulating religion was necessary to make this phenomenon possible. Here we will review the political change in the Chinese Communist state's regulations on religion, particularly around the 1990s when many Christian leaders chose to join the patriotic associations.

The year 1978 marked the end of the CCP's militant attitude toward religion—especially evident during the Cultural Revolution—as the pendulum began to swing from "the distorted religious policy"[16] to viewing the religious problem

---

16   Xiao Hong, "Ruhe zhengque kandai Zhongguo de zongjiao zhengce," *Zhongguo zongjiao*, 2004.5: 57.

pragmatically and thus tackling it in tolerant ways. The party-state, which prioritized economic progress much more than ideological struggle, announced that it would permit "legal" religious activities. The slogan "Dispel chaos and restore righteousness" (*boluan fanzheng* 拨乱反正) was proclaimed, and religious venues were reopened. The resumption of religious activities coincided with the gradual restoration of church leaders. The central United Front Work Department (UFWD) surveyed clergy and rehabilitated many, arranging for them to return to religious work. The UFWD further ensured that important religious figures' jobs were secure and their needs met, and made sure that the children of these figures would not be discriminated against when applying for jobs, education, or entrance into the Party. Institutionally, the RAB, which was established in 1954, annexed to the UFWD in 1961, and deactivated in 1975, resumed functioning at both the central and local levels in 1979 and officially cooperated with the UFWD to tackle "normal religious affairs." However, in reality the church-state relationship was still dominated by the political-legal sector and the Public Security Bureau, which I call the "rigid-suppression" apparatuses of the Chinese regulatory regime. The RAB and UFWD, which we may understand as "soft-governance" apparatuses, were still marginalized at this stage and served as little more than a symbol of the party-state's renewed openness to religion.

The reform-era Chinese Communist state took religious affairs lightly until the end of the 1980s. Things began to change in the 1990s, however, because of significant domestic and international events. After dreams of political reform were shattered in the Tiananmen Square Incident of 1989, many disappointed Chinese flocked to religion, particularly Christianity, for new hope or salvation.[17] In addition, Christian churches played a decisive role in toppling communist regimes in Eastern Europe, such as in Poland, where the national Catholic Church called for greater popular support of political protests. With both international and domestic crises threatening political stability, the central state became aware of the importance of managing religion and started to take seriously both the administrative and legal construction of religious regulations. For example, in 1990, Chen Yun, then second in command under Deng Xiaoping, wrote a letter to remind Jiang Zemin, Deng's future successor, of how serious religious infiltration from domestic and international enemies was and of how important it was for the Party to tackle this "critical matter"

---

17   Fenggang Yang, "What about China? Religious Vitality in the Most Secular and Rapidly Modernizing Society," *Sociology of Religion* 75.4 (2014): 564–578.

of religious affairs for the sake of national stability.[18] Following the call of his predecessor, Jiang, in his first year in power, issued a document titled "Highly Emphasizing Ethnic and Religious Work," confirming the state principle that "religious affairs are never trivial" (*zongjiao wu xiaoshi* 宗教无小事).

Thus, the party-state put a lot of effort into including various nonofficial religious groups into the government-sanctioned structure. Abundant official resources were infused into the soft-governance apparatuses, to an unprecedented extent, in order to attract religious groups to answer the state's rationale. In the early years of the reform era, the RAB of the State Council (*Guowuyuan zongjiao shiwuju* 国务院宗教事务局) was a symbolic institution, largely irrelevant to the top leadership of the CCP. But the heightened attention given to religious affairs led to the expansion of the RAB, resulting in significant increases in the number of religious affairs cadres in 1988 and again in 1994. In 1998, the RAB expanded again and was renamed the State Administration of Religious Affairs (*Guojia zongjiao shiwuju* 国家宗教事务局, hereafter SARA) and was given an elevated administrative status within the central government.[19] The basic direction followed what Jiang announced in 1993 as the key goal of religious work under his rule: "intensifying the management of religious affairs according to law" (*yi fa jiaqiang zongjiao shiwu de guanli* 依法加强宗教事务的管理). Many legal documents on religious regulations were released from 1994 onward, establishing fundamental guidelines that defined the official relationship between the state and religious groups. The local RAB, which was granted more resources, discretion, and power in tackling religious affairs, started to endeavor to "rally with patriotic religious people" (that is, to form a united front) by including as many religious groups as possible within the state-sanctioned patriotic structure. Here we see that the state opened the door of the government-sanctioned religious structure and provided incentives (such as the establishment of seminaries for the cultivation of new clergy and salaries for registered religious leaders) to attract Christian groups to join the structure.

The new generation of Christian leaders emerging in the 1990s, in comparison with their previous counterparts, were much more pragmatic and capable of handling relations with the state. Many of them were eager to grasp the opportunities offered by the state in order to enhance the religious

---

18 Beatrice Leung, "China's Religious Freedom Policy: The Art of Managing Religious Activity," *China Quarterly* 184 (2005): 905.

19 Fenggang Yang, *Religion in China*, 79. In 2018, this organization became further entrenched in the UFWD and its official English name was changed to the National Religious Affairs Administration.

development of their churches. Although religious groups might not be able to comply with every regulation officially issued, local bureaucrats tended to tolerate minor transgressions in order to allow as many religious leaders as possible to be officially included. Thus, it was not uncommon to see a variety of informal adaptive practices negotiated between local officials in charge of religious affairs and Christian leaders.[20] For example, some Christian leaders liked to invite prestigious overseas Chinese pastors to hold mass evangelical conventions. If they complied with the regulations and went through the whole bureaucratic process, it might take more than half a year to gain approval, as an elder told me. To bypass such inconveniences, they often relied on tacit agreements or favors from friendly officials. The officials considered it necessary to grease the newly formed relationship and to help religious leaders by overlooking minor infractions that would not cause any damage to their own careers.

4 Deciding to Be "Patriotic": Religious Cleavages and Resource Seeking

I now shift the analytical focus of this chapter from macro-level questions of leadership and state policy on religion to the micro-level, grassroots situations where Christian leaders make the decision to join the state-sanctioned structure. The reader will see that such decisions are often the outcome of a power struggle within a church and are made when one faction seeks additional resources. The agency of religious leaders is illustrated in the cases discussed below, which suggest that leaders' willingness to be included in the patriotic associations seems less "patriotic," as expected by the literature, and stems more from religious reasons.

Generally speaking, the factional divides that end with one group within a church joining the patriotic association can be ascribed to one of two causes: conflict between older and younger members of a church, or conflict between parties defined by doctrinal differences.

4.1 *Generational Conflict*
In the reform era, there is much more information about, as well as interaction with, overseas Christianity. Rapid social changes have pushed young Christians in China to reflect on how their faith is lived out and how the church

---

20 Ke-hsien Huang, "Dyadic Nexus Fighting Two-Front Battles: A Study of the Microlevel Process of the Official-Religion-State Relationship in China," *Journal for the Scientific Study of Religion* 53.4 (2014): 706–721; Liu and White, "Old Pastor and Local Bureaucrats."

is managed. Compared to the older generation, many young Christians have different opinions on how faith should be interpreted and practiced.[21] I have witnessed or heard about several instances in which young church members could not stand the old leaders' authoritarian decrees on matters of faith and exited to form new groups. For example, Elder Hsu, the old head minister of one church, used prophecies, visions, dreams, and revelations to condemn new church practices that had been instituted in the last two years. He and his followers dismissed orderly worship services and new reform practices as spiritually dry or even blasphemous. They continued old-fashioned boisterous worship services filled with physicality, laughter, and tears—traits that the founders of the TJC proclaimed as features of orthodox worship passed down from the apostolic age. However, young believers thought such worship was bizarre and boring and lacked any intellectual enrichment; they wanted a sermon that was better organized, articulated in clear language, and biblically based. This difference in worship styles led to a schism in the church, and one side eventually joined the patriotic structure while the other remained unregistered.

In other cases, old-guard elders made appeals to their congregants regarding the legitimacy of their authority, which had remained unchallenged for decades. The most extreme example I witnessed occurred in the Henan city of Zhuokuo: an elder suddenly confronted a congregation during a service and disbanded the newly elected church officers on the authority of a self-proclaimed "miraculous sign from God"—that is, he raised what he claimed was a paralyzed arm above his shoulder. Such dramatic proclamations are unconvincing to many urban TJC personnel but legitimate in the eyes of local congregants, who are accustomed to showing complete deference to long-established elders. The elder justified his action by citing the Bible, but the young cohort in the congregation did not accept his interpretation and judgment. This later led to the division of the church.

4.2 *Doctrinal Conflict*

Officially, the TSPM claims that Chinese Christianity has entered a postdenominational era. There are no formal denominational structures within the TSPM. Without institutional support and surveillance, the maintenance of a denominational tradition became difficult. Although some religious leaders recognized a denominational tradition and wanted to preserve it, this was difficult to do without guidance or structure. Some leaders have relied on

---

21 Ke-hsien Huang, "Sect-to-Church Movement in Globalization: Transforming Pentecostalism and Coastal Intermediaries in Contemporary China," *Journal for the Scientific Study of Religion* 55.2 (2016): 407–416.

improvisation and unreliable memories in explicating the intricacies of faith. Even within a denominational tradition such as the TJC, it is common to see different approaches to certain main doctrines. Such differences have ignited serious disputes between different TJC churches. One group of churches may condemn others for betraying the faith or practicing heterodoxy. For example, the question of whether speaking in tongues is a necessary criterion for verifying baptism of the spirit (which is the most fundamental, defining doctrine in the TJC) has triggered a major dispute among True Jesus churches in Jiangsu. Hundreds of thousands of members belonging to the TJC tradition are divided into two main camps. Legal accusations, veiled defamation, and even violent attacks have been employed in this conflict. The leaders of the camps do not talk to each other and forbid their members from interacting with those in the other camp, except for the purpose of recruiting them to "forsake darkness and come to the light." One pastor involved in the dispute explained to me, "In order to be saved in the end times, you must be baptized in the correct way, namely by the spiritual authority of the Holy Spirit. So, if you were previously baptized wrongly, without the Holy Spirit, you should be rebaptized in our church." But this kind of rebaptizing has made the other side very angry. They view it as disrespectful and as an indication that their religious legitimacy has been dismissed.

The chasm within this religious community led one side to consider creating a relationship with the state, a provider of immense resources. The side that was not in power sought help outside of the church, while the other side had to find new resources to compensate for what it had lost in the schism. The state became a partner in that process. In my fieldwork in Hubei, I met one elder who had differing opinions on how to keep the denominational tradition alive and finally decided to cease all contact with other churches sharing the TJC tradition. Suddenly, he found that his church had lost access to a lot of manpower and theological materials for preparing sermons, since these resources were supplied by the neighboring TJC churches and even overseas preachers. The regular sermons became less edifying and indeed so boring that believers stopped attending worship services or even switched to neighboring churches. It was impossible for the elder, as a poorly educated peasant, to salvage this situation on his own. The only rope he could grasp was the TSPM, which promised him theological teachers and preachers to fill the gap of religious manpower. During my visit to his church, he gladly displayed new sermon-related textbooks to me.

Sometimes TSPM or RAB officials took the initiative to approach churches embroiled in an ongoing split and to encourage the weaker side to establish a new meeting point. By encouraging such splits, officials hypothetically simplify the management of local religious affairs, since the new leaders whom they helped to gain independence are expected to be more submissive to the officials' command. I visited one registered church in southern Anhui in 2011 and 2014. During my second visit, I found that the leadership had changed; the old female charismatic leader (who often prophesied about the future) had stepped down, while the new leader (a much younger man) who used to be her second-in-command had taken over. I asked him what happened. He said that the old lady became very stubborn in teaching her visions, which worried young generations within the church as well as the RAB officials. Thus, "we forced her to retire despite her protests." It was said that the RAB had long been dissatisfied with her unwillingness to cooperate and had been hoping to find new leadership to end her long dictatorship. I asked the new leader if he was concerned about the church's closer relationship with the state. He told me confidently that it was they who were using the government, and not vice versa. For some other churches that were not experiencing internal discord, joining the TSPM was a strategic way to acquire more resources for evangelism. Every year, they could send a quota of their own young people to official theological schools for free in order to gain a preaching certificate, which supported the churches' evangelical work in and even beyond the province. Maintaining a presence at TSPM meetings could be beneficial, too. If other registered Protestant groups condemned the evangelical activities of the TJC-affiliated churches, the latter could speak in their own defense during meetings.

5 Preliminary Conclusions: A New Situation in Xi's Era

In light of the preceding discussion, the inclusion of Protestant churches into the patriotic structure in contemporary China requires a nuanced understanding. Joining the TSPM should not be interpreted as either a victory for the state or a betrayal of the official churches. In my research, from the perspective of Protestant leaders, joining the TSPM was a legitimate strategy to maximize religious interests and to help preserve the faith. State officials, beginning in the 1990s, made reasonable efforts to encourage as many churches as possible to join the state-sanctioned structure in order to advance the policy on religious regulation. Thus, the "patriotic" movement of churches toward the state was the joint result of the pragmatic considerations of religious individuals and state-initiated efforts.

However, since Xi Jinping's administration took power in 2012, the political winds have changed. "Western-contaminated" Christianity hardly fits into Xi's new nationalist vision of "the China Dream" (*Zhongguo meng* 中国梦),

and the decade-long cooperative relationship between the state and official Christianity has been rendered fragile, if not broken altogether. To realize this Chinese dream in the religious realm, the state has launched a series of struggles against Christianity, particularly in areas where it is strategically important for the CCP to reassert its ideological dominance. It has been reported that, at the local level, the restrictive atmosphere toward Christianity has manifested itself in a tendency by local governments to crack down on often-tolerated Christian practices in many places where religious freedom has been taken for granted. The "undesirable" religion of Christianity has faced its most serious persecution in more than a decade. The harsh actions targeting Christianity are considered part of the party-state's response to the growing number of Christians in China, which was recently forecasted to be the country with the most Christians in the world by 2030.[22] Each Christmas since 2014, reports have circulated that this "Western" holiday has been boycotted, or that celebrations surrounding it have been forbidden by local authorities. The CCP's ban on granting membership to believers has been reasserted again in some provinces. The most dramatic event illustrating the break in cooperative state-Christianity relations is certainly the "Three Rectifications and One Demolition" (*sangai yichai* 三改一拆) campaign started in October of 2013 by the Zhejiang government. According to Christian Solidarity Worldwide, more than five hundred crosses were removed, demolished, modified, or covered up in the campaign, thirty-seven churches were demolished, and more than one hundred people were arrested, detained, or summoned in 2014 in connection with these events.[23] Pastor Joseph Gu, a prestigious and well-known Hangzhou pastor who led one of the largest churches in China and was head of the Zhejiang Christian Council, was accused of embezzlement and arrested. Observers believe that the state's action might be related to the fact that Gu had published an open letter denouncing the "Three Rectifications and One Demolition" campaign.

Under this brand-new, state-initiated situation, there may be some changes in the cooperative ties built between Christian leaders and the state that I have discussed in this chapter. The political opportunities seem to be closed, or at least narrowed. Christian laity and leaders may experience more

---

22 Tom Philips, "China on Course to Become the 'World's Most Christian Nation' within 15 Years," *The Telegraph*, April 19, 2014, https://www.telegraph.co.uk/news/worldnews/asia/china/10776023/China-on-course-to-become-worlds-most-Christian-nation-within-15-years.html (accessed August 20, 2019).

23 "Zhejiang Church Demolitions: Timeline of Events," CSW website, https://www.csw.org.uk/zhejiangtimeline (accessed August 20, 2019).

harassment and hostility from the Communist regime. It is very likely that more churches will be more reluctant to align themselves with the government and will turn to seek aid from overseas Christians or domestic allies belonging to a particular domination. As the golden age of church-state relations in contemporary China seems to have passed, optimism toward the state could vanish, and hardline positions on church-state relations may become further entrenched. In the coming years, more Christian churches may join a trend of disaffiliation from or indifference to the government-sanctioned TSPM, now that official government sanction is not as beneficial to religious causes as before.

Bibliography

Allès, Élisabeth, Leïla Chérif-Chebbi, and Constance-Hélène Halfon. "Chinese Islam: Unity and Fragmentation." *Religion, State and Society* 31.1 (2003): 7–35.

Barnett, Robert. "Symbols and Protest: The Iconography of Demonstrations." In *Resistance and Reform in Tibet*, edited by Robert Barnett and Shirin Akiner, 238–258. London: Hurst & Company, 1994.

Bays, Daniel. "A Tradition of State Dominance." In *God and Caesar in China*, edited by Jason Kindopp and Carol Lee Hamrin, 25–39. Washington, DC: Brookings Institution Press, 2004.

Chan, Cheris Shun-ching. "The Falun Gong in China: A Sociological Perspective." *China Quarterly* 179 (2004): 665–683.

Dunn, Emily C. "'Cult,' Church and the CCP: Introducing Eastern Lightning." *Modern China* 35.1 (2009): 96–119.

Goossaert, Vincent, and David Palmer. *The Religious Question in Modern China*. Chicago: University of Chicago Press, 2010.

Huang, Ke-hsien. "Dyadic Nexus Fighting Two-Front Battles: A Study of the Microlevel Process of the Official-Religion-State Relationship in China." *Journal for the Scientific Study of Religion* 53.4 (2014): 706–721.

Huang, Ke-hsien. "Sect-to-Church Movement in Globalization: Transforming Pentecostalism and Coastal Intermediaries in Contemporary China." *Journal for the Scientific Study of Religion* 55.2 (2016): 407–416.

Kindopp, Jason. "Fragmented Yet Defiant: Protestant Resilience under Chinese Communist Party Rule." In *God and Caesar in China*, edited by Jason Kindopp and Carol Lee Hamrin, 122–145. Washington, DC: Brookings Institution Press, 2004.

Kindopp, Jason, and Carol Lee Hamrin. *God and Caesar in China: Policy Implications of Church-State Tensions*. Washington, DC: Brookings Institution Press, 2004.

Kipnis, Andrew. "*Suzhi*: A Keyword Approach." *China Quarterly* 186 (2006): 295–313.

Koesel, Karrie J. *Religion and Authoritarianism: Cooperation, Conflict, and the Consequences*. New York: Cambridge University Press, 2014.

Leung, Beatrice. "China's Religious Freedom Policy: The Art of Managing Religious Activity." *China Quarterly* 184 (2005): 894–913.

Liu, Jifeng, and Chris White. "Old Pastor and Local Bureaucrats: Recasting Church-State Relations in Contemporary China." *Modern China* 45.5 (2019): 564–590.

Marsh, Christopher. *Religion and the State in Russia and China: Suppression, Survival, and Revival*. New York: Continuum, 2011.

McLeister, Mark. "A Three-Self Protestant Church, the Local State and Religious Policy Implementation in a Coastal Chinese City." In *Christianity in Contemporary China: Socio-Cultural Perspectives*, edited by Francis Khek Gee Lim, 234–246. London: Routledge, 2013.

Philips, Tom. "China on Course to Become the 'World's Most Christian Nation' within 15 Years." *The Telegraph*, April 19, 2014. https://www.telegraph.co.uk/news/worldnews/asia/china/10776023/China-on-course-to-become-worlds-most-Christian-nation-within-15-years.html (accessed August 20, 2019).

Potter, Pitman B. "Belief in Control: Regulation of Religion in China." *China Quarterly* 174 (2003): 317–337.

Qu, Hong. "Religious Policy in the People's Republic of China: An Alternative Perspective." *Journal of Contemporary China* 20.70 (2011): 433–448.

Reny, Mari-Eve. *Authoritarian Containment: Public Security Bureaus and Protestant House Churches in Urban China*. New York: Oxford University Press, 2018.

Tang, Edmond, and Jean-Paul Wiest, eds. *The Catholic Church in Modern China*. New York: Orbis, 1993.

Vala, Carsten T. *The Politics of Protestant Churches and the Party-State in China: God above Party?* Abingdon, Oxon: Routledge, 2018.

Wenger, Jacqueline. "Official vs. Underground Protestant Churches in China: Challenges for Reconciliation and Social Influence." *Review of Religious Research* 46.2 (2004): 169–182.

White, Chris. "The Haicang Voice: Modernity, Cultural Continuity, and the Spirit World in a 1920s Church." In *Protestantism in Xiamen, Then and Now*, edited by Chris White, 103–139. London: Palgrave, 2019.

Wielander, Gerda. "Protestant and Online: The Case of Aiyan." *China Quarterly* 197 (2009): 165–182.

Xiao Hong 肖虹. "Ruhe zhengque kandai Zhongguo de zongjiao zhengce" 如何正确看待中国的宗教政策. *Zhongguo zongjiao* 中国宗教 2004.5: 57–59.

Xie Xiaheng. "Religion and Modernity in China: Who Is Joining the Three-Self Church and Why." *Journal of Church and State* 52.1 (2010): 74–93.

Yang, Fenggang. *Religion in China: Survival and Revival under Communist Rule*. New York: Oxford University Press, 2012.

Yang, Fenggang. "What about China? Religious Vitality in the Most Secular and Rapidly Modernizing Society." *Sociology of Religion* 75.4 (2014): 564–578.

Zhao Tianen (Jonathan Chao) 赵天恩 and Zhuang Wanfang (Rosanna Chong) 庄婉芳. *Dangdai zhongguo jidujiao fazhanshi* 当代中国基督教发展史, 1949–1997. Taipei: Zhongguo fuyin hui, 1997.

"Zhejiang Church Demolitions: Timeline of Events." CSW website, https://www.csw.org.uk/zhejiangtimeline (accessed August 20, 2019).

CHAPTER 2

The Transformation of Mentuhui (Society of Disciples)

Constructing Legitimacy and Adapting to a Changing Religious Economy

YUAN Hao

The relationship between the state and society has undergone considerable restructuring since China's reform and opening up. As the state began to retreat from the economic and social realms, the restoration of the policy of religious freedom in 1979 opened up space for some degree of autonomy in the realm of religion. Additionally, the rise of a civil society is indicative of an altered relationship between the state and society. Protestant Christianity, as a component of civil society, has enjoyed rapid development in reform-era China, especially in rural areas. At the same time, however, Christian cults have surged.

Fenggang Yang's tricolor market theory has become the dominant framework under which scholars examine the internal transformations of the religious market under strict regulation in the interior of China.[1] However, the constant transformation and metamorphosis of Christian sects calls for further research. For example, groups that are officially declared to be "cults" and banned nevertheless remain active and continue to expand in rural areas. Mentuhui 门徒会, or the Society of Disciples, is a prime example of such a religious movement in China. It has a large number of followers and has come to occupy a gray area in the religious market, which allows it not only to survive but also to expand. What are the tenets of Mentuhui? How is it organized? How does it manage its relationship with the government? This chapter examines Mentuhui in the framework of the tricolor religious market theory and against the backdrop of a church-state relationship in a heavily regulated environment. It seeks to articulate Mentuhui's transition from the black to the gray market and discuss the mechanisms of such evolution in the religious market.[2]

---

1 Fenggang Yang, *Religion in China: Survival and Revival under Communist Rule* (New York: Oxford University Press, 2012).
2 The research for this chapter was carried out by YUAN Hao and a colleague, who wishes to remain anonymous. Much of the fieldwork, including many of the interviews, was carried out by this researcher and shared with the author.

1 Background and Theoretical Framework

Two major approaches to theorizing the evolution of religious organizations can be identified: the typology of religious organizations and the mechanisms of their evolution. Religious sociologists have classified religions (or religious organizations) on the basis of various criteria in order to examine their development and transformation. Ernst Troeltsch was the first to theorize the "church-sect typology," which Max Weber later incorporated into the sociology of religion.[3] Depending on the degree of tension between an organization and society, religious organizations can be divided into two types, church or sect. A sect is often at odds with mainstream society, whereas a church tends to maintain an amicable relationship with society at large.[4] Ronald Johnstone mentions a third type of religious organization that is distinguishable from church and sect, namely cult.[5] He observes that this type of religious organization employs new religious terminology and symbols. Compared with other religious organizations, a cult emphasizes inspirations and revelations from supernatural forces; it also revolves around charismatic leaders. These leaders are believed to be endowed with special revelations and knowledge and thus have the ability to guide their disciples to the truth. Scholars have posited church and cult as the two ends of a religious continuum, placing sects somewhere in the middle.

Regarding the respective evolution of church, sect, and cult, Johnstone argues that as a sect continues to grow, subgroups inevitably form within the organization, and charismatic leaders who are deemed holy also become normalized.[6] All of these changes can cause a sect to evolve. A sect may transform into a church or move in the opposite direction and turn into a cult. The formation and subsequent operation of a cult tends to rely heavily on the personality of a charismatic leader. This type of organization often experiences division or transformation when a leader passes away.

The works of Rodney Stark and Roger Finke are also helpful in thinking about the development of religious organizations. In *Acts of Faith*, Stark and Finke apply the concept of religious economy and construct a model to explain the structure and process of a religious economy. They posit that the religious

---

3 Ronald Johnstone, *Religion in Society: A Sociology of Religion*, 8th ed. (Abingdon, UK: Routledge, 2016), 60; translated by Yuan Yayu and Zhong Yuying as *Shehui zhong de zongjiao–yizhong zongjiao shehuixue* (Chengdu: Sichuan renmin chubanshe, 2012), 95.
4 Benton Johnson, "On Church and Sect," *American Sociological Review* 28 (1963): 539–549.
5 Ibid.
6 Ibid.

economy consists of all economic activities in a society, including existing and latent "markets" of believers, one or more organizations that attract or retain followers, and religious cultures shaped by these organizations.[7] The subjects of Stark and Finke's study are American religious groups in a free, unregulated religious market. They seek to understand the relative places of sects and churches in the interplay between supply and demand, as well as the evolution of each relative to the other. When a sect is established, its messages tend to be provocative and cause conflicts with society at large. Such tension reduces the number of "free riders," which strengthens the followers' devotion and evangelical fervor. Sects that have a strained relationship with the outside world also tend to enjoy the most substantial expansion.[8] On the flip side, as a sect grows in scale, it also tends to tone down its messages and adjust its survival strategy, and thus becomes more moderate in its interaction with the outside world.

All of the above conclusions are derived from the Euro-American religious experience. Since the implementation of the policy of reform and opening up in 1979, the Chinese state has abandoned suppressive policies toward religion and has adopted a multi-pronged strategy in managing religious organizations. This change led to further splits within religious organizations, as well as unprecedented complications in religious affairs. Strict governmental control does not fully suppress religious activities. Tight regulation of the red market of legal religions has the unintended consequence of driving organizations and believers from the red into the black and gray markets, which further complicates the overall religious market. Lu Yunfeng's study of Yiguandao 一贯道 in Taiwan offers a fresh perspective on the religious black market. He argues that, in response to the government's stringent regulations, Yiguandao reformed both its tenets and organizational structure. These measures effectively reduced the tension between church and state, which also allowed Yiguandao to expand rapidly at a time of heightened governmental control.[9]

---

7 Rodney Stark and Roger Finke, *Acts of Faith: Explaining the Human Side of Religion* (Berkeley: University of California Press, 2000); translated by Yang Fenggang as *Xinyang de faze—jieshi zongjiao zhi ren de fangmian* (Beijing: Zhongguo renmin daxue chubanshe, 2004), 237.
8 Thomas Robbins, Dick Anthony, and James Richardson, "Theory and Research on Today's 'New Religions,'" *Sociological Analysis* 39.2 (1978): 95–122.
9 Lu Yunfeng, "Chaoyue jiduzongjiao shehuixue—jianlun zongjiao shichang lilun zai huaren shehui de shiyongxing wenti," *Shehuixue yanjiu*, 2008.5: 81–97. Also see Yunfeng Lu, *The Transformation of Yiguan Dao in Taiwan: Adapting to a Changing Religious Economy* (Plymouth, UK: Lexington Books, 2008).

In my opinion, current scholarship is limited in its ability to explain groups like the Mentuhui. Stark and Finke examine the sect-to-church transformation in an unregulated, highly developed, competitive, and specialized religious economy. However, their model does not fully describe and explain religious evolution in a highly regulated and constrained environment. Fenggang Yang's tricolor religious market theory directly addresses that insufficiency. Nevertheless, Yang has not fully addressed the issue of the internal operations of each of the three markets, nor has he fully explained how groups move from one market to another. Lu Yunfeng's study of Yiguandao is indeed an original contribution to the field, and yet his conclusions are not entirely applicable to the religious landscape in mainland China, especially with regard to the internal competition and evolution within the Chinese religious market.

Challenges to the tricolor religious market theory aside, it remains the most effective interpretative framework for the transformation of the religious market in China. This chapter argues that by applying this model to specific cases it is possible to develop it further. In particular, we should seek to validate and expand upon this model by investigating new religious groups or cults within Chinese Protestant Christianity. An analysis of Mentuhui will complement the existing understanding of how the black market actually operates and morphs. This study, therefore, applies both the church-sect-cult typology and the tricolor religious market theory to the case of Mentuhui in order to reach a better understanding of the operation and evolution of both the black and the gray markets. I also seek to identify the process of religious evolution in the Chinese context.

2   Mentuhui: A Case Study

A considerable number of indigenous Christian cults have emerged in rural China since the 1980s. This was a consequence of the merging of a rapidly expanding Protestant Christianity with local folk religion. Three Grades of Servant 三班仆人, the Lingling Sect 灵灵教, Mentuhui, the Lord God Sect 主神教, and Established King 被立王 are some of these groups. They have three characteristics in common. First, they appropriate Christian teachings, especially Christology and apocalypticism, for their own ends. Second, they deify religious leaders who are venerated as the second coming of Christ. Third, they seek out miracles and supernatural phenomena. Mentuhui, founded by Ji Sanbao 季三宝, is a case in point. It falls into the academic category of a cult and is one of the most representative cases.

2.1   The Founder: Ji Sanbao (1940–1997)

Hailing from Tongchuan, Shaanxi, Ji converted to Christianity in 1979. He joined the True Jesus Church (*Zhenyesu jiaohui* 真耶稣教会) the following year and was baptized there. Ji then joined the Local Church (*Zhaohui* 召会) and soon became a church leader. In 1983, the Chinese state began its suppression of the Shouters sect (*Huhan pai* 呼喊派), which prompted Ji to start his own sect. Ji composed a *Seven-Step Spiritual Journey* (*Qibu lingcheng* 七步灵程) in 1985 to present the tenets of his sect; it teaches apocalyptic ideas, casts Ji Sanbao himself as the savior, and anticipates the establishment of a "heavenly kingdom of Christ" (*Jidu tianguo* 基督天国). By 1989, Ji had preached in the rural areas of southern Shaanxi, Henan, and Hubei and attracted a following. In the same year, he hosted an assembly in his home, summoned twelve disciples, and declared himself a prophet and the personification of God. Mentuhui was thus established and it expanded rapidly into several provinces.

In November 1995, the General Office of the Communist Party and the General Office of the State Council issued a proclamation against the Shouters that also included information on Mentuhui, affirming its cult status and declaring a ban on the organization.[10] Ji was sentenced to seven years in prison by a Shaanxi court in 1992 and was released before the sentence expired in 1997. Ji died in a car accident later that year.

2.2   Becoming a Cult (1995)

The authorities declared Mentuhui a cult and explained this designation by providing a set of criteria. According to the official document, Mentuhui, also known as Narrow Gate (*Kuangye zhaimen* 旷野窄门) in Hubei Province, was established by farmer Ji Sanbao of Yao County 耀县, Shaanxi Province, in early 1989. The cult has a hierarchy of seven ranks, including the headquarters (*zonghui* 总会), main churches (*dahui* 大会), main branches (*dafenhui* 大分会), sub-branches (*xiaofenhui* 小分会), main branch points (*dafendian* 大分点), sub-branch points (*xiaofendian* 小分点), and meeting places (*juhuidian* 聚会点). By early 1995, Mentuhui had expanded into over three hundred counties in fourteen provinces and had more than 350,000 members. In crafting his *Seven-Step Spiritual Journey*, Ji claimed to be "Christ anointed by God" and the "son

---

10   "Concerning the Investigation and the Banning of the 'Shouter Sect' and Other Cultic Organizations and Their Situation and Suggestions for Action issued by Ministry of Public Security" 中共中央办公厅、国务院办公厅下发《关于转发〈公安部关于查禁取缔"呼喊派"等邪教组织的情况及工作意见〉的通知》. *Ting zi* 厅字 50 (1995). This proclamation was meant to be confidential, but its contents have been leaked.

of God" and allegedly performed miracles such as fasting for thirty-two days, healing the blind and the crippled, and resurrecting the dead.

Officials further commented that the leadership of the organization disseminated disinformation and spread superstitions. Their messages include "prayers and exorcism to cure diseases," "two taels of grain are sufficient for daily nourishment; farming is a futile effort," and "faith in the Lord makes a perfect student." The disinformation has caused an alarming number of families to withdraw their children from primary- and secondary-school. Followers have abandoned their livelihoods and sold off their material possessions to prepare for the "rapture." Some have refused to seek medical attention for illnesses, and many have died out of such negligence. The core personnel of the organization have engaged in illegal dealings such as human trafficking, rape, and swindling in the name of "evangelization." The leadership of Mentuhui have openly challenged the party and the government and threatened to "seize the people's heart before seizing political power" by agitating the masses. They protest the one-child policy, agitate crowds to surround local party and government agencies, and retaliate against party officials who have enforced the ban on illegal Mentuhui activities. All of these acts have severely threatened the social and political stability of affected areas.

The text of the official November 1995 proclamation banning Mentuhui reveals that Mentuhui enjoyed rapid growth and expansion. The government designated Mentuhui a cult based on the following criteria. First, Mentuhui distorts Christian teachings. Ji Sanbao compiled a new scripture, the *Seven-Step Spiritual Journey*, which effectively deified Ji, referring to him as "Christ anointed by God" and "son of God." The scripture also records Ji's miracles, such as resurrecting the dead. Second, Mentuhui profoundly impacts the family and social order. Both its tenets and religious practices challenge and attack existing organization of family life and social norms. For example, Mentuhui's excessive attention to the impending apocalypse and an overwhelming enthusiasm for evangelism cause followers to neglect family life, education, and agricultural production. Additionally, the organization advocates prayer and exorcism as cures for illnesses rather than promoting science, medicine, and personal hygiene. Moreover, some of the key personnel deceive and defraud their followers in the name of evangelism. Finally, Mentuhui challenges the political order. Official records indicate that "the leadership of Mentuhui have openly challenged the party and the government and threatened to 'seize the people's heart before seizing political power' by agitating the masses. They protest the one-child policy, agitate crowds to surround local party and government agencies, and retaliate against party officials who have enforced the ban on illegal Mentuhui activities."

With regard to the issue of alignment with mainstream society, there is still much difference between Mentuhui and mainline Christian churches (including the Catholic Church) that evangelize openly and widely in the public space. From the perspective of the sect-church typology, Mentuhui should be categorized as a sect situated on the fringe of mainstream society. According to the tricolor religious market theory, in the context of strict governmental regulation, religious groups pay a steep price by entering the black market. Both the leaders and believers of such groups are bound to face suppression and prosecution. It follows that only religious zealots would choose to pay the hefty price for entering the black market. In a system of religious regulation, Mentuhui has been banned and officially marked as a cult. Mentuhui is a typical "black-market sect," as it has never been able to acquire legal status.

The concept of a black-market sect, however, does not sufficiently describe Mentuhui's current state or the transformations it has undergone. An online search shows that Mentuhui has nationwide appeal.[11] Mentuhui's centralized organization and widespread influence set it apart from a typical, loosely organized underground sect. The price of joining Mentuhui is not exorbitant. Moreover, the group has differentiated itself within the black market; its mechanism of operation is distinguishable from that of other black-market sects such as the Church of Almighty God (*Quanneng shen* 全能神, also known as Eastern Lightning). Furthermore, albeit a black-market sect, Mentuhui has proactively adjusted its strategy for expansion, carving out a sphere of activity by pursuing legal recognition. Liu Yanwu's 刘燕舞 research shows that Mentuhui activities around Dongtinghu 洞庭湖 in Hunan have been normalized. The organization's internal operation is sufficiently organized, standardized, and institutionalized. It maintains a nonconfrontational working relationship with the government. Not only are its activities partly open, but the organization even publishes annual reports.[12]

A colleague's interest in Mentuhui was piqued during an annual visit to his hometown, Lancheng.[13] A relative of my colleague, who I will call Mr.

---

11   A Google search for "Mentuhui" generated about 1,290,000 results, suggesting that Mentuhui's influence is widespread. Its scripture, *Shanguang lincheng* (闪光灵程), spiritual songs, and testimonies are all available in the public domain. Tang Xiaofeng 唐晓峰 corroborates our search results: "I began a research project after hearing about the many 'followers of Jesus' in W Banner in Inner Mongolia in late 2008. Once I was on location, the Christians I encountered were all 'Mentuhui' members, even though there were no registered Protestant churches in W Banner." See Tang Xiaofeng, *Gaige kaifang yilai de Zhongguo jidujiao ji yanjiu* (Beijing: Zongjiao wenhua chubanshe, 2013), 1–50.

12   Liu Yanwu, "Mentuhui zai Hunan de chuanbo," *Zhanlüe yu guanli*, 2009.8: 20–28.

13   The name of this city and of the individuals discussed in this paper are pseudonyms.

Hong, tirelessly tried to recruit him, Bible in hand, to join his group. In fact, he is a follower of Thrice Redeemed Christ (*Sanshu jidu* 三赎基督), a part of Mentuhui. Out of curiosity, my colleague conducted fieldwork in Lancheng in May 2008 and during the Spring Festival of 2009.[14] The primary research methods employed were interviews and participant observation of Mentuhui activities. He took part in Three-Self Patriotic Movement (TSPM) activities multiple times and interviewed a former member of the Church of Almighty God in order to gain insights into these two organizations. He also interviewed local government officials to better understand the authorities' attitudes toward these organizations. The following discussion is based on this fieldwork, which was shared with me, as well as my own interaction with Mentuhui and analysis of existing research, information, or documents relating to the group.

3 The Mechanisms of Operation in the Religious Black Market

How are groups in the religious black market organized? How do they manage their operations? What are their rituals and rhetoric? How do they maintain unity and group cohesion? I will examine such questions regarding the religious black market in this section.

3.1 *Organization and Structure*

This research indicates that Mentuhui has an elaborate organization. Designated personnel are in charge of seven different ranks of organizations. Each subgroup has a base, with designated contact points. Interviews revealed that the higher a member ranks in the organization, the more cautious and discrete he or she tends to be. Group leaders are rather reticent about the specific details of the organization. Questions about the organization were posed during church meetings. A female follower gave a generic statement every time she received such questions, saying that evangelization is good work that is not dictated by a stratified organization, or that there is no need to concern oneself with church organization and hierarchy. She appeared to be anxious and on high alert about the line of questioning; she also seemed to be suspicious of the interviewers' true identity and motivation. Afterward it was learned that this female follower was one of those in charge of Mentuhui in Lancheng. She and another female member were, in fact, responsible for transcribing

---

14 Lancheng is located in central Hunan. It is a small city with a limited downtown area, consisting primarily of townships and small towns.

and copying the "word" and "testimonies" of the leaders at the next level up and distributing them to those in charge of branch churches in Lancheng. My colleague attempted to learn more about Mentuhui's organization during gospel meetings but did not gain much useful insight. In the end, my colleague was able to gather information by turning to Mr. Hong and following him to meetings. Hong only opened up about the organization of Mentuhui once he had verified that my colleague and I did not present any political threat to the organization.

According to Mr. Hong, there is a sub–branch church in Lancheng that was incorporated into the stratified management structure in April 2008. Prior to that, the heads of sub–branch churches, main branch points, and sub–branch points all attended meetings for testimonies and evangelization. Once the stratified management has been implemented, communication and meetings only extend to the next level up or down. For example, the head of a sub–branch point meets only his or her counterpart at the main branch center when they are due to receive "instructions" from leaders at higher levels. The "instructions" are passed from the top down once or twice a month. For fear of government suppression, Mentuhui adjusts its communication strategy to avoid contact between units of the same rank within the organization; units at any given level only report to the next level up. Such a vertical structure minimizes horizontal connections within the organization, which helps to reduce conflicts with government authorities. Mentuhui's vertical and centralized structure is comparable to that of Yiguandao under the authoritarian rule of the Nationalist regime in Taiwan.

The basic unit of Mentuhui in any locality is the sub-branch. It consists of twenty members who are under the charge of three deacons. A member becomes eligible for deaconship when he or she has been with the church for at least a year, has actively participated in church affairs, and has studied the deacon's code. Meetings tend to be small. Each of the three deacons holds a meeting with six or seven members (such a meeting is known as a meeting place). One interviewee highlighted the fact that church activities are banned by the government. Following the rules is important to her and other members, and thus the church avoids large-scale instructional activities or gatherings.

Notably, the church has prohibited communication among its members by telephone. Instead, it requires members to communicate spiritually through prayer, claiming that believers can sense one another's calls. In Mr. Hong's words, "If you pray to God and tell God that you are going to visit a fellow believer the night before, that believer will be home waiting for you the next day." In his opinion, God reveals his greatness in his believers' ability to arrange visits with fellow believers through prayer and telepathy, although outsiders may interpret the ban on telephone communication as a means of skirting government scrutiny.

Our fieldwork experience suggests that Mentuhui's organization and structure is highly planned and that church leaders exercise caution against outsiders, even though ordinary members tend to be welcoming. Mentuhui evangelists may appeal to unthreatening outsiders by citing the church's national popularity. Under the current state of religious regulation, however, a national organization runs the risk of attention and hence government suppression. It follows that Mentuhui members treat outsiders differently depending on their intentions. They are especially discreet when interacting with outsiders with unstated intentions. Even though my colleague was a relative of Mr. Hong, he was not able to win the trust of leaders at a higher level. His experience suggests that in this pyramid structure, the higher one goes up the organizational ladder, the fuller one appreciates the leaders' apprehension of the weak legal position of the church. Thus, leaders who sit closest to the top of the pyramid are vigilant about the regulatory power of the government.

3.2 *Rituals and Rhetoric*

A religious organization depends on routine rituals to stimulate and strengthen the collective identity of its members. The primary Mentuhui rituals include Bible study, regular meetings, giving testimonies, and group prayer on the Sabbath. Through rituals, believers reinforce their sense of membership in a group, construct a sacred community, and produce as well as reproduce a collective social identity.

Mentuhui members observe a day of rest weekly, when they study the transcripts of the "word" and testimonies passed down from higher-ranking leaders of the church. Meetings typically take place in the homes of enthusiastic members, at somewhat regular meeting times determined by all participants (which may be adjusted occasionally). At a meeting, participants sing spiritual songs, share their "testimonies," engage in Bible study, and pray together. Spiritual songs are adaptations of familiar folk tunes or pop music with spiritual lyrics. The lyrics are also a kind of "word," calling for repentance and a new life in God, cautioning against damnation to hell, and promising eternal life in heaven. After the testimonies and instructions of the "word" come prayers. Typically, there is a red cross in each member's home. As participants pray, they kneel and face the cross, repeatedly calling out "My Lord! My God! Thrice Redeemed (*sanshu* 三赎)!"

The discussion during a meeting typically revolves around two topics: the "word" and testimonies. The "word" refers to a manually transcribed guidebook for studying the Bible (*Shengjing xuexi zhinan* 圣经学习指南). The study of the "word" entails the reading of every single verse of the Bible and the associated commentary, with the evocation of awe and admiration for God in mind. This Mentuhui practice is almost identical with Bible study at the Three-Self Church. During fieldwork, we realized that the Mentuhui term for "word" (*dao* 道) is with the same as that used in the study guides in mainline Protestant churches. However, because the term "word" is theological in nature, it is easily perceived as a foreign concept by people who have no prior experience with theology. Therefore, even though the "word" has theological significance, the concept's practical significance lies in the Christian veneer it lends to Mentuhui rhetoric.

Testimony is by far the most important idiom through which believers spread the Mentuhui message. Testimonies are typically transcribed and copied manually. They recount the miracles that believers throughout the country have experienced after their conversion, such as blind persons who have regained their sight, physically disabled persons who have regained the ability to walk, or individuals who have been cured of a severe illness or demonic possession. In the meetings, participants devote the bulk of the meeting to promoting testimonies and spend hardly any time on the reading and interpretation of the Bible. A truly devout believer can only transcribe the "word" and testimonies by hand; photocopying and circulation over the phone are strictly forbidden. Similar to Mentuhui's method of internal communication, this process guarantees that the only printed material in circulation within the sect is the Bible, which is approved by the state. The circulation method also adds yet another shroud of mystery to the organization and reinforces a sense of collective identity.

Based on the testimonies' relevance to the believers' actual lived experiences, they can be divided into two general categories: mundane events and miraculous happenings (miracles). Any testimony that only concerns an individual believer is usually trivial and mundane. Below are two examples of mundane testimonies:

> The belief in God does not require money or grain. It requires faith. Once I scolded my wife for playing mahjong, and I got a sore throat the next day. I knew immediately that this was God's way of reprimanding me for pointing fingers at others and of steering me in the direction of spreading the good news. I prayed to God for his forgiveness and had my wife join me in prayer. My throat felt fine the following day.

> Another time I got very sick with a cold. A relative came to visit me and ridiculed my faith in God, asking why my God had not protected me. I immediately prayed to God and pleaded to Jesus for a cure so that I could

be a testament to God's greatness. It happened to be the sixtieth birthday party of a relative a couple of days later, and my cold was cured on that day. I knew that God had revealed his omnipotence, allowing me to give testimony to others and be a messenger of God at this family gathering.

Testimonies tend to emphasize that, as far as physical illnesses are concerned, chances of recovery are proportionate to a believer's degree of devotion. Failure to be cured of a disease is an indication of lack of devotion. Only prayer and preaching can fully cure illnesses. Testimonies about events that have no immediate temporal or geographical relevance tend to have a much stronger miraculous overtone than mundane minutiae, similar to the biblical stories of the blind receiving sight, the lame walking, and the deaf hearing. One of the manually copied testimonies reads as follows:

> An old and crippled man in Hunan has had chronic heart problems. He is stubborn and refuses to believe in God. His son refuses to give up on bringing him to God. As the old man was dying, he thought that he had nothing to lose and reluctantly accepted God to appease his family. Although his faith was wavering, other believers' love made him see the truth. He finally said, "I believe in God." As soon as he uttered these words, he was able to walk. His heart disease was cured instantaneously! He was saved by the power of God. This old man now openly and sincerely shares his story with everyone in the hopes that people will get to know God, fear God, and thank God!

Testimonies of God the savior, such as the one below, surged shortly after the May 12, 2008, Sichuan earthquake.

> Brother Chen of the suburb of Beichuan 北川 [near the earthquake epicenter] gives testimony along with his family, all of whom are now the children of the Lord. On May 12, right before the earthquake hit Sichuan, Chen was praying alone at home while his family worked in the field. He sat down in a chair after his prayers and immediately heard a voice in the sky, saying, "Get out of the house!" He saw a man in white flashing by; a big hand grabbed him out of the chair and hurled him to a safe spot twenty meters away. At that instant, the ground started trembling, mountains were shaking, and everything was destroyed. Two minutes later, there were dead bodies everywhere, and houses lay in ruins. But all three members of the Chen family were unharmed. They thanked God profusely. They immediately started searching for brothers and sisters

under their pastoral care and found all of them safe and sound. Sisters Li and Jing at Ruxian Hospital were also saved. At the moment when the earthquake struck, Li was moved by the Holy Spirit and walked into the courtyard; Jing was helping a patient to the restroom and happened to be in the middle of the courtyard as well. Everyone in the hospital died except for these three. A big hand carried Old Sister Li Qiongying to safety when she was praying at home, as the building was collapsing. God saved all of these individuals. Now they travel around and give testimonies to God's grace. They have successfully brought more than twenty brothers and sisters who are weak in faith back to God, along with an additional twenty relatives and family members. They are continuing their tours of testimonies.

Other testimonies are similar in nature. They recount stories of angels descending from heaven and rescuing believers. In them, God either warns and denies aid to nonbelievers or performs miracles and imparts grace on the devout.

Testimonies to divine miracles set Mentuhui apart from mainline Christian denominations. For instance, the Three-Self Church rarely circulates contemporary miracles. Most of the testimonies shared in Three-Self churches are mundane family matters that teach moral lessons without any tinge of the miraculous. Pastors in Three-Self services do speak of miracles, but these are typically limited to those recounted in the Bible and are used to demonstrate God's omnipotence. Contemporary miraculous happenings have little place in the Three-Self Church.

Mentuhui testimonies are impossible to substantiate, as they usually take place in faraway places. The testimonies are also revelations of divine power and profoundly miraculous. Witnesses usually give very personal and highly relatable testimonies. Repeating testimonies allows believers to feel God's power over and over again and envision an eternal life in "heaven."

4   The Pursuit of Legitimacy

Mentuhui's development has shifted course as the government continues to enforce strict regulations on religious affairs. Changes are revealed in the following aspects: the reform of teachings, the adoption of moderate religious practices, and highlighting a gray identity in the competition within the religious black market. Through these means, Mentuhui attempts to establish legitimacy in a variety of dimensions.

4.1 The Reform of Teachings

Mentuhui members do not deny their Christian identity. What sets them apart from other Christians, though, is their faith in the "Thrice Redeemed Christ" and their belief that Ji Sanbao is Christ incarnate. Due to this major divergence from orthodox Christian teaching, Mentuhui attempts a renewed interpretation of the Thrice Redeemed Bible in order to ameliorate its tension with Christian orthodoxy. The new interpretation associates the Bible with specific Chinese conditions. When novices inquire about the doctrines of Mentuhui, members begin by explaining the biblical origin of the Three Redemptions.

Mentuhui members cite biblical verses to demonstrate that the Chinese people are destined to deliver the promise of salvation through Christ. For instance, they may cite Genesis 2:8, "Now the LORD God had planted a garden in the east, in Eden; and there he put the man he had formed," and Isaiah 49:12, "See, they will come from afar—some from the north, some from the west, some from the region of Aswan." In *Mentuhui* interpretation, the "east" in Genesis refers to China and "Aswan" refers to Shaanxi province.[15] Shaanxi is situated in the northwest. All of these messages are received as signs from God.

The first verse of the Gospel of John is another biblical text that has received a localized interpretation: "In the beginning was the Word, and the Word was with God, and the Word was God" (John 1:1). In this verse, "Word" corresponds to the *dao* 道 referenced by *Laozi* 老子. As far as Mentuhui is concerned, this verse is an indication that ancient Chinese sages had perceived the existence of Yahweh.

The first step of Mentuhui's self-legitimization is to associate its own tenets with Christian tradition, by claiming to be a Christian denomination and appropriating select biblical verses to connect indigenous sages to their Christian counterparts. This alliance of East and West capitalizes on Christianity's perceived mysterious quality in the popular imagination.[16] The Chinese people, generally speaking, do not challenge the legitimacy of Christianity and are even intrigued by it, partly because of the status that Christianity enjoys in advanced, Western countries. At the same time, Mentuhui's interpretation of the Christian scriptures connects Christianity and the Three Redemptions to create a sense of cultural affinity between the Chinese people and the Christian tradition. By these means, Mentuhui argues for the legitimacy of its

---

15   In the Chinese Union Version of the Bible, Aswan is rendered as 秦国 (*Qinguo*). In Chinese history, the Qin Dynasty 秦朝 was based in Shaanxi.

16   James Thayer Addison, "Chinese Ancestor-Worship and Protestant Christianity," *Journal of Religion* 5 (1925): 140–149.

tenets by appropriating biblical verses and reinterpreting the Christian tradition through the prism of Chinese cultural heritage, even though it maintains the belief in the Three Redemptions.

4.2 Church-State Relations: A Focus on Obedience

According to the official document mentioned above, one of the grounds on which the state designated Mentuhui a cult is its challenge to the political status quo. Responding to this accusation, an officer of a Mentuhui meeting place explained:

> We've always avoided the topic of politics, let alone challenging the Party. Our higher-ranking leaders often ask us to pray for government officials and political leaders. They also instruct us to submit to higher powers. Because political authorities are ordained by God and by the supreme power, they are not to be disobeyed or resisted. People say that we are a cult banned by the state. They don't understand us, and they are ignorant. As members of Mentuhui, we support the state, and the state wouldn't ban us.

Mentuhui members repeatedly stressed their submission to governmental authority during the interviews. They also recited biblical verses that commanded so. For example, Romans 13:1–7 is often referenced:

> Let everyone be subject to the governing authorities, for there is no authority except that which God has established. The authorities that exist have been established by God. Consequently, whoever rebels against the authority is rebelling against what God has instituted, and those who do so will bring judgment on themselves. For rulers hold no terror for those who do right, but for those who do wrong. Do you want to be free from fear of the one in authority? Then do what is right and you will be commended. For the one in authority is God's servant for your good. But if you do wrong, be afraid, for rulers do not bear the sword for no reason. They are God's servants, agents of wrath to bring punishment on the wrongdoer. Therefore, it is necessary to submit to the authorities, not only because of possible punishment but also as a matter of conscience. This is also why you pay taxes, for the authorities are God's servants, who give their full time to governing. Give to everyone what you owe them: If you owe taxes, pay taxes; if revenue, then revenue; if respect, then respect; if honor, then honor.

We can see from these verses that Mentuhui pursues political legitimacy by articulating proper church-state relations. That is, by declaring its members' obedience to the authorities and governmental regulations, Mentuhui seeks to increase its presence in the political realm. To Mentuhui members, these biblical verses are evidence that the organization is harmless to the political order. Moreover, during interviews, the officers of meeting places repeatedly emphasized that they abided by the rules, did not hold large-scale assemblies, and kept meeting sizes small, allowing no more than twenty participants.

Online searches provide yet another perspective on Mentuhui's transition from the "black" to the "gray" market. Ever since its suppression in 1991, Mentuhui has endeavored to reshape its organization, practices, and identity. These efforts have contributed to the group's movement in the direction of a gray market.

4.3 Competition among Religious Groups

Mentuhui has clearly distinguished itself from "orthodox" Protestant Christian churches, on the one hand, and black-market sects, such as the Church of Almighty God, on the other. It aims to prove its legitimacy through competition in the religious market.

Mentuhui is critical of the practice of soliciting donations, which is commonplace in "orthodox" Christian churches. In Lancheng, at the end of every Sunday service at TSPM churches, church leaders would announce the individuals and matters in need of prayer (prayers are usually solicited for illnesses), and the congregation would pray together while making donations of about 200 RMB (30 USD) or more each.

Mr. Hong recounted an incident of competition between two churches: "Once a fellow believer became sick, and we prayed for his recovery wholeheartedly. When he got better, people from the [TSPM] church went and collected donations from him, saying that his illness was cured by prayers at the church." Mentuhui's adamant rejection of donations or any form of financial support, in fact, gives its members a sense of superiority, which is also leveraged as moral capital in its criticism of the TSPM. Moreover, Mentuhui's principled refusal of all donations also presents a counterargument against the state's allegation of swindling and defrauding, as stated in the 1995 official document that banned the sect.

Mentuhui members have no hesitation about calling another black-market sect, the Church of Almighty God, a cult. They support the government's suppression of it. A Mentuhui leader in Lancheng shared a story about the denunciation of the Church of Almighty God. According to him, the Church of Almighty God receives financial and material aid from overseas, and the organization even agitates to topple the government. But collusion with foreign powers in a potential coup d'état is a capital offense in the eyes of Mentuhui members. Since the local Church of Almighty God often competes with Mentuhui for recruits, Mentuhui members are eager to report the illicit activities of their rival and may even demand disciplinary action by the government.

Both in rhetoric and in practice, Mentuhui is quite distinguishable from the Church of Almighty God. Mentuhui members' attitude toward the government is one of submission, as opposed to the apocalyptical messages and clandestine activities of the Church of Almighty God (CAG). A Mentuhui member who had formerly belonged to the CAG revealed: "I used to buy into the rhetoric that the end is near, that only by joining our group [CAG] can one escape the apocalypse. The government will be damned because it tries to suppress us. Let's ignore the government."

4.4 Preservation of the Family and Social Order

An avalanche of official propaganda has portrayed Mentuhui as a cult that challenges the family and social order. When asked if Mentuhui is a cult, our interviewees were forthcoming and articulated their thoughts in a matter-of-fact manner.

> Why does the government see Mentuhui as a cult? My fellow church members and I are very willing to help others. To start, the church prescribes ten commandments. The first four teach us to worship God and forbid idolatry. The fifth commandment onward are: obeying and honoring our parents; prohibitions on killing, scolding, loathing, and promiscuity; abstinence toward women; stealing or taking from others, regardless of the amount, is theft and forbidden; prohibitions on giving false testimony, avarice, or greed. There are six additional rules. First, be tolerant; second, be congenial; third, moderate in temper; fourth, adopt a friendly attitude; fifth, do onto others as you would have them do to you; sixth, obey and care for one's parents. If everyone abided by the ten commandments and six rules, harmony and peace would reign in our society! If only everyone were a Mentuhui member! In that case we wouldn't ever have to keep an eye out for thieves!

Mentuhui's revised rhetoric presents a brand-new self-image. No longer is Mentuhui the destroyer of the family and social harmony portrayed in the 1995 official document. Quite to the contrary, Mentuhui members love their God, their parents, and their neighbors; they uphold the moral order and promote family unity. This message is yet another means of claiming social legitimacy.

4.5 Donations to the Church

My research shows that Mentuhui has limited sources of revenue. For example, the amount of revenue it derives from donations is far less than that of the Three-Self Church. Interviewees insisted that it costs them nothing to join Mentuhui, with the exception of the purchase of a Bible, which is sold at a fixed price. Their Bible is the same as the standard edition used by the TSPM, and it even sells at a slightly lower price: 10 RMB (1.50 USD) for a copy of the Bible. Mentuhui charges 15 RMB (just over 2 USD) for a cross (i.e., a red cross printed on white canvas), but I learned that some Mentuhui members have made crosses for themselves using their own materials, and thus the crosses generate little to no profit.

The church does not need donations, and it further forbids members from making donations. As the organization expands, I have not observed any hints of wrongdoing or swindling in the name of evangelization on the part of the deacons in county-level cities. With limited resources, Mentuhui has to keep the costs of its activities down. Mentuhui never has the need to rent venues for large-scale events, nor does it have to provide honoraria for guest pastors or participate in public charitable activities. Evangelism does not require much capital investment.

Moreover, with the exception of the Bible, all Mentuhui study materials are copied by hand. Manual reproduction significantly reduces the financial burden on members by eliminating printing costs. Anyone with inexpensive pens and paper can study the Bible. Devout members are also exposed to God's greatness through the repetitive transcription of testimonies. On average, every member receives a shipment of the "word" and testimonies every two weeks. Each package consists of roughly four sheets of "word" and six sheets of testimonies. Working with total concentration and without interruption, it takes about two hours for a member to transcribe one package. The transcripts are then forwarded to branches at the appropriate levels in the organization, and the quantity of copies is determined by the numbers reported by the officers at each level.

In 2006, Mentuhui spent 40,000 RMB (approximately 6,100 USD) on Bible purchases (all together about 4,000 copies). I was told that one of the members fronted the church these funds, thanks to his wealthy son. This member's home also serves as a meeting place and as a guesthouse for church members from out of town. Whenever the organization gains a new recruit, the deacon goes to him to purchase a copy. Mentuhui's officer-in-charge in Lancheng believes that the number of Bibles sold roughly represents the number of members. Mentuhui members believe that their church is the "narrow gate" to Heaven (see Matthew 7:13–14), and thus their numbers have to be limited.

All of the aforementioned practices have contributed to Mentuhui's continuation and expansion in three important ways. First, the prohibition of donations satisfies a sense of moral superiority vis-à-vis the Three-Self Church. It is commonplace to ask for donations at the end of each Sunday service at the local Three-Self church. Mentuhui, on the other hand, insists on free and voluntary mutual aid between believers, with no money involved. This strategy appeals to ordinary people. Second, the Three-Self Church's legitimacy is evidenced by its ability to openly solicit donations. Mentuhui, on the other hand, by forbidding donations, is able to refute the allegation that it is a cult engaged in racketeering and thus avoids legal intervention. Third, the method of dissemination and distribution of study materials (including commentaries on the Bible and testimonies) reduces the cost of running the organization. Additionally, copying is an exercise that only the most devout members are willing to do. In a way, transmission of the tenets by hand helps to weed out insincere members and ensure the purity of members' devotion. Furthermore, as members copy the study materials, they are also exposed to the teachings of the church. On the whole, such exercises enhance members' conviction in the central teachings and the collective identity of Mentuhui, as well as strengthen the moral community of the church. An added benefit is the reduced risk of legal disputes caused by publication, since the texts are not printed.

4.6 *Cure through Prayer or Medicine?*

The following story about leukemia is an allegory of the "power" and "powerlessness" of faith. In 2007, the oldest son of a member suddenly fell ill. The family tried to pray his illness away, but to no avail, so they took him to the hospital as a last resort. The son was diagnosed with leukemia at the best hospital in Hunan. After undergoing treatment that cost more than 40,000 RMB (approximately 6,100 USD), the patient still showed no sign of improvement. His father decided to take him home, and fellow Mentuhui members prayed for his recovery. The patient himself even started preaching, as a testament to his faith in God, in the hope of a cure. He died two weeks later.

The father, who is a devout believer and a deacon of a main branch, said, "Many people say that my belief killed my child. But they are wrong. How could I kill my son? His mother cried every day when he was being treated." He then showed us the receipts and test results from the hospital. The father continued,

> My son insisted on receiving treatment in the hospital, refusing to pray like we asked him to. Then we took him to the hospital—the best one [in the province]. His treatment lasted for nearly a month; it cost us dearly every single day. The test results showed that he was not getting better

> but even worse [than before the treatment]. I've kept all the receipts as proof that I spared nothing on my son's treatment. It was my son who said he wanted to go home and believe in God. Once he believed in God and started to pray, he began to feel a lot better and regained his appetite. God signaled to us in our prayer that our son should go out and spread the good news. After a few days of evangelizing, he felt much better and looked healthier. Alas, when he was out spreading the good news many relatives and acquaintances ridiculed him. They tried to talk him into returning to the hospital and ignoring our advice. His confidence in God was wavering; feeling embarrassed, he stopped evangelizing. He left us after all. On his deathbed, he said to us and his brother, "I'm leaving. God is good, but he can't save me just now." He left us. But we will meet again in the eternal life.

The father lives in a close-knit community in which everyone knows everyone else. Our research indicates that all of his neighbors condemned his course of action. They blamed him for not getting his son proper treatment and resorting instead to the irrational "collective prayer." Gambling with his son's life like this delayed treatment and eventually cost him his child, according to his neighbors.

This case illustrates the negotiation between belief and lived experience. Such negotiation, in fact, rarely occurred in the foundational period of Mentuhui; it used to be considered incompatible with the prevailing rhetoric of cure by prayer or cure by exorcism. Nevertheless, the fact that such negotiation takes place indicates that prayer for healing is not the sole guiding principle in Mentuhui members' practices of faith. This is a case in which religious practice converges with the expectations of mainstream society.

On the whole, recent developments show that Mentuhui has successfully carved out a sphere of activity. According to the government agencies in Lancheng, Mentuhui remains under close scrutiny. The government, however, will not take any action to ban the organization as long as it does not agitate protests, deceive the masses, or coerce people into joining the church. No disciplinary action will be taken without higher-lever orders or complaints from the public. Regarding another black-market cult, the CAG, the government takes a much firmer stance. An official at the Religious Affairs Bureau in Lancheng confirms that Mentuhui members denounced the CAG. According to this official,

> The Church of Almighty God definitely has notoriety and always instills fear in people. It claims to be an international organization, putting on

a foreign air to deceive ordinary people and acting suspiciously. We pay special attention to areas where they engage in clandestine activities. We also broadcast the potential harm of the Church of Almighty God to the general populace. We are applying the same strategy we used to employ in dealing with Falun Gong members to the Church of Almighty God.

Judging by the way in which local government officials compare the different illicit organizations, it is clear that Mentuhui is no longer an organization worthy of suppression in the religious black market in the eyes of the government.

In 1995, the state declared Mentuhui a cult based on its tenets and practices. Mentuhui was said to be a major challenge to the family, social order, and political status quo. This case study of Lancheng reveals that, in the context of strict governmental regulation, Mentuhui has reformed itself, pursued legitimacy, and reduced the likelihood of conflict with the government, and in the event of conflict, it has endeavored to reduce the damage. Legally speaking, Mentuhui is still a cult. In practice, however, Mentuhui's status has undergone a transformation in the religious market. Through the reformation of its teachings and its strong support of the family and social order, as well as its expressed obedience to the government, Mentuhui's renewed religious practices have pushed the organization into the gray market.

5   Conclusion and Discussion

When we situate Chinese religious organizations on a continuum based on their respective spheres of activity, we find the five legal religious organizations (including the TSPM) on one end, and various officially banned cults, such as the Church of Almighty God, on the other. Although Mentuhui technically is not an unregistered church in the gray market, it has been steadily moving toward the gray end of the black-market section on this spectrum. My analysis of the differences among Mentuhui, the TSPM, and the Church of Almighty God in the previous pages is summarized in Table 2.1.

In the framework of the tricolor market theory, the TSPM falls in the red market, as its legal status is approved by the state, whereas the CAG and Mentuhui both find themselves in the black market, banned by the state. This is a static display of their respective places in the religious market. However, we may ask whether and in what ways the status of each organization has changed in the overall transformation of the religious landscape in the last decade or so. A comparison of the characteristics of these organizations can shed light on each group's movement within the religious market.

TABLE 2.1   Comparison of characteristics of religious organizations: Three-Self Patriotic Movement (TSPM), Mentuhui, and the Church of Almighty God (CAG)

Characteristic	TSPM	Mentuhui	CAG
Church-state relationship	Supports the government while downplaying its support	Openly supports the government and emphasizes obedience	Resists, attacks, and challenges the government
Spheres of activity	Open and legal; large-scale, public Sunday services	Semi-open; no large-scale gatherings	Fully underground activities
Government's response	Supports churches	No open suppression	Heavy suppression; close scrutiny of communication and networks
Resources	Openly accepts donations from members in a ritual setting	Limited resources; prohibition of donations in a ritual setting	Claims to receive foreign financial aid
Rhetoric	Focuses on Bible study and commentaries; promotes upright living and behavior	Miracles are rather important	Miracles are central to its teachings
Recruitment strategy	Combination of open preaching and private evangelization	Semi-open private evangelization	Clandestine private evangelization
Level of piety	Diverse membership with varying degrees of devotion; many "free riders"	Rather homogeneous membership with a higher degree of devotion; no "free riders"	Perceived as fanatical
Perceptions of the other two sects	Views Mentuhui and CAG as cults	Believes TSPM has ulterior motives and distorts Christian teachings; views CAG as a cult	Views TSPM and CAG as insincere and excluded from the eternal life

With regard to the church-state relationship, Mentuhui is similar to the TSPM in its attitude toward the government and willingness to submit to authorities. Whereas Mentuhui emphasizes obedience to political authority, the CAG holds a completely opposite view of state power. On the other side of the relationship, the government's stance toward the three ranges from approval to acquiescence and stringent regulation. Although Mentuhui and the Church of Almighty God are both in the black market, the former has successfully softened the government's intransigence and transformed its long-held policy of suppression. From its recruitment strategy to its sphere of activity, it is clear that Mentuhui has left the CAG behind as it marches toward the gray market. Finally, Mentuhui has also shed the self-identity of a cult, and members no longer view themselves as operating in the black market. As far as Mentuhui members are concerned, their church has obtained legitimacy.

It has been more than two decades since the state put a ban on Mentuhui in 1995. Mentuhui has managed to move from the black market in the direction of the gray market over the last twenty years. Our analysis concludes that, despite the strict regulation of local governments in certain locations, Mentuhui in Lancheng is a case of a successful transition from the black to the gray market. I have examined Mentuhui's transformation into its current state from different perspectives. Regarding self-identification, individual Mentuhui members make a clear distinction between their organization and "illegal" groups. Mentuhui's multi-pronged strategy for expanding its sphere of activity and increasing recruitment is also revealed in this chapter. In particular, the organization cites biblical verses to substantiate its support of the political authorities. The rejection of donations, the circulation of manually transcribed testimonies, and a cap on the number of meeting participants have not only allowed Mentuhui to avoid disciplinary and legal action by the state, but they have also effectively solidified the "moral community" within the organization.

To conclude, in the context of strict governmental control, Mentuhui has both reduced the state's inclination to suppress its activities and expanded its sphere of activity by demonstrating its legality through its teaching, its influence on the family, and its role in society. This case study also sheds light on the mechanisms of religious transformation from the black into the gray market. The government's strict control is, in fact, a motivator for a religious organization to reform and adjust itself. In the Chinese context, fierce competition within the black market is yet another powerful contributing factor to such transition.

Looking ahead, the next phase of Mentuhui's transformation will make an interesting topic for sociological research. Even though Mentuhui was pushed into the black market due to stringent government regulation, it has now carved out a sphere in the gray market. The color gray signifies uncertainty. Mentuhui's future is unpredictable. Maintaining the status quo as it marches into the gray market is a possible development. However, when the status quo changes, Mentuhui may have to move in one of two divergent directions. First, it is possible that the government will resume its suppression of Mentuhui and push it into the black market once again. My online research shows that negative comments and criticisms targeting Mentuhui are quite common, given its wide reach. In the event that Mentuhui members cause unrest in a locality, the government will likely crack down on their activities. That would put Mentuhui back where it started in the early 1990s—in the black market along with Falun Gong and the CAG. The other possibility is assimilation. Indeed, mainstream religious groups and the state alike have regarded Mentuhui as a cult since its formative years mainly because of its sensational and unorthodox messages. Through negotiation with mainstream religious culture and internal adjustment, Mentuhui has assimilated into mainstream society and gained social approval. The Mormon Church's assimilation into the dominant culture is a useful frame of reference. The relaxation of religious regulations can result in the institutionalization of a sect, which makes the sect acceptable to society at large. The best example of such acceptance is the evolution of Yiguandao in Taiwan. In the end, whether or not a sect is able to assimilate into mainstream society depends on negotiations among state, sect, and believers, as well as the respective stance each party takes.

Bibliography

Addison, James Thayer. "Chinese Ancestor-Worship and Protestant Christianity." *Journal of Religion* 5 (1925): 140–149.

"Concerning the Investigation and the Banning of the 'Shouter Sect' and Other Cultic Organizations and Their Situation and Suggestions for Action issued by Ministry of Public Security" 中共中央办公厅、国务院办公厅下发《关于转发〈公安部关于查禁取缔"呼喊派"等邪教组织的情况及工作意见〉的通知》. *Ting zi* 厅字 50 (1995).

Johnson, Benton. "On Church and Sect." *American Sociological Review* 28 (1963): 539–549.

Johnstone, Ronald. *Religion in Society: A Sociology of Religion*. 8th ed. Abingdon, UK: Routledge, 2016. Translated by Yuan Yayu 袁亚愚 and Zhong Yuying 钟玉英 as *Shehui zhong de zongjiao–yizhong zongjiao shehuixue* 社会中的宗教——一种宗教社会学. Chengdu: Sichuan renmin chubanshe, 2012.

Liu Yanwu 刘燕舞. "Mentuhui zai Hunan de chuanbo" 门徒会在湖南的传播. *Zhanlüe yu guanli* 战略与管理, 2009.8: 20–28.

Lu, Yunfeng. *The Transformation of Yiguan Dao in Taiwan: Adapting to a Changing Religious Economy*. Plymouth, UK: Lexington Books, 2008.

Lu Yunfeng 卢云峰. "Chaoyue jiduzongjiao shehuixue—jianlun zongjiao shichang lilun zai huaren shehui de shiyongxing wenti" 超越基督宗教社会学—兼论宗教市场理论在华人社会的适用性问题. *Shehuixue yanjiu* 社会学研究, 2008.5: 81–97.

Robbins, Thomas, Dick Anthony, and James Richardson. "Theory and Research on Today's 'New Religions.'" *Sociological Analysis* 39.2 (1978): 95–122.

Stark, Rodney, and Roger Finke. *Acts of Faith: Explaining the Human Side of Religion*. Berkeley: University of California Press, 2000. Translated by Yang Fenggang 杨凤岗 as *Xinyang de faze—jieshi zongjiao zhi ren de fangmian* 信仰的法则—解释宗教之人的方面. Beijing: Zhongguo renmin daxue chubanshe, 2004.

Tang Xiaofeng 唐晓峰. *Gaige kaifang yilai de Zhongguo jidujiao ji yanjiu* 改革开放以来的中国基督教及研究. Beijing: Zongjiao wenhua chubanshe, 2013.

Yang, Fenggang. *Religion in China: Survival and Revival under Communist Rule*. New York: Oxford University Press, 2012.

CHAPTER 3

Between Interests and Politics

The Changing Status of Two Protestant Churches in China's Tricolor Religious Market

Li Hui

In 2004, Fenggang Yang introduced Chinese scholars to Rodney Stark and Roger Finke's *Acts of Faith: Explaining the Human Side of Religion*.[1] This book has generated a great deal of discussion among sociologists of religion in China, especially with respect to its presentation of the religious market theory and the rational choice approach to religion.[2] Although *Acts of Faith* is a seminal work on the religious market theory, it has been critiqued on many fronts. For instance, Yang argues that the application of religious market theory to the Chinese context ought to take into consideration the distinctive religious history and environment in China. In particular, writes Yang, China's widespread unapproved religious groups and unorganized religious practices on the individual level require a more critical understanding. Moreover, the opposite side of the religious market, that is, state control of religion, is an influential actor in the Chinese religious market.[3] In his *Religion in China: Survival and Revival under Communist Rule*, published in 2012,[4] Yang further articulates the strengths and shortcomings of the religious market theory as an interpretive

---

[1] Rodney Stark and Roger Finke, *Acts of Faith: Explaining the Human Side of Religion* (Berkeley: University of California Press, 2000); translated by Yang Fenggang as *Xinyang de faze—jieshi zongjiao zhi ren de fangmian* (Beijing: Zhongguo renmin daxue chubanshe, 2004).

[2] Ji Zhe, "Ruhe chaoyue shisuhua lilun?—ping zongjiao shehuixue de sanzhong houshisuhua lunshu," *Shehuixue yanjiu*, 2008.4: 55–75; Chan Bing, "Zongjiao ye you shichang?—Luodeni Sidake de zongjiao shichang lilun pingshu," *Daqing shifan xueyuan xuebao*, 2009.5: 45–50; Li Xiangping and Yang Linxia, "Zongjiao, shehui yu quanli guanxi—'zongjiao shichang lun' de shehuixue jiedu," *Huadong shifan daxue xuebao (zhexue shehui kexue ban)* 43.5 (2011): 1–7; Li Feng, "Huidao shehui: dui dangqian zongjiao shehuixue yanjiu fanshi zhi fansi," *Jianghai xuekan*, 2013.5: 95–100.

[3] Fenggang Yang, "The Red, Black, and Gray Markets of Religion in China," *Sociological Quarterly* 47.1 (2006): 93–122. Translated and abridged by Yang Fenggang as "Zhongguo zongjiao de sanse shichang," *Zhongguo renmin daxue xuebao* 6 (2006): 41–47.

[4] Fenggang Yang, *Religion in China: Survival and Revival under Communist Rule* (New York: Oxford University Press, 2012).

framework. In the final analysis, Yang has proposed a "tricolor market" theory with the distinctive Chinese religious policies and religious landscape in mind.

1   The Tricolor Religious Market Theory

Yang's book title clearly reflects his thesis: religion has survived and revived under Communist rule in China. Yang argues that not only have draconian religious policies been unsuccessful in suppressing religious activities, but they have also effectively diversified the religious market. Some religious groups have gone underground, and others have managed to survive in a gray zone of the religious market. The result is the emergence of the red, gray, and black religious markets. The gray market is further divided into two categories. The first encompasses illicit religious activities sponsored by approved religious organizations, individuals, or unspecified groups. State-sponsored religious endeavors, such as the construction of a temple for the sake of boosting tourism, also fall into the first category. The second category is represented by quasi-religious activities, that is, religiosity expressed in the forms of cultural traditions or health sciences, such as *qigong*.

Yang further makes three key points regarding the three different religious markets. First, the more the state restricts the membership and operation of religious organizations, the more likely a black market will emerge, even though believers have to pay a steep price. Second, when the red market is constrained and the black market is suppressed, a gray market will emerge. Finally, the greater the constraints that are put on religious engagements, the larger the gray market will grow.[5] Yang's primary goal is to establish an overarching interpretive framework for religious change under the rule of the Chinese Communist Party.[6] The official atheism of the Chinese Communist regime inevitably puts it at odds with religious organizations and practices. Indeed, religion has always existed in a suppressed state under Party rule. Specifically, the state's regulation of religion has targeted underground churches in the hope that illegal groups could be brought under the oversight of religious patriotic associations. In practice, the state has had limited success in regulating underground churches.

Although the tricolor religious market is easy to understand, we cannot escape the complex fact that groups often simultaneously occupy many different

---

5   Ibid., 89–92.
6   Ibid., xi–xii.

parts of this spectrum. Because state policies regarding religious affairs in the Hu Jintao era (2004–2012) were more relaxed than before, church-state relations improved during these years.[7] For instance, local governments acquiesced to the prevalence of house churches. Under the banner of "mutual adaptation between religion and Socialism," local governments typically refrained from overtly suppressing house churches. Under such circumstances, it is imperative that we revisit the features of the tricolor market, especially those forces that will move a religious community from one part of the market to the other.

The complexity of the tricolor market can be seen in China's Christian organizations. The churches that are members of the China Christian Council (CCC)/Three-Self Patriotic Movement (TSPM) and are approved by the state find themselves in the red market. Christian churches that are not members of the TSPM are viewed as underground churches and thus are cast into the black market. However, a Three-Self church may support certain activities that are not sanctioned by the state and thus exist in the gray market. Moreover, even though house churches have been declared illegal by the state, in recent years they have enjoyed greater degrees of freedom. That is, the state has turned a blind eye to many unregistered churches, acquiescing to their existence in a gray area. The line between legal and illicit churches is, in effect, blurred. Furthermore, local governments have employed "unofficial means" and exhibited great flexibility in their management of religious affairs.[8] On the whole, an examination of the enforcement of religious policies on the ground and how religious groups actually operate suggests the following: house churches that are not explicitly suppressed by local state authorities operate in the gray market, and those that are outlawed remain in the black market.

As the political environment has eased, it is key to consider the factors that have contributed to a further diversification within the religious market. How do religious groups shift from one space to another within the tricolor market? What is the mechanism of transition? How does knowledge of this mechanism affect scholarly appreciation of the church-state relationship at the local level? Examining the Christian religious markets in two cities, which I will refer to as Anhong and Bentu, gives us a pair of case studies that are helpful for understanding the interpretive framework of the tricolor market theory.[9]

---

7   Yoshiko Ashiwa and David L. Wank, *Making Religion, Making the State: The Politics of Religion in Modern China* (Stanford, CA: Stanford University Press, 2009).
8   Zhou Xueguang, "Weiquan tizhi yu youxiao guanli: dangdai Zhongguo guojia zhili de zhidu luoji," *Kaifang shidai*, 2011.10: 67–85.
9   Pseudonyms are used for the names of these cities, as well as the local individuals referenced in this chapter. "Christianity" in this chapter refers exclusively to Protestantism.

Even though official religious policies have a direct influence on the formation of the Christian tricolor market in the two localities, individual as well as group interests are the major drivers of shifting status within the religious market. When communication between church and state breaks down, and when each party becomes less tolerant of the other's bottom line, the more powerful party-state often reacts by mercilessly suppressing churches. Yet a comparative study of Christian churches in Anhong and Bentu will demonstrate that governmental suppression has not yielded the desired outcomes. Rather, suppression has stimulated further development and expansion of Christian churches.

2   The Christian Tricolor Market in Anhong

Anhong, a city in Shanxi Province, used to be within the sphere of influence of the China Inland Mission (*Neidihui* 内地会, hereafter CIM). The Christian population has seen significant growth since China's reform and opening up. By 2014, the Christian population of Anhong had reached 132,000, roughly 3 percent of the total population.[10]

In 2009, a church in Anhong clashed with the local government over property rights. This incident even attracted international attention. At the time, I was a student and was intrigued by the respective perspectives of the government and the church on this matter. When I tried to interview a person of interest about this incident, he was observably reluctant to disclose much about the conflict to a student. However, his enthusiasm for evangelization could not be overstated. In 2014, I once again came face to face with this controversy. The church leaders who ended up being incarcerated were venerated as martyrs by church members. Their reputation and influence have also spread to other cities in the province and even to the neighboring provinces. An official government document indicates that the church began to flourish after the release of all convicted church members in late 2013. It is clear that the local government keeps a close watch on the house churches in Anhong.

Other Christian traditions such as Catholicism and the Orthodox Church are not considered.
10   See "Anhong tianzhujiao jidujiao jiben qingkuang" (安红天主教基督教基本情况), Anhong Religious Affairs Bureau Records (Anhong: Anhong Religious Affairs Bureau, 2014).

2.1 Transitioning from the Red to the Gray Market in Anhong

The major house churches in Anhong have no ties to their counterparts that were active prior to the Cultural Revolution.[11] The current house churches were founded after the reforms in the early 1980s. Initially, most house church members were members of religious patriotic associations, namely the religious red market. The largest church in Anhong, referred to here as Endian Church, underwent a schism in 1992, and a new house church system took shape in the aftermath. A charismatic leader, Enhua, heads this well-established house church system along with her husband, Chaoyang. Enhua's father was also a preacher. Enhua and Chaoyang married after she graduated from university and then assumed a teaching position at the university where her father-in-law taught. She was forced to leave her teaching position when the university restructured its faculty. Due to Enhua's family background and her university education, she was well suited for ministry and served at Endian Church full-time. Enhua and Chaoyang remained preachers at Endian until 1992.

Elder Wei was in charge of both the TSPM/CCC and Endian Church in the 1980s and 90s. According to one of the pastors, Elder Wei "made a mistake" by grooming two preachers at once for leadership—Enhua and Lingge—and yet he was too indecisive to pick one of the two as his successor. In 1990, Lingge started her training for ministry at Yanjing Theological Seminary and completed the program in late 1991. Undoubtedly, formal training made her a very competitive candidate for the position of head of the church. In the meantime, Enhua's older brother also graduated from seminary and wanted to assume ministry at the church, but his request was denied.

The tension over this situation caused a rift between Enhua and Elder Wei, even though, unbeknownst to Enhua, Elder Wei had already taken steps to pass the baton to her in late 1992. Yet another development in Enhua's favor was Lingge's pending return to Beijing, as the latter had originally been an educated youth dispatched from Beijing to serve in Anhong. Lingge's impending departure left the church leadership to Enhua. Without knowledge of either of these developments, Enhua conspired with supporters in the congregation, planning a coup to seize control of the church. They held a "planning meeting" and assigned specific tasks to specific individuals—one person would take control of the circuit breaker panel, and a second person would seize the official stamp of the church. One of the conspirators left the minutes of the secret

---

[11] Leung Ka-lun (Liang Jialin), *Gaige kaifang yilai de Zhongguo nongcun jiaohui* (Hong Kong: The Alliance Bible Seminary, 1999).

meeting in an office of the church, where they were found by Elder Wei. As soon as Wei learned about the planned "coup," he took the official stamp and keys and hid them at his home.

In the aftermath of the failed takeover, Enhua left Endian Church. Eighty percent of the congregants followed, leaving only two to three hundred members, most of whom were elderly. The choir was stripped down to twelve members. In the weeks that followed the exodus, Enhua sent followers to disrupt services at Endian Church, accusing Elder Wei of fraudulently appropriating donations for personal use. An audit conducted by the Anhong Municipal Audit Bureau revealed that not only was Elder Wei innocent of the embezzlement accusation, but he had even funded the church's operations out of his own pocket. At the conclusion of the investigation, the church issued a public letter to underscore Elder Wei's innocence. Pastor Enli was a witness to this episode. She recalls that after Enhua's "betrayal" of the church, her attack on Elder Wei exclusively focused on the amount of donations received while purposefully neglecting to mention the expenses of the church. Those were simpler times, and congregants were easily misled. Enli thinks that Enhua consolidated her authority by trolling. After the schism, Elder Wei began to recruit an increasing number of younger coworkers to the ministry in order to cultivate successors. Intramural power struggles and the subsequent schism turned a red religious group into a gray one.

Enhua and her followers started a new church in a rented location. She quickly gained celebrity with her charisma and engaging preaching. A former congregant of Enhua's house church, Mr. Wang, described her conduct as follows:

> When we first split from Endian Church, Enhua had indeed done a great deal for the new church. She was attentive to the needs of individual congregants, which gained her large numbers of followers. Her evangelism was dynamic, and her renderings of salvation through the Lord and the healing power of faith were true crowd-pleasers. However, few knew about the backstory of her rise to leadership. No one would listen to me when I tried to tell him or her the truth. The congregants are too credulous ...
>
> She claimed that the construction of the church cost 8,000,000 RMB (1,230,000 USD), and yet we had no clue about the church's sources of revenue or its expenditures. We didn't even know who our donors were. A few congregants and I demanded a disclosure of donations. She dismissed us, saying God is informed of the details of the expenses, and that is the only thing that matters ...

Enhua would only invite her acquaintances as guest speakers. We understood that she did so to protect her flock. But the sermons were one-note, for the most part, and even though the preachers were dynamic, the sermons were devoid of intellectual stimulation. A coworker from Beijing visited one of Enhua's churches and intended to give a short sermon. When he arrived, the congregation was still singing. Enhua prompted congregants to circle the visitor and prevented him from giving a sermon. Why wouldn't she let him speak? She could have cut the sermon short if his messages were deemed inappropriate …

Mr. Wang and a group of congregants left Enhua's church shortly afterward. One of Enhua's former chauffeurs, Mr. Ma, confirmed the above characterizations. He observed a sharp contrast between the current Enhua and what she was like at the time of the exodus in 1992:

She is very clever and well educated. She manages the church with efficiency, but she makes church officials spy on one another. Once you are defeated in a power struggle, you lose all of your friends as well. Any opposition to Enhua would be branded as Eastern Lightning (*Dongfang shandian* 东方闪电) …

She gave a loan at high interest to a sister of the church to help her start a business. The sister's venture failed and she couldn't pay Enhua back. Enhua claimed that the loan did not come from her own savings and sued the sister in the name of the church. She instructed the congregants against a number of wrongdoings, but she dipped her toes in every single one of them …

At the time I wanted to run a factory and rented forty houses in the village for a fifteen-year term. The village governing body extended my lease to twenty-five years to help stimulate the local economy, at a rent of 400,000 RMB (61,500 USD). I didn't have enough money to pay the rent. Enhua claimed that the church would contribute 170,000 RMB (26,000 USD) to supplement my lease, saying that the church could hold study groups or build new churches on the property in the future. On that account, I signed a formal lease with the village and an agreement with the church in private. But the church cut me loose after the incident of 2009. I understand that the church has its own difficulties, but now that I've been negotiating with higher-ups of the church, they are refusing to acknowledge the signed agreement. Meanwhile, the village authorities keep pressuring me to pay the rent. I am currently involved in a lawsuit with the church. The way I see it, the government should publicize all the wrongdoings of this church to save other Christians from all the deception ...

In Pastor Enli's words, Enhua "mobilized the rural areas to encircle the cities" as a tactic to harass Endian Church. Endian's pastor responded with an equal degree of tenacity, as the leadership readies itself for impending attacks. Enhua made meticulous plans before every act of harassment, and she has a solid knowledge of the law. Moreover, Enhua has established positive relationships with local government officials ever since her exodus, and the local authorities have turned a blind eye to the activities of Enhua's church.

2.2 *Transitioning from the Gray to the Black Market in Anhong*

In 2008, Enhua started the construction of a new church in Anhong. It was a house church, so the local government did not approve of the construction. In an encounter with local authorities, Enhua sent elderly congregants to the church entrance to block law enforcement from halting the construction. When the new church was built, it became the largest in the city. The municipal government did not want to demolish the unapproved church, lest it cause unrest during the Summer Olympic Games. In the following year, 2009, Enhua founded a second new church under the pretext of building a shoe factory. This time, the municipal government forcefully demolished the church building, citing the failure to obtain official approval. Some congregants were injured in a clash with local authorities. On the day of the demolition, Enhua and her congregants marched to the city hall for a sit-in. A younger congregant was arrested for streaming the protest live on the Internet.[12] The year 2009 was the sixtieth anniversary of the People's Republic of China. The Municipal Office of Complaints decided to settle with Enhua privately to minimize negative publicity. The city agreed to compensate Enhua's church for its loss in the amount of 1,400,000 RMB (215,400 USD) but refused to release the congregants under arrest. The municipal government further demanded that the congregants stop attending services at house churches. Enhua declined these terms and proceeded to appeal to a higher court.[13] Shortly after this incident, municipal authorities arrested Enhua as she was traveling to visit the Shanxi provincial government.

---

12 Anonymous, "Defense Statement: En Hua, a Member of Anhong Church," *Chinese Law & Religion Monitor* 6.1 (2009): 45–52.
13 Chinese Christian Rights Defense Lawyers Association, "Summary of the Seminar on the Anhong Church Case and Religious Freedom," *Chinese Law & Religion Monitor* 6.1 (2009): 101–120.

Enhua's defense indicated in court that the government had accused the church of two violations: the unlawful appropriation of protected basic farmland and failure to obtain a permit for construction from the Religious Affairs Bureau (RAB). The newly established church was thus deemed illegal and warranted demolition. But one of the leaders of Enhua's church maintained that, first of all, citizens have the constitutional right of freedom of religion, and second, house churches have continued to grow. With more than 10,000 congregants, the church was in dire need of a proper meeting place. The church leadership has tried to register with the municipal government and obtain legal status, but to no avail.[14]

2.3 Consequences of State Suppression of Religion

By now, most of the congregants who were arrested during the incident of 2009 have been released from prison, except for Enhua, who was still serving her sentence when I concluded my research. Incarceration did nothing to undermine Enhua's influence. On the contrary, she has been able to dictate church affairs from behind bars, and even neighboring cities have felt the influence of Enhua's church. Congregants continued to seek her input on critical matters of the church. The incident of 2009 has put Enhua on a pedestal; she is venerated as a martyr and a saint, and this has only further strengthened the convictions of her followers. Officials at the RAB are dissatisfied with the handling of the "Anhong Incident." They have come to the realization that the outcome of this conflict has enhanced Enhua's name and elevated her to a saintly status. The new chief of the RAB has also become controversial and is shunned by many.

Enhua's career started in the Three-Self church headed by Elder Wei, where she was well respected. She found herself in a weak position in the contest for leadership of her church. Her failed attempt to seize control of the church in 1992 ended with an exodus of her supporters and the subsequent establishment of her own house church. In 2009, Enhua's church clashed with the local government, resulting in severe governmental suppression, the official designation of the house church as an "extreme force," and the incarceration of Enhua, as well as some of her followers. Rather than undermining Enhua's house church, however, this incident and its aftermath helped to consolidate the congregation. Under Enhua's leadership, this church has traveled the full spectrum of the tricolor religious market—shifting from the red to the gray market, and further moving from the gray into the black market. The congregants who left

---

14   Anonymous, "Defense Statement: Wan Xian, a Member of Anhong Church," *Chinese Law & Religion Monitor* 6.1 (2009): 53–58.

Enhua's church as a result of internal disagreements, on the other hand, managed to move out of the black market and enter the red market.

3 The Christian Tricolor Market in Bentu

Historically, the predominant Protestant denominations in the Henan city of Bentu were CIM and the Norwegian Lutheran Church. Today, the city's major Protestant churches have all benefited from the foundations laid down by the Norwegian Lutheran Church. The ministries of Jonathan Goforth (Gu Yuehan 古约翰)[15] and Marie Monsen (Meng Muzhen 孟慕真) in Henan instilled the concepts of confession and being "born again" among Christians in Bentu.[16] After a period of anonymity, Christians in Bentu began clandestinely preaching toward the end of the Cultural Revolution. They secretly groomed a group of young preachers, who would become instrumental to the revival of house churches after the Cultural Revolution.[17] Bentu chronicles reveal that the Shouters sect (*Huhanpai* 呼喊派) claimed a large membership in the 1980s. The municipal government outlawed the Shouters in July 1983. In the early 1980s, the largest church in Bentu reopened. According to municipal officials, the Christian population in the city reached 250,000 by 2011. When I visited Bentu on Christmas in 2012, members of the TSPM/CCC shared that the Christian population in the city had reached 800,000, among whom nearly 500,000 were members of the Three-Self Church.

Since the reform, more than any other province, Henan has witnessed the most rapid growth of Christians. This has earned the province the nickname "the Galilee of China."[18] However, due to the generally low education level and the lack of structured theological training among Christians, cults

---

15 Rosalind Goforth, *Goforth of China* (Grand Rapids, MI: Zondervan, 1937).
16 Marie Monsen, *The Awakening: Revival in China, a Work of the Holy Spirit*, trans. Joy Guinness (London: China Inland Mission, 1961).
17 Alan Hunter and Chan Kim-Kwong, *Protestantism in Contemporary China* (Cambridge: Cambridge University Press, 1993); Tony Lambert, *The Resurrection of the Chinese Church* (Wheaton, IL: Harold Shaw, 1994); Tony Lambert, *China's Christian Millions* (Oxford: Monarch, 2006); David Aikman, *Jesus in Beijing: How Christianity Is Transforming China and Changing the Global Balance of Power* (Washington, DC: Regnery; Lanham, MD: National Book Network, 2003); Paul Hattaway, *Henan: The Galilee of China* (Carlisle, UK: Piquant Editions, 2009); Xi Lian, *Redeemed by Fire: The Rise of Popular Christianity in Modern China* (New Haven: Yale University Press, 2010); Zhang Yinan, *Zhongguo jiating jiaohui liushi nian* (Hong Kong: Revival Chinese Ministries International (HK) Ltd., 2010).
18 Hattaway, *Henan*; Liu Yi, "Pentecostal-Style Christians in the 'Galilee of China,'" *Review of Religion and Chinese Society* 2 (2014): 156–172.

have gained a stronghold in the province.[19] Churches originating in Henan, including Fangcheng Fellowship (*Fangcheng tuanqi* 方城团契), the China Gospel Fellowship (*Zhonghua fuyin tuanqi* 中华福音团契), and the Word of Life Church (*Shengming zhi dao jiaohui* 生命之道教会), have garnered considerable attention from both academics and Christians.

I traveled to Bentu in 2012 to witness the outcome of the prophecy of the apocalypse disseminated by Eastern Lightning (or Church of the Almighty God). From December 22 to 28, I conducted field research in the city and was introduced to its complicated religious history for the first time. I returned to the city a few months later in February 2013, when I engaged in in-depth interviews. Both visits generated a wealth of data.

As noted above, Bentu has a large Christian population, over 500,000 of whom are members of the Three-Self Church. A church at the city center, Gospel Church (*Fuyin tang* 福音堂), claims the largest congregation. It was initially established by Lutheran missionaries. The church reopened its doors to worshipers following the start of the reform era, making it the first church to be restored in the city. As Gospel Church is situated in the old town center, it has a small courtyard, and the street offers limited parking space. Congregants often park their vehicles in the parking lot in a nearby shopping center and walk five minutes to attend Sunday services. The shopping center seems to have breathed new life into the old church.

3.1 Transitioning from the Red to the Gray Market in Bentu

Gospel Church holds three services each Sunday. Gospel Church is deeply rooted in the historical memories of citizens. It is natural that this church claims the largest congregation in the city. Wang Jiangshan is the current chief pastor; he is skilled at making biblical teachings relatable to everyday encounters for diverse congregants. The pews are segregated by sex, and one-sixth of the seats are reserved for male congregants. The single-sex seating arrangement, as a preacher explains, is designed to prevent male and female worshipers from socializing during the service. In the 1990s, Gospel Church was

---

[19] Zheng Xiaochun, *Zheng ye Henan, xie ye Henan?—tantao Henan heyi chengwei jidujiao ji "xiejiao" dasheng* (Hong Kong: The Alliance Bible Seminary, 2006). For a historical perspective, see Erleen J. Christensen, *In War and Famine: Missionaries in China's Honan Province in the 1940s* (Montreal: McGill-Queen's University Press, 2005). For more on Protestant Christianity in Henan, see Wang Ying, *Shenfen jiangou yu wenhua ronghe—zhongyuan diqu jidujiaohui gean yanjiu* (Shanghai: Shanghai renmin chubanshe, 2011); Li Huawei, *Xiangcun jidutu yu rujia lunli—yuxi licun jiaohui gean yanjiu* (Beijing: Shehui kexue wenxian chubanshe, 2013).

in desperate need for new blood to revitalize the congregation. Pastor Kang noticed the keen and youthful Wang Jiangshan and invited him to give sermons from time to time. Wang wrote his own sermons; he was engaging and his audience-centered preaching style won him considerable popularity, as well as the trust of the congregants.

Born before the Cultural Revolution, Pastor Kang comes from a long line of Christians. He studied at a Lutheran seminary and was ordained immediately after the Cultural Revolution, when there was a shortage of ministers. Kang is upright and yet uptight, lacking the soft skills to be an effective manager. Wang Jiangshan joined Kang's congregation while the latter was combatting an illness. As Wang's popularity grew in the church, the tension between him and pastor Kang also rose. In addition to Gospel Church, Kang was in charge of the city's TSPM/CCC at the time, working out of an office in Gospel Church. Meanwhile, Wang Jiangshan had already gained control over the governance of the church. To counter Wang's influence, Pastor Kang named a Nanjing Theological Seminary graduate, Liu Muyun, to be his successor.

Kang and Wang clashed over the construction of a senior home affiliated with the church. Pastor Kang was opposed to having the senior residents pay a fee, while Wang maintained that this income would help relieve the financial strains of the senior home. After the completion of the home, Kang did not collect the fees, and when he did not submit any money, Wang accused him of appropriating rent payments for personal use. The church's accountant at the time, Wenhua, cleared Pastor Kang of the corruption accusation, stating that Wang and Kang simply did not see eye to eye on the financing of the senior home and the construction of a clinic. In the end, Wang doubled down on his accusation and put the rumor mill in overdrive. Wang and his supporters eventually drove Pastor Kang out of the church, leaving Wang in charge of the largest church in the city.

Wang took a further step and withdrew from the municipal Three-Self system. In early 2000, Liu Muyun completed his graduate training at Nanjing Theological Seminary and took over the leadership of the city TSPM/CCC. Due to the tension between Wang and Liu, the TSPM/CCC was forced to move out of its office in Gospel Church. Some among the Gospel Church congregation felt that Wang himself was corrupt and was scheming and rallying congregants to purge opponents. These congregants followed in Liu Muyun's footsteps and left Gospel Church. The schism was thus complete. In the meantime, the TSPM/CCC found an office in a small church in the city center.

None of the pastoral personnel of Gospel Church were members of the state-approved Three-Self Church. It is likely that the local government has refrained from suppressing this well-respected and populous church for fear of popular backlash. And yet, ordinary Christians often do not know the distinction between a state-approved church and an unregistered one. After the schism, Gospel Church was no longer affiliated with the Three-Self Church, transitioning from the "red market" into a "gray market." Despite its physical space and the size of the congregation, Gospel Church, in essence, has now become indistinguishable from a house church.

As the city center has continued to expand, it has become increasingly inconvenient for elderly congregants who live on the outskirts of town to attend services at Gospel Church. Thanks to the church's abundant endowment, Wang Jiangshan was able to construct a modern-style church on the south side of the city. This new church surpasses all churches in the city in size and boasts a modern design. The church is equipped with a computer lab, a piano room, and a library holding a sizeable collection of Christian publications. On the upper level of the building, one finds a small "seminary," so to speak, providing room and board for seminarians. Because the seminary has not been incorporated into the Three-Self system, its sheer existence violates the law. The middle-aged woman who keeps watch over the church is reticent about this seminary. In addition, Wang Jiangshan continues to establish churches around the city and dispatches preachers to deliver sermons every week. Wang's church has now far exceeded the Three-Self Church in scale and influence.

3.2 *Transitioning from the Gray to the Red Market in Bentu*

The foundation of Grace Church can be seen as the outcome of a rivalry between Wang Jiangshan and the TSPM/CCC. The accountant of Gospel Church, Wenhua, lived on the north side of the city at the time. In 2003, she rented an abandoned factory west of the city on behalf of the church and turned it into a venue for Sunday services for the convenience of congregants living on the north side. When the church first opened, fewer than forty congregants were in attendance. Over time, as the congregation grew, Gospel Church purchased the factory for 600,000 RMB (92,300 USD) and renovated it. Within a year, the factory proved to be too small to accommodate all the congregants. Wenhua proposed to expand the church building so that the overflow congregants would not have to remain outside during the service. The church did not have sufficient funds to add an extension to the old factory, so the leadership opted to build a makeshift structure. The construction company's quote for such a structure turned out to be about the same as for a more permanent addition. Wang Jiangshan was in favor of building the temporary structure, considering the church's financial situation, whereas Wenhua insisted on building the permanent addition. The conflict between Wenhua and Wang Jiangshan escalated as a result.

Wang Jiangshan demanded that Wenhua work full-time at Gospel Church as an accountant in 2007. Wenhua refused to comply and resigned. She thereafter devoted her time entirely to the ministry at Grace Church. The congregation at Grace Church never ceased growing, to the extent that a physical expansion had become a necessity. This development prompted Wenhua's decision to build a new and larger church to benefit Grace Church's long-term growth. When Wang Jiangshan gave a sermon at Grace Church in April of 2008, he declared the church financially independent, even though Gospel Church still controlled Grace Church's preaching agenda. Wenhua believed that Wang Jiangshan intended to shield Gospel Church from potential financial trouble incurred by the renovation of Grace Church's original building. At the time, Grace Church had already paid back 520,000 RMB (80,000 USD) out of the 600,000 RMB (92,300 USD) that Gospel Church had contributed to the renovation, and it fully intended on making the remaining payments. A much heavier financial burden at the time was the 5,000,000 RMB (769,000 USD) budget for the construction of a new church; Grace Church only had 200,000 RMB (30,800 USD) in cash, which had already been set aside for the architectural design and laying the foundation. But the husband of a congregant owned a construction company, and he offered to advance the church 2,000,000 RMB (308,000 USD) for the building project. Construction began in 2010. After covering its regular expenses, Grace Church put all the donations it received into repaying its debts. Two years and nearly 6,000,000 RMB (923,000 USD) later, a new church was finally erected.

TSPM/CCC chair Liu Muyun reached out to Wenhua when the new church was under construction. He helped Grace Church obtain the appropriate certificate for land use. Wenhua was in charge of Grace Church's finances when the new church was completed. Wang Jiangshan immediately sent the accountant and treasurer of Gospel Church to take over the treasury of Grace Church. Wenhua dared them to take over the church and yet insisted on clearing all of the debts before handing over the finances. From then on, Wang started sending congregants from Gospel Church to block the entrance of Grace Church, scolding and accusing Wenhua of selling her church to Liu Muyun. Wenhua defended Liu, who "didn't take a single brick" from the church. She proudly declared that the new church was built on the donations of the brothers and sisters in the congregation. Wenhua explained that Liu helped Grace Church obtain the appropriate certificates and register with the municipality, and that she was grateful for Liu's assistance.

Wang's incessant harassment of Grace Church prompted Wenhua to seek assistance from the district RAB. Because Gospel Church fell under the jurisdiction of the RAB of a different district bureau, the officials advised Wenhua not to hand over the church treasury and, instead, told her to refer the Gospel Church leadership to that bureau when the next incident occurred. Once the authorities were involved, Wang Jiangshan had no choice but to sit down with Wenhua at the negotiation table. They reached an agreement on preaching. Gospel Church would assign a preacher to Grace Church on the first Sunday of every month, leaving the municipal TSPM/CCC effectively setting the preaching agenda for the remaining Sundays of the month.

To summarize, in the case of Bentu, Wang Jiangshan rose to a position of power on account of his dynamic preaching and distinctive abilities and wrested control of Gospel Church from its pastor. In the competition for leadership of Bentu's TSPM/CCC, however, Wang was unsuccessful and consequently withdrew from the Three-Self Committee. Nevertheless, he skillfully rallied his supporters in Gospel Church and undermined his rivals at the TSPM/CCC without resorting to extreme measures. In this way, he led his church out of the red market and marched it into the gray market. Regarding Grace Church, Wang was willing to support its expansion at its inception. And yet, tension between the leaders of the two churches continued to increase, as the Three-Self Committee intervened on the side of Grace Church. In the end, Grace Church not only came out of the struggle victorious, but it also succeeded in moving out of the gray market and entering the red market.

3.3 *Increased Complexity in the Religious Market*

Conscious of his age, Wang Jiangshan has been proactively grooming younger coworkers for church leadership. The current chief pastor of Gospel Church, Enqiang, is a young graduate from a seminary overseas. He and Wang do not share the same attitude toward the Three-Self Committee, however. In Enqiang's opinion, Gospel Church must reenter the Three-Self system because both its scale and membership have grown too large for the church to remain unregistered. Without securing legal status for the church, it would be difficult to find legal ways to hire clergy.

Meanwhile, the Three-Self Committee in the city has taken measures in response to the significant expansion of Gospel Church. It has established a seminary, with state approval, to supply the city and subordinate townships with training programs to educate clergy. Under the leadership of Liu Muyun, the church that serves as the main office for the TSPM has continued to expand, so much so that it has purchased a piece of land for the construction of a new church. At the same time, urbanization and globalization have brought local churches into contact with international Pentecostal movements. A Three-Self pastor who came to embrace the Pentecostal style of worship established connections to a wide network of churches and Pentecostalism into his own church in Bentu. But both the Three-Self Church and Gospel Church were opposed to Pentecostalism. This pastor had to leave the Three-Self system and start his own church in his hometown. Other house churches, along with the local Three-Self Church, are suspicious of this newly founded Pentecostal church.

4 Conclusion

The three religious markets are by no means isolated from one another; instead, they are fluid and interchangeable.[20] On the whole, the markets shift in response to state control. However, the case studies of Christian churches in two cities provided here have shown that the causes and drivers of the markets' transformations are much more complicated than state control alone.

Figure 3.1 summarizes the various shifts from one market to another discussed in this chapter. In Anhong and Bentu respectively, Enhua and Wang Jiangshan clashed with the leadership of the local Three-Self Church, which resulted in the establishment of their respective house churches. The local governments did not outlaw these new churches immediately after their founding but acquiesced to their existence. In this instance, both house churches have transitioned from the red into the gray market (1). Some discontented congregants of Enhua's church decided to return to the Three-Self Church in response to active recruitment efforts as well as the encouragement of the RAB. In this way, they moved out of the black market and transitioned directly into the red

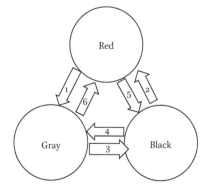

FIGURE 3.1   Transformations in the Tricolor Market

---

20   Fenggang Yang, *Religion in China*, 121.

market (2). For the first fifteen years of the new millennium, the state loosened its control on religious affairs and outright suppression of churches was rare. It was only when the actions of church and state became intolerable to each other that the state suppressed house churches and these churches challenged state authority. Such open confrontation left the already weakened churches in the gray market with no choice but to enter the black market (3). Governmental suppression of Enhua's house church in Anhong is a case in point. In this instance, certain congregants of Enhua's fledgling church became dissatisfied with her authoritarian leadership style and left. They were, however, unwilling to return to the Three-Self system. Thus, they transitioned from the black into the gray market (4). Movements from the red market directly into the black market were rather rare. There were, nevertheless, situations in which "cults" recruited Christians in the red market, turning these believers into outlaws and pushing them into the black market (5). Grace Church of Bentu was born out of a disagreement between its leader and the leader of Gospel Church over the foundation of a new church. With the assistance of both the Three-Self Church and the municipal RAB, Grace Church managed to obtain legal status and successfully transitioned from the gray market into the red market (6). Both the Anhong and Bentu case studies have demonstrated that clashes between individuals or groups can push churches from the two ends of the spectrum—the red and black markets—toward the gray market in the middle. The gray market, indeed, serves as an important buffer zone for house churches.

The consideration of interests, whether those of individuals or cliques, is a key contributing factor to transformations within the tricolor religious market. Disputes over interests often lead to internal division. In addition to disagreements over the management of church property and the pursuit of positions of authority, congregants also argue about church teachings. Divisions are commonplace within both the Three-Self Church and house churches. When compounded by external forces such as the state's religious policy, internal divisions are likely to trigger movements within the tricolor market. Specifically, churches in the black and gray markets, when suffering from internal rivalry, may transition into the other two markets under the influence of the Three-Self Church or the government.

State control of religion remains the major driver of the emergence of the tricolor religious market, as the state is an ever-present variable in the change of status of the churches in question. Nevertheless, the state is a major player only in a church's transition from the gray into the black market. As social order and general stability are the local governments' priorities, the government's bottom line, therefore, is to maintain the status quo. On the one hand, many religious affairs officials are military veterans who have little knowledge of religion. When they suppress house churches without a full grasp of the local and religious contexts, the outcomes are often counterproductive. On the other hand, even though certain churches are not registered with religious patriotic associations, their leaders have maintained good working relationships with religious affairs officials. Local officials usually turn a blind eye to these unregistered churches unless they are ordered to suppress them and unless the churches directly challenge state authority. The general leniency of local governments helps sustain a religious gray market, although Christians in the gray market are always at risk of forced movement into the black market.

On the whole, state suppression at the local level does little to undermine Christians and their practices in the black market. The comparative study of Anhong and Bentu supports my conclusion. When a house church was harshly suppressed by the local government in Anhong, it not only survived, but even extended its influence beyond the provincial borders. A house church in Bentu split into two because individual and group interests clashed. Yet, the communication channel between church and state remained open, and positive church-state relations also facilitated the church's long-term success.[21] Moreover, the local government has largely stayed out of internal church affairs; the RAB, for example, refrained from taking sides in any church disputes. To the extent that internecine conflicts stay within the churches, local governments welcome schisms and divisions, as they tend to weaken the churches in general.

Bibliography

Aikman, David. *Jesus in Beijing: How Christianity Is Transforming China and Changing the Global Balance of Power*. Washington, DC: Regnery; Lanham, MD: National Book Network, 2003.

"Anhong tianzhujiao jidujiao jiben qingkuang" 安红天主教基督教基本情况. Anhong Religious Affairs Bureau Records. Anhong: Anhong Religious Affairs Bureau, 2014.

Anonymous. "Defense Statement: En Hua, a Member of Anhong Church." *Chinese Law & Religion Monitor* 6.1 (2009): 45–52.

Anonymous. "Defense Statement: Wan Xian, a Member of Anhong Church." *Chinese Law & Religion Monitor* 6.1 (2009): 53–58.

Ashiwa, Yoshiko, and David L. Wank. *Making Religion, Making the State: The Politics of Religion in Modern China*. Stanford, CA: Stanford University Press, 2009.

21　Zhong Zhifeng, "Multiple Modernizations, Religious Regulations and Church Responses: The Rise and Fall of Three 'Jerusalems' in Communist China" (Ph.D. diss., Baylor University, 2013).

CHAN Bing 陳彬. "Zongjiao yeyou shichang?—Luodeni Sidake de zongjiao shichang lilun pingshu" 宗教也有市場?—羅德尼·斯達克的宗教市場理論述評. *Daqing shifan xueyuan xuebao* 大庆师范'学院学报, 2009.5: 45–50.

Chinese Christian Rights Defense Lawyers Association. "Summary of the Seminar on the Anhong Church Case and Religious Freedom." *Chinese Law & Religion Monitor* 6.1 (2009): 101–120.

Christensen, Erleen J. *In War and Famine: Missionaries in China's Honan Province in the 1940s*. Montreal: McGill-Queen's University Press, 2005.

Goforth, Rosalind. *Goforth of China*. Grand Rapids, MI: Zondervan, 1937.

Hattaway, Paul. *Henan: The Galilee of China*. Carlisle, UK: Piquant Editions, 2009.

Hunter, Alan, and Kim-Kwong Chan. *Protestantism in Contemporary China*. Cambridge: Cambridge University Press, 1993.

Ji Zhe 汲喆. "Ruhe chaoyue shisuhua lilun?—ping zongjiao shehuixue de sanzhong houshisuhua lunshu" 如何超越经典世俗化理论?—评宗教社会学的三种后世俗化论述. *Shehuixue yanjiu* 社会学研究, 2008.4: 55–75.

Lambert, Tony. *China's Christian Millions*. Oxford: Monarch, 2006.

Lambert, Tony. *The Resurrection of the Chinese Church*. Wheaton, IL: Harold Shaw, 1994.

Leung Ka-lun 梁家麟. *Gaige kaifang yilai de Zhongguo nongcun jiaohui* 改革开放以来的中国农村教会. Hong Kong: The Alliance Bible Seminary, 1999.

Li Feng 李峰. "Huidao shehui: dui dangqian zongjiao shehuixue yanjiu fanshi zhi fansi" 回到社会：对当前宗教社会学研究范式之反思, *Jianghai xuekan* 江海学刊, 2013.5: 95–100.

Li Huawei 李华伟. *Xiangcun jidutu yu rujia lunli—yuxi licun jiaohui gean yanjiu* 乡村基督徒与儒家伦理—豫西李村教会个案研究. Beijing: Shehui kexue wenxian chubanshe, 2013.

Li Xiangping 李向平 and Yang Linxia 杨林霞. "Zongjiao, shehui yu quanli guanxi—'zongjiao shichang lun' de shehuixue jiedu" 宗教、社会与权力关系—"宗教市场论"的社会学解读. *Huadong shifan daxue xuebao (zhexue shehui kexue ban)* 华东师范大学学报（哲学社会科学版）43.5 (2011): 1–7.

Lian, Xi. *Redeemed by Fire: The Rise of Popular Christianity in Modern China*. New Haven: Yale University Press, 2010.

Liu Yi. "Pentecostal-Style Christians in the 'Galilee of China.'" *Review of Religion and Chinese Society* 2 (2014): 156–172.

Monsen, Marie. *The Awakening: Revival in China, a Work of the Holy Spirit*. Translated by Joy Guinness. London: China Inland Mission, 1961.

Stark, Rodney, and Roger Finke. *Acts of Faith: Explaining the Human Side of Religion*. Berkeley: University of California Press, 2000. Translated by Yang Fenggang 杨凤岗 as *Xinyang de faze—jieshi zongjiao zhi ren de fangmian* 信仰的法则—解释宗教之人的方面. Beijing: Zhongguo renmin daxue chubanshe, 2004.

Wang Ying 王莹. *Shenfen jiangou yu wenhua ronghe—zhongyuan diqu jidujiaohui gean yanjiu* 身份建构与文化融合——中原地区基督教会个案研究. Shanghai: Shanghai renmin chubanshe, 2011.

Yang, Fenggang. "The Red, Black, and Gray Markets of Religion in China." *Sociological Quarterly* 47.1 (2006): 93–122. Translated and abridged by Yang Fenggang 杨凤岗 as "Zhongguo zongjiao de sanse shichang" 中国宗教的三色市场, *Zhongguo renmin daxue xuebao (shehui kexue ban)* 中国人民大学学报（社会科学版）. 2006.6: 41–47.

Yang, Fenggang. *Religion in China: Survival and Revival under Communist Rule.* New York: Oxford University Press, 2012.

Zhang Yinan 张义南. *Zhongguo jiating jiaohui liushi nian* 中国家庭教会六十年. Hong Kong: Revival Chinese Ministries International (HK) Ltd., 2010.

Zheng Xiaochun 郑晓春. *Zheng ye Henan, xie ye Henan?—tantao Henan heyi chengwei jidujiao ji "xiejiao" dasheng* 正也河南，邪也河南？——探讨河南何以成为基督教及"邪教"大省. Hong Kong: The Alliance Bible Seminary, 2006.

Zhong, Zhifeng. "Multiple Modernizations, Religious Regulations and Church Responses: The Rise and Fall of Three 'Jerusalems' in Communist China." Ph.D. diss., Baylor University, 2013.

Zhou Xueguang 周雪光. "Weiquan tizhi yu youxiao guanli: dangdai Zhongguo guojia zhili de zhidu luoji" 权威体制与有效治理：当代中国国家治理的制度逻辑. *Kaifang shidai* 开放时代, 2011.10: 67–85.

CHAPTER 4

State Appropriation of Society
Refashioning the Miao through a Public Display of Christianity

Kong Deji

The construction of a Christian church in the Miao Village 苗族寨 of the Yunnan Ethnic Theme Park 云南民族村, a major tourist attraction in Kunming, began in 2006. On May 1, 2007, the prominent Christian church officially began operations. In the Chinese context, Christianity is often associated with foreign culture, and yet, in this instance, it has been appropriated as a cultural characteristic of an ethnic minority. That a Christian church should be put on display as a tourist product at a theme park spotlighting ethnicity is unusual and deserves further investigation.

Over the past century, both the Republic of China and the People's Republic of China have adhered to the principle of separation of church and state. Ever since the Chinese Communist Party (CCP) took power seven decades ago, the state has upheld atheism. The Communist regime severely suppressed various religions prior to reform in the 1980s. In the wake of this reopening came a steady growth of the Protestant population. The presence of the Christian faith and the establishment of churches are common in both mainstream Han society and in ethnic minority communities on the periphery of China.

The interplay between state and society is a prevalent analytical framework employed by scholars of religion in China, and specifically of Chinese Christianity, to examine church-state relations. The central concern of these scholars is the question of legitimacy. Moreover, the state-society paradigm can be further expanded into a model of dominance and resistance or of central vs. local governments. The dominance-resistance model is most noticeable in, for example, Richard Madsen's study of Chinese Catholicism and Fenggang Yang's works on the tricolor religious market.[1] Louisa Schein's "internal orientalism" and Adam Chau's analysis of the Great Black Dragon King in northern

---

[1] Richard Madsen, *China's Catholics: Tragedy and Hope in an Emerging Civil Society* (Berkeley: University of California Press, 1998); Fenggang Yang, "The Red, Black, and Gray Markets of Religion in China," *Sociological Quarterly* 47.1 (2006): 93–122.

Shaanxi both represent the central vs. local government model.[2] Liang Yongjia 梁永佳, furthermore, has indicated the problem of oversimplifying the binary opposition between state and society.[3]

A church is a religious site, an embodiment of faith. A church is also a prerequisite for the Chinese state to grant permission to a religious group for its incorporation into the official religious management apparatus. Nevertheless, the lawful presence of a Christian church in a state-sponsored tourist attraction crosses the boundaries of the church-state relationship as it is defined in the conventional scholarly interpretation. Why would an atheist state allow this to happen? A number of forces have come into play as the Miao's Christian faith has gradually gained legitimacy. The chairman of the prefecture's Political Consultative Conference helped organize a Miao Christian choir and trained it for a chorus contest. The propaganda machine of the party and the state was a positive force in forming the award-winning Miao Christian choir. The writings of Han scholars, such as Dong Renda 东人达 and Chen Xiaoyi 陈晓毅, have also played a significant role in documenting Miao Christianity.[4] All of these factors have led to favorable policies toward ethnic minorities.

In this chapter, I examine the construction of the Miao Christian church in the Yunnan Ethnic Theme Park from conception to completion. My fieldwork has led me to the following conclusion: by participating in state-approved art-and-cultural contests, Miao Christian choirs have successfully raised the public's awareness of the Christian faith of the Miao. In addition, they have desensitized Christianity in the public sphere. The outcome is the reformulation of the public imagination of the connection between Christianity and the Miao. In the process, Miao choirs at one and the same time have been appropriated by the local government and have become the embodiment of mainstream ideology as well as political rituals. In addition to the frequent interaction between the representatives of the state and the Christians who represent

---

2   Louisa Schein, "Gender and Internal Orientalism in China," *Modern China* 23 (1997): 69–98; Louisa Schein, *Minority Rules: The Miao and the Feminine in China's Cultural Politics* (Durham, NC: Duke University Press, 2000); Adam Chau, *Miraculous Response: Doing Popular Religion in Contemporary China* (Stanford, CA: Stanford University Press, 2006); Adam Chau, "Modalities of Doing Religion and Ritual Polytropy: Evaluating the Religious Market Model from the Perspective of Chinese Religious History," *Religion* 41.4 (2011): 547–568; Adam Chau, ed., *Religion in Contemporary China: Revitalization and Innovation* (London: Routledge, 2011).
3   Liang Yongjia, "Zhongguo nongcun zongjiao fuxing yu 'zongjiao' de Zhongguo mingyun," *Shehui* 1 (2015): 161–183.
4   Dong Renda, *Dianqian chuanbian jidujiao chuanbo yanjiu* (Beijing: Renmin chubanshe, 2004); Chen Xiaoyi, *Zhongguo shi zongjiao shengtai: qingyan zongjiao duoyang xing ge'an yanjiu* (Beijing: Shehui kexue wenxian chubanshe, 2008).

society, a variety of interested groups have also contributed to this unexpected outcome. The political elites in the religious affairs sector of the government and Miao elites, together with non-Christian and non-Miao academic elites, have all played their respective parts.

This case of state appropriation illustrates the complexity in the interplay between the state and the populace. As a tourist attraction, the Miao church in the Ethnic Theme Park serves to convert tourists to Christianity. And yet it is neither a state-approved religious site nor an underground church seeking to circumvent state scrutiny. Instead, this church belongs to a third category, falling beyond the interpretive parameters of the state-society paradigm. Moreover, in this instance, the local government is not the coequal of the "state," and not all nongovernment action can be attributed to "society." The interplay between the two, therefore, far exceeds the analytical capacity of a dominance-resistance model, as much compromise, negotiation, intentional misrepresentation, and even complicity are in play.

The branding of a Miao choir as a Yizhou 彝州 group is a case of intentional misrepresentation.[5] Whether deliberately or accidentally, the local government overlooks the potential damage to Yizhou's cultural capital by misbranding both Christians and the Miao. Such refashioning may be construed as a kind of appropriation, but in this case the state appropriates symbols of society, rather than the more typical process in which the ethnic elite appropriate symbols of the state.[6] In fact, it is common for tourist sites as well as art and cultural products to refashion ethnic minorities into public images that are inconsistent with a lived reality. Dru Gladney's research on artistic pieces at a tourist attraction in Beijing, China Ethnic Culture Park (*Minzu yuan* 民族园), has elaborated on the "representations" of ethnic minorities.[7] Gladney views China as a successful example of carrying out a nationalist project. It has not only constructed the world's largest ethnic group—the Han—but has also created a new polity sustained by fifty-six different ethnic groups. Gladney seems to suggest that as ethnic diversity gradually takes central stage, it may threaten the status quo of national unification.

---

5 Yizhou refers to the Chuxiong Yi Autonomous Prefecture (*Chuxiong yizu zizhizhou* 楚雄彝族自治州), a prefecture adjacent to the Yunnan capital of Kunming.
6 Liang Yongjia, "'Diexie' de xiandu—yige Dali jieqing de difang yiyi yu feiyihua," in *Zongjiao renleixue (disi ji)*, ed. Jin Ze and Chen Jinguo (Beijing: Shehuikexue wenxian chubanshe, 2013), 127–143; Nicholas Tapp, "In Defence of the Archaic: A Reconsideration of the 1950s Ethnic Classification Project in China," *Asian Ethnicity* 3.1 (2002): 63–84.
7 Dru C. Gladney, *Dislocating China: Muslims, Minorities, and Other Subaltern Subjects* (Chicago: University of Chicago Press, 2004).

1 Building a Church in a Tourist Site

Situated on the shores of Kunming Lake (also known as Dianchi 滇池), the Yunnan Ethnic Theme Park is an AAAA-level tourist site.[8] The site opened its doors on February 18, 1992, and instantly became a "must-see" attraction in Kunming. By design, the park represents twenty-six different ethnic cultures in Yunnan and offers visitors a firsthand experience of the lives and customs of minority populations. Additionally, the site serves as an ethnic cultural base for the State Ethnic Affairs Commission (*Guojia minwei* 国家民委), as well as a base for CIOFF's[9] China Commission for folk culture, and it is one of the State Ethnic Affairs Commission's first points of contact in ethnic affairs.

The administrators of the Ethnic Theme Park assigned a section of the park to each ethnic minority. Each group would build a "village" and put its way of life and customs on display. Villages were built and opened for operation in succession. To date, twenty-six villages named after corresponding ethnic minority groups have been set up. On May 1, 2007, the Miao village, which has a Christian church at its center, opened to visitors, along with a few other newly renovated villages. The Miao village covers an area of two to three *mu* (one-third to one-half of an acre), a quarter of which is taken up by the church while the remaining is open space, where public performances such as singing and dancing is held. A section of the open space was carved out for a dart-blowing game around 2010.

The Miao Christian church resembles a typical church in design and style. Each of the four sides of the church has a door to accommodate tourists, and three of these doors are typically open. At the far end of the nave is a counter functioning as a gift shop, offering merchandise bearing traditional Miao motifs, including batik featuring biblical stories.

When I visited this church in 2009, Liu Yinghua[10] sat on a bench in the middle of the church wearing traditional Miao clothing and welcoming visitors. His duty was to speak with tourists about matters of faith. Before Liu assumed this post, he had studied at the Yunnan Theological Seminary and had been

---

8 Tourist sites in China are awarded A's based on a number of factors, including significance and management of the site. The highest category is AAAAA. The city of Kunming has only two AAAAA sites.
9 The International Council of Organizations of Folklore Festivals and Folk Arts. This organization is an official partner of UNESCO.
10 Here and throughout this paper, all personal names are pseudonyms except for those of high-ranking government officials.

recruited by the Ethnic Theme Park to work in the Miao section. Liu became a full-time employee at the Ethnic Theme Park in 2007.[11]

Liu led religious services for fifty to one hundred employees of the Ethnic Theme Park every Sunday. Among the congregants were members of groups who have had a longer history with the Christian faith, such as the Lisu 傈僳族, Lahu 拉祜族, and Derung 独龙族, as well as those who converted after the completion of the Miao church, such as congregants of the Shui minority 水族. Before the construction of the Miao church, ethnic minority Christians attended services at a church in a nearby village. The completion of the Miao church eliminated an obstacle that Christian employees had faced concerning their religious lives. Previously, they would have had to travel long distances to attend a church. As the church was the property of a tourist agency nestled in the Ethnic Theme Park, it was not officially designated a religious site. Liu Yinghua's occupation, therefore, was as a hospitality professional and not clergy.

The Miao church serves at least four major functions. It provides a place of worship for employees of various villages in the park; it offers a platform for tourism products and cultural performances; it is a public arena for evangelization; and finally, it legitimizes ethnic minority groups' belief in a "foreign" religion. In this way, Christianity has become an integral part of the constant renewal and representation of ethnic minority traditions and characteristics.

2   The Situation of Miao Christians

Those who have visited the Christian church in the Miao village in the Yunnan Ethnic Theme Park have often left with the impression that the Miao people are heavily influenced by Christianity. It would seem that a significant number of the Miao population are Christians, and that Christianity is an integral part of Miao culture. However, my study on the Miao population in Guizhou, Hunan, and Yunnan, as well as of the religious lives of ethnic minorities in Yunnan, shows that the above impressions are not correct. Christian missions enjoyed considerable success among many ethnic minorities in Yunnan for more than a century, and the Miao are one of the groups that have been most receptive to the Christian faith. Nevertheless, the Miao claim neither the largest Christian

---

11   When I returned to the Ethnic Theme Park in 2015, more of the interior space of the church had been appropriated for commercial use, and Liu was running the dart-blowing game in the open space outdoors.

population nor the highest percentage of Christian converts among the ethnicities in Yunnan.

Christians make up less than 10 percent of the Miao population. According to the 2000 national census, the population of the Miao nationwide was 8,940,116. The Miao population in Guizhou, a total of 4,299,951, was the largest in the country with half of the national Miao population. Hunan had the second-largest Miao population, amounting to 1,921,495 in total. Relatively few Miao residents in Guizhou and Hunan are Christians; the vast majority are practitioners of traditional folk religion. By contrast, there are more Miao Christians in Yunnan, where the total Miao population is 1,043,535—the third-largest Miao population in China, and one-ninth of the national Miao population. Yunnan's Miao population is concentrated in Wenshan Prefecture 文山州 (422,991), Honghe Prefecture 红河州 (274,147), and Zhaotong City 昭通市 (155,766). The combined Miao population of Wenshen and Honghe makes up about 66.8 percent of the province's total Miao population, few of whom are Christians.[12] The most Christianized Miao population tends to be concentrated in northeastern Yunnan, on the Yunnan-Guizhou-Sichuan border, as well as in central to northern Yunnan. All the same, Wenshan and Honghe have a small Miao population, and neither has a majority Miao county that can claim a proportion of Miao exceeding 1 percent of the national Miao population.[13]

The Christian church in the Miao village in the Ethnic Theme Park is highly symbolic and has effectively reshaped the popular imagination of ethnic minority groups. Nonetheless, Christianity has only touched a sliver of the Miao population. Although the Christian church in the Yunnan Ethnic Theme Park positions itself as a landmark of Miao culture, it does not represent the majority of the Miao. This observation suggests new questions. How has a subgroup of the Miao that comprises less than 10 percent of the total population come to represent the collectivity of the ethnic group? Is the misconception of the Miao's "intimate relationship" with Christianity purely a coincidence?

2.1　*The Opposition of Non-Christian Miao*

An investigation into the validity of allowing a minority to represent the majority in an ethnic group only addresses half of the "mystery" about the Miao church. The small percentage of Christians in the Miao population aside,

---

12　Data derived from the Yunnan Provincial Religious Affairs Bureau in 2003 indicates that the total ethnic minority Christian population in Wenshan was roughly 930.

13　Fumin County 富民县, part of Kunming, is known for its Miao choir and will be discussed below. The county's Miao population is so small that it is not represented in the census.

it is imperative that we consider my initial question: In the context of a tense church-state relationship, what made the building of a Christian church in a public space possible in the first place? Interviews with Christian leaders, professionals in the tourism industry, and scholars of the Miao, as well as employees in the Ethnic Theme Park, have allowed me to reconstruct the beginnings of the project.

We can glean from Liu Yinghua's professional identity and his entry into his current role that the church is not primarily conceived as a religious space but is, first and foremost, a tourist product. The general manager of the Ethnic Theme Park at the time, Mr. Yan, had a Christian mother. The art director of the department of cultural development at the park, Mr. Yu, also grew up around Christian culture. These men were instrumental in the building of the church. Their Christian upbringing appears to have been a major determinant in the church's conception, and the two managers' personal preferences also influenced the design of the church.

Certain non-Christian Miao elites in Yunnan reacted strongly against the proposal to build a Christian church. Sharing my view of its political connotations as well as its implications for how Miao identity would be perceived, they quickly organized to protest its construction. Under the name of the Miao Studies Committee (*Miaoxuehui* 苗学会) of Yunnan they reported the plan to the appropriate authorities and visited the provincial government of Yunnan to voice their objection to the construction of a Miao church. Their rationale was that "the majority of the Miao are not Christians." On account of this protest, the secretary of the Yunnan Provincial Party Committee, Bai Enpei 白恩培, visited the Ethnic Theme Park in an unofficial capacity. He also sat in on a prayer session in the Miao church during the day. According to Liu Yinghua's recounting of this visit, Bai Enpei felt that Christianity could purify the soul, and seemingly acquiesced to the building of the Miao church. This event also gave greater legitimacy to the Miao church in the Yunnan Ethnic Theme Park.

Religion, as an important part of culture, inevitably affects national identity, which is why non-Christian Miao elites protested against the construction of a Christian church in the Miao village. In 1993, Jiang Zemin pointed out in a speech at the National United Front Work Conference that "there are no trivial matters concerning nationalities and religions" (*minzu, zongjiao wu xiaoshi* 民族、宗教无小事). Over the following twenty years, the issue of nationalities and religions has often been treated as a sensitive issue. However, this case demonstrates that it is possible for Chinese local governments to desensitize and depoliticize ethnic and religious issues. The CCP and the government do not always suppress religion.

3   The Miao Choir: Between Faith, Culture, and Politics

3.1   *The Choir as Political Capital*

A newly developed tourist activity in Yunnan in recent years is visiting churches in Miao or Lisu villages to enjoy renditions of world-famous pieces and hymns by ethnic minority choirs. On the one hand, tourists are impressed by the choirs' outstanding performances, but the choirs' prioritization of internationally renowned classics in their repertoires has also reinforced the preconception that Christianity is a "foreign religion." The contrast between everything foreign and the preconception of an underdeveloped ethnic minority in the interior of China cannot be more pronounced in this instance.

In the opinion of Liu Yinghua, the rationale for building a church in the Miao village or, for that matter, for any kind of construction project in the park, is first and foremost the proper presentation of the signature culture for an ethnic group. Religion is an indispensable part of culture, and the Christian faith, of which the choir is a key component, is central to Miao life. The superb quality of the Miao choirs is well known.

Liu's assessment aligns with the decision-making process of the Ethnic Theme Park's managers. They decided to build a church in the Miao village to represent the Miao's perceived signature cultural characteristic, which is Christianity. This perception is further reinforced in the popular imagination by the Miao choirs.

A choir is an indispensable component of a church. The expression of religiosity through the collective singing of religious music, moreover, is an integral part of the Sunday service. At the same time when Christianity was taking roots in China, nascent political parties as well as their organizational capabilities were also exerting influence on religious culture. The mobilizing and propagandizing abilities of political organizations are on display in events such as artistic and cultural festivals or singing contests.

In May 1942, Mao Zedong delivered a speech at the Yan'an Forum on Literature and Art in which he put forward his position on the role that literature and art should play in the nation. In the reform era, artistic endeavors have also been promoted by top leaders of the CCP. On September 28, 1986, the Sixth Plenary Session of the Twelfth Central Committee of the CCP adopted the "Resolution of the Central Committee of the CCP on the Guidelines for the Construction of Socialist Spiritual Civilization," emphasizing the construction of a "spiritual civilization" together with the reform of the economic and political systems. In 2014, Xi Jinping made an important speech at the New Literature and Art Symposium, pointing out that the cause of literature and art is important to the Party and the people, and that the literary and art front is an important front of the Party and the people.

However, the rural population rarely has the opportunity to cultivate or display such talents. When Yunnan first started coordinating artistic and cultural events, local government officials identified Christian choirs as an important piece of cultural capital. Miao choirs were heavily "recruited" by the organizing bodies not only to promote these events but also to participate in singing contests. It is worth noting, however, that the Christian identity of the participating members was often concealed.

3.2   *The Mountain-Dweller Chorus*

In order to participate in various promotional activities and literary competitions, in 2005, Yang Wenbiao 杨文彪, the chair of the Political Consultative Conference of the Yunnan Chuxiong Yi Autonomous Prefecture, recruited more than two hundred Miao choir members from three counties (Lufeng 禄丰, Wuding 武定, and Yuanmo 元谋) and organized them into one choir. Yang arranged a concert, the "Night of Peace and Harmony" (*Xianghe zhiye* 祥和之夜), for the annual Chuxiong Yi Autonomous Prefecture celebration of the traditional Yi Torch Festival (火把节). On July 29, the newly formed Miao choir performed at the concert, which proved to be a highlight of the Torch Festival. "United China" (*Hexie zhonghua* 和谐中华), "Harmonious Society" (*Xianghe shehui* 祥和社会), "Blissful Life" (*Huanle shenghuo* 欢乐生活), and "Wholehearted Blessing" (*Zhencheng zhufu* 真诚祝福) were the four acts of the concert, featuring world and Chinese classics, such as "I Love Our China" (*Ai wo zhonghua* 爱我中华), "Hallelujah," "Auld Lang Syne," and "Ode to Joy," as well as Miao folk songs. The local government issued an official statement reporting on the success of the concert, stating that the event abundantly illustrated the unity and harmony among the ethnic groups in Yizhou, making the Torch Festival a breathtaking spectacle.[14]

The year 2005 was the sixtieth anniversary of the Chinese victory in the Sino-Japanese War. It was also the seventieth anniversary of the death of Nie Er 聂耳, the composer of the national anthem of the People's Republic of China and a Yunnan native from Yuxi 玉溪市. The first chorus festival in commemoration of the native son, called the Nie Er Cup, opened on September 14. The event was sponsored by the Yunnan Provincial Party Committee Publicity Department, the Provincial Department of Culture, the Provincial Federation

---

14   Yunnan Chuxiong Prefecture Ethnic Affairs Commission, "Miaozu daxing yanchanghui zai Yunnan Chuxiong yanyi 'Xianghe zhiye,'" August 4, 2005.

of Literary and Art Circles, the Kunming Municipal Party Committee, and the Kunming Municipal Government. Yang Wenbiao led the choir he had formed earlier in the year, now dubbed the "Mountain-Dweller Chorus" (*Shanmin hechang tuan* 山民合唱团), to first place in the contest, beating out 120 other choirs from throughout the country.

A total of four Miao choirs participated in this contest. Two choirs from Kunming—one from Wuhua district 五华区 and the other, the better-known Xiaoshuijing 小水井 Miao choir, from Fumin County 富民县—shared first place. The choir from Luquan County 禄劝县, Kunming, won second place with its rendition of "Graduation Song" (*Biye ge* 毕业歌).

Nearly all choirs representing rural counties are Miao, and the members of these choirs are exclusively Christian. Both the state's ideology and official religious policies have prevented open expressions of Christian culture. Even though church choirs have won awards in state-organized singing contests, they largely concealed their Christian identity and fashioned themselves as a "Mountain-Dweller Chorus." *Guangming Ribao*, a national newspaper published in Beijing, reported on the newly formed choir:

> Hoes on the ground and livestock in the barn, the farmers flicked the dust off their arms. Clearing their throats, they begin to sing. ... It's incredible that these singers with such remarkable voices are Miao farmers from the remote mountains of Yunnan.
>
> The Chuxiong Prefecture Miao "Mountain-Dweller Chorus" was formed in July 2005, consisting of two hundred members with equal numbers of male and female singers. They are young and middle-aged Miao farmers from the mountains of Chuxiong. Chuxiong Prefecture Political Consultative Conference Chairman Yang Wenbiao discovered these farmer-singers and organized them into a chorus.
>
> Self-taught from books and DVDs, these farmers helped one another learn. Even though some lack formal education, all had exceptional talent in music. A music-infused upbringing, combined with soulful interpretations of beloved pieces, turns the farmers into true musicians. They are able to sight-read numbered musical notation, and some have even advanced to reading staff notation. Tireless study and practice not only led the Miao farmers to master Chinese and world classics alike, but also led them out of the remote mountains and onto the national stage.[15]

---

15   Ren Weidong, "Hongdong shengcheng de miaozu shanmin hechangtuan," *Guangming ribao*, September 20, 2005.

The Chuxiong Political Consultative Conference reported that the key to the "Mountain-Dweller Chorus" was the farmers' "natural talent." Their accomplishment was lauded as "a great honor for Yizhou." Thanks to the excellent organizational efforts of the Prefecture Political Consultative Conference, the Miao choir members performed to perfection world-famous pieces as well as patriotic and revolutionary songs.

Even though the Christian identity of the Miao choirs was not a secret, media reports and public acknowledgments of their accomplishments neglected to disclose this. On the surface, avoiding any mention of the choirs' Christian identity may be construed as the state's suppression of "society." The reality is more complicated than this. For instance, the chair of the Prefecture Political Consultative Conference at the time, Yang Wenbiao, took an interest in folk religion. After his retirement, he raised funds for the construction of a "blessing-themed" tourist attraction in the prefecture, called the Blessed Tower (*Futa* 福塔). In fact, this structure is a cross between a Buddhist temple and one for the veneration of folk deities. The deities worshipped both within and beyond the confines of the main tower bear little difference from other Buddhist statues. In addition to this project, Yang was heavily involved in the organization of the Miao Christian choir and actively led the choir to perform at concerts and win prizes in contests. Yang's actions, together with the Ethnic Theme Park management's interest in building a Christian church, suggest the complexity of the "state," as revealed in the degree of state involvement in cultural and religious affairs and the multifaceted nature of the officials' motivations.

By participating in contests, the Miao choirs have effectively become a cog in the state's propaganda machine. In addition to Christian music, choir members have also performed a number of revolutionary-themed pieces, such as "March of the Volunteers" (*Yiyong junjin xingqu* 义勇军进行曲), "Song of the Motherland" (*Gechang zuguo* 歌唱祖国), "Defend the Yellow River" (*Baowei Huanghe* 保卫黄河), "Song of Selling Newspapers" (*Maibao ge* 卖报歌), and "Ode to Our Motherland" (*Zuguo song* 祖国颂). The Miao church has earned political legitimacy that allows it to demonstrate its Christian faith in public, precisely because the choirs have performed revolutionary-themed music to satisfy the state's expectations. Notably, the interplay between state and society far exceeds the parameters of the resistance model, in which much negotiation, debate, and compromise, as well as willful misrepresentation and complicity, are put on display. Presenting a Miao Christian choir in Chuxiong as a "Mountain-Dweller Chorus" and packaging it under the Yizhou brand is a clear case of willful misrepresentation. It is clear that the local government, both by design and inadvertently, has concealed the choir members' dual identity as Christian and Miao to prevent any erosion of Yizhou cultural capital. This manner of repackaging is a form of appropriation. In it, the state appropriates society, which is contrary to the conventional pattern of ethnic elites appropriating symbols of the state.

The state-society relationship is a commonly invoked framework in the analysis of religion in China, and of Christianity in particular. The primary scholarly concern is the question of legitimacy. When it comes to the issue of legitimacy, conventional wisdom tends to simply replace the state-society model with the paradigms of dominance-resistance or central vs. local government. However, the case of the Miao choirs has shed considerable light on the complex interaction between state and society in practice. The state and society appropriate and yet complement one another with no apparent ill intent.

The Miao choirs were successful at the Nie Er Cup competition in 2005, but after winning the prize, the group's Christian identity was hidden in media reports. But as the influence of the Miao choirs continually expanded, they received more and more attention and the "secret" of their identity was eventually brought to light. From October 12 to 15, 2007, the "Mountain-Dweller Chorus" went to Zhongshan City in Guangdong Province to attend the National First New Socialist Countryside Choir Congress, where it won first prize in the national competition, which featured twenty-five choirs from thirteen provinces. In early 2008, *China Religion*, a magazine published by the State Administration of Religious Affairs, released an article on the Miao "Mountain-Dweller Chorus" in Chuxiong Prefecture with the title "Color Clouds Flowing from Afar" and made clear the Christian background of the choir.[16]

3.3 The Xiaoshuijing Chorus

Even better known than the Chuxiong "Mountain-Dweller Chorus" is the Miao Xiaoshuijing "Farmer Chorus" (*Nongmin hechang tuan* 农民合唱团) from Fumin, Kunming (Table 4.1). The choir represented Yunnan and entered CCTV's Young Singer TV Contest in 2008, in the group category. As the choir performed music in the Miao language in national singing contests, both the Miao church and the Miao people actively took part in the grand project of nation-building. Participation in singing contests grants official state approval and acceptance to a foreign religion hitherto suffering institutionalized discrimination. It also earns a religious group a legitimate space for public display. Furthermore, as these Miao choirs perform world classics that are Christian in nature (such as "Hallelujah"), Miao Christians have succeeded in demonstrating their faith,

---

16   Long Wende, "Yuanfang piao lai de caiyun," *Zhongguo zongjiao* 2008.3: 56–57.

through organized artistic expressions, in both the public sphere and the political arena.

Even with their extraordinary accomplishments, none of the Miao choirs that competed in the Nie Er Cup in 2005 publicly demonstrated their Christian faith. Nevertheless, the choirs have continued to accumulate substantial cultural capital ever since. As tourism thrives and society becomes increasingly open, the performances of Miao choirs have also become a major topic in news media. Moreover, Christianity has gained legitimacy through both the art of singing and the economic benefits of this art form, making it possible for Christians to live their faith publicly. Whereas the choirs had concealed

TABLE 4.1 Performance schedule for the Fumin Xiaoshuijing Chorus, 2003–2008

October 2003	The First Western China Chorus Festival "Meili cai Yunnan" 美丽彩云南 Ethnic Cup Contest
April 10, 2004	CCTV "Tongyi shouge, zoujin Yunnan" 同一首歌·走进云南 concert
September 2005	The First Yunnan Nie Er Music Week and Nie Er Cup chorus contest
January 2006	Performance with the National Philharmonic of Russia in Kunming and Qujing 曲靖
December 2006	Performance with the Russian National Ballet at Yunnan Art Theater
May 1, 2007	2007 Kunming International Tourism Festival opening performance
May 20, 2007	The Seventh National Special Olympics of China opening performance
June 2007	Naming ceremony for the Kunming Intangible Cultural Heritage & Ethnic Folk Dance and Song Gala 民族民间歌舞乐晚会
October 14, 2007	The First National Socialist New Countryside chorus contest, Zhongshan, Guangdong
November 2007	The First Chinese Fubao 福保 Rural Cultural and Art Festival
March 2008	CCTV Lonliqi Cup 隆力奇杯 Thirteenth Young Singer TV Contest
April 2008	The Thirteenth Farmers Games opening performance in Kunming

their Christian status at the Nie Er Cup in 2005, by 2008, most reporting on the choirs acknowledged the members' Christian identity. For example, a feature on Xiaoshuijing published in *Kunming Daily* stated that 85 percent of the adults in this village community were Christians. The story went on to recount the origin of the Miao "Farmer Chorus" in a church and how its unadulterated, heavenly four-part harmony propelled the choir onto the international stage.[17]

With the development of tourism and the spread of the Miao's reputation, their musical ability has become not only a news source, but also a source of tourism available to local governments. As early as the mid 2000s, officials in Fumin County built a "small well" Miao-style village with a chorus as a tourist attraction. On December 29, 2010, the "China Kunming Xiaoshuijing Miao Ethnic Style Eco-village" project, developed by Fumin Xiaoshuijing New Rural Industrial Development and Management Co., Ltd., was inaugurated with an investment of 6 billion yuan (approximately 923 million USD).

The popularity of the choir has been quite profitable financially and has also enriched the existing cultural and propaganda system of the CCP. On May 15, 2016, the "National Best Family" was unveiled and the National Conference for the Recognition of the "Five Good Civilized Families" was held in the Great Hall of the People. Long Guangyuan, conductor of the Miao Chorus of Oishui Farmers, and He Yingyu, director of the Investment Cooperation Bureau of Yunnan Province, were invited to attend the unveiling ceremony in Beijing as representatives of the twenty-five "Most Beautiful Families" in Yunnan Province. From February 16 to March 2, 2018, the "Little Well Choir" (Xiaoshuijing) was invited by the New York Philharmonic Orchestra and the London Philharmonic Orchestra to perform at Chinese New Year concerts in the United States and Britain. The event was funded by the Beijing International Music Festival Foundation and was led by world-renowned conductor Yu Long; he and his team helped to arrange the international trip of the Xiaoshuijing Choir. Yu commented that the choir well represents the ethnic minorities and international culture of China. Their international performances further helped to promote Kunming's image as an international city under China's "One Belt, One Road" policies.

All in all, the political plasticity of the choir is very strong and can be endowed with various political meanings. Participating in cultural exchanges with political significance in the form of literature and art has made foreign religions that were originally discriminated against accepted by the official

---

17 Jia Wei et al., "Fuming Xiaoshuijing jiangban qian? Shiren danyou miaozu 'tianlai zhisheng' congci yakou," *Kunming Daily*, March 23, 2009.

system and become a very representative model. The Miao Choir, as a religious group, has obtained the opportunity to display its faith in a public space.

The choirs built a repertoire for singing contests primarily consisting of Miao-themed music, which effectively reduced the tension caused by the state's scrutiny of religious activities. Additionally, the economic benefits of the choirs' success in singing contests help justify the performance of religious music. The prospect of economic reform and growth not only gives legitimacy to the choirs, it also removes the institutional and cultural shackles from religious activities, hence making the public expression of faith possible. It follows that the expression of faith can effectively be facilitated by the society's cultural, political, and economic needs. While the ruling class views religion as an object to be eliminated, it is also a piece of political capital to be appropriated to satisfy mainstream ideology. For religious people, on the other hand, political power is at once a threat to the existence of religion and a means for the latter's fulfillment.

The legitimization of Miao Christian choirs reveals that, although politics and religion operate on different and yet parallel playing fields, they reciprocate and complement each other. Nationwide initiatives such as China's campaign to develop the western regions (*Xibu da kaifa* 西部大开发), the Construction of a New Socialist Countryside (*Xin nongcun jianshe* 新农村建设), the plan for developing Cultural Countrysides (*Wenhua xiaxiang* 文化下乡), Rural Tourism (*Xiangcun lüyou* 乡村旅游), Intangible Cultural Heritage, Cultural Ecological Villages (*Wenhua shengtai cun* 文化生态村), and the "One Belt, One Road" initiative have in one way or another benefitted from the Miao Christian choirs.[18] They are, at the same time, resources for the Miao Christian population to appropriate. Additionally, the growth of Christianity in Yunnan has not negatively affected the efficiency or effectiveness of local religious affairs agencies. On the contrary, Yunnan, as a multiethnic and multireligious province, is often lauded as an exemplar for areas with a similar demography. It seems that measured and studied management of religious affairs can serve as a valuable resource for local administrations as well as research institutions.

Additional forces have facilitated the reciprocity between politics and religion. Former Chuxiong Prefecture Political Consultative Conference Chairman Yang Wenbiao is a strong advocate for traditional folk religion. The China Federation of Literary and Art Circles Vice Chairman, Dan Zeng 丹增, and

---

18   Dou Zhiping, "Shehuizhuyi xin nongcun jianshe yu xiangcun lüyou xietiao fazhan yanjiu: you Fuminxian xiaoshuijingcun wei li," *Kunming daxue xuebao*, 2007.2: 7–11.

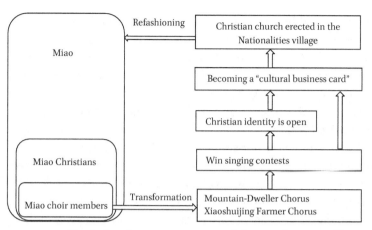

FIGURE 4.1   The choir as the primary source in refashioning the Miao public image

renowned literary figure Yu Qiuyu 余秋雨 were both judges at the Young Singer TV Contest at which Xiaoshuijing performed. Developers co-opted by the government, in this instance, managers of the Ethnic Theme Park, responded to market demands. All of the above forces have been instrumental in making possible the Miao choirs' performance careers (Figure 4.1).

4   Conclusion

The construction of a Christian church in the Ethnic Theme Park has sufficiently demonstrated that the state-society relationship is more complicated than a straightforward binary opposition, to the extent that the state-society dichotomy is rendered invalid. The successful construction of the church can be interpreted as an act of the state, a product of market forces, or an expression of religiosity. However, none of the above fully explains the phenomenon. As state policy discourages the establishment of churches, the developers at the Ethnic Theme Park devised a coping mechanism—they never registered the church with the local government. Without an official registration, the church is not a "religious site" in the eyes of the law, and thus it will never be subject to the rules and regulations that would otherwise apply. In the framework of a state-society dichotomy, an unregistered church is typically designated an "underground church." However, this label does not represent the Miao church in the Ethnic Theme Park. It is, notably, not a meeting place intending to circumvent governmental scrutiny, even though it does serve congregants. It is, more accurately, a tourist destination, even a stunt. In this sense, the Miao church should be characterized as a "third category" outside of the state-society dichotomy, and it challenges the conventional binary opposition.

The process of solidifying Christianity as a signifier of the Miao is dynamic and complex, and yet the majority of the Miao people have been excluded from it (see Figure 4.1). An interpretive model that only recognizes two entities—state and society—in the process of a discursive construction fails to take into account the lived realities of the society. The silent majority lacks proper channels and means of self-expression, nor does it have sufficient access to accurate information. This case illustrates a process in which the Miao have become closely associated with a key symbol of Christianity, regardless of the fact that Christians only account for a small fraction of the total Miao population. Moreover, the state-society framework tends to emphasize the role of Christian elites in the discursive practice. Miao and non-Miao intellectuals alike have participated in the construction of the Miao-as-Christian discourse. Nevertheless, we would be ill-advised to equate these intellectuals with "society" simply by dint of their active participation.

Furthermore, it is arguable that political and socioeconomic elites might be genuinely interested in the belief in animism held by the majority of the Miao. Their appropriation of media reports and relevant texts about the Miao's religious life is selective at best. In the final analysis, we can see that various strands of internal and external forces have collectively crafted a Miao-as-Christian discourse that is far from the reality. Elites in different fields at once collaborated and competed with one another. It is impossible to identify all of the entities that have exercised some degree of agency in this discursive process. But one thing is clear: since the Miao as a people have increasingly been identified with Christianity, ordinary Miao have had little say in the matter. Louisa Schein's "internal orientalism" provides a useful tool for analyzing the construction of a complex discourse of "ethnic characteristics."[19] Internal orientalism is far more sophisticated than the simplistic binary oppositions of state-society, or its variations of dominance-resistance and central vs. local governments. Schein argues that a discourse takes on a life of its own once it has been formulated; neither its proponents nor its opponents can escape from its discursive power.

The Christianity of the Miao is precisely such a powerful discourse that resists challenges and discourages revision. Not even Schein's internal orientalism is sufficient to capture the disenfranchisement of the non-Christian Miao who have been left out of the construction of a discourse about their people.

---

19   Schein, "Gender and Internal Orientalism in China."

Worse, they are ignorant of the falsehood of such a narrative. In the end, the silent majority is represented by statistical data. Alternatively, they may be tourists visiting the Ethnic Theme Park or the viewers of televised singing contests.

Bibliography

Chau, Adam. *Miraculous Response: Doing Popular Religion in Contemporary China*. Stanford, CA: Stanford University Press, 2006.

Chau, Adam. "Modalities of Doing Religion and Ritual Polytropy: Evaluating the Religious Market Model from the Perspective of Chinese Religious History." *Religion* 41.4 (2011): 547–568.

Chau, Adam, ed. *Religion in Contemporary China: Revitalization and Innovation*. London: Routledge, 2011.

Chen Xiaoyi 陈晓毅. *Zhongguo shi zongjiao shengtai: qingyan zongjiao duoyang xing gean yanjiu* 中国式宗教生态：青岩宗教多样性个案研究. Beijing: Shehui kexue wenxian chubanshe, 2008.

Dong Renda 东人达. *Dianqian chuanbian jidujiao chuanbo yanjiu* 滇黔川边基督教传播研究. Beijing: Renmin chubanshe, 2004.

Dou Zhiping 窦志萍. "Shehuizhuyi xin nongcun jianshe yu xiangcun lüyou xietiao fazhan yanjiu: Yi Fuminxian xiaoshuijingcun wei li" 社会主义新农村建设与乡村旅游协调发展研究——以富民县小水井村为例. *Kunming daxue xuebao* 昆明大学学报, 2007.2: 7–11.

Gladney, Dru C. *Dislocating China: Muslims, Minorities, and Other Subaltern Subjects*. Chicago: University of Chicago Press, 2004.

Jia Wei 贾薇 et al. "Fumin Xiaoshuijing jiangban qian? Shiren danyou miaozu 'tianlai zhisheng' congci yakou" 富民小水井村将搬迁？ 世人担忧苗族"天籁之声"从此哑口. *Kunming Daily* 昆明日报, March 23, 2009.

Liang Yongjia 梁永佳. "'Diexie' de xiandu—yige Dali jieqing de difang yiyi yu feiyihua" "叠写"的限度——一个大理节庆的地方意义与非遗化. In *Zongjiao renleixue (disi ji)* 宗教人类学（第四辑）, edited by Jin Ze 金泽 and Chen Jinguo 陈进国, 127–143. Beijing: Shehui kexue wenxian chubanshe, 2013.

Liang Yongjia 梁永佳. "Zhongguo nongcun zongjiao fuxing yu 'zongjiao' de Zhongguo mingyun" 中国农村宗教复兴与"宗教"的中国命运. *Shehui* 社会 35.1 (2015): 161–183.

Long Wende 龙文德. "Yuanfang piao lai de caiyun" 远方飘来的彩云. *Zhongguo zongjiao* 中国宗教, 2008.3: 56–57.

Madsen, Richard. *China's Catholics: Tragedy and Hope in an Emerging Civil Society*. Berkeley: University of California Press, 1998.

Ren Weidong 任维东. "Hongdong shengcheng de miaozu shanmin hechangtuan" 轰动省城的苗族山民合唱团. *Guangming ribao* 光明日报, September 20, 2005.

Schein, Louisa. "Gender and Internal Orientalism in China." *Modern China* 23 (1997): 69–98.

Schein, Louisa. *Minority Rules: The Miao and the Feminine in China's Cultural Politics.* Durham, NC: Duke University Press, 2000.

Tapp, Nicholas. "In Defence of the Archaic: A Reconsideration of the 1950s Ethnic Classification Project in China." *Asian Ethnicity* 3.1 (2002): 63–84.

Yang, Fenggang. "The Red, Black, and Gray Markets of Religion in China." *Sociological Quarterly* 47.1 (2006): 93–122.

Yunnan Chuxiong Prefecture Ethnic Affairs Commission 云南楚雄州民委. "Miaozu daxing yanchanghui zai Yunnan Chuxiong yanyi 'Xianghe zhiye'" 苗族大型演唱会在云南楚雄演绎"祥和之夜." August 4, 2005.

Zhao Dianhua 赵殿桦. "Miaozhai feichu jinfenghuang—ji Fuminxian Xiaoshuijing miaozu nongmin hechangtuan" 苗寨飞出金凤凰—记富民县小水井村苗族农民合唱团. *Jinri minzu* 今日民族, 2008.5: 21–24.

CHAPTER 5

Worship of the God of Wealth and a Portrait of Rural Public Life

Zhao Hao

Religion in China has grown in recent years, both in terms of the establishment of worship sites (such as temples) and a surging number of worshipers. In addition to the five officially approved religions, a wide variety of folk religious groups have also flourished. The loosening of governmental and ideological control over religious practices coincides with the general promotion of traditional local culture as well as specific folk traditions. Temples have been restored or built and temple fairs have also become more dynamic and engaging. In short, many temples have no shortage of visitors. In terms of spatial distribution, the location in which a particular folk worship originally developed tends to become the center of a wider sphere of faith, drawing worshipers from neighboring rural villages. Regarding the composition of the body of worshipers, there is no clear indicator of group identity. Folk religion believers tend to be ordinary people who choose the object of their religious practice out of geographical convenience rather than agreement with the specific tenets of a religion. The most popular forms of folk religion seem to be temples that are not staffed by religious professionals such as monks or Daoist priests (*daoshi* 道士), as well as Tudigong (Earth God, 土地公) temples, Dragon King (*Longwang* 龙王) temples, Guandi temples, or trees and boulders believed to be infused with spirits.

The emerging research on folk religion in China has continued to blossom, as evidenced by an abundance of published monographs and articles.[1] These studies have provided a broad overview of the current state, typology, and characteristics of folk religion in China. Extensive field research has also generated literature analyzing specific forms of folk religion or specific regional practices of folk religion. International scholars have long engaged in the study of Chinese folk religion, indicating its contributions to Chinese society, and have

---

1   For example, Gao Bingzhong, "Zuowei feiwuzhi wenhua yichan yanjiu keti de minjian xinyang," *Jiangxi shehui kexue*, 2007.3: 146–154. See also Lu Yao et al., *Zhongguo minjian xinyang yanjiu shuping* (Shanghai: Shanghai renmin chubanshe, 2012).

proposed an array of interpretive frameworks.[2] More field research is necessary to analyze this vast variety of folk religion, the complexity in the practices of folk religion, and the interrelation as well as the interdependence between folk religion in a specific locality and its particular social context. Studies from specific locations help us situate the practices of a particular form of folk religion in its proper cultural-geographical environment, allowing for a faithful portrayal of context-specific religious practices.

This chapter presents a thick description of the worship of the God of Wealth, Caishen 财神, observed in Yan County, Sichuan.[3] I examine the interactions among the Caishen temple, its worshipers, and the government. My analysis focuses on the ways in which the Caishen temple has shaped and affected communal life among the local population in order to demonstrate an important social function of folk religion, namely, to stimulate the germination of publicness in rural society.

1 Survey of the Geography and the Temple

An area referred to as Caishen Ya 财神垭 is located on the border of Linshan township 林山乡 and Shuangbei township 双碑乡 in Yan County, between Hulu Mountain 葫芦山 and Guanding Mountain 关顶山. "Ya" refers to a narrow strip of land between two hills or mountains, typically a small hill or a strip of flat land. On one side of the hill is a village in Linshan township, about four kilometers from the town of Linshanchang 林山场镇. On the other side of the hill is a village in Shuangbei township. At the foot of the hill is a large pond. Caishen Ya falls under the jurisdiction of Shuangbei township. The residents believe Caishen Ya to be superbly positioned, with excellent *fengshui*, as the area is surrounded by mountains on three sides with a body of water at the bottom of the hill. The encircling features of the mountains, claim the residents, reflects their ability to "enclose" and hence their capacity to accumulate and

---

2 Below is a select list of studies that have offered varying perspectives on Chinese folk religion: C. K. Yang, *Religion in Chinese Society: A Study of Contemporary Social Functions of Religion and Some of Their Historical Factors* (Berkeley: University of California Press, 1961); Daniel Overmyer, *Folk Buddhist Religion: Dissenting Sects in Late Traditional China* (Cambridge, MA: Harvard University Press, 1976); translated by Liu Xinyong et al. as *Zhongguo minjian zongjiao jiaopai yanjiu* (Shanghai: Shanghai guji chubanshe, 1993); Meir Shahar and Robert Weller, *Unruly Gods: Divinity and Society in China* (Honolulu: University of Hawaii Press, 1996); Stephen C. Averill, ed., *Zhongguo dazhong zongjiao*, trans. Cheng Zhongdan (Nanjing: Jiangsu renmin chubanshe, 2006).

3 Pseudonym.

store wealth. The only access to Caishen Ya from either direction, however, is unpaved dirt roads. Four-wheel-drive vehicles cannot enter these windy mountain roads; one has to either go by foot or ride a motorcycle over bumpy paths. As Caishen Ya is located in a remote location, far from the center of everyday activities, it has more in common with temples in rural areas than a typical Tudigong temple or Yaowang 药王 (Medicine King) temple found in the center of a town that is accessible by better means of transportation.

Looking out from the top of the hill of Caishen Ya, we can spot three other temples, Gaoling Guan 高灵观, Feilong Si 飞龙寺, and Jinzi Shan 金子山, in the surrounding hills.[4] Gaoling Guan is a Daoist temple without a priest; Feilong Si is a Buddhist temple that worships Guanyin but is not managed by any Buddhist monks. A Buddhist monk with no specific credentials runs Jinzi Shan and is assisted by a Daoist priest. Because of their remote locations, worshipers tend not to discriminate against these temples on the basis of the religious tradition each represents. Accessibility is the primary consideration for the worshipers, many of whom frequent all four temples. The temples also host their respective temple fairs at different times of the year to avoid competing for attendees. Villages scattered in the gaps of the mountains are the main suppliers of worshipers.

The temples seem to have taken turns in achieving fame and popularity. The worship of Caishen has flourished in the past three years. Although Feilong Si and Gaoling Guan were popular among locals in previous years, Caishen Ya is now the most sought-after folk religious site, thanks to its distinct history and worshipers' dissemination of reports of the miraculous power of worshiping Caishen.

The narrow strip of land limits Caishen Ya's area. In the front of the temple is a small brick structure, housing the oldest extant statue of Caishen. Behind it is a lush, large fruit tree; it is encircled by piles of stone and marked by an iron plate. The main building, the Caishen temple, is situated behind the fruit tree. It houses a statue of Caishen who is guarded by Yaowang Bodhisattva (Yaowang pusa 药王菩萨) and Manjusri Bodhisattva (Wenchang pusa 文昌菩萨) on its left and by Guanyin 观音 Bodhisattva and Leizu 嫘祖 on its right. Straw cushions are scattered on the floor for kneeling. Incense, candles, paper money, and firecrackers are stashed in one corner for purchase. Beside the Caishen

---

4   I am comparing Caishen Ya with the three neighboring folk religious sites because of their intricate relationship. On the one hand, the four sites compete with one another for worshipers. On the other hand, they strengthen each other as they collaborate and learn from one another's experiences. Each seeks to expand its own capacity to serve the community while benefiting from the others' presence.

altar is a locked donation chest. Three rundown cottages with a few stone tables outdoors are found behind the Caishen temple.

The architectural style as well as the interior layout of the Caishen temple resemble those of any typical Daoist or Buddhist temple—they share the same floor plan, rituals, and notion of merit through donation. Apart from Caishen, other deities are also worshipped at Caishen Ya. For example, Yaowang Bodhisattva is a sought-after intercessor, as he has influence over health and sickness. Manjusri Bodhisattva oversees standardized tests, and Guanyin is the most accessible of all Buddhist deities. It is said that Yan County is Leizu's hometown, and I will discuss the implications of this fact in the following pages. In any case, the blending of Daoist and Buddhist deities in one temple is commonplace. Caishen often finds a home in either a Daoist or a Buddhist temple, and it is not uncommon that the worship of Caishen is integrated into the tenets of both Daoism and Buddhism.[5]

2   Caishen Ya: A Forgotten Tradition and a Restored Memory

What distinguishes the worship of Caishen from other forms of folk religion? Neither Yan County gazetteers nor the county archives can provide historical documentation of Caishen Ya. According to Wang Zhiyuan (pseudonym), who watches over Caishen Ya, the worship of Caishen began in the late Qing period (1644–1911) and never ceased. When the Communist Party took over China, the worship of Caishen was condemned as feudal superstition in the ensuing mass social movements. Despite the condemnation, villagers continued to worship Caishen in secret, and the cottage in front of the main temple was preserved from destruction during the Cultural Revolution. The worship of Caishen has regained its popularity in recent years. The custom of "welcoming Caishen" in Shanghai has undergone a similar journey.[6] Even though empirical documentation or official written records cannot be found to corroborate Wang's account, his story is considered authoritative as his family has watched over Caishen temple for three generations.

The deity venerated at Caishen Ya seems to be a mix of personifications of Caishen. The statue in the small brick cottage has fine and delicate facial

---

5   Li Xiaoguang, "Daojiao yu minjian caishen xinyang wenhua beijing zhi bijiao," *Zongjiaoxue yanjiu*, 1997.4: 117–120; Jiayang Pingcuo, "Guandi xinyang yu Gesaer chongbai—yi Lasa pamari gesaer lakang wei zhongxin de taolun," *Zhongguo shehui kexue*, 2010.2: 200–291.
6   Huang Jingchun, "Shanghai jie caishen xisu de lishi yu xianzhuang yanjiu," *Minsu yanjiu*, 2010.3: 134–145.

features and wears the vestments of a civil official; it is an image of the civil God of Wealth, Fan Li 范蠡. The Caishen in the main temple, on the other hand, has ferocious and sinister features with thick brows and a dark complexion. The statue holds a scepter in one hand and wears the clothing of a military commander, which suggests the personification of Zhao Gongming 赵公明 or Guangong 关公. Little systematic research on representations of Caishen is available in China.[7] Articles on the subject are published for a popular readership and to introduce folk customs.

The fact of the matter is that the personifications and the theology behind these representations are of little importance to worshipers. A long history of the worship of a deity and confirmed miracles are, on the other hand, quite significant. Thus, my interviewees typically stress the following regarding their religious practices: that Caishen Ya has a long, uninterrupted history, and that this is the one and only Caishen temple in the entire province of Sichuan.[8] For the latter reason, worshipers even travel all the way from Chengdu and Mianyang to venerate Caishen and make wishes. It is said that someone saw a place looking exactly like Caishen Ya in his dream and found his way to the temple. He made a wish for prosperity and ended up making a big fortune. He started making annual donations of 3,000 RMB (460 USD) to fulfill his vows.

My interviewees maintain that the main attraction of Caishen Ya is its miraculous power. Worshipers typically wish for prosperity and safety for family members seeking work out of town, and Caishen makes their wishes come true. Through word of mouth, the worship of Caishen continues to flourish. A case in point is the temple fair held on the tenth day of the first month of the lunar calendar in 2016. More than one hundred worshipers visited Caishen Ya that day, and the temple also received 16,000 RMB (2,460 USD) in donations in the ten days leading up to the temple fair. The donations were managed by a coordinating committee consisting of officials of the township, local village officials, and members of the Wang family, who have watched over the temple for generations.

The history and traditions of Caishen Ya are not attested in archival and historical records and thus cannot be substantiated with empirical evidence.

---

7 Lu Wei, *Yinyu shijie de laifangzhe: Zhongguo minjian caishen xinyang* (Beijing: Xueyuan chubanshe, 2001). See also Huang Jingchun, "Sanshi nianlai caishen xinyang jiqi yanjiu zhuangkuang gaishu," *Changjiang daxue xuebao (shehui kexue ban)*, 2008.6: 12–16.
8 This perspective has not been substantiated. To be sure, there is a plethora of folk religion in Sichuan, yet there is no record of any other Caishen temple like the one in question. Nonetheless, Caishen often resides in Buddhist and Daoist temples. That there is only one Caishen in the entire province of Sichuan is likely an overstatement.

On the other hand, through the oral transmission of miracles and past experiences, a version of the historical memory of the worship of Caishen has been restored. The renewed tradition has also established Caishen Ya as the center of communal activities for neighboring villages. At present, rural villages in Sichuan are facing the challenges of a declining population and a decline in public life in general. As significant numbers of the rural population seek work out of town, spaces that villagers used to gravitate toward for public events no longer exist. For example, ancestral halls that lay in ruins are not being restored. Traditional places of gathering, such as the pond or the threshing ground, have also lost their functions due to the depletion of the population. Today, one can only find large-scale gatherings on occasions such as rallies, market days, and temple fairs. However, rallies are by nature political and compulsory, and market days often do not serve to bond attendees. The temple fair seems to be the only public sphere born out of the voluntary and organic association of individuals who have shared desires and needs. Although individuals' religious desires are private matters, the temple fair formalizes such desires and effectively transforms a private, utilitarian demand for religion into an observable public phenomenon.

3 Caishen Worshipers: Reciprocity and the Emergence of an Ethical Community

Reciprocity is the overarching principle of the relationship between folk religion and its worshipers. The religion supplies products that satisfy the worshipers' demands, and worshipers return the favor by making donations to sustain the operation and boost the reputation of the folk religion. The two parties thus establish a solid social relationship in this reciprocal process. Research has shown that folk religion operates on its ability to fulfill specific social needs: Tudigong oversees local harvests; Matchmaker Yuelao 月老 exercises influence over romance and marriage; the Dragon King helps bring favorable weather for the crops; and Caishen is associated with good fortune and wealth.

The basic needs and demands of the Chinese rural population have largely remained unchanged for millennia, with slight variations in priorities during different time periods. For example, in a traditional agricultural society, people tend to solicit blessings from Tudigong and the Dragon King for good harvests. Yaowang Bodhisattva and Songzi Guanyin 送子观音 also may attract worshipers for their ability to promote family harmony, continuation of the bloodline, and personal health, as well as to ward off harm and hardships. Manjusri Bodhisattva's popularity has increased as standardized tests have come to dominate education. In recent years, as the rapid expansion of the market economy has drawn an ever-increasing rural population to cities, money has come to dominate social values, and enrichment has become the priority of most families. Naturally, the popularity of Caishen has risen dramatically.

Caishen Ya offers a wider variety of religious products than merely an object of worship—Caishen—and an exclusive focus on wealth and fortune. The deities that are most commonly sought after by the rural population, such as Yaowang Bodhisattva, Manjusri Bodhisattva, and Guanyin, are also venerated in the Caishen temple. This mode of veneration creates a new phenomenon that constantly blurs the boundaries of the deities' spheres of influence. That is, a deity may expand his or her original charge to oversee other areas of religious demands. For instance, Caishen has transformed from a deity that fulfills wishes for enrichment into an all-encompassing god. Interviewees who have come to seek out Caishen at Caishen Ya have wished for health, the safe delivery of a child to an expecting mother, smooth sailing in a career in the government, and a good future spouse, in addition to wealth and fortune. When Caishen answers demands, worshipers return the favor in the form of generous donations. In the first few days of the lunar New Year, streams of worshipers fulfill the vows they made to Caishen in the previous year by making donations.

The record of donations tells us that Caishen Ya can collect a handsome sum in the first ten days of the lunar New Year; the revenue in 2015 amounted to nearly 60,000 RMB (9,200 USD). Caishen Ya maintains a reciprocal relationship with worshipers and manages income in the form of donations. Three members from the Wang village at the foothill of Caishen Ya typically oversee the temple's operations. They purchase incense, candles, paper money, and firecrackers; they also give visitors tours of the temple and assist them in their worship. Worshipers leave donations of various amounts in the donation chest. Incense, candles, paper money, and firecrackers are complimentary for everyday worshipers, and donations are made at will.

A voluntary committee manages income from donations with collective and democratic governance, which not only avoids corruption and abuse but also effectively disperses donations to appropriate outlets. Names of worshipers who have disclosed their donations are publicly displayed on a blackboard in the temple to ensure transparency. According to Wang Zhiyuan, donations are appropriated in three major ways. First, donations are used toward everyday expenses of the temple, including the purchase of supplies for worship and food preparation for the temple fair. Second, donations fund the maintenance and expansion of the buildings of the temple. The temple that is currently standing is the fruit of donations received in the past few years, and the committee plans to expand the current structure once donations reach a desired amount. Finally, donations will be used toward paving dirt roads with cement to give access to four-wheeled vehicles. Complimentary lunches at the temple fair, complimentary supplies for worship, and better roads and more convenient access are all provided to repay the worshipers' support.

The first major temple fair in 2016 took place on the tenth day of the first month of the lunar calendar. Caishen Ya prepared lunch for more than one hundred worshipers from across the region. There were two rounds of dinner, each with twelve tables. A temple fair is probably the most public of all temporal and spatial situations in a rural society. Actions that have a public quality are arguably the byproducts of the reciprocal relationship between Caishen Ya and its worshipers. Renovation of roads is a case in point. Renovating roads not only allows Caishen Ya to afford its worshipers more convenient access, it also helps to connect several villages in Linshan and Shuangbei townships. Currently, most folk religious organizations do not have the capacity to engage in works of charity beyond the activities of their own organizations. That Caishen Ya engages in public works independent of the government's agenda is a contribution to the public good. Incidentally, Feilong Si, Gaoling Guan, and Jinshan Ze share this tendency: Gaoling Guan has constructed a major road leading to the mountaintop, and Jinshan Ze is also constructing new buildings for the temple.

The Caishen temple fair usually lasts an entire day. Attendees cross paths with relatives and acquaintances from neighboring villages, and they meet complete strangers. There are four major temple fairs in a year, on the tenth day of the first, third, sixth, and ninth months on the lunar calendar. Another major event is Caishen's birthday. All five events attract a large number of energetic worshipers and are marked by firecracker noises, incessant lighting of incense and candles, and, most importantly, a constant stream of donations. This positive cycle of reciprocity has inspired Caishen Ya to implement a simple measure of membership retention in recent years. The temple has set up a modest teahouse to function as a satellite center in the town. When worshipers arrive on market days, they gather at the meeting place to enjoy a cup of tea and watch a few episodes of TV shows or movies about Caishen and Guanyin. The teahouse is a place for friendly conversations where people can share the latest news about various villages.

This community of Caishen worshipers has developed out of a voluntary association whose members have moved it from a private sphere into a public one. In it, individuals are free to express ideas and make actionable plans; they are released from political restrictions and are able to exercise greater personal liberties. When this public and private divide is applied to the conditions of contemporary rural society, we may consider the "private" as the sphere of the home and the family, in which public mutuality and reciprocity do not exist. The "public," it follows, exists outside of the home. It implies associating oneself with strangers and unrelated individuals to form a new community, as well as engaging in activities that do not concern either private family matters or public engagement imposed by the government.

Approaching folk religions from this private/public perspective, this kind of religious group possesses the traits of an ethical community. Such a group occupies a social and public sphere outside of both the family and the state. Its "ethical" qualities are not only revealed in its "public"—as opposed to "private"—character, but "ethics" also exceeds the parameters of a political identity and begins to forge a social identity rooted in a moral and ethical entity. A social sphere thus generated is transient and cyclical, yet it nonetheless provides a model for the transition of a disconnected rural society into a coherent community. Myriads of temples exist in the rural area, and an equal number of folk religious sites host endless temple fairs. Worshipers' chosen objects of devotion overlap and intersect with one another. A distinctive expression of publicness is essentially an unintended consequence of a social network created by folk religion in the rural society. This phenomenon demands scholarly attention. The ethical community formed as such is by no means inactive. A shared folk belief will exercise its social functions in organization and mobilization when faced with decisions that would impact public interest.

4 Caishen Ya and Government-as-Symbol: Surviving the Gray Market

According to Fenggang Yang's theory of the tricolor religious market, Caishen Ya operates in a gray area.[9] The government neither approves its activities nor directly restricts or suppresses its operation. Caishen Ya is understandably concerned about its status because of the vicissitudes in its history as well as the state's official stance against feudal superstition. However, at present, the state encourages local communities to promote traditional culture and to pass down distinctively local customs. This gives Caishen Ya a potential opening into the red market. Two seminal studies offer compelling analyses of folk religion's transition from the gray into the red market as well as the challenges it faces while in legal limbo. Adam Chau has examined the worship of the Black

---

9 Fenggang Yang, "The Red, Black, and Gray Markets of Religion in China," *Sociological Quarterly* 47.1 (2006): 93–122; translated and abridged by Yang Fenggang as "Zhongguo zongjiao de sanse shichang," *Zhongguo renmin daxue xuebao (shehui kexue ban)* 6 (2006): 41–47.

Dragon King (*Hei longwang* 黑龙王) in northern Shaanxi,[10] and Jun Jing 景军 has studied the memory of the Kong 孔 family in Gansu.[11] Both investigate the ways in which folk religions negotiate the gray and red markets, resulting in legitimization. Feilong Si and Jinzi Shan are both folk religious sites like Caishen Ya, but they craftily take on the label of Buddhism. In recent years, Buddhism has experienced a renaissance in Yan County. A magnificent, brand-new main hall (*Daxiong baodian* 大雄宝殿) was erected in nearby Fenghuang Shan 凤凰山. Along with an imposing Four-Faced Awakened Buddha (*Simianfo* 四面佛), the main hall has become a landmark, or the face, so to speak, of the county seat. Smaller Buddhist temples have also benefited from the larger temple's fame. For instance, both Feilong Si and Jinzi Shan claimed to be subordinate institutions of Fenghuang Shan (there is, in fact, no such organizational hierarchy). Caishen Ya, meanwhile, finds itself in a difficult position. The worship of Caishen is not widespread in Sichuan. Under such circumstances, it behooves Caishen Ya to skillfully navigate the risks associated with promoting its tenets while seeking legitimization, so that it can continue to host temple fairs and attract worshipers.

Caishen Ya has attempted self-promotion on two fronts: beliefs and practice. Caishen Ya's central teachings resemble those of Buddhism and Daoism; however, it does not publish any brochures, nor does it have any teachings in writing. By imitating the Buddhist and Daoist rituals and temple fairs, Caishen Ya projects a sense of familiarity to its worshipers. Worshipers have said in interviews that they see little difference between the worship of Caishen and bodhisattvas, except for their respective deity statues. Caishen Ya has put up banners and painted slogans on the walls to spread its tenets. Moreover, these slogans incorporate the state's policy guidelines on the practices associated with belief in Caishen and state them in plain language. These ideas include the pursuit of social harmony, the core values of socialism, and the prospect of an overall well-off society. Some of the most noticeable slogans on the wall of Caishen Ya are "peace in all four directions," indicating a wish for all to be peaceful and safe within the realm, and "the good will prosper and the evil will perish," which aligns with the traditional Chinese concepts of reward for do-gooders and retribution for evildoers. By associating itself with

---

10   Adam Chau, *Miraculous Response: Doing Popular Religion in Contemporary China* (Stanford, CA: Stanford University Press, 2006).
11   Jun Jing, *The Temple of Memories: History, Power, and Morality in a Chinese Village* (Stanford, CA: Stanford University Press, 1996); translated by Wu Fei as *Shentang jiyi: yige Zhongguo xiangcun de lishi, quanli yu daode* (Fuzhou: Fujian jiaoyu chubanshe, 2013).

the state-approved religions of Buddhism and Daoism, Caishen Ya dispels the suspicion of superstition and troublemaking.

Caishen Ya operates as a space for community, but particularly for the elderly. The three brick cottages behind the main temple are venues for local voluntary associations. On the building in the middle hangs a sign, "Caishen Ya Community of Villages." It is a nonpolitical organization. The fact that one of the cottages serves as a venue for communal activities suggests the community's approval of Caishen Ya. To the right of the "Community of Villages" sign hangs a "Caishen Ya Seniors' Association" sign. Another sign reading "Caishen Ya Community Seniors' Leisure Hall" hangs on the right-hand side of the main hall of the temple. The government has, in recent years, promoted seniors' associations throughout the country. Care for the elderly, as well as issues relevant to the elderly's leisure activities and mental or physical health, have become a key area of rural development. Even though few senior citizens frequent Caishen Ya, the provision of a space for a seniors' association gives the temple a politically correct reason for existing. Despite the official condemnation of the worship of Caishen, the government has no reason to disapprove of Caishen Ya as a venue for senior citizens' socialization. Given that Caishen Ya fosters this kind of seniors' association, it show the group's willingness to support the official policy, as well as the government's compromise.

Caishen Ya also actively incorporates distinctive local traditions into its religious practices. Yan County is the hometown of the renowned Leizu 嫘祖 and the land of the silkworm. Leizu is one of the four guardian deities in the main hall of the Caishen temple. Yan County has also invested handsomely in the construction of a mausoleum for Leizu (*Leizu ling* 嫘祖陵), which is a popular pilgrimage destination for Leizu's worshipers. The Leizu statue in Caishen Ya is situated right next to Guanyin. A "Yan County Caishen Ya Community of Villages Leizu Cultural Promotion Site" sign hangs at the main entrance of the Caishen temple. It shows that Caishen Ya fashions itself as a venue for the promotion of Leizu's legacy, which aligns with the overall cultural atmosphere of the county and "downplays" the worship of Caishen.

During our interview, Wang Zhiyuan was up front about his concern for governmental suppression of Caishen Ya as a manifestation of feudal superstition. After all, Caishen Ya cannot compare with a large and government-approved temple like Fenghuang Shan. Any misstep could lead to suppression. I explained to Wang that the government had loosened its grip on folk religious practices, that the state's formal opposition to folk religions was not backed up by enforcement and thus it would not forcefully and directly suppress Caishen Ya. Wang felt that under the cover of the seniors' association and Leizu cultural promotion site, Caishen Ya might be able to avoid the limelight and remain on the right side of the official policy. Caishen Ya also plans to renovate the cottage for the seniors' association once its revenue grows. Once this project is completed, the elderly will be even more inclined to make Caishen Ya their gathering place.

Negotiation between Caishen Ya and the local government has resulted in the community of villages and the seniors' association, both of which are social organizations that manifest publicness, existing outside of the home. As far as the current state of rural development is concerned, the most public of the social organizations is the seniors' association. Because so many locals have headed to cities or other provinces to find work, elderly people, women, and children comprise the majority of the people remaining in the countryside, and thus rural society acutely feels the burden of an aging population. For instance, more than half of the attendees of Caishen Ya's fairs are elderly. The existence of a seniors' association is also a consideration during the audit of local governments. Although the seniors' association at Caishen Ya was originally a front and is barely active, it is conceivable that this organization might serve its full function once the cottage is renovated and roads are paved. Moreover, the negotiation between Caishen Ya and the government has further stimulated the interaction between the government and civil society, which may allow increased agency for the latter. Furthermore, folk religion provides a platform for such negotiation to play out on a small scale. All of these are benefits of publicness, which overcomes a "top-down" fashion of interaction and enables meaningful communication and reciprocity.

5 "The Three-Headed Snake": An Ethical Community and the Birth of Publicness

The emergence, operation, and growth of Caishen Ya helps us delineate its everyday operation and practices at the micro level. This organization further reveals the growing sense of publicness within this rural religious community, in particular its increasing role as a rudimentary ethical community. The question of the formation of a civil society in China has captured much scholarly attention. It is worth noting that the politico-philosophical notion of a civil society implies universality, and thus it is fruitless to search for local expressions of civil society per se within China. On the other hand, it may be methodologically possible to focus on one element of a civil society, such as communitarianism, and treat its presence in a community as a transformational stage in the movement toward a universal, civil society. As the essence of a civil society is the dialectic relationship between "public" and "private," the development of publicness is inherent in a civic community. In my fieldwork and research on Caishen Ya I have captured an expression of publicness among the worshipers of folk religion whose source of legitimacy is not the state. Rather, publicness is revealed through their identification with an ethical community.

With regard to the spatial organization of folk religion, I have found John Lagerwey's imagined rural community helpful in thinking about this community.[12] An archetype of an ethical community founded upon religious ties is none other than the "community-church" model in Western society. Churches are ubiquitous. A church is both the physical and emotional heart of a community. Not only does a church provide a gathering place for community members, but it is also a spiritual haven as well as a venue for interpersonal connections. The easy accessibility of churches fully satisfies individual needs. More importantly, a church-based subcommunity offers a buffer between the state—an abstract entity—and the individual. Community, rather than the state or society, is at the forefront of individuals' minds. Furthermore, the community has an important and highly symbolic place in a civil society. A community provides the public with services such as elder care, medical care, and education.

Common interests, such as individuals who attend the same school, hold the same faith, or share a common ethnic background, form communities organically. Consider Caishen Ya and the neighboring Shanlin and Shuangbei townships. The impact of modernization on traditional rural communities occurs at a deep, structural level. The exodus of the rural labor force has made a dent in the population. The mechanization of agriculture has severed the rural population's tie to the land. The consequences of fundamental social change have introduced new sources of stress in individuals' lives. Individuals are eager to find spiritual solace, while the collapse of traditional forms of communal bonding and the disappearance of traditional rural public spaces have also driven individuals to seek out new types of communal association. Temples have become hubs that connect neighboring villages, and the fact that worshipers frequent multiple temples also helps connect these hubs of religious activities. Caishen Ya, Gaoling Guan, Feilong Si, and Jinzi Shan each occupy a hill and yet are close to one another, offering worshipers multiple options for their spiritual needs and connecting worshipers through their dynamic and lively temple fairs. Folk religion serves as the thread that ties individuals and

---

12   John Lagerwey, "Du caractère rationnel de la religion locale en Chine," *Bulletin de l'École française d'Extrême-Orient* 87.1 (2000): 301–315; translated by Fan Lizhu as "Zhongguo zongjiao de helixing," in *Faguo hanxue (di 4 ji)* (Beijing: Zhonghua shuju, 1999), 338–354.

various communities together; it also becomes the center of communal activities as well as a spiritual haven for community members.

Huang Yinong 黃一農 has offered a useful analytical tool for examining the formation of an ethical community through the multiple practices of interaction among the belief system, worshipers, and the government. Huang proposes the image of a "two-headed snake" in his analysis of first-generation Chinese Catholics during the dynastic transition of the seventeenth century.[13] The religious practices centered around Caishen Ya appear to be a "three-headed snake." The snake evokes cunning and craftiness; these are arguably the qualities necessary for a folk religion to cope with its position in the gray market.

The snake's first head is the question of Caishen Ya's legitimacy. The legitimacy of Caishen worship has thus far been sustained by an unquestioned oral-historical tradition, as well as by the ongoing worship of Caishen. The extant oral tradition of Caishen Ya began to circulate in the late Qing. Claims of superior geography or *fengshui* and stories of the temple's waxing and waning over time can only appeal to unsophisticated worshipers. Moving forward, Caishen Ya cannot avoid confronting the issue of legitimacy head-on. Caishen Ya's prospects will be affected by the likelihood of the worship being written into the county chronicle, as well as the temple's ability to circulate its own brochures or its teachings in writing. Additionally, it is in Caishen Ya's interest to devise a feasible plan of development, with a timeline for the renovation and expansion of the temple, as well as one for paving the roads.

As Caishen Ya reexamines its own pursuit of legitimacy, it should also reassess its public relations while transitioning into the public sphere. In addition to the examples of other successful temples, it would benefit Caishen Ya to consider its place in society and its contributions to worshipers and the local community alike. In consideration of its own prosperity and continuation, the small temple of the God of Wealth between the hills inevitably has to think broadly and appeal to worshipers drawn from the nearby townships, the county seat, and an even wider geographical area. The supervisor of the temple has mentioned that Caishen Ya has been featured in Russian media. He anticipates more and similar interest in the temple in the future.

The snake's second head is the continuation of the reciprocity between the belief system and its worshipers in the long term. Worshipers' spiritual needs are generally utilitarian and concern private matters such as prosperity,

---

13   Huang Yilong, *Liangtou She: Mingmo Qingchu diyidai tianzhujiaotu* (Shanghai: Shanghai guji chubanshe, 2006).

enrichment, family harmony, safety, good health, and longevity, which accurately reflect the social needs in today's rural villages. The miraculous power of Caishen not only fulfills the spiritual needs of worshipers by providing a religious product, but it has also earned the trust of believers as well as their monetary donations. Caishen Ya's growth is furnished by the worshipers' monetary contributions, and in turn, the temple offers even more appealing services to incentivize even more donations. The plan to renovate a building to house the seniors' association, the meeting place in the town center, and a complimentary feast at the temple fair are all ongoing efforts that concern the public and hence exhibit a degree of publicness. Worshipers, on the other hand, exercise their agency in the process, as they engage with fellow attendees at the temple fair and strengthen their social bonds in communal gatherings.

The snake's third head is Caishen Ya's relationship with the local government. The state's authority and power are manifested in the predominance of state ideology as well as its constantly changing religious policies. Caishen Ya's response to state authority has transitioned from avoidance to voluntary contact and now to the current and active pursuit for recognition. By forming a community of villages and the seniors' association, Caishen Ya's actions not only give back to the community, but the temple is also well received by government bureaucrats for its service. Moreover, Caishen Ya helps preserve a cherished cultural-historical legacy by venerating Leizu in the modest Caishen temple. The designation of a Leizu cultural promotion site has effectively shielded the worship of Caishen from governmental scrutiny. An equally noteworthy outcome of the negotiation between Caishen Ya and the government is the latter's effort at collaboration with folk religious groups and the abandonment of an uncompromising policy of prohibition. The ingenuity revealed in the process of negotiation is a valuable lesson for the formation of a civil society.

6 Conclusion

Interaction between the government and worshipers has not been addressed in this essay, as the worshipers have not broken the law, nor have they associated with religious groups that are publicly suppressed by the government. Other religious groups, such as churches in Wenzhou, Shouwang Church in Beijing, Falun Gong, and Eastern Lightning have all crossed the state's bottom line, resulting in outright and fierce confrontations. Indeed, Caishen Ya is not immune from legal action. It remains in the gray area of the religious market, for there is no specific legislation regarding religion to facilitate Caishen Ya's transition into the red area. In the end, the interplay among the three heads of the snake has given birth to an ethical community. Such public character is still developing—at the forefront is the formation of a civil society and the socialization of worshipers—and struggling to achieve some degree of community-building while continuing the negotiation between folk religion and the local government.

Though small and remote, the case of Caishen Ya reveals the role played by folk religions in Chinese religiosity. Unlike other "folk" religious temples nearby, Caishen Ya is not a registered Buddhist or Daoist site, but it has strategically situated itself as a provider of social services, such as an entertainment venue for senior citizens, in order to avoid state interference. Furthermore, this study of Caishen Ya underscores the publicness of religious practices by highlighting the ways in which folk religious practices have stimulated the formation of an ethical community of worshipers. There are many different social organizations outside of religious groups that serve a similar function, such as the "stone dumbbell association" or the "association of theater lovers." Local communities have also restored ancestral halls, reconstructed genealogies, and reorganized social life around the household and the clan. Similarly, this chapter has argued that the activities promoted by Caishen Ya, such as the annual temple festival and seniors' association, have created a public space and encouraged the development of a civil society.

Bibliography

Averill, Stephen C., ed. *Zhongguo dazhong zongjiao* 中国大众宗教. Translated by Cheng Zhongdan 陈仲丹. Nanjing: Jiangsu renmin chubanshe, 2006.

Chau, Adam. *Miraculous Response: Doing Popular Religion in Contemporary China*. Stanford, CA: Stanford University Press, 2006.

Gao Bingzhong 高丙中. "Zuowei feiwuzhi wenhua yichan yanjiu keti de minjian xinyang" 作为非物质文化遗产研究课题的民间信仰. *Jiangxi shehui kexue* 江西社会科学, 2007.3: 146–154.

Huang Jingchun 黄景春. "Sanshi nianlai caishen xinyang jiqi yanjiu zhuangkuang gaishu" 30年来财神信仰及其研究状况概述. *Changjiang daxue xuebao (shehui kexue ban)* 长江大学学报（社会科学版）, 2008.6: 12–16.

Huang Jingchun 黄景春. "Shanghai jie caishen xisu de lishi yu xianzhuang yanjiu" 上海接财神习俗的历史与现状研究. *Minsu yanjiu* 民俗研究, 2010.3: 134–145.

Huang Yilong 黄一龙. *Liangtou She: Mingmo Qingchu diyidai tianzhujiaotu* 两头蛇：明末清初第一代天主教徒. Shanghai: Shanghai guji chubanshe, 2006.

Jing, Jun. *The Temple of Memories: History, Power and Morality in a Chinese Village.* Stanford, CA: Stanford University Press, 1996. Translated by Wu Fei 吴飞 as *Shentang jiyi: yige Zhongguo xiangcun de lishi, quanli yu daode* 神堂记忆：一个中国乡村的历史、权力与道德. Fuzhou: Fujian jiaoyu chubanshe, 2013.

Lagerwey, John. "Du caractère rationnel de la religion locale en Chine," *Bulletin de l'École française d'Extrême-Orient* 87.1 (2000): 301–315. Translated by Fan Lizhu 范丽珠 as "Zhongguo zongjiao dehe lixing" 中国宗教的合理性. In *Faguo hanxue (di 4 ji)* 法国汉学（第4辑）, 338–354. Beijing: Zhonghua shuju, 1999.

Li Xiaoguang 李小光. "Daojiao yu minjian caishen xinyang wenhua beijing zhi bijiao" 道教与民间财神信仰文化背景之比较. *Zongjiaoxue yanjiu* 宗教学研究, 1997.4: 117–120.

Lu Wei 吕微. *Yinyu shijie de laifangzhe: Zhongguo minjian caishen xinyang* 隐喻世界的来访者：中国民间财神信仰. Beijing: Xueyuan chubanshe, 2001.

Lu Yao 路遥 et al. *Zhongguo minjian xinyang yanjiu shuping* 中国民间信仰研究述评. Shanghai: Shanghai renmin chubanshe, 2012.

Overmyer, Daniel. *Folk Buddhist Religion: Dissenting Sects in Late Traditional China.* Cambridge, MA: Harvard University Press, 1976. Translated by Liu Xinyong 刘心勇 et al. as *Zhongguo minjian zongjiao jiaopai yanjiu* 中国民间宗教教派研究. Shanghai: Shanghai guji chubanshe, 1993.

Shahar, Meir, and Robert Weller. *Unruly Gods: Divinity and Society in China.* Honolulu: University of Hawaii Press, 1996.

Yang, C. K. (杨庆堃). *Religion in Chinese Society: A Study of Contemporary Social Functions of Religion and Some of Their Historical Factors.* Berkeley: University of California Press, 1961.

Yang, Fenggang. "The Red, Black, and Gray Markets of Religion in China." *Sociological Quarterly* 47.1 (2006): 93–122. Translated and abridged by Yang Fenggang 杨凤岗 as "Zhongguo zongjiao de sanse shichang" 中国宗教的三色市场, *Zhongguo renmin daxuexuebao (shehui kexue ban)* 中国人民大学学报（社会科学版）. 2006.6: 41–47.

PART 2

Group Competition

CHAPTER 6

Competing Interests and Conflicting Beliefs
A Case Study of a Seaside Church in Zhejiang

ZHAO Cuicui

1   Introduction

On September 14, 2011, a strange event occurred in a seaside community of Zhejiang province.[1] The Christian members of the community, around four hundred in number, were in the process of constructing a church on the edge of a village, when suddenly, according to reports from villagers, a sacred tree ignited. Flames shot forth from the tree, a sign that some took to mean that local deities were angered over the construction of the new church. Protests erupted and accusations were made, resulting in the halting of the construction of the church. This chapter recounts the events leading up to the incident of the fiery tree and discusses how the relationships between Christianity and local folk religions are mediated.

Fieldwork is my primary research method. I interviewed a total of 92 individuals in three two-month periods from 2013–2014. Research data is derived from textual sources, participant observation, and in-depth interviews. The 92 interviewees can be sorted into roughly three social groups: 34 were registered party members, 57 were ordinary citizens, and one was a Communist Youth League member (*tuanyuan* 团员). Of the interviewees, 26 were Christian and 66 were non-Christian. All the interviewees were, in one way or another, involved in the incident in question. They can be further identified as worshipers of folk religion, Christians, local party officials at the town and village levels, villager representatives, senior citizens, and members of the senior associations, as well as average villagers.

Interviews were typically conducted in the homes of the interviewees as social calls. The setting of the home and the social nature of my interaction with the interviewees helped create a relaxed and pleasant environment and guided the conversations in the desired direction. The privacy of the home also

---

1   "Seaside community" refers to a collective of six different villages, all of which are densely populated with disorganized settlement patterns.

eliminated external interference during the interviews. In addition to the incident of the burning tree, I also examined the demographics, economy, genealogy, land use, and belief systems at the field site to help contextualize and formulate my research questions.

To ensure the interpretive effectiveness of my data, I have based my discussion on interview notes, which have been analyzed for their accuracy and the credibility of their descriptions of the event in question. I take the relation/event approach to evaluate the interaction between folk religion and Protestant Christianity.[2] A series of interconnected incidents generates a host of relations/events. The relation/event approach opens a window into the significance of a singular incident. An examination of the relations/events helps crystalize interpersonal, divine-human, and group dynamics, as well as the flexible, strategic decisions that people of faith make in a highly volatile situation. My approach will reveal the dynamic nature of the study of the relationship between Christianity and folk religion. I use the term "interfaith relationship" to refer to the interactions between worshipers of all varieties of folk religion and Christians, as well as the practices of different beliefs. Here, "interfaith relationship" is viewed as a process of practicing one's belief.

2   The Incident and Its Background

This seaside community has a long history. The "ten temples and nine ancestral halls" have dominated the local folk belief system for years. As the state's policy toward religion has continually loosened since the 1990s, religious sites such as Buddhist and Daoist temples or monasteries have also been gradually restored with the overwhelming support of devout men and women.

More than twenty Buddhist and Daoist temples and monasteries stand in the seaside community; there is only one Christian church. In terms of the number of believers, out of a population of eight thousand, we can only count three or four hundred Christians, among whom about two to three hundred are regular attendees of services. The number of attendees at services may reach four to five hundred on major holidays, such as Christmas. Christians are not evenly distributed across the six villages of the seaside community. Dongwei village has the largest Christian population, while Jiujing village only has about

---

2   Gilles Deleuze, *The Logic of Sense* (New York: Columbia University Press, 1990); Gilles Deleuze, *The Fold: Leibniz and the Baroque* (Minneapolis: University of Minnesota Press, 1993).

twenty. Some of the Christians come from neighboring villages of the seaside community.

As the Christian population has reached a healthy number, the church has also steadily grown. The synthesis of ideas between the Christian faith and folk religion has been one of the major contributing factors in Christianity's growth. For example, the seaside church largely relies on oral transmission for its evangelization. Testimonies of miracles, ideas that "the Lord is the eternal life" or stories about healings appeal to the local population. A period of rapid expansion preceded a slow but steady growth in the Christian population. When compared with the number of worshipers of folk religion, Christians remain the minority, claiming about 5 percent of the total population.

While traditional folk religion has deep roots in the seaside community, Christianity, in comparison, lacks a deep historical connection to the local population. Additionally, there is tension between Christians and non-Christians due to the inherent differences between the two belief systems. Moreover, the two religions' respective histories, population sizes, codes of conduct, and ritual practices are also different. All of these factors have contributed to verbal and even physical conflicts in everyday life.

2.1　*The Incident of the Sacred Fiery Tree*

For the most part, Christians and worshipers of folk religion have mutual respect for one another. However, the latent tension between the two groups is manifested when competing interests are provoked by a particular incident. The incident of the "sacred fiery tree" that occurred during the construction of a new Christian church is one of those events that disrupted this peaceful coexistence.

While a new seaside church was under construction, someone spotted sparks coming out of two holes in a tree on the hill near the church at around eight o'clock in the evening on September 14, 2011. The story of the burning sacred tree quickly spread throughout the seaside community the following day. Before long, the story had morphed into an absurd rumor that the construction of the church had angered the tree god. The flames were signs of the tree's wrath. In the meantime, provocateurs agitated the public, claiming that the construction work had displeased the tree god and instigating the locals to take their anxiety out on the church.

These agitators rallied a mob and launched a premeditated attack on the church on the morning of September 19, 2011, which became known as the "storming." A mob of thirty to forty people gathered at the seaside church, smashing everything at the construction site. They broke the cement-filled pillars, tore apart the wooden boards ready for concrete fillings, and struck the construction workers on site. A leading church member rushed to the site and forcefully stopped the attack.

2.2   The Escalation of the Conflict

The incident of the sacred fiery tree did not end there. The provocateurs spread a rumor about a second sighting of sparks coming out the same tree, which drew even more locals to the construction site. Even though there was no substantive connection between the tree fire and the construction of the church, the seaside community's general reverence toward the tree god turned the incident of the fiery tree into a major episode.

Some folk religionists believed that the tree god objected to the construction of the church. A Daoist priest had also warned against continuing the construction work lest it bring misfortune to the entire population. The Christians were convinced that more and more locals would reject the church's construction as a result.[3] Folklore has it that spirits reside in old trees. The tree behind the construction site is hundreds of years old. One community member was convinced that a host of spirits in the tree were displeased with the construction of the church. He cited the elders in the community, explaining that the tree god was vexed because the renovated church would oppress the tree's spirit.[4] These perceptions turned an innocent construction project into the direct cause of "the wrath of a sacred tree."

Worshipers of folk religion also subscribed to a local sorceress's warning that the completion of the new Christian church would bring disaster to the seaside community and cause the death of half of the male population.[5] The woman's words spread like wildfire. Locals became even more deeply convinced of the woman's prophetic power and credibility. They believed that the seaside community would be in turmoil, as the newly constructed church would block the tree and thus block the light for the community.[6] Once the church was erected, they thought, the cross might cast a shadow on this tree and affect the good *fengshui*. Moreover, as the church stood near the East Gate (*dongmen* 东门) of the community, it would block not only the views of the sea and the scenery but also the farmers' line of sight to observe agricultural activities. Some devout worshipers of folk religion also viewed the east as the most auspicious of the four cardinal directions, likening it to a person's face with respect to the rest of

---

3   Interview, March 29, 2014.
4   Interview, March 28, 2014.
5   Interview, March 20, 2014.
6   Interview, October 5, 2013.

his body. The face should not be covered.[7] This discursive construction of the sacred quality of the tree and the east further instilled anxiety in the locals, creating an overall atmosphere of uncertainty, confusion, and uneasiness.

Such is the holiness attributed to the maple tree that stands by the East Gate of the seaside community.[8] The tree is also viewed as having powerful *fengshui*, a symbol of the safety of the community. The incident of the sacred fiery tree was inexplicable, verging on the miraculous. It not only drew the locals' attention to the construction of the Christian church, but it also became an instrument for the provocateurs to spread falsehood and rumors. The truth about the burning tree, therefore, is buried in the discursive construction of holiness through folk religious idioms.

2.3   *The Outcome: The Construction Interrupted*

People on both sides of the conflict felt immense pressure. In the aftermath of the incident of the tree, congregants of the seaside church suffered from the accusations of folk religion believers. They lamented that even the simple pursuit of spiritual solace seemed like an insurmountable obstacle. Out of desperation, Christians kept vigil in the church and prayed to God for a way out, in the hope that the construction project would be completed as planned and that the investment of 2,000,000 RMB (308,000 USD) would yield positive returns.

The incident of the burning tree, as a case of interfaith conflict, was complicated by the belief in *fengshui* and the construction of a new church. The tsunami of public opinion drowned out the local Department of Agriculture's efforts to determine the natural causes of the incident. The locals, rather, reacted with multiple attempts at disrupting the church's construction. Not only has the incident of the sacred fiery tree cast a spotlight on the underlying tension between folk religion believers and Christians, but it has also unified folk religion believers, along with a broader range of locals, against the construction of the new church. The widespread opposition was supported by deep-rooted folk belief and overwhelming public opinion.

The fire department declared the tree fire a case of arson. When a local TV station reported on the incident, it likewise described the incident as man-made and not caused by the "wrath of the tree god." Nevertheless, public

---

7   Interview, April 9, 2014.
8   This tree is at least three hundred years old and is designated a protected tree by the County Agricultural Department. Some of the elderly villagers call it the "village tree." Others have said that this tree helped defend the seaside community during the Japanese aggression, because it was situated at the strategic location of the East Gate, shielding the villages with its luxuriant foliage and wide-reaching branches.

opinion in the village quickly silenced outside judgment, forcing the church to halt construction.

Although the incident came to an end, the agitators never stopped their opposition. They have continued to mobilize opponents against the church. Whenever they detected any sign of the resumption of construction, a mob descended on the site and disrupted its progress. Consequently, the construction of the seaside church was put on hold for years. The "incomplete construction project" also came to symbolize the conflict and tension between folk religion and Christianity in the community.

3 Conflict and Stalemate

Under normal circumstances, believers of different religions coexist peacefully without incident. Villagers manage to be polite and respectful to one another even if the politeness is primarily motivated by self-interest. The interaction between worshipers of folk religion and Christians in this seaside community is no exception. However, the construction of a new Christian church and the incident of the burning tree unexpectedly introduced variables into a status quo that had been predicated upon self-interest, disrupting the delicate interfaith relationship. More importantly, the incident invoked other types of competing interests, such as profits from real property, the belief in *fengshui*, the question of legality, and power dynamics at the grassroots, all of which have cast a spotlight on deeper structural tensions. An end to the ensuing conflict is nowhere to be seen.

3.1   *The Transfer of Land and the Appropriation of Rules for Self-Interest*

The cause of the conflict between folk religion and Christianity is by no means singular. Although direct confrontations between the two groups were isolated incidents, their seeds had been sown further back in time. Prior to the tree incident, a bill of debt in the value of 10,000 RMB (1,500 USD) had instilled animosity.[9] The burning tree itself became the catalyst of a confrontation in which both sides appropriated rules and religious capital to satisfy their own interests, thus engaging in a battle fought in a web of private discourses and private relationships.

---

9 The bill of debt states, "I, the undersigned, hereby confirm and acknowledge to the creditor, Su Yegen 苏页耕, that I am indebted to the creditor in the amount of 10,000 RMB. The amount includes the land expropriation fee up to the date set forth herein: August 20, 2011. Signed: Qin, Accountant, Seaside Church. Date: June 12, 2011."

While the church was under construction, Zhang Lingguang 张陵洸, a representative of the original land owners, presented a bill of debt in the value of 10,000 RMB.[10] The church's accountant, Qin Ziyao 秦子耀, secretly promised Zhang Lingguang the money without the knowledge of the church leadership. To make matters worse, Qin failed to make the payment on time. When the seaside church leadership learned about this private agreement after the fact, it also failed to properly resolve this dispute over profit and self-interest. Claiming that the land transaction had already been completed, instead of fulfilling the promise made under the table, the seaside church leadership refused to pay Zhang Lingguang the additional 10,000 RMB before the completion of the building. Members of the coordinating committee of the church were in agreement that the additional payment ought to be made upon the completion of the new church, in consideration of the typically upward trend of land value in the rural area.

The church's postponement of the payment aggravated Zhang Lingguang and other villagers. They threatened to sabotage the construction. The incident of the burning tree took place not long after. The incident, together with the overwhelming obstruction from folk religion believers that followed, clarified for the church coordinating committee that they had handled the bill of debt poorly. The 10,000 RMB bill effectively escalated the existing tension.

Open conflict between Christians and folk religion believers broke out as the hitherto latent tension reached a boiling point. What started out as an interpersonal disagreement over group interests was hijacked by a "sacred discourse" of *fengshui* in the public arena, and the religious capital of *fengshui*, in turn, was appropriated as an instrument in the competition between the two sides' interests. An under-the-table property transaction became the catalyst of a case of public, interfaith conflict. The sellers of the land appropriated the

---

10   In 2004, twenty-eight households in the village, including that of Zhang Lingguang, agreed to transfer 1.36 *mu* 亩 (less than a quarter of an acre) of land to the church. The agreement was acknowledged by the thumbprints of all parties involved, in the amount of 13,000 RMB per *mu* (17,680 RMB in total, or 2,700 USD). At the time, the church did not have a plan for the land; it was fenced off and lay vacant. The idea for constructing a new church arose as the congregation grew larger and when cracks began to show on the existing church building. By late 2010, after two additional land transactions, the seaside church had accumulated a total of four *mu* of land (around two-thirds of an acre). The newly acquired land enabled the seaside church to create a steering committee to plan the construction of a new building. Villagers did not object to the project when the Christians broke ground and laid the foundation for the building. But this inspired Zhang Lingguang to demand additional payments from the church. The bill of debt is evidence of this new development.

concept of *fengshui* as well as reverence for the sacred tree in pursuit of personal gain, all because they did not receive the payment promised by a church member on time. The incident of the fiery tree provided an opening in which varying considerations of self-interest were subsumed under the belief in *fengshui*, which escalated the interfaith conflict.

3.2   A Conflict Exacerbated by Competing Interests

It has become clear that the bill of debt debacle and the incident of the burning tree are connected. Moreover, the incident exacerbated the tension between folk religion believers and Christians.

As far as the Christian congregants are concerned, the twenty-eight households in the village, as the collective owner of the piece of land on which the church stands, agreed to the sale of the property in May 2004. When construction of the new church finally started in 2011, the original sellers had no right to raise the property value and demand additional payment. The congregants were of the opinion that even if the church were to agree to the adjusted sale price, it would be reasonable for the church to make up for the difference in land value after the completion of the new building. The original landowners, represented by Zhang Lingguang, in fact agreed to such a compromise.

Nevertheless, considerations of profit sat at the core of subsequent conflicts, and open confrontations further intensified the existing animosity between the two religious groups. Although the church was not ready to make the 10,000 RMB payment, Zhang Lingguang, representing the original landowners in the village, reached out to the church's accountant Qin Ziyao several times to collect the funds in May and June of 2011.[11] These communications were conducted in secret, without the knowledge of the church leadership.

Driven by the pursuit of profit and self-interest, Zhang negotiated with Qin the payment of the difference in land value. Out of desperation, Qin produced a bill of debt and signed it in his own name on June 12, agreeing to make the 10,000 RMB payment to Zhang by August 20, 2011. The land expropriation fee owed to Su Yegen referred to in the bill is the amount demanded by the twenty-eight households residing in the tenth division of Dongwei village. The bill of debt signed in Qin's name presented a difficulty to the church's coordinating committee, because it was a private agreement between Zhang and Qin made without the knowledge of any other church member. The church did not want to endorse a debt ostensibly owed to a single person, Su Yegen. From the

---

11   Zhang Lingguang believed that Qin Ziyao, as the accountant of the seaside church, ought to be able to come up with 10,000 RMB.

church's perspective, making the payment to Zhang might also antagonize the rest of the landowners, despite Zhang's assurance that all twenty-eight households were the creditors of the church.

August 20 came and went. Zhang did not receive the 10,000 RMB payment and proceeded to try to collect from the church leadership. To the annoyance of Zhang and other villagers, however, the church leadership had no knowledge of this agreement. Regulations regarding land transfer in rural areas are very lax. The value of a property can continue to rise in the middle of a transaction or even after the transaction is complete. Variations in land price often lead to disputes between the two parties in a deal. Moreover, the two parties in this deal represented two different belief systems. Failure to make a profit propelled one side to leverage the difference between belief systems.

In this way, failure to collect the payment of 10,000 RMB justified Zhang and company's strong and passionate objection to the construction project: if there was no payment, there would be no church. Although neither party pointed to the 10,000 RMB payment as the direct cause of the incident of the sacred fiery tree, the correlation between the two incidents cannot be overlooked.

It is now obvious that the dispute over the 10,000 RMB indeed foreshadowed a major conflict between folk religion believers and Christians. However, at the time, the church leadership did not foresee the damage that a single bill of debt could have on the construction project. Church leaders did not imagine that folk religion believers would use the incident of the burning tree as a pretense to spread rumors, manipulate public opinion, and provoke large-scale confrontations, all of which highlighted the underlying competing interests. In the end, all six villages in the seaside community were opposed to the construction of the new church.[12] Some on the side of folk religion even reported the church to the authorities for illegal construction. The main opponents produced official documents to prevent the church from erecting a new building. A middle-aged female villager summed up the villagers' fierce opposition to the construction project with strong sentiments and harsh language:

> We don't care that the church is buying the land, and we don't mind selling the land to the church. But the villagers simply won't let them build a [new] church. To start, they still owe us 10,000 RMB, and we will not let off our complaints until they pay up. If they [the church] want to get their money, I'll collect money from the villagers and bring it back to the church. But they [the church] never followed the proper procedure [in

---

12   Interview, March 16, 2014.

the transaction]. The church didn't put its stamp on a contract, and the village representatives didn't sign the agreement, either. For these reasons, we decided to bring the church to the county court. All five of us went to the Bureau of Complaints at the county seat and filed our complaints with the secretary of the county committee.[13]

Not only is this woman a major opponent of the construction of the church, but she is also a core member of the group who filed complaints. I obtained an important document from her detailing the grievances against the church. Written on September 25, 2011, this document detailed for the Urban and Housing Construction Bureau the folk believers' opposition to the construction of a new church. In it, the plaintiffs demanded the return of the property. Six village committees put their official stamps on the document. This document effectively publicized the conflict, making it known to the entire seaside community. All the villagers now felt involved in this dispute.

In this way, interfaith relationships became a signifier of competing interests. Believers in folk religion frame the conflict as an interfaith matter: "a battle between *fengshui* and the cross." In the public arena, however, the conflict represents an intricate web of *fengshui*, competing interests, and legality. Taken together, these factors have altered the rules of engagement for both parties in the conflict and further intensified the distrust and misunderstanding between the two.

3.3   *The Structural Causes of Conflicts and Opposition*

Ostensibly, the bill of debt led to a disagreement, which subsequently developed into a conflict between two religious groups. The interfaith confrontation, however, essentially signified claims over land, morality, and religious resources. The symbolic power of sacralization and normalization was maximized when the dispute over the bill of debt turned into a challenge of the legality of the land transfer. The disagreement between *fengshui* believers and the church also morphed into a major public debate involving all six villages of the seaside community. In this process, both sides constantly reflected on their own actions and behaviors and corrected their courses of action accordingly. They manipulated personal networks to gain an upper hand in this battle over legitimacy.

---

13   Interview, April 4, 2014. This woman was one of the representatives newly elected in late 2013, representing the tenth division of the village.

The folk religionists opposed the construction of the church on the basis of their shared belief in *fengshui*; the landowners were motivated by their very particular and personal interest (the 10,000 RMB) in their opposition to the construction of a new church. The private concerns of *fengshui* believers and landowners overlapped but were not identical.

In a striking fashion, folk religionists managed to rally individuals with diverse interests and social identities to form an interest group. They did so by creating a narrative about a deified tree, drawing on the idioms of *fengshui* and dragon veins. This narrative served to absorb divergent private interests into the overarching concept of *fengshui*. It was effective in mobilizing a large group of villagers in opposition to the construction of a new church. As the *fengshui* believers interacted with outsiders, they made a compelling argument against the church's lack of legality and its failure to follow proper bureaucratic procedures. The sacred tree narrative invoked a privately motivated opposition against what the church represents. The legal argument rested on the rules of land expropriation and transfer in the public sphere. In the end, the belief in *fengshui* supplied the dominant narrative that encompassed private interests and public rules, to the extent of dictating the language of opposition to the construction of the church.

Upon close analysis, we find that although the *fengshui* believers condemned the church for its lack of legality, they clearly glided over their own failure to comply with proper legal and bureaucratic procedures when it comes to the construction of temples. They strategically avoided making an argument for good *fengshui* in their dealings with the government. Believers in *fengshui* understand that the government perceives their belief as superstition. The most effective complaint has to be the church's lack of legality, not its contradiction to good *fengshui*.[14]

In this sense, the belief in *fengshui* serves as religious capital to be invoked when believers see fit. Although the state does not identify with such belief, it does not take a hardline stance against it. Nevertheless, the *fengshui* argument has little lasting power as a legitimate tool of opposition. After all, the seaside church was registered with the local government, and the construction of a new church had been approved by the town's administration in order to replace a derelict building.[15] The construction was indeed legitimate. Additionally, the

---

14 Interview, March 28, 2014.
15 The original building in which the seaside church had resided was very old. As the congregation grew, signs of dilapidation, such as cracks in the walls, began to show. The building was, by then, deemed too run down to stay in operation. During routine inspections, relevant agencies at the town and county levels had repeatedly indicated this major safety

concept of *fengshui* in folk belief is predicated upon the sacralization of persons, the land, and deities. There are no specific ordinances that regulate *fengshui*. Thus, belief in *fengshui* is a tacit understanding, an informally agreed-upon rule for internal consumption. Only through the complaint about land use did the *fengshui* believers have the moral leverage and legal standing to condemn the construction of a new church.[16]

Folk religion believers appropriated the religious capital of *fengshui* and dragon veins to consolidate internal cohesion, on the one hand, while on the other hand they utilized an idiom of the public, one of "procedural legality," to build up fierce opposition to the construction of a new church. In the ensuing stalemate, the church has justified its legitimacy on account of the understanding of the town administration—that the local government promised to proceed with the bureaucratic procedure while the construction was underway. Moreover, the Christian church has also challenged the "procedural legality" of many folk religious temples, a subject which the *fengshui* believers have avoided addressing. All the same, this conflict has crystalized the ways in which both sides appropriated the idioms of procedural legality, religious capital such as *fengshui* and dragon veins, and the capital of authority as well. Through repetitive iterations of these idioms, both sides have relied on private concerns as well as available capital to strengthen their respective group interests and rebuke the opponent.

4   Arbitration and Quagmire

The interfaith conflict originated in the folk believers' opposition to the construction of a new Christian church in the seaside community. The confrontation can be summarized in six phases:

---

concern. They also deemed the building derelict. The condition of the building motivated the seaside church to plan for the construction of a new building.

16   One interviewee explained: "The church requested permission for renovation, but, in fact, the project was a new construction. There are three kinds of construction projects: new construction after a demolition on the same site, an expansion or renovation, and a brand-new construction. What the church was doing falls under the first category." Assuming this assessment is accurate, the construction of a new church was indeed illegal. Construction started when the town's party officials agreed to "build the church while awaiting approval." Regardless, the church did request permission for a renovation, and the request was still under consideration while the construction was underway. In the meantime, the "sacred fiery tree" incident happened, and it prevented the village committee from approving the renovation request, resulting in the permanent interruption of the construction.

1. Individual protests (March to August 2011)
2. Group protests (September 14–19, 2011)
3. Subsequent group protests (September 19 to November 2011)
4. Hiatus (December 2011 to March 2013)
5. Group protests (March to April 2013)
6. Hiatus (May 2013 to the present[17])

The conflicts were fiercest during the "storming" shortly after the tree incident (September to October 2011) and the mass protest and boycott in March and April of 2013. After a few episodes of mass protest, the town organized several meetings in an attempt at arbitration. These efforts failed, as there had been too much bad blood between folk believers and Christians and neither side was willing to compromise its group interests. More interestingly, even though those attending the meetings reached some sort of agreement, protests ensued as soon as the construction resumed.[18] Constant reversal of positions resulted in an indefinite halt to the construction.

Director Wu of the seaside community committee office explained that several mediation meetings, both formal and informal, had been held in the hope of resolving the stalemate. Every meeting ended in disagreement and bad feelings without any concrete conclusion, including the four formal arbitration sessions. There are two forms of arbitration: multilateral and unilateral.[19] In multilateral arbitration, representatives of both the folk believers and Christians were present. Unilateral arbitration involved only one of the two parties involved. To the dismay of the town administration, both sides insisted on guarding their group interests, as neither was willing to compromise.

Furthermore, party officials at the town and village levels are the representatives of governmental authority, with the power to influence decisions based on public interests. However, in the process of mediation, these officials were equally affected by personal relationships and self-interest and therefore failed to exercise their authority according to the demands of justice. Below I will examine four groups of government agents and discuss their conflicts of interest as well as their dereliction of duty. They are former officials who handled the conflict and were later reassigned to other areas; newly appointed officials

---

17   I.e., in 2015, when this chapter was written.
18   Interview, March 20, 2014.
19   One respondent explained: "They have come to our office for arbitration more than three times already. We've also talked to the two parties separately. We've had at least four formal meetings when both parties were present. I can't even recall the number of unilateral mediations we've had."

in the town administration; the mayor and secretary who sat on the village committee; and village representatives.

4.1 Personal Promises from Former Officials

The officials who were involved in the early stage of the construction of the Christian church have been reassigned. They adopted the approach of "building the church while awaiting approval" due to the lack of clear policy guidelines for approving and registering religious sites. They hoped to find a way to grant the church a permit for construction while the dilapidated building was being renovated. Local officials hoped to rely on personal relationships rather than the rule of law to resolve the matter, as one Christian explained to me:

> Officials in the town administration allowed us to "build the church while awaiting approval" out of the goodness of their hearts. They could have traded their land quotas with others for a profit. Giving us the land quota didn't earn them a dime, unlike other departments who often profit from their land holdings. They didn't get additional tax revenue by helping us. When the officials suggested that we just start building as they figure out a way to approve the land use, no one objected to the idea. They thought that they wouldn't have to deal with the issue of land quotas when the new church was complete, as long as no one protested the construction. Who'd have guessed that the tree would just start burning one day? This led to a general opposition to the construction. And the construction had to stop. Now, if you ask the officials about "building the church while awaiting approval," I bet they'll deny ever saying that.[20]

At first glance, "building the church while awaiting approval" is a practical and viable solution. Indeed, building a new church is of upmost importance to the Christians in the seaside community; after all, the church was, at the time, housed in a derelict building. The fact of the matter is, however, that local officials prioritized personal relationships and abused their land quotas when dealing with a matter of public interest. Moreover, it seems like the officials were trying to fast-track the request for construction to avoid bearing any responsibility for the use of a dilapidated building as a church. All the same, the officials appropriated public resources to meet private ends, such as profiting from the land quota. This behavior reveals a lack of consideration for rules and regulations in the management of religious affairs.

---

20   Interview, January 18, 2014.

4.2   *The Newly Appointed Officials' Principle of Stability*

While the new church was under construction, the officials who employed the strategy of "building the church while awaiting approval" had already been reassigned elsewhere. The newly appointed officials did not give the matter sufficient attention. They prioritized local economic development and largely neglected this historical case. However, the newly appointed officials were sympathetic with the Christian church and its need for a new building. All the same, they adopted a conservative position in favor of stability.

In several mediation meetings, relevant officials expressed sympathy for the church and were generally in favor of "building the church while awaiting approval." They regarded this as a matter of the well-being of a few hundred Christians who deserved a reasonable explanation as to why the construction had to stop.[21] However, sympathy was not a solution. The new officials also failed to follow through on their predecessors' promise to find legal support for the church's construction. So that they would not lose face as the representatives of governmental authority, the officials sought to take advantage of loopholes. One interviewed official stated:

> My thinking was to exploit the loophole. Even though the construction of the church was not entirely legitimate, once the construction is complete and the building is in use, it will be a hassle to tear it down. But, for example, if they [Christians] reported an illegal temple while it was under construction and protested it, no matter what our executive order says, I would have to order its demolition. Any illegal construction without permission has to be stopped. My official title aside, I hope for communal harmony in the village. If no one objected to the construction of a temple until after it was completed, we would not interfere. The same applies to the church. The problem is that they [non-Christians] protested when the construction was ongoing.[22]

The effectiveness of exploiting loopholes as a policy relies on a lack of opposition. "No opposition" is a justification for the construction of a new church. Conversely, opposition or protest from the folk believers was taken to justify halting construction. Consequently, the challenge to the church's procedural legality voiced by the folk believers became the primary measure that determined how local government officials mediated the relationship between

---

21   Interview, January 19, 2014.
22   Interview, January 19, 2014.

folk believers and Christians. In choosing which rules to follow, the officials revealed their exploitation of the rhetoric of the public for self-interest, as well as a preference for folk religion.

4.3   Party Officials in the Village and the Web of Power Relations

The village's mayor and the secretary of the village committee have typically acquiesced to the construction of folk temples. Relevant authorities in the local government usually turn a blind eye to the appropriation of land resources. That, together with the intricate web of power relations woven by party officials in rural villages, has facilitated the construction of temples as well as rampant private transactions of real estate. One interviewee summed up the reality thus: "What would be the point of us visiting village party officials everyday if lobbying didn't work?"[23] In other words, a temple is considered "legal" so long as village party officials do not report it prior to its completion. For the most part, approval for the appropriation of the land on which a temple-in-construction stands is left incomplete.

The village mayor and the secretary of the village committee, as members of a grassroots self-governing body, tend to stay out of land transaction and construction projects. Some of them are sponsors of temples. To put their attitudes in plain language, the construction is justified by the lack of opposition to the process. The mayor has even referred to folk temples as a historical and cultural legacy.[24] Such rhetoric not only gives legitimacy to the construction and renovation of temples but also justifies the officials' involvement in such construction projects.

The construction of Christian churches, however, is subject to a set of standardized rules, including the "Regulations on Religious Affairs" issued by the central government, as well as a strict process of land-use approval. Whereas the mayor and village committee secretary tended to downplay the legal aspect of the construction of folk religious sites and justify the presence of temples by their historical significance, they insisted on abiding by the rules when it comes to the construction of the seaside church. The persistent emphasis on the church's failure to comply with bureaucratic procedure, on the one hand, and the deliberate exoneration of temples from the standard of legality, on the other, clearly illustrate an abuse of rules concerning public matters to suit private ends.

---

23   Interview, January 19, 2014.
24   Interview, April 9, 2014.

4.4 The Ambiguity of the Village Representatives' Positions

In keeping with the deliberately noncommittal attitudes of officials at the town and village levels, village representatives have also kept their positions ambiguous. By dint of their elected office, village representatives have the right and obligation to take a stand in committee meetings on matters of great significance. However, in consideration of the overwhelming number of folk religion believers—the source of their influence—representatives have largely remained silent or neutral in the mediation meetings. Their inaction was driven by considerations of self-interest, reputation, and interpersonal dynamics. Not only have private concerns curtailed the committee's ability to preserve justice, they have also diminished the impact of the multiple mediation meetings hosted by Dongwei village.

Without the expressed position of the Dongwei village representatives, the review and approval of the necessary paperwork came to face an even greater obstacle. The proper procedure of land transfer requires the signed consent of all twenty-four representatives of Dongwei village. It is a necessary step before requesting a construction permit so that ownership of the 1.36 *mu* of land on which the church's foundations stand can be legally transferred to the seaside church. Without taking this step, the village committee would remain the rightful owner of the land.

However, village representatives began to exercise extra caution after the incident of the burning tree. Whenever the matter of the new church came up, they refrained from expressing their opinions one way or the other. Two of the village representatives were Christian, but they followed the lead of their peers and never betrayed their positions.[25] One explained, "After the election last year, more than forty village representatives and party members attended a meeting. No one uttered a word in opposition to the church's construction at the time. But once the construction was underway, they [the opponents] came and tore down the walls."[26]

At the core is the village representatives' unwillingness to bear the blame for offending fellow villagers. In the face of two competing forces, the majority of the representatives have chosen to remain silent, and yet their silence broadcasted their reluctance to assume responsibility loud and clear.

This examination of the actions of four different groups of agents of the government reveals their primary motivations. Their decisions were primarily driven by the desire to preserve private interests and to maintain a balance in

---

25 Interview, January 19, 2014.
26 Interview, March 20, 2014.

power relations. This is essentially an abuse of rules concerning the public, compounded by negligence of duty and an ambiguity in the rule of law.

The conflict between folk religion and Christianity is far more than a simple matter of legality. Rather, it weaves interpersonal relationships, the reciprocity of interests, power relations, and religious practices into an intricate web of interests. The four groups of governmental agents refused to state their position and failed to propose an effective solution to interfaith conflict, either through formal or informal means. That is mainly because they each made a calculated decision based on personal preferences and self-interest, and decisions made on the basis of personal interest have further illuminated the private rules by which they operated.

The implementation of private rules and self-interest to resolve interfaith tension conflated the public and private spheres. More importantly, it failed to formulate a universally applicable set of principles for the management of interactions between folk religion and Christianity. There is, moreover, no sign of any effort to strike a balance between practical problem-solving and the rule of law. Furthermore, a standardized procedure for the application of rules and resources to the management of interfaith relationships is practically nonexistent. Thus, any solution to conflict is to be determined by context. Private appropriation of rules concerning the public may ease the symptoms, but it does little to remedy the deep-rooted structural ills.

5   Conclusion

Many factors contribute to the volatility in the interaction between folk religion believers and Christians. These include the relationship between religion and government or society, as well as the intricate web of Chinese social relations consisting of interpersonal relationships, power dynamics, competing interests, and the influence of family and clan. Despite the underlying tension, folk religion and Christianity typically manage to coexist peacefully in rural society. When friction arises in the manifold relationships described above, however, conflict ensues. In the analysis of such conflict, it is critical to point out factors that have affected the respective status, functions, and religious practices on both sides.

It is noteworthy that interfaith conflicts are manifested in different manners in different geographical locations and contexts. The interactions between folk religion believers and Christians in the seaside community in Zhejiang also take place in a power ecosystem, not unlike cases in other regions. However, the case of the seaside community stands out for the volatility of the conflict.

The dispute over the 10,000 RMB foreshadowed an open, direct conflict, catalyzed by the incident of the sacred fiery tree. The conflict escalated as disputes over land, competing interests, power struggles, and debates over legality surfaced.

The interaction between folk religion believers and Christians in the seaside community in Zhejiang showcases the interweaving of multiple factors: interfaith relationships, competing interests, power dynamics, interpersonal relationships, and family connections. Notably, the number of adherents to a belief system is indeed an indicator of its strength and influence in a community. The religion with the greater population may also exercise more influence in the power structure. All the same, numbers alone do not account for the relative rise and fall of religions. The relative strengths of folk religion and Christianity should not be weighed from a perspective of binary opposition.

To be clear, folk religion and Christianity are by no means in a zero-sum relationship. The experiences of individuals interacting with those in other belief systems can be affected by local religious history, economic development, the demand for religion, and the restoration of religious sites, as well as local religious elites. Whether or not a religious group succeeds in establishing a mutually beneficial relationship with local authorities in terms of interest- and resource-sharing also plays an important role. Indeed, the relationship between folk religion and Christianity presents a challenge in the field of religious sociology. But it is also a fruitful topic for research. The defining features of the interaction between the two belief systems are shaped by the interplay between religion and society, as well as the two systems' respective entanglement with the local culture, social composition, and power structure.

Bibliography

Deleuze, Gilles. *The Fold: Leibniz and the Baroque.* Minneapolis: University of Minnesota Press, 1993.
Deleuze, Gilles. *The Logic of Sense.* New York: Columbia University Press, 1990.

CHAPTER 7

House Churches in Northern Jiangsu

Patterns of Transformation and the State Effect

Xiao Yunze

1   Introduction

As Christianity enters a local society, its localization is a twofold process. First, the religion transitions from an entity led by charismatic leaders to an institutionalized church. Second, the state effect manifests itself during the change.[1] Take, for example, the Christianization of the West. Jeffrey Russell and Douglas Lumsden propose a "pendulum theory," arguing that Western Christianity originated in a charismatic prophet "endowed with a free-flowing spirit" and afterward transformed into a formal "institutionalized church."[2] While much of this transformation was due to the state, the inception of Christianity was not political in nature. Rather, the religious movement initially centered on Jesus's demand for a singular allegiance from his disciples as well as their renunciation of other loyalties. The encounter between a Christianity distinct from Judaism and Roman religion as well as state institutions generated a state effect, which engendered a host of strategies for action, including conflict, avoidance, interaction, or assimilation.[3]

Chinese Christianity experienced a "revival" after the disruption of the Cultural Revolution. In the era of reform and opening up, Christianity expanded further into Chinese local society. As the Three-Self Patriotic Movement (TSPM) has been fully incorporated into the state's governing apparatus, it represents the state's will, and exhibits a high degree of homogeneity. In contrast, Christianity in local society reveals a greater degree of idiosyncrasies,

---

1 Timothy Mitchell, "Society, Economy, and the State Effect," in *The Anthropology of the State: A Reader*, ed. Aradhana Sharma and Akhil Gupta (Oxford: Blackwell Publishing, 2006), 169–180.
2 Jeffrey Burton Russell and Douglas W. Lumsden, *A History of Medieval Christianity: Prophecy and Order* (New York: Peter Lang: 2000), 1–7.
3 James D. G. Dunn, *The Partings of the Ways between Christianity and Judaism and Their Significance for the Character of Christianity* (Salem, OR: Trinity Press International, 1991); translated by Yang Hui as *Fendao yangbiao: Jidujiao yu youtaijiao de fenli jiqi dui jidujiao texing de yiyi* (Hong Kong: Logos and Pneuma Press, 2015).

especially in the autonomous house churches. Despite the disputes and divisions among house churches over the last three decades, there is an observable pattern in their transformation. These groups rose in the 1970s and 80s and did not conform to the positions of the Three-Self Church.[4] They revived the theological legacies of major preachers of indigenous fundamentalist movements, such as Watchman Nee 倪柝声, John Sung 宋尚节, and Wang Mingdao 王明道. As such, they fashioned forms of worship on the basis of existing charismatic Christian traditions, including miracles or spiritual leadership, and drew on the traditional Chinese social practice of voluntary association.

House churches have furthermore distanced themselves from the state. Compared to the Three-Self Church, house church leaders are deeply influenced by fundamentalist ideas and seek a strict separation from the secular world. This has caused house churches to keep the state at arm's length. Pastors have consistently rejected state demands for allegiance and resisted state interference in religion. In a sense, the tradition of disobedience developed among house churches has created the state effect.[5] Consequently, house churches are often viewed as a disruptive force in society, and their legitimacy is commonly questioned.

Unlike early Christianity in the West, which developed as an urban phenomenon, Chinese local Christian churches started out as a rural movement. The core bases of operation for Western churches were cities, which were centers of evangelization and religious worship as well as bastions of rationalism. Farmers were dismissed as heretics or lesser Christians. The recognition of a genuine faith among rural Christians is a relatively modern development.[6] Rodney Stark has made a similar argument about Western Christianity, adding that churches provided a mechanism for association among strangers in cities, while their charitable services gave birth to a host of public characteristics.[7] In contrast, the practices of Christianity in Chinese local society were born out of

---

4   Quite a few house church leaders were involved in the TSPM and were incarcerated for this. After 1978, they became the core leadership of house churches. These experiences, in a sense, have contributed to an "anti-Three-Self" tradition among house churches.
5   Yuan Hao, "Zhongguo jidujiao yu bufucong de chuantong: yi Wang Mingdao, Tanghe jiaohui yu Shouwang jiaohui weili," *Daofeng*, no. 44 (2016): 87–122.
6   Max Weber, *Sociology of Religion*, trans. Ephraim Fischoff (Boston: Beacon Press, 1963); translated by Kang Le as *Zongjiao shehuixue* (Guilin: Guangxi shifan daxue chubanshe, 2011).
7   In *The Rise of Christianity*, Rodney Stark explains that early Christianity was an urban movement. The religion spread rapidly across European cities. More recently, in *The Triumph of Christianity*, Stark further argues that the European countryside was barely Christianized, as Christianity in rural Europe had an abundance of pagan elements. See Rodney Stark, *The Rise of Christianity: A Sociologist Reconsiders History* (Berkeley: University of California Press, 2000), translated by Huang Jianbo and Gao Mingui as *Jidujiao de xingqi: yige shehuixuejia dui lishi de zaisi* (Shanghai: Shanghai guji chubanshe, 2005), 176; Rodney Stark,

rural movements. Specifically, house churches in Henan, Anhui, and northern Jiangsu rose out of movements in which peasants yearned for transcendental experiences and self-identified as the defenders of this monotheistic religion. These peasants were more concerned with personal salvation than public service. The church turned into a spiritual family, providing a mechanism for socialization.

Chinese house churches currently face different kinds of challenges as rural communities transition into urban entities. Internal changes have also impacted the church order. In the meantime, as the state has not formalized a policy for managing house churches, government agencies in different localities or different departments have adopted varying management systems. Certain localities have even developed unofficial, tacit mechanisms of religious control. As the Chinese state is moving toward the rule of law in its administrative actions, some local governments have begun to employ nonreligious methods in the management of religious affairs in their engagement with Christian house churches. Thus, different house churches may generate varying state effects, and thus divergent strategies, in response.

Studies of house churches have identified many of these changes. For example, scholars have highlighted three types of house churches. The first are traditional house churches. More open-minded house churches are known as open house churches, and those established in urban areas are identified as emerging churches in the cities.[8] However, the existing scholarship tends to consist of general surveys rather than case studies. This has prevented scholars from being able to sufficiently analyze the impact of both internal and external changes on house churches. The most notable changes include the effects of internal rules of governance, mechanisms of operation, and the state effect.

For these reasons, it is imperative that we conduct a case study based on one location or one specific house church to appreciate the formation of local Christianity in China. Here, focusing on the countryside-to-city transition, we will identify the pattern according to which house churches departed from both rural communities and the household, how they standardized church operation, and how they managed their engagement with the state.[9] In practice, the

---

The Triumph of Christianity: How the Jesus Movement Became the World's Largest Religion (New York: HarperOne, 2011), 255.

8   Yu Jianrong, "Zhongguo jidujiao jiating jiaohui hefahua yanjiu," *Zhanlüe yu guanli* 战略与管理, 2010.3–4, featured on Aisixiang, http://www.aisixiang.com/data/70584.html (accessed August 20, 2019).

9   Jie Kang has analyzed this pattern as it is manifested in unregistered churches in a city in Shandong. Jie Kang, *House Church Christianity in China: From Rural Preachers to City Pastors* (Cham, Switzerland: Palgrave, 2016).

study of Christianity in Chinese local society is in and of itself a process of analyzing "society through religion and vice versa"[10] or examining "the state through religion and vice versa."

2 Research Methods and Fieldwork Site

In early 2016, I conducted fieldwork in house churches in Mingcheng (pseudonym) in northern Jiangsu. Yu Jianrong 于建嵘 has identified this areas as the "Huai River basin religious belt."[11] My original objective was to construct a broad picture of house churches through in-person visits, participant observation, and in-depth interviews. However, I ended up uncovering a host of stories about Vineyard Church.[12] Out of ethical considerations, I have given pseudonyms to all locations and interviewees, as well as most of the interviewees' congregations.

My journey into the field began with an introduction arranged by a congregant at Wenzhou House Church 温州家庭教会. I arrived at a branch of Vineyard Church, in the suburbs of Mingcheng, on January 21.[13] I attended the youth fellowship camp of this church for the next four days, camping in sub-freezing temperatures with Christian youths. This was my first personal experience of the "discipline" (order) of Vineyard Church. It was also during the camp that I started hearing more stories of the church, further fueling my interest.

Upon my return from camp on January 26, I interviewed Mao Biao, the preacher of the Mengzhuang Church, another branch of Vineyard Church, and other congregants and leaders within the Vineyard Church structure and other house churches in and around Mingcheng.[14]

---

10 Li Feng, *Xiangcun jidujiao de zuzhi texing ji shehui jiegou xing weizhi—Huanan Y xian X zhen jidujiao jiaohui zuzhi yanjiu* (Shanghai: Fudan daxue chubanshe, 2005), 361.
11 House churches dominate two major areas: the Huai River 淮河 basin and the Min-Zhe 闽浙 (northern Fujian and southern Zhejiang) coastal region. See Yu, "Zhongguo jidujiao."
12 This church was formerly known as the Zhujia Church 朱家教会.
13 For more on the term "branch" (*zhiti* 肢体), see below.
14 I have combined the two churches into one case study because at one time they had been a single church. They separated from one another in the time frame of our narrative. To further strengthen our argument, I have also included interviews conducted with church leaders and congregants (of both house churches and the Three-Self Church) in February, August, and November of 2016.

3   "Everything Done in Order": The Rise of Zhujia Church in Mingcheng

3.1   *The Beginning: Fundamentalism and an Evangelical Base*
Situated in the flat plains in the northern part of Jiangsu, Mingcheng has historically been a major battlefield. It has been a key industrial city and a railway hub of Jiangsu since 1949. Christian missions sponsored by the American Baptist Church, the Presbyterian Church (USA), and the Seventh-Day Adventist Church have all left their footprints in Mingcheng, followed by indigenous denominations such as the Christian Assembly Hall 聚会处 and the Jesus Family 耶稣家庭. Among these, the Presbyterian Church (USA) saw the most success. It built the first Protestant church in Mingcheng in 1897, established the first hospital practicing Western medicine in 1900, and founded the first Christian school in 1905. In 1910, the first Presbyterian church in northern Jiangsu was established to manage the evangelization of several cities in the Jianghuai 江淮 region.[15] A document compiled in 1934–1935 indicates that the Presbyterian church had 1,771 adult congregants, along with 1,800 unbaptized members. By 1947, there were 123 churches and 7,960 Christians in the city.[16]

Two kinds of Christianity emerged in Mingcheng. The first has Presbyterian roots and is disposed toward fundamentalism and pietism. The Presbyterian Church (USA) established a North Jiangsu mission in 1910, as well as four levels of government and administration. This mission was known as a "heavily evangelical and ultra-conservative organization," partly due to the poverty and cultural conservatism of this region, and partly because this mission favored the conservative theology of the traditional Presbyterian Church. Not only did the mission come to represent fundamentalist missionaries in China, but it was also involved in a heated debate between fundamentalists and liberals in the 1920s and 30s.[17] Latecomers such as the Christian Assembly Hall and Jesus Family operated within the same theological framework, adding a pietistic flair to the Christianity in Mingcheng.

---

15   G. Thompson Brown, "Jidujiao zai Jiangsu Mingcheng diqu chuanjiao jianshi, 1884–1941," in *Mingcheng wenshi ziliao*, vol. 31, trans. Yang Naizhuang, ed. Zhongguo renmin zhengzhi xieshang huiyi Jiangsu sheng Mingcheng weiyuanhui wenshi weiyuanhui (Mingcheng, Jiangsu, China: Zhongguo renmin zhengzhi xieshang huiyi Jiangsu sheng Mingcheng weiyuanhui wenshi weiyuanhui, 2010).

16   Huang Dianchi, ed., *Mingcheng minzu zongjiao zhi* (Mingcheng: Mingcheng shi minzu zongjiao shiwuju, 1991).

17   Yao Xiyi, *Wei zhendao zhengbian: zaihua jiduxinjiao chuanjiaoshi jiyaozhuyi yundong (1920–1937)* (Hong Kong: China Alliance Press, 2008), 101.

The second kind of Christianity in Mingcheng was shaped by evangelist groups who also took root in the area. In the first half of the twentieth century, northern Jiangsu was an economically underdeveloped region, plagued by floods and banditry. The locals were hostile to foreign missionaries, and religious conflicts in Mingcheng were as common as those in the more prosperous and culturally autonomous southern part of Jiangsu. In fact, Mingcheng was once the center of anti-Christian movements.[18] Nevertheless, missionaries laid down roots during this tumultuous time by building hospitals, running schools, and offering relief to peasants. Furthermore, they deliberately cultivated indigenous pastors and missionaries who were actively involved in church governance. When anti-Christian movements dissipated, indigenous preachers established two middle schools, run solely by Chinese. American missionaries left Mingcheng in 1941 when the Pacific War broke out. Afterward, the Presbyterian churches in northern Jiangsu joined forces and formed the Suhuai Chinese Christian Church 苏淮中华基督教会. A Chinese Christian Jianghuai Synod 中华基督教江淮大会 was established in 1947, which joined the national Church of Christ in China 中华基督教会 shortly afterward.[19] By then, Christianity had laid down deep roots for evangelization in the communities of Mingcheng.

3.2 The Zhu Family House Church: The Emergence of Fundamentalist House Churches in Mingcheng

A series of mass political movements between 1949 and 1978 caused rifts among Christians throughout China; those in Mingcheng were not exempt from these campaigns. In 1950, highly respected Chinese pastors in the Jianghuai 江淮 Synod launched a Three-Self reform movement. Christians of all denominations were summoned to Xiguan Church 西关教堂 for worship services in 1959, while services in the other seven churches were banned.[20] From 1966 to 1976, during the Cultural Revolution, all religious activities were outlawed, which had a profound impact on both the TSPM and religious specialists. Church buildings were appropriated and pastoral personnel were evicted. The churches and evangelical networks established by missionaries of various

---

18 Gao Jun, "Qingmo Jiangsu minjiao chongtu de qiluo," *Anqing shifan xueyuan xuebao (shehui kexue ban)*, 2014.6: 111–114; Gao Jun, "Jiangsu feijidujiao yundong shimo," *Puyang zhiye jishu xueyuan xuebao*, 2014.4: 40–42.
19 Mingcheng difangzhi bianzuan weiyuanhui, ed., *Mingcheng shizhi* (Beijing: Zhonghua shuju, 1994), 2123.
20 Ibid., 2123, 2125.

denominations were effectively destroyed. Nevertheless, the deep, evangelical traditions of Mingcheng were not completely uprooted.

Wang Yuena, a daughter-in-law of the Zhu family in Mingcheng, attended the Chinese Christian Bible Institute (*Zhongguo jidujiao lingxiu xueyuan* 中国基督教灵修学院) in the 1940s.[21] She returned to Mingcheng after 1949 and started preaching at Nanguan Church 南关堂. When the church shut its doors in 1966, Wang also stopped preaching. Her husband had been attending a Christian Assembly Hall. His congregation had only 115 members in its heyday and was suppressed by the local government for resisting the Three-Self movement after 1949.[22] In 1966, Wang had a spiritual experience while recovering from a severe illness. She began to host clandestine services in her own home. Her oldest son, Pastor Zhu Bide, a sixty-year-old high school math teacher, told me that his mother was a student of Pastor Jia Yuming 贾玉铭. She had dedicated her life to the service of God but had to stop preaching due to political suppression. She then opened an eye clinic to help raise her four children. The Three-Self pastors and elders had been derelict in their pastoral duties, and she felt God had called her to service through her illness.[23] With a small congregation consisting of kinsmen, Zhujia (or Zhu family) Church came into shape. Older Christians in Mingcheng were also aware that the Zhu family had started a new church.[24] Not long after this, however, the Public Security Bureau outlawed the church, and its female preacher was labeled a reactionary. Accused of "engaging in anti-revolutionary activities in the name of religion," "competing with the Communist Party for the souls of the next generation," and "being a special agent for Hong Kong," she was sentenced to one year in prison.

In January of 1977, the state redressed Wang's case. For an emerging church or church leaders, hardships can help generate unintended religious capital and reputation; the more harshly the state suppresses religion, the more energized religious groups may become.[25] The Zhu family's rehabilitation as well as

---

21   The Chinese Christian Bible Institute was founded by Jia Yuming 贾玉铭in Nanjing in 1936. When the Sino-Japanese War broke out, the school relocated to Sichuan and found a new home in Chongqing. After the war, in 1945, the Institute returned to Nanjing and relocated again to Shanghai in 1949. It was forced to close its doors in 1956. See *Huaren jidujiaoshi renwu cidian* (Biographical Dictionary of Chinese Christianity), http://bdcconline.net/zh-hans/stories/jia-yuming (accessed August 20, 2019).
22   Huang Dianchi, *Mingcheng minzu zongjiao zhi*, 158, 160.
23   Interview with Pastor Zhu Bide, Vineyard Church, Mingcheng (January 31, 2016).
24   Zhu Bide likens the establishment of a church to the act of "releasing." This turn of phrase is suggestive of his self-identity as a church leader.
25   Lu Yunfeng, "Kunan yu zongjiao zengzhang: guanzhi de feiyuqi houguo," *Shehui*, 2010.4: 200–216.

its subsequent resumption of services drew Christians from both Mingcheng and the surrounding rural and urban areas. By 1978, nearly one hundred congregants filled the two houses of the Zhujia Church each week. In contrast, the municipal Three-Self church reopened its doors at Xiguan Church only in 1980.[26]

Christianity in northern Jiangsu grew exponentially in the 1980s and 90s, especially in rural villages.[27] One Christian I spoke with reminisced about the 80s, when evangelization resumed, saying that as most of the villagers were Christian, many new believers simply followed the others' examples. A pastor revealed that a production brigade warehouse in his village had been converted into a church. Several interviewees recounted that Buddhist and Daoist temples had sustained severe damage in the period of "doing away with the four olds," especially as northern Jiangsu was one of the earliest Communist and revolutionary bases. The destitute farming villages had no means of restoring temples. Moreover, while the state was constructing its religious policies, it also exercised tight control over religious sites and their establishment, leaving a vacuum in the religious landscape in rural villages. As a result, the fundamentalist, communal, and embodied devotional style of house churches emerged as a timely solution to peasants' spiritual needs. Both primary and secondary conversions took place at a large scale.[28]

The first house church I visited in Mingcheng, Beixiang Church 北乡教会, is a product of Zhujia Church's evangelism. This church has grown into a large organization, consisting of nearly sixty smaller house churches and more than three thousand congregants. The church is in the home of a rural preacher in Mengzhuang, Mao Biao, and remains a humble meeting site in the style of

---

26 Mingcheng difangzhi bianzuan weiyuanhui, *Mingcheng shizhi,* 21–25.
27 Much scholarship has addressed the rapid development of Christianity in northern Jiangsu since 1978. The religious inclination in the region's rural villages, in particular, showed a stark contrast to the predominantly Buddhist region of southern Jiangsu. The "Buddhist South" vs. "Christian North" landscape was a cause for concern for many government officials. See Jiangsu sheng shehui kexueyuan ketizu, "Jiangsu sheng nongcun zongjiao zhuangkuang ji duice yanjiu," *Jiangsu sheng shehuizhuyi xueyuan xuebao,* 2003.3: 7–10; Zhang Hua and Xue Heng, "Zai shehui zhuanxing zhong chuangxing zongjiao shiwu guanli Jiangsu xin nongcun jianshe zhongde zongjiao hexie guanxi yanjiu," *Zhongguo zongjiao,* 2013.8: 66–67.
28 Primary conversion refers to the voluntary conversion of an individual "who plays a critical role in his or her conversion experience. Typically, the convert carefully assesses a faith prior to becoming a devout follower, although the social connections among members of the faith also play a significant part." Secondary conversion is a more passive form of conversion. "It is a reluctant acceptance of a faith, which is usually contingent upon a primary conversion." See Stark, *Rise of Christianity,* 99–100.

the 1990s, outfitted with a simple cross, a blackboard, and a few benches and kneeling cushions. The only major difference between the Beixiang Church and Zhujia Church is that most of the current congregants in Mengzhuang are elderly.

3.3 Encountering "Order" at Zhujia Church

"Order" is a concept frequently invoked by leaders and congregants alike at Zhujia Church. They refer to the church as a "limb." Branches at the grassroots call themselves "lampstands," rather than "meeting places," and the overseer of a branch is a "watcher of the lampstand." "Limbs" and "lampstands" form a hierarchical structure, in which Christians of each "limb" must abide by a host of tacit rules that represent the authority of church leaders as well as the governing order. These terms are biblical in origin. Through the metaphor of the body, the church establishes a symbolic order. For example, in his First Letter to the Corinthians, Paul compares the church to the "body" of Jesus, which is connected to all the limbs. Limbs and the body suffer hardships and celebrate glories as one.[29] Paul also highlights the importance of "order" in the prevention of chaos, demanding Christians to "let all things be done decently and in order."[30]

As Zhujia Church continued to open new churches, the mother church sought to consolidate its authority by establishing order. When I, an outsider, first approached the north-country branch of Zhujia Church, the preacher who received me stressed the importance of "everything being done in order." He had to report my request for a visit and an interview to his superiors—first to the supervisor of the meeting site, who then forwarded the request to coworkers at a higher level. In the end, the head of the "limb" gave me permission. When a Christian friend asked to visit me at this location, we had to submit a formal request to the head of the church. The answer to this request was no.

Regardless, I remained curious about the ways in which the "parent" church in the Zhujia system constructed such a rigorous power structure. How did it establish a watertight order for the church? How does an exclusive community disseminate the ostensibly welcoming and inclusive message of the Gospels? Perhaps most surprising is the fact that the Zhu family might no longer be the master of its limbs—Zhujia Church seemed effectively a shell.

---

29   1Corinthians 12:26–27: "If one part suffers, every part suffers with it; if one part is honored, every part rejoices with it. Now you are the body of Christ, and each of you is a part of it."
30   1Corinthians 14:40.

4 The Grace to the City Movement: The Collapse of the Old "Order" and a Renewed "Order"

4.1 *From Zhujia to Four Major Families to Dozens of Families*

Buddhist monks commented on the widespread destruction of temples in Mingcheng during my fieldwork. Unable to compete with folk religious household-based religious services such as Shen Mama 神妈妈,[31] Buddhist temples have only recently restored their visible presence, helped by their formal registration status with the state. It appears that household- or family-based religious worship is the predominant form of folk belief in Mingcheng. Conceivably, Zhujia Church is a household-based form of worship. It differs from other household-based religious providers in that religious services are not the church's livelihood. Nonetheless, a family-based church is prone to division, especially in the local society of northern Jiangsu where splits within households have a long tradition.[32] According to the records of the TSPM/CCC (China Christian Council) in Mingcheng, the city currently has 370,000 Christians registered with the Three-Self Church, and house churches claim a comparable size of membership. However, house churches disagree with this number, maintaining that their membership exceeds that of the TSPM, but neither party can provide evidence to support its claims. The specific number may well be irrelevant, since house churches in Mingcheng are suffering from serious internal friction.

Although Zhujia Church was the first house church in Mingcheng, it has suffered internal discord since its inception. According to the account of Zhu Bide, those congregants who refused to submit to Zhu's governance broke away. In the 1980s and 90s, as segments broke away from the Zhu family house church, four major branches became well known. Today, Christians in Mingcheng can recall the four major house churches, which I will refer to using the surnames Zhu, Li, Dong, and Jin. Each carved out its own sphere of influence and they competed with one another. The "parents" of the four families became strangers to each other, and they demanded that their followers conform to the same rules of engagement.

Division is the overarching theme for house churches in Mingcheng. The four families have failed to sustain their respective operations. The Jin family turned to heresy, the Li family collapsed due to economic strains, and the Dong

---

[31] Zhou Yue (Adam Chau), "Zhongguo minjian zongjiao fuwu de jiahu zhidu," trans. Zhang Xixiang, *Xuehai*, 2010.3: 44–56.

[32] He Xuefeng, "Lun Zhongguo nongcun de quyu chayi—cunzhuang shehui jiegou de shijiao," *Kaifang shidai*, 2012.10: 108–129.

father and son broke with one another. These instabilities caused even greater division among and within churches.[33] The attitude that "if you can start a church, why can't I?" contributed to further splits. To date, there are several dozen house church networks in the area.[34]

Even Zhujia Church, ostensibly intact and legitimate, suffers from constant rifts within. Wang Yuena handed over the church to her two sons as she was nearing retirement. Her eldest son, Zhu Bide, naturally took over as a new generation of "parent" and oversaw the first church that Wang established. Interestingly, Wang's sons have caused division in Zhujia Church.

Zhu Bide's younger brother, Zhu Yage, became estranged from him in 1993. Zhu Bide appeared indifferent when the subject of his younger brother came up during my interview with him, saying that they were no longer of one mind. Some congregants have observed that Zhu Yage is well-spoken, capable, reform-minded, and overall superior to his older brother. Churches under his supervision engaged in organizational reform and opened Sunday schools for children. He also partnered with other house churches in Mingcheng to engage in collaborative projects, encouraging churches to get involved in local communities by providing social services and acting in the manner of a young leader of all house churches. Unfortunately, this descendant of the Zhu family died of a heart attack while engaged in missionary work in Yunnan in 2014.

4.2 Jiamishan Church and the Grace to the City Movement

Many Christians brought Jiamishan Church to my attention when I first began researching churches in Mingcheng. I was encouraged to learn more about the church's pastor, Xiang Tianle, and its Christian school and theological training, as well as its community services. This church of nine hundred congregants has become the new paradigm for house churches in the region. Pastor Xiang was born into the household of a high-ranking party official. He was baptized at Zhujia Church in 1989 and quickly found himself entangled in an internal conflict. In 1992, Zhu Bide felt that Xiang Tianle had connected with members of Lijia Church without the permission of his home church, thus violating church "order." Zhu issued an ultimatum, stating that Xiang would either discontinue his interaction with Lijia Church or leave Zhujia Church for good. As Xiang reflected on his options, he realized that the "order" of house churches was nothing but a paternalistic and authoritarian regime without any written rules.

---

33 Interview with preacher Zhou Yisa, Dongjia Church, Mingcheng (January 31, 2016).
34 Interview with Pastor Zhu Bide, the Vineyard Church, Mingcheng (January 31, 2016).

In the spring of the same year, Xiang, along with twenty followers, left the Zhu family and joined Lijia Church. The Li brothers had created a Jesus Christ Church (*Yesu jidu jiaohui* 耶稣基督教会) whose influence spanned from Lianyungang in the east to the Henan and Anhui borders in the west and from the Yellow River in the north to the Yangtze River in the south. It also designated "ten districts" and "eight departments" within the church system. Xiang Tianle was appointed to oversee the Mingcheng district. On the pretext that the church had accepted funds from Taiwan, the Public Security Bureau outlawed churches in Xiang's jurisdiction in 2000. According to a Religious Affairs Bureau official in Mingcheng, "Taiwanese Christians founded an illegal organization, which has seen rapid growth. The Religious Affairs Bureau does not have jurisdiction over illegal entities, and thus the state must outlaw it."[35] Xiang was sentenced to a year of reeducation through labor. Due to his health conditions, he was granted a noncustodial sentence and was permitted to serve his time outside of prison. The incident of the "illegal organization" was a traumatic experience for Xiang and sowed the seeds of his departure from Lijia Church, the establishment of Jiamishan Church, and a shift to the Reformed tradition (Calvinism).

In 2002, Jiamishan Church achieved de facto independence and claimed a membership of six hundred, albeit existing outside of a structured organization. Lacking a clear plan for future development, however, the church also reached a bottleneck. Pastor Xiang summarized the period of hardship in terms of the overall challenge facing all rural churches. He observed,

> The most flourishing churches in the 1990s were rural churches. The four major families emerged in the countryside, and their organizations were based on the infrastructure of rural churches. Although Zhujia Church is based in the city, it still maintains a rural structure and primarily serves the countryside. Granted that we are an emerging urban church, our belief system is comparable with that of a rural church. Our tenets, style of worship, and method of governance are nearly identical to those of a rural church as well.[36]

It was also in 2002 that Chinese Christian denominations came to embrace the reformed tradition on a large scale, thanks to the efforts of overseas Chinese pastors such as Stephen Tong (Tang Chongrong 唐崇荣). The

---

35   Interview with Deputy Chief Zhang of the Religious Affairs Bureau of Mingcheng (July 25, 2016).

36   Interview with Pastor Xiang Tianle, Jiamishan Church, Mingcheng (February 2, 2016).

Reformed soteriology of predestination and its emphasis on a distinctly stratified church organization appealed to Xiang Tianle. Between 2006 and 2007, he pushed for institutional reform after the fashion of the Presbyterian system. In 2007, Xiang was appointed senior pastor. He resigned from his post at a state-run organization in 2008 and devoted himself to pastoral service full-time. In the same year, Jiamishan Church established a school, Mingxian Academy.

The congregation at Jiamishan Grace Church grew to eight hundred in 2010. Although the church still largely consisted of the traditional church-going demographics—the elderly, women, and the poor—the number of white-collar Christians showed a noticeable increase.[37] Between 2010 and 2012, Xiang Tianle connected with prominent Chinese Christians of the reformed tradition in North America. These religious elites were promoting the Grace to the City Movement among Chinese house churches. This movement was inspired by the theology of Timothy Keller, senior pastor of Redeemer Presbyterian Church in New York, and Xiang became an enthusiastic surrogate. A "Grace to the City" convention took place in Hong Kong in 2014, and Keller was the keynote speaker. Xiang took part in the convention and, as one of the representatives of four house churches from mainland China, shared his experiences with fellow convention attendees.

Xiang's advocacy for the "Grace to the City" Movement has not only contributed to strengthening the Presbyterian system, but it has also advanced the church's cultural mission as well as its involvement in urban society. Xiang told us that the church had been following Timothy Keller's "Gospel DNA" course and implementing a church incubator. On the one hand, church leaders drew an evangelical map based on Mingcheng's subway system, with the intent of establishing churches in all four directions. On the other hand, the selection of new church locations was deliberate, targeting rental properties in residential buildings in the city. Xiang thought that with a narrow evangelical focus on cities and urban communities, church reform could reshape believers' overall religious and social lives, achieving a fundamental renewal of "order." Jiamishan Church's "Grace to the City" Movement has had ripple effects. Some traditional house churches in Mingcheng have begun to transition into urban churches.

---

37   These Christians primarily come from a white-collar (*bailing* 白领) background, forming the core (*gugan* 骨干) and elite (*jingying* 精英) elements of society, hence the nickname "Baigujing Christians." See Li Xiangping, "Gongmin jidutu yu jidujiao de Zhongguohua wenti," *Wenhua zongheng*, 2014.8: 108–109.

4.3 Vineyard Church and "The Wild Boar in the Vineyard"

Zhu Bide cannot help but sense an impending crisis, as he has witnessed the numerous splits within house churches over the years, as well as the rapid expansion and growth of Jiamishan Church. In fact, Zhu has been seeking an opening to expand his own church. Jonathan Chao (Zhao Tianen 赵天恩) arrived at Mingcheng in 1997 in the hopes of uniting the four major families through standardized theological training. Three families declined the opportunity due to political considerations. Eager to grow his resources, Zhu Bide positively responded to Zhao. He recruited twenty young preachers from the church to receive theological training for two years, while Jonathan Chao sent several Chinese pastors from North America, Taiwan, and Hong Kong to offer instruction. The training program had a significant impact on Zhujia Church in two respects. First, the Calvinist reformed tradition came to exercise a deep influence on a group of middle-aged and young Christians. Second, Christians have generally been in favor of the decentralization of church governance, preferring a reorganization of the church into districts that run democratic elections.

Zhu Bide did not agree with Calvinist theology, but he regarded the decentralized model of governance as biblical. Because Zhu was stretched thin by his full-time job and church affairs, he favored a separation of powers and devolution. In 2000, Zhujia Church reformed the organization of the church, transitioning from an authoritarian and paternalistic style of governance into a decentralized system based on a democratic process. Regardless of the biblical nature of the democratization of church governance, the reform of Zhujia Church was indicative of the effects of institutionalization.[38] Granted that the Chinese state has exhibited a tendency of returning to authoritarianism in recent years, in the first two decades of reform and opening up, national politics indeed leaned toward democratization and reform.

The democratic tendency in China presented new concepts and opportunities for change in civil society, allowing the notion of modernity to trickle down to the localities. Specifically, as civil society began to question the validity of paternalism, the traditional form of governance also began to lose its legitimacy as a form of social organization. In the West, the Protestant Reformation facilitated a democratic form of church organization, whether Congregationalism or Presbyterianism. Increased contact with overseas Christians also facilitated

---

38 Zhou Xueguang, *Zuzhi shehuixue shijiang* (Beijing: Shehui kexue wenxian chubanshe, 2003).

the dissemination of the concept of democracy among Christian youths in China. At the very least, there was a generally favorable view of church governance through the democratic process. The theological training sponsored by Jonathan Chao offered a direct exposure to a democratic notion of the church as well as a democratic organization of the church. As a result, family- or household-based Christianity as a form of religious association lost much of its legitimacy.

The democratization of church governance in 2000 was, therefore, a logical conclusion of the above developments. In 2000, Zhujia Church was divided into three districts: the city, the northern countryside, and the western countryside. The congregants elected twelve grassroots coworkers who were appointed to twelve different specialized units, overseeing church affairs such as parliamentary procedure, accounting and finance, and logistics. Each of the twelve coworkers was fully responsible for the operations of their respective unit. Zhu Bide, the director of the church, oversaw the operation of the entire organization. Moreover, Zhujia Church abandoned the family-based model of worship. Its city district began to hold services in rental units in office or commercial buildings. There were plans to build new churches in the western and northern districts. These efforts, in Zhu Bide's view, could help legitimize the church and attract more young Christians.

The democratization of the church was not accomplished without growing pains. Zhu Bide had some grievances about the unintended consequences of democratization. First, the decentralization of the treasury stripped the director of the power to appropriate funds. Zhu Bide regretted not requiring a portion of district funds to be submitted to the central treasury when the reform was implemented. That left the main district without a standing fund for the training of preachers, public relations, and the mobilization of coworkers. Zhu had assumed that his long-term friends and companions would come to his aid whenever the church had needs, and prior to the reform, he was also wary of suspicions or even accusations of personal corruption relating to church finance. Once the delegation of powers was a fait accompli, his district directors began to resist requests for assistance. At one point, leaders of the church reached a compromise whereby districts would submit 1,000 RMB annually for training and public relations expenses. But twenty years of inflation had rendered 1,000 RMB a miniscule amount; it was hardly enough to cover the expenses of one service, let alone organize a seminary. Additionally, as the director of the church system, Zhu incurred many travel and discretionary expenses, all of which had to go on public record and be reported to the districts for reimbursement. His district directors never traveled for church business, and, as they held the purse strings, they were often critical of the amount of expenses Zhu incurred, making the reimbursement process unpleasant and difficult.[39]

Secondly, Zhu Bide had much difficulty adjusting to the democratic system of governance. He was especially frustrated with the parliamentary procedure in the branch churches in the city district. Although Zhu was in favor of the democratic process, he perceived that decentralization effectively stripped him of any authority in decision-making. Every coworkers' assembly meeting turned into a shouting match; there was no hope for consensus. In Zhu's view, the average coworker was sometimes shortsighted. Even when a motion was passed by the majority, coworkers would not implement the decision fully. A leader might have a sound vision, but his opinion did not carry more weight than anyone else's. Thus, a leader's proposal would fail to pass, and due to either indecision or a poor decision, important issues concerning the church would not move forward. Zhu complained that the leader was, after all, not perfect. His hard work would always invite criticism and contempt. This puts the leader in a difficult position, and internal rifts become almost inevitable, Zhu maintained.[40]

Arguably, the democratization of Zhujia Church has brought the previously concealed negotiations among coworkers out in the open. Zhu Bide has had a difficult time adjusting to these public negotiations; he was even convinced that the coworkers' demand for democratization was not so much a rejection of his authority, but that of God.[41]

5 Management by Force and Management by Communication: State Control and the State Effect

5.1 *Management by Force and Zhu Bide's Passive Response*

The history of governmental control of house churches in Mingcheng parallels the development of the churches themselves. Suppression is often carried out by state agencies of violence. A rural preacher related to me that Public Joint Defense Force members raided his house church, confiscating benches and blackboards, and forbade future meetings. He vividly recalled the secretary of the brigade taunting him that it was shameful to believe in Jesus.

Today, house churches have carved out a space for themselves. The likelihood of incorporation into a formal regulatory mechanism under state institutions

---

39 Interview with Pastor Zhu Bide, the Vineyard Church, Mingcheng (November 25, 2016).
40 Interview with Pastor Zhu Bide, the Vineyard Church, Mingcheng (January 31, 2016).
41 Interview with Pastor Zhu Bide, the Vineyard Church, Mingcheng (August 11, 2016).

has also increased. Some of my interviewees mentioned receiving questionnaires from the local government that requested information on preferences for management methods. Zhu Bide's preference was for house churches to be institutionalized by the state while staying outside of the Three-Self Church's jurisdiction. To prevent the intrusion of "five entries and five transformations" into his church, however, Zhu specified on the questionnaire that he would accept state control as long as measures of institutionalization conform to biblical teachings.[42]

According to Zhu Bide, "house churches used to be like sheep"—they took the brunt of governmental suppression and always caved under pressure.[43] Governmental suppression has subsided considerably in recent years, as state management of house churches has become increasingly regular and institutionalized. Nevertheless, as China has yet to produce formal laws regarding religious affairs, the competent authorities tend to impose draconian measures on religious practitioners.

While his church was engrossed in internal conflict and continued down the path of decline, and while his personal credibility was caught in a downward spiral, Zhu Bide maintained that he was a primary target of government intervention. Through his interaction with governmental authorities, he has gained clarity on the state's typical strategy regarding churches like his. Zhu has been arrested four times in his own home for hosting Christmas and Easter celebrations. He believes that because he was the leader of a church, the authorities specifically targeted him. His teaching duties were also affected. After being summoned to the police station a few times, he was put on a list of usual suspects and was subjected to surveillance.[44]

Ordinary congregants seem to agree that their leaders have been targeted by the authorities. As one church member explained, "the Party likes to harass our leaders, and it puts tremendous pressure on our leadership." Zhu Bide often recounts two episodes in his dealings with relevant authorities. Both are indicative of the government's bottom line.

The first episode concerns Zhu's failed attempt to apply for an exit/entry permit for traveling to and from Hong Kong and Macau. When Zhu applied for the permit, the clerk informed him that he was on the blacklist and thus denied exit. Zhu filed a complaint and was told that he had to be under surveillance by government agents whenever he traveled outside of mainland China. He responded jokingly that he would happily be put under surveillance if the

---

42   Ibid.
43   Ibid.
44   Ibid.

state were to cover his travel expenses. Zhu reminisced on this incident with a sense of humor, while producing a wry smile.[45]

The second episode has to do with the government's intervention with major church events. Zhujia Church established a seminary in its northern countryside district. At the second commencement of the seminary, Zhu Bide invited the dean of a theological seminary in Hong Kong as the guest of honor. Shortly after the ceremony had started, agents from a government bureau surrounded the venue. Church workers concealed the guest in the audience and helped him leave through the back door, which averted a crisis. Due to Zhu's history with the authorities, he was able to de-escalate the situation, saying "we are a legitimate church, and a legitimate church provides instruction on the Bible. This is our way of fending off heresies and cults. Our efforts will save you much trouble."[46]

These are only two examples of the many dealings Zhu has had with the authorities. Over time, he has gained a clear understanding of the boundaries set by the state on his activity. The absolute red line is a travel ban and a ban on communications with overseas organizations. Large-scale events must be limited and permission must be secured in advance. As Zhujia Church continues to decline, the authorities are especially cautious about its resistance to state control.

For better or worse, Zhu Bide appreciates that the authorities wish his cooperation. The requirements to file reports and obtain permission for events and gatherings, however, would risk exposing every detail about the church's operations. Zhu does not want to become the "Judas of his church."[47] For preachers like Zhu, whose religious existence has always been accompanied by draconian state control, the state is the embodiment of violence, irrationality, and cruelty. Such preachers have kept the state, or "the secular ruler," at arm's length. The solution is to move their churches more underground. Going underground then turns into a self-fulfilling prophecy, in which the more clandestine the churches become, the greater the state's scrutiny; the more draconian the state's approach is, the more secretive the churches become.

As more and more intellectuals have converted to Christianity in recent years, the more intellectually inclined religious elites have come to urge house churches to come out of hiding and engage the state through institutional means.[48] Zhu Bide is not unaware of these calls, yet he is not a proactive

---

45 Interview with Pastor Zhu Bide, the Vineyard Church, Mingcheng (January 31, 2016).
46 Ibid.
47 Ibid.
48 Sun Mingyi, "Renshi Zhongguo chengshi jiating jiaohui," *Jumu* (*Behold*), no. 26 (2007): 12–17.

supporter of such measures, but rather a passive responder. This situation became even tenser when Zhou invited a member of the Wenzhouren Church 温州人教会 to lead Sunday schools in 2005. A hundred congregants from the western countryside attended, but the guest speaker discovered that he was surrounded by the authorities, an experience that dissuaded him from further contact with Zhu.[49] The authorities broke up the training session and raided the venue, confiscating DVDs, camcorders, cameras, TVs, and reading materials.

Afterward, the authorities warned the Wenzhouren Church against interaction with Zhu Bide's church. This incident was a wake-up call for Zhu. He refused to be a docile sheep, as he perceived his actions to be legitimate and free of any intent to challenge the authorities. The legal training that he received prior to this incident has further strengthened his conviction. Given that China had joined the World Trade Organization and was on track to adopt the rule of law, Zhu perceived that it was imperative that house churches be sufficiently informed of the law and prepared to defend themselves.

Therefore, Zhu hired an attorney from Beijing and sued the relevant authority for neglecting due process; specifically, he accused the authorities of failing to produce a warrant or present identifications at the raid. The church, on the other hand, was armed with ordinances issued by the Religious Affairs Bureau, arguing that the authorities had conducted a search without a warrant and had failed to produce an inventory for the confiscated items. The church further accused the authorities of disrespectful behavior and crude language while interfering with religious life and forcefully terminating their gathering.[50]

This lawsuit produced positive outcomes. The authorities acknowledged the procedural illegality of their actions and returned half of the confiscated items. Moreover, the case was reopened, even though the training session was still judged an illegal assembly. Armed with the legal knowledge he acquired through training and the lawsuit, Zhu Bide articulated the church's position with legal backing.

> My church is illegal because it is not registered with the state. We wanted to be registered, but the government did not allow it. You continued to force us to join the Three-Self Church despite our multiple appeals to be registered separately. We have stated that our belief is different from that of the Three-Self. Article 36 of the Constitution stipulates the freedom

---

49   Interview with a preacher of the Wenzhouren Church, Mingcheng (May 30, 2016).
50   Interview with Pastor Zhu Bide, the Vineyard Church, Mingcheng (August 11, 2016).

of religion. You, the government, have specified that religious freedom means the freedom to choose different denominations. We hired an attorney and took you to court. We were standing on solid ground. The Three-Self Church is liberal, and house churches are fundamentalist. Due to the freedom of religion, you have no right to force us to join the Three-Self. Doesn't the government follow the rule of law?[51]

Admittedly, Zhu's second lawsuit did not produce a satisfactory outcome or a definitive solution. Afterward, the relevant authorities laid down even more rules for Zhu's church, forcing him to continue to test the boundaries of governmental constraints. Recently, as more social issues have surfaced, scholars have proposed various theories of resistance, among which "lawful protest" has received broad attention.[52] House churches have become practitioners of lawful protest. Nevertheless, Christians in traditional house churches have not gained much ground in their demand for rights through lawful protest. The litigation even pushed Zhu Bide to distrust the state completely.

Litigation simply doesn't work. In China, all Christian attorneys end up being persecuted. A Christian lawyer in Beijing was just sentenced to prison not long ago. He was accused of disrupting the social order. The law doesn't carry the same weight in China as it does in countries that follow the rule of law. I figure that because our country adheres to atheism and rejects God, its overarching policy [regarding religion] won't change.[53]

This incident clarified for me why congregants of the northern countryside district of Zhujia Church were so strict about abiding by "order." There have been other run-ins with the authorities in addition to the training incident noted above. For example, the district has been denounced for constructing a church in the dark of the night, and a camp for university students was dispersed. Thus, all church leaders are extremely suspicious of outsiders. Zhu Bide has no other recourse than to conceal information about Zhujia Church.

---

51   Ibid.
52   Ying Xing, "Caogen dongyuan yu nongmin qunti liyi de biaoda jizhi—sige gean de bijiao yanjiu," *Shehuixue yanjiu*, 2007.2: 1–23; Yu Jianrong, "Dangdai Zhongguo nongmin de 'yifa kangzheng'—guanyu nongmin weiquan huodong de yige jieshi kuangjia," *Wenshi bolan* (*lilun*), 2008.12: 60–63; Wu Changqing, "Cong 'celüe' dao 'lunli' dui 'yifa kangzheng' de pipingxing taolun," *Shehui*, 2010.2: 198–214.
53   Interview with Pastor Zhu Bide, the Vineyard Church, Mingcheng (August 11, 2016).

And yet, as his power is in decline, there may not be much information for him to conceal after all.

5.2 Management by Communication and the Proactive Strategy of Xiang Tianle

Xiang Tianle has an accurate grasp of the state's management strategy for house churches and his own Jiamishan Church. He understands that Pastor Zhu suffers from extra scrutiny because his church is historic. The authorities are interested in Xiang's church because it has a large congregation and a high profile.[54] With years of experience dealing with the authorities, Xiang does not regard engagement with the government as a negative. In his view, engagement improves knowledge of the state's attitude and stance.

Xiang's upbringing in the household of a party official as well as his employment history in a state-run organization have likely helped familiarize him with the administrative procedures of government bureaus. Xiang understands that the authorities have a duty to carry out the charges given by the state. One of the responsibilities is to monitor and control any unregistered religious activity and to maintain stability in the local religious community. Managing relationships with relevant authorities, therefore, is an ongoing and practical lesson on church-state relations relevant to all house churches in China.

Given the rapid rise to prominence of Xiang's emerging church, along with his frequent communication with overseas organizations, the head of the relevant bureau makes regular contact with Xiang. They catch up over meals or tea; officials see him off when he leaves the country and pick him up upon his return. In short, the authorities treat Xiang with courtesy as a means of managing an emerging church. In a joint prayer meeting with other house churches in Mingcheng, Xiang learned that few church leaders had even been introduced to the head of the bureau. In the past, the authorities did not treat Xiang with the same respect they accord him today. As he rose to the position of senior pastor of an established church, Xiang experienced an upgrade in treatment firsthand. This transition has left an impression on Xiang.

Through frequent contact and engagement, Xiang Tianle has mastered church-state relations. He abides by three principles. First, Xiang ensures that the channel of communication remains unobstructed. "Secrecy invites anxiety; transparency encourages trust."[55] Xiang has increasingly appreciated the authorities' efforts to maintain professionalism and transparency in

---

54 Interview with Pastor Xiang Tianle, Jiamishan Church, Mingcheng (February 2, 2016).
55 Ibid.

communication. He responds with a comparable degree of openness to cultivate mutual trust.

Second, Xiang has established a clear boundary for engagement with the government. Authorities have access to information regarding the church's elections, district assembly meetings, internal organization, communal activities, and plans for expansion. However, Xiang adamantly defends information about the core interests of the church, as well as matters concerning individuals outside of the church, against governmental interference. He firmly holds that the state does not have an unlimited right to violate individual privacy.

Finally, both the government and the church make their respective boundaries known. For example, the governing authorities demand that Xiang refrain from contact with foreigners and simply focus on running his church. However, it is impossible to sever all connections to overseas organizations. Hence, Xiang reassures the authorities that he will limit his overseas visits to the religious realm and shun politicians, foreign funds, and democratic activists. In return, Xiang expects the government to respect his church's right to assemble openly without forcing members to join the Three-Self Church, and to refrain from interfering with the church's teachings and internal affairs.

As Zhu and Xiang see it, the church-state relationship, as it applies to house churches, is mainly defined by the authorities' attempt to standardize their dealings with entities that have an ambiguous, unofficial status. In other words, the authorities are trying to devise ways to tolerate unregistered churches. For both Zhu and Xiang, successful church-state engagement is contingent upon a mutual trust established on a case-by-case basis, as well as a tacit understanding of each other's bottom line. Xiang, however, is more at ease with this approach than Zhu is. In Xiang's words, "this country is no longer Mao's China." The current Chinese government rests on the principles of separation of powers and specialization, with vast regional variations. The state provides channels of communication and negotiation, revealing its limited and rational characteristics. Through active engagement with government officials, Xiang has managed to befriend some government employees and even sought their assistance in times of need. At the same time, Xiang was concerned about the possibility of transferring house churches to the jurisdiction of the Religious Affairs Bureau, "which is not as professional as the current authority and doesn't know the first thing about house churches."[56]

---

56 Interview with Pastor Xiang Tianle, Jiamishan Church, Mingcheng (May 8, 2016).

6 Conclusion and Discussion: Christianity in Local Society from the Countryside to the City

The above case study analyzes the transformation of church "order" in house churches in northern Jiangsu. In particular, it sheds light on the impact of the state apparatus on churches and helps us understand the conditions facing the majority of house churches in China. Christianity is undergoing a transformation that replaces charismatic leadership with a church organization as it puts down roots in local society, and in the process, the state effect is created. These processes are evident in house churches in Mingcheng.

In addition to a transformation in the geographical sense, the transition from the countryside to the city also incurs changes in the logic of practice, as well as an evolution of social order. The countryside and the city also represent two divergent approaches, and thus different types of relationships emerge. Traditionally, social relationships in the countryside are built on a concentric association of acquaintances, emanating outward from the parent at the core to lesser relationships. A modern city operates on interactions among egalitarian strangers, and public order is established on contract-based relationships.

One of our cases, the Jiamishan Church, represents a transition out of the paternalistic order. The church seeks to keep up with the latest theological trends, democratizes its governance, and advocates for social and communal services. These acts are public in character.

The Chinese state adopts panopticism in its management of religious affairs. The specific tactics vary over time, but the strategy remains unchanged. A widely circulated article by Pastor Wang Yi 王怡 argues that Christians appear far more menacing than they truly are.[57] The title is political in character, and yet the content of the article is religious. All the same, such sensational and unsubstantiated rhetoric as this contributes to the power of the state effect.

In reality, the state's suppression since reform and opening up has exacerbated the inward-looking tendency of house churches. House churches have come to self-identify as secret societies. Their fear of the state intensifies their reservations about outsiders, and fear of outsiders is manifested in reservations about the state. Newly emerged urban churches, as represented by Jiamishan Church, have managed to resist the state with selective submission. When churches do submit to the state, however, they maintain an air of disobedience. We may argue that such behavior reveals an identification with

---

57 Wang Yi, "Jidutu shi yige quntixing shijian," *Xinghua* (Fall 2010): 80–88.

both Jesus and the values that Jesus upholds; that is, the values that Jesus represents align with certain ideals of a modern society, which the Chinese state happens to share. Therefore, urban churches manage to balance their loyalty to Jesus with their allegiance to the state. This balancing act allows them to devise a host of proactive strategies.

Granted, the relationship between house churches in Mingcheng and the local government has improved quite a bit. Xiang Tianle observes that the government wishes to appropriate churches as resources to combat social problems, but it is cautious about selecting the appropriate churches for these tasks.[58] In an atmosphere of collaboration, certain Christian churches are deemed as positive forces in the creation of a peaceful and harmonious society. However, it is important to realize that the Chinese state has many faces; some rely on personal and informal communication, and others take on a public character and are managed through institutional and legal means. The modes of engagement between Christians and the state determine which face of the state is shown.

Bibliography

Brown, G. Thompson. "Jidujiao zai Jiangsu Mingcheng diqu chuanjiao jianshi, 1884–1941" 基督教在江苏明城地区传教简史 (1884–1941). In *Mingcheng wenshi ziliao* 明城文史资料, vol. 31, translated by Yang Naizhuang 杨乃庄 and edited by Zhongguo renmin zhengzhi xieshang huiyi Jiangsu sheng Mingcheng weiyuanhui wenshi weiyuanhui 中国人民政治协商会议江苏省明成城委员会文史委员会. Mingcheng, Jiangsu, China: Zhongguo renmin zhengzhi xieshang huiyi Jiangsu sheng Mingcheng weiyuanhui wenshi weiyuanhui, 2010.

Dunn, James D. G. *The Partings of the Ways between Christianity and Judaism and Their Significance for the Character of Christianity.* Grand Rapids, MI: Eerdmans, 1999. Translated by Yang Hui 杨慧 as *Fendao yangbiao: Jidujiao yu youtaijiao de fenli jiqi dui jidujiao texing de yiyi* 分道扬镳：基督教与犹太教的分离及其对基督教特性的意义. Hong Kong: Logos and Pneuma Press, 2015.

Gao Jun 高俊. "Jiangsu feijidujiao yundong shimo" 江苏非基督教运动始末. *Puyang zhiye jishu xueyuan xuebao* 濮阳职业技术学院学报, 2014.4: 40–42.

Gao Jun 高俊. "Qingmo Jiangsu minjiao chongtu de qiluo" 清末江苏民教冲突的起落. *Anqing shifan xueyuan xuebao (shehui kexue ban)* 安庆师范学院学报（社会科学版）. 2014.6: 111–114.

---

58 Interview with Pastor Xiang Tianle, Jiamishan Church, Mingcheng (February 2, 2016).

He Xuefeng 贺雪峰. "Lun Zhongguo nongcun de quyu chayi—cunzhuang shehui jiegou de shijiao" 论中国农村的区域差异—村庄社会结构的视角. *Kaifang shidai* 开放时代, 2012.10: 108–129.

Huang Dianchi 黄殿墀, ed. *Mingcheng minzu zongjiao zhi* 明城民族宗教志. Mingcheng: Mingcheng shi minzu zongjiao shiwuju 明城市民族宗教事务局, 1991.

Huaren jidujiaoshi renwu cidian 华人基督教史人物词典. http://bdcconline.net/zh-hans/stories/jia-yuming.

Jiangsu sheng shehui kexueyuan ketizu 江苏省社会科学院课题组. "Jiangsu sheng nongcun zongjiao zhuangkuang ji duice yanjiu" 江苏省农村宗教状况及对策研究. *Jiangsu sheng shehuizhuyi xueyuan xuebao* 江苏省社会主义学院学报, 2003.3: 7–10.

Kang, Jie. *House Church Christianity in China: From Rural Preachers to City Pastors*. Cham, Switzerland: Palgrave, 2016.

Li Feng 李峰. *Xiangcun jidujiao de zuzhi texing ji shehui jiegou xing weizhi—Huanan Y xian X zhen jidujiao jiaohui zuzhi yanjiu* 乡村基督教的组织特征及其社会结构性位秩—华南Y县X镇基督教教会组织研究. Shanghai: Fudan daxue chubanshe, 2005.

Li Xiangping 李向平. "Gongmin jidutu yu jidujiao de Zhongguohua wenti" 公民基督徒与基督教的中国化问题. *Wenhua zongheng* 文化纵横, 2014.8: 108–109.

Lu Yunfeng 卢云峰. "Kunan yu zongjiao zengzhang: guanzhi de feiyuqi houguo" 苦难与宗教增长：管制的非预期后果. *Shehui* 社会, 2010.4: 200–216.

Mingcheng difangzhi bianzuan weiyuanhui 明城地方志编纂委员会, ed. *Mingcheng shizhi* 明城市志. Beijing: Zhonghua shuju, 1994.

Mitchell, Timothy. "Society, Economy, and the State Effect." In *The Anthropology of the State: A Reader*, edited by Aradhana Sharma and Akhil Gupta, 169–180. Oxford: Blackwell, 2006.

Russell, Jeffrey Burton, and Douglas W. Lumsden. *A History of Medieval Christianity: Prophecy and Order*. New York: Peter Lang, 2000.

Stark, Rodney. *The Rise of Christianity: A Sociologist Reconsiders History*. Princeton: Princeton University Press, 1996. Translated by Huang Jianbo 黄剑波 and Gao Mingui 高民贵 as *Jidujiao de xingqi: yige shehuixuejia dui lishi de zaisi* 基督教的兴起：一个社会学家对历史的再思. Shanghai: Shanghai guji chubanshe, 2005.

Stark, Rodney. *The Triumph of Christianity: How the Jesus Movement Became the World's Largest Religion*. New York: HarperOne, 2011.

Sun Mingyi 孙明义. "Renshi Zhongguo chengshi jiating jiaohui" 认识中国城市家庭教会. *Jumu* 举目 (*Behold*), no. 26 (2007): 12–17.

Wang Yi 王怡. "Jidutu shi yige quntixing shijian" 基督徒是一个群体性事件. *Xinghua* 杏花 (Fall 2010): 80–88.

Weber, Max. *Sociology of Religion*. Translated by Ephraim Fischoff. Boston: Beacon Press, 1963. Translated by Kang Le 康乐 as *Zongjiao shehuixue* 宗教社会学. Guilin: Guangxi shifan daxue chubanshe, 2011.

Wu Changqing 吴长青. "Cong 'celüe' dao 'lunli' dui 'yifa kangzheng' de pipingxing taolun" 从"策略"到"伦理"对"依法抗争"的批评性讨论. *Shehui* 社会, 2010.2: 198–214.

Yao Xiyi 姚西伊. *Wei zhendao zhengbian: zaihua jiduxinjiao chuanjiaoshi jiyaozhuyi yundong (1920–1937)* 为真道争辩：在华基督教新教传教士基要主义运动 (1920–1937). Hong Kong: China Alliance Press, 2008.

Ying Xing 应星. "Caogen dongyuan yu nongmin qunti liyi de biaoda jizhi—sige gean de bijiao yanjiu" 草根动员与农民群体利益的表达机制——四个个案的比较研究. *Shehuixue yanjiu* 社会学研究, 2007.2: 1–23.

Yu Jianrong 于建嵘. "Dangdai Zhongguo nongmin de 'yifa kangzheng'—guanyu nongmin weiquan huodong de yige jieshi kuangjia" 当代中国农民的"以法抗争"——关于农民维权活动的一个解释框架. *Wenshi bolan (lilun)* 文史博览（理论）. 2008.12: 60–63.

Yu Jianrong 于建嵘. "Zhongguo jidujiao jiating jiaohui hefahua yanjiu" 中国基督教家庭教会合法化研究. *Zhanlüe yu guanli* 战略与管理. 2010.3–4. Featured on Aisixiang 爱思想, http://www.aisixiang.com/data/70584.html.

Yuan Hao 袁浩. "Zhongguo jidujiao yu bufucong de chuantong: yi Wang Mingdao, Tanghe jiaohui yu Shouwang jiaohui weili" 中国基督教与不服从的传统：以王明道、唐河教会与守望教会为例. *Daofeng* 道风, no. 44 (2016): 87–122.

Zhang Hua 张华 and Xue Heng 薛恒. "Zai shehui zhuanxing zhong chuangxing zongjiao shiwu guanli Jiangsu xin nongcun jianshe zhong de zongjiao hexie guanxi yanjiu" 在社会转型中创新宗教事务管理 江苏新农村建设中的宗教和谐关系研究. *Zhongguo zongjiao* 中国宗教, 2013.8: 66–67.

Zhou Xueguang 周雪光. *Zuzhi shehuixue shijiang* 组织社会学十讲. Beijing: Shehui kexue wenxian chubanshe, 2003.

Zhou Yue 周越 (Adam Chau). "Zhongguo minjian zongjiao fuwu de jiahu zhidu" 中国民间宗教服务的家户制度. Translated by Zhang Xixiang 张细香. *Xuehai* 学海, 2010.3: 44–56.

CHAPTER 8

Demands for Faith, Institutional Constraints, and Niche Choices of an Urban Church in China

Zhang Zhipeng

A variety of newly emerged religious groups are present in many large cities in China, most notably Protestant Christian and Buddhist groups. Over the years, not only have these communities established regular meeting places, but they have also consolidated their memberships, which have continued to grow. These groups are similar in the following ways: they developed in cities in the last decade, they do not have regular clergy, and they are not registered as religious sites and therefore are not officially recognized by the state.

Whether a religious group is able to offer the services in demand is contingent upon the relevant institutional conditions. Diverse demands, corresponding supplies, and institutional conditions together generate a variety of forms of religious organization. For example, when sociopolitical institutions are tolerant, converts are satisfied with the services provided by their chosen religious group, and the church may be approved by the state and permitted to operate legally and openly. And yet, in a highly constrained environment, a religious group may fail to satisfy converts' expectations and demands. In this instance, converts may choose to leave their current organization and establish a new one. In the following pages, I present a case study of an urban church to demonstrate the interplay among three factors: individual expectations for conversion, the niche choices of a church, and the state's religious policies.

One can find hundreds of newly emerged religious groups in my city of residence, Nanjing, Jiangsu. They are ubiquitous.[1] The subject of this study is JM Church.[2] My first encounter with its congregation took place in the fall of 2014, when I was a member of a book club at DN University. Some of my fellow members were core congregants of JM Church, and I learned about the Christian faith of Professor Xu at DN University during that time.[3] Professor

---

1 Nanjing is home to not only Protestant Christian churches, but also folk religious groups as well as Buddhist organizations. I have participated in Buddhist group events, as well as collective meditations hosted by a group called Wang Fengyi Shanrendao 王凤仪善人道.
2 Throughout this chapter, I use initials to represent churches or organizations.
3 Throughout this chapter, pseudonyms are used for names of people.

Xu shared with me that JM Church had experienced difficulty finding suitable preachers, as there were many university professors with advanced degrees among its flock. This remark piqued my interest in this church, and I began interviewing the friends I had made among the congregants.

In December 2015, I started attending Sunday services regularly, observing and interviewing the congregants. My inquiries focused on the following: How and why was this church formed? How does self-governance function without a full-time pastor? How did the church find its niche? Finally, since this church is still growing, I hope the conclusions of this study will serve as an appraisal of their current challenges, and I make tentative suggestions for future research. My research methods are participant-observation, interviews, analysis of financial records, and textual analysis of sermons, and I will use the results of my research to formulate answers to the above questions.

1   Converts as Drivers for Growth

JM Church is situated in an office building at the center of Nanjing, a stone's throw from metro and bus stops. In addition to a central room, the unit has two side rooms typically used for Sunday school and coworker meetings. In one room, one finds the Bible and relevant Christian publications, and in the other, instructional materials for kids.

The central room is a spacious area of about 40 square meters. There are seven rows of about fifty chairs in total, four on each side, with one aisle in the center and another on the left side. A magnetic whiteboard is hung on the right side of the entrance, displaying miscellaneous forms such as a "schedule of worship and services," statements of expenses and revenue, and utility bills. Further along the right wall, one finds two framed texts: the Ten Commandments and the Apostles' Creed. To the right of the chairs is a computer desk, facing the pulpit. The distance between the pulpit and the window behind it is no more than a meter. A projector screen covers the center of the window. A wooden cross is hung on the wall to the left of this window, and a smaller cross is stationed on the top of a window unit in the upper left corner. A keyboard occupies the space between the window unit and the first row of chairs, but it is only used when a pianist is present. For the most part, singing is accompanied by guitar music or simply a tambourine. A framed copy of the Lord's Prayer hangs on one of the room doors, and the other door is decorated with red cutouts reading "JM is our family."

As a matter of fact, JM found this secure and cozy "home" after several relocations. Among the new congregants, few can remember the precise dates of the relocations. In the beginning, meetings were held in congregants' homes, making the church a literal house church. It had rented several places for services and meetings until one of the congregants purchased the current location three years ago and helped the church settle down.

JM transformed into an independent religious entity with a proper name in 2008. In fact, JM broke from a larger house church, JY, and formed its own church. The leader of JY church was Professor Qiu. He held a doctorate in comparative literature and was an assistant professor at a local university. He was baptized as a Christian in 1997 after a long period of consideration. Shortly afterward, Qiu started JY Church, which was also one of the best-known house churches in Nanjing.

It was Ms. Wang who broke ties with JY Church and established JM Church. Wang is also an assistant professor at the same university as Qiu, with a doctorate in literature. It remains unclear why JM Church first split from JY Church. It seems that divergent views and disagreements about rituals drove some congregants away. JY Church also had a conservative and fundamentalist streak. For instance, the congregants were only allowed to sing hymns from the biblical book of Psalms, and modern hymns were forbidden. The founding congregants of JM Church were mostly university professors. However, they left the church for one reason or another over the years, leaving Ms. Wang alone in the service of the church as a coworker. Wang resigned from the ranks of coworkers in late 2015.

Two professors at DN University, Xu and Zhou, joined JM Church in quick succession around 2010. Professor Xu, who was already a baptized Christian, joined the faculty at DN University after receiving a doctorate in philosophy. Zhou is a professor of engineering. At present, there are a number of professors at DN University in the congregation, whose conversions were likely inspired by Xu and Zhou. Brothers Wei, Yang, and An are also in the philosophy department of DN University and are currently in charge of the daily operations of the church. Another congregant from DN University is Professor Hao.

A successful entrepreneur, Mr. Lin, joined JM Church around 2012. Before he entered the world of business, he participated in the Tiananmen student movement of 1989 and was imprisoned for a year. He discovered JM Church on his own and, over time, has become a key member of the team of coworkers. He helped purchase the space in which the church is currently located and gave the congregation a regular meeting place.

Yet another core member of JM joined the church in 2012—eighty-year-old Brother Mao. Mao grew up in a Christian family and has experienced many significant historical events. He has an important responsibility in the church: he plays the guitar for the choir during Sunday service. In the 1930s, Mao's mother was attracted to Dr. John Sung's (Song Shangjie 宋尚节) street preaching and decided to be baptized as a Christian. Mao never abandoned his faith, even during the Cultural Revolution. Prior to joining JM, Mao attended services at a large Three-Self church in Nanjing. He left it due to what he viewed as the corruption of the pastors there.

There are three major categories of congregants. The first consists of family members of the founding congregants. Many coworkers brought their spouses, children, and parents to attend services. Colleagues and friends of the founding members form the second group; some are seekers, and others are baptized Christians from other churches. The last category is made up of individuals who are looking for a church and, through one way or another, landed on JM. Seekers are encouraged to join Bible studies to learn more about the faith. Despite some departures over time, JM has maintained a healthy, albeit small congregation of forty to fifty members.

Although JM Church does not yet have a full-time pastor, it has grown into a self-sustaining community with a rudimentary organization and hierarchy. At the core of church governance is a committee of five coworkers, three of whom are university professors. Anyone who desires to become a coworker must do so out of their own volition. An assembly of coworkers, consisting of regular members of the congregation, approves a candidate by voting. The candidate must receive a majority vote to join the ranks of coworkers. Brothers Wei, Yang, and Lin, along with Sister Zhao, are coworkers who were baptized at JM Church after 2010. They have grown and matured at JM Church and have become the backbone of the church. Some coworkers started a Bible study group on the DN University campus to accommodate the professors in the area, which is far from the church. This Bible study group grew into the JL Church in 2014. JM Church contributed 25,000 RMB (3,800 USD) to assist JL with rent and other expenses.

2   Regular Meetings and Annual Reports

Worship services on Sunday mornings, prayer meetings on Wednesday evenings, and Bible study sessions on Tuesday evenings are the three major weekly events at JM Church. Each of the four Sunday services in a typical month has a different agenda. The coworkers lead the first two weekly worship services, which center on sermons. For the third service of the month, the church invites a guest minister to give a sermon and administer communion, and the congregants make donations. The last worship service of the month is followed by a communal meal, attended by all congregants. A Sunday school runs in tandem with each worship service. The children are divided into two groups according to age and receive lessons in two separate rooms under the supervision of designated congregants.

Below is a detailed account of a typical Sunday worship service at JM Church in full. On January 17, 2016, forty-five congregants—nineteen men and twenty-six women—attended Sunday service. Among those in attendance, five were over 60 years old, and nine were under 30 years of age; nine were university professors, and eight were children attending Sunday school. About a quarter of the attendees at any given service are unbaptized seekers.[4] The service started at 9:30 in the morning. The vast majority of the congregants arrived before this time.

A typical Sunday service, which does not include the administration of communion, runs as follows:

1. 9:00: The congregants rehearse hymns for the day's worship service. Congregants trickle in.
2. 9:32: The presider announces the commencement of the worship service and requests the congregation to silence their mobile phones. The projector screen displays the words "Please be silent and prepare yourselves for the worship of the Lord."
3. 9:33: Group singing of "The Lord is in His Holy Temple" ("*Zhu zai shengdian zhong*" 主在圣殿中);[5] the screen displays the full text.
4. 9:34: The screen displays "Call to Worship"; the presider leads a group reading of two passages in Psalms.
5. 9:35: The presider leads the singing of "Praise the Lord, O My Soul" ("*Wo de xinli chengsong Yehehua*" 我的心里称颂耶和华) at the prompt of the projector screen.
6. 9:36: The screen displays "Gospel Reading"; the congregants read aloud select verses in Isaiah, Corinthians, and John.
7. 9:42: The screen displays "Apostles' Creed," while the presider leads the congregants in reading the Apostles' Creed aloud. The presider then prompts the congregants to pray individually and silently. The congregants engage in individual prayers to give thanks to God and beseech God to impart grace on fellow congregants.

---

4 The estimated unbaptized-to-baptized ratio is derived from the number of congregants who received communion at a service held on the third Sunday of a month, as only baptized congregants are eligible for this. A typical communion service is described below.

5 Full text: "The Lord is in his holy temple / The Lord is in his holy temple / Let all the earth keep silence / Let all the earth keep silence before him / Keep silence, keep silence before him."

8. 9:48: Blessing of children. Six children approach the pulpit to be prayed over by the presider.
9. 9:50: Coworker Wei (a university professor) gives a sermon on "Faith-driven Deeds" (*Zhenxin xingshan* 真心行善). The sermon begins with a group reading of relevant Bible verses, followed by individual prayers. Wei proceeds with the sermon after the prayers. The sermon teaches that faith demands that God, rather than man, is the source of morality. The righteous are justified by faith, not fulfilled by deeds. The congregants are prompted to offer vocal prayers after the sermon.
10. 10:52: Group singing of "O, To Be Like Thee" ("*Zhu, wo yuan xiang ni*" 主，我愿像你); the screen displays the song sheet.
11. 10:55: The screen displays "Response"; the congregants pray and give thanks to God. The presider leads the congregation to recite the Lord's Prayer to conclude the service.
12. 11:05: The screen displays "Adult Sunday School" while the presider reads questions out loud and the congregants respond accordingly.
13. 11:06: The screen displays "New Friends, Welcome"; first-timers stand up to introduce themselves, followed by the singing of "The Bond of Love" ("*Ai shi women xiangju zaiyiqi*" 爱使我们相聚在一起).[6]
14. 11:09: "Reports"; the coworker in charge of the treasury reports on the revenues and expenses of the year.

The service ends after the financial report. First-timers converse with coworkers; some congregants stay to chat, while others leave after the service.

The communion and donation services held on the third Sunday follow a similar schedule, with slight variations. First, JM Church invites Pastor Li from a local theological seminary to administer communion and give a sermon. The coworkers also assist him at this worship service. The pastor receives an honorarium of 300 RMB (46 USD) for each service. JM Church approves of Pastor Li's conviction and character, even though he belongs to the Three-Self system. Second, Pastor Li gives a sermon, as in step 9 of the regular Sunday schedule. Third, communion is administered after the sermon, following these steps:

1. The projector screen displays a script for the pastor and the congregants to follow. The pastor leads a prayer after the call-and-response.

---

6 Full text: "We are one in the bond of love / We are one in the bond of love. / We have joined our spirit with the Spirit of God / We are one in the bond of love. / Let us sing now, every one / Let us feel His love begun. / Let us join our hand that the world will know / We are one in the bond of love."

2. Pastor Li elaborates on the meaning of communion, namely, that it is a sacrament, imbued with meaning and significance in "four fundamental ways."
3. Pastor Li summons baptized congregants to receive communion and withholds the sacrament from the unbaptized. He then refers to the Apostle Paul's teachings to the Corinthians, and the full text of 1 Corinthians 11:23–29 is projected on the screen. After the sermon, Pastor Li invites the congregants to contemplate the sins and offenses that they have committed against others and against God. While the congregants contemplate in silence, Pastor Li prays on the congregation's behalf. Afterward, he gives the dismissal benediction. Congregants shake hands with one another and wish each other peace.
4. Pastor Li washes his hands and puts on gloves. As he raises the wafer, he recites, "The Lord Jesus, on the night he was betrayed, took bread, and when he had given thanks, he broke it and said, 'This is my body, which is for you; do this in remembrance of me.'" Then Pastor Li breaks the wafer into small pieces; the coworkers distribute them to the baptized congregants standing to receive communion. Meanwhile, the pastor leads the congregation in singing "Receiving the Bread and the Cup" ("*Lingshou bingbei ge*" 领受饼杯歌) as the song sheet is displayed on the screen. After communion is complete, Pastor Li leads a prayer on behalf of a variety of individuals.

The final step is the collection of donations, which is preceded by vocal readings of Malachi 3:10–11 and 2 Corinthians 9:6–11. As the ushers pass a canvas donation bag across the rows, from the back toward the front, the congregants sing the hymn "I Surrender All" ("*Yiqie quan xian shang*" 一切全献上), making donations of varying amounts at will.

Bible study is another important and regular event at JM Church. The sessions are held to help seekers learn the Bible and the tenets of Christianity. In short, Bible study is the pipeline for baptism. Bible study sessions are held every Tuesday evening from 7:00 to 9:00. Among the dozen or so attendees, seven or eight of them are seekers. The group practices singing hymns until 7:30 and then proceeds to Bible-reading and discussion. Each person in the group takes turns reading the verses in a chapter. A coworker leads a prayer and then comments on the chapter in segments. Each commentary is followed by questions and discussions. The session concludes with a final discussion and a prayer led by the coworker.

The success of a church depends, to a great extent, on its revenue. Even though JM Church does not have a regular pastor, it has managed to meet the congregants' expectations and take in sufficient donations. This is a notable accomplishment on the part of the church. Here we briefly examine the church's revenue and expenditures in 2015 to assess its financial health.

According to the public records of JM Church, it had a balance of 52,895.71 RMB (8,100 USD) at the end of 2014. In 2015, it took in 172,899.41 RMB (26,600 USD) and spent 117,627 RMB (18,100 USD), including the expenses of both JM and its branch, JL Church, ending the year with a balance of 108,169.12 RMB (16,600 USD). Based on the balances of these two years alone, we may conclude that, despite greater expenses in 2015, the church also took in a considerably greater amount of revenue in the same year. That, of course, only takes into account the monetary cost and does not reflect the unpaid services provided by the coworkers. The balance would have been reduced to nearly nothing if the church had hired a full-time minister, and the coworkers are conscious of this fact. The church's annual revenue streams include 155,193.62 RMB (23,900 USD), or 89.76% of the annual revenue, in "regular donations;" 10,290 RMB (1,600 USD), or 5.95% of the annual revenue, in "ad-hoc donations" (donations requested for exceptional situations, such as providing financial aid to members with medical needs at other churches); 7,200 RMB (1,100 USD) in rent collected from JL Church; and 215.79 RMB (33 USD) in interest. Donations, by far, make up the lion's share of the church's revenue.

JM Church's major expenditures include "rent and management fees" (56% of the annual revenue); "ad-hoc expenses," primarily contributions to charities such as Da Liangshan 大凉山 children's ministry (16%); discretionary expenses (10%); and travel (5%). Other minor expenses include utilities, supplies for Bible study groups and Sunday school, compensation for sermons (guest preachers), books and reading materials, and overall hospitality. The total expenditures of the branch church, JL Church, amount to 39,557.5 RMB (6,100 USD), of which 30,000 RMB (4,600 USD) covers rent and management fees. Before JL Church was able to receive donations, JM Church was completely responsible for its financial support.

We can draw the following conclusions from the financial records of JM Church. First, the amount of donations received each month rarely fluctuates. With the exception of April (exceeding 20,000 RMB, or over 3,000 USD), the average revenue from donations hovers around 10,000 RMB (1,500 USD). Additionally, on average, forty congregants give a total of 13,000 RMB (2,000 USD) monthly. The average donation comes out to 325 RMB (50 USD) per person per month. The average annual income in Nanjing in 2015 was 46,103.62 RMB (7,100 USD); the average donation per person per month, therefore, amounts to 8.64% of the average individual monthly income. Furthermore, congregants not only give regularly, but they also make additional donations in times of need. Finally, it is safe to assume that there is much room for growth in

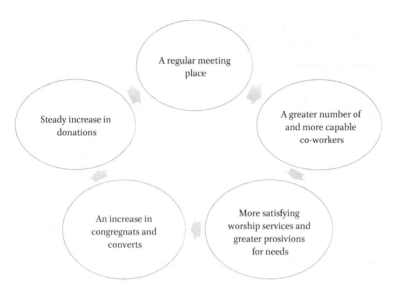

FIGURE 8.1 Conditions for maintaining a healthy cycle of growth in a house church

terms of revenue from donation, as the congregation continues to grow while the fluctuation in rent and management fees is minimal. In the span of eight years, JM Church has created a positive environment that has contributed to a healthy cycle of growth (see Figure 8.1). It has, above all, a regular meeting place to host various events. Regular services draw capable coworkers to the church, and committed coworkers improve the quality of the services provided to congregants. An increasing number of congregants brings an increasing revenue stream; this allows the church to continue to grow and expand.

3   Converts with Varying Demands

Eight men and women were baptized at JM Church on October 16, 2016. This was one of the few occurrences of multiple simultaneous baptisms at the church. This tells us that the expansion of urban Christian churches is not progressing at as quick a pace as we may imagine. Indeed, large numbers of urban dwellers are seekers in search of faith, and yet relatively few commit to being baptized as Christians. On the flip side, urban churches hold their congregants to a high standard; they often require new converts to go through a probationary period of a year in which they learn the Bible and solidify their convictions. When a convert is ready for baptism, he or she gives a testimony before the pastor administers the sacrament of baptism.

The testimonies of eight new converts revealed their respective journeys from discovery, to understanding, to accepting Christianity, as well as their deeper individual desires for faith. Mr. Wu was in his 70s; he openly declared his opposition to the Chinese regime and state propaganda. Ms. Liu was a university professor who came of age in 1989. She revealed in her testimony that she strongly supported a free and democratic government based on the rule of law. The university had penalized her for her ideology and action. Ms. Wen was also a university professor. She divulged that when growing up, she had simply followed a path of schooling and employment that was paved for her. Realizing her aimlessness, she desired guidance and direction. Earning a doctorate in philosophy and becoming a high school teacher did nothing to help her gain a new perspective. Her solution to questions in life has been nothing but reading, learning, and studying. However, it seemed that the more she learned about history and present conditions, the more aimless she felt. Ms. Wang was a housewife and had struggled with depression. Ms. Zhao was a university student. Prior to her experiment with Christian churches, she had struggled with psychological and emotional troubles. She would reach a hysterical state, burning with rage, which no one among her family and friends, including herself, was able to comprehend. Another university student, Mr. Deng, was frustrated by some encounters at the university. Even though his parents had been supportive, he felt empty inside and questioned the meaning of life. Another university student, Mr. Cao, admitted that he had been very selfish and apathetic with respect to human relationships. He did not like to go home to his parents because they quarrel constantly. The people at the church appealed to him because everyone was authentic.

Indeed, converts are driven by a variety of motivations, such as different concerns about rights and different demands for faith. Their expectations for a church also vary. A church can find it challenging to satisfy every single congregant. For example, if a church acts as a platform to demand political rights, it runs the risk of driving away those congregants who seek mainly solace and community. If it fashions itself as a mutual-aid association, the reform-minded and progressive congregants may be disinclined to stay. If it serves primarily as a charitable organization or a counseling service, it may disappoint congregants who aspire to a higher level of intellectual engagement. Furthermore, the church must walk a fine line between the demands of the congregants and scrutiny from the state. In fact, a few government officials were among the attendees at the baptism ceremony that I have just described. The officials gave the church advance notice of their visit, and the coworkers also cautioned the congregants against speaking out against the government.

4 Finding a Niche between the Push and Pull

No single religious organization can satisfy every single demand. Theories of religious economy posit that religious economies include a set of relatively stable niches. Niches are defined as "market segments of potential adherents sharing particular religious preferences (needs, tastes, and expectations)."[7] Rodney Stark and Roger Finke's scholarship indicates that these niches are met by religious organizations in the following ways:

> Proposition 76: Even where competition is limited, religious firms can generate high levels of commitment to the extent that the firms serve as the primary organizational vehicles for social conflict.[8]
>
> Proposition 79: The capacity of new religious firms to enter relatively unregulated markets successfully is inverse to the efficiency and variety of existing religious firms.[9]
>
> Proposition 80: Religious organizations mainly originate through sect formation.[10]
>
> Proposition 81: Sect movements that endure and grow will tend to reduce their tension with the sociocultural environment, thereby moving away from the market niche(s) in which they originally were based (a process referred to as the sect-to-church transformation).[11]
>
> Proposition 90: Religious organizations are easier to form to the extent that they can be sustained by a small number of members.[12]
>
> Proposition 91: Most religious groups will begin in a relatively high state of tension.[13]

---

7   Rodney Stark and Roger Finke, *Acts of Faith: Explaining the Human Side of Religion* (Berkeley: University of California Press, 2000), 202–207; translated by Yang Fenggang as *Xinyang de faze—jieshi zongjiao zhi ren de fangmian* (Beijing: Zhongguo renmin daxue chubanshe, 2004), 240, 248–252.
8   Ibid., 202.
9   Ibid., 203.
10 Ibid., 205.
11 Ibid.
12 Ibid., 207.
13 Ibid.

My examination of JM Church attests to the validity of the above propositions. A niche is not formed solely by design; rather, it is shaped by the constant interplay between church leaders and congregants, as well as by the innovations generated from the processes of these interactions. For example, church leaders design and offer services based on an assessment of both the church's needs and the congregants' demands. Feedback from congregants serves as a reference for improvement. As the church becomes more in tune with the congregants' expectations, it is more successful in attracting new converts and will grow into a larger organization. A larger and more established organization is better equipped to satisfy the congregants' demands.

The experiences of JM Church demonstrate how this niche is formed. First, in the specific institutional setting of China, citizen demands for faith encourage the formation of new, urban religious groups. Propositions 76 and 79 cited above help explain how newly emerged religious groups blossom in cities. On the one hand, "social conflict" is the status quo, and on the other hand, "the efficiency and variety of existing religious firms" are weak. The growth and expansion of JM Church sufficiently illustrates both characteristics. Congregants and seekers alike share a tendency toward critical thinking, which is revealed in their interest in the deeper meaning of life and of society. Although their respective life experiences and living environments stimulate such tendencies, their introspection is, to a greater degree, a response to external and institutional forces. The university professors among the congregants are by no means satisfied with material sufficiency. Rather, they reflect on their own lives while critiquing current affairs and social conditions. They engage in activism that has the potential of affecting positive change in society as a whole. Nevertheless, in the current sociopolitical climate, their engagement is often construed as impropriety or eccentricity, rendering them subjects of criticism and even attack.

The majority of the founding members of JM have undergone that journey. At present, registered religious organizations and churches have neither the capacity to provide high-quality experiences nor the ability to satisfy a diverse range of demands. As a consequence, the "seekers" who are able have turned to establish their own churches. A case in point is the group of philosophy professors from DN University at JM Church. Philosophy has served as their framework for thinking about the most fundamental questions about life and the world. Yet, it does not seem to offer satisfactory answers to either the ultimate questions about life or the most immediate challenges in their current surroundings. The Christian faith seems to be a viable alternative that fulfills their needs. In addition to the professors at DN University, Professors Zhang and Tang at NL University are both researchers and instructors of philosophy. Some of the JM congregants advocate for freedom and rights and demonstrate their intellectual concerns with action. Frustrated with the institutional obstacles, they turn inward and seek the meaning of life in a higher power. Businessman Lin's personal journey provides another example. His quest for meaning began with the study of the Confucian Four Books and Five Classics; he then moved on to the Buddhist Diamond Sutra and the Christian Bible. Eventually, Lin found himself visiting churches. Professor Li at RK University and Professor Su at ZX University are both seekers. They undertook a similar journey as their concerns about society and sociopolitical institutions morphed into a preoccupation with the meaning of life and faith. Their attitudes and behaviors have transformed as they have grown as members of the church. Because these professors have found personal fulfillment in the church, they tend to invite their students and their students' friends to church as well.

The Christian faith has also brought institutional "oppression." The state denies house churches legal status. The Christian identity of the congregants of house churches is also rejected. As far as university professors who operate within the educational system are concerned, they are free to read the Bible and attend Sunday services. Any effort at evangelization, however, would cross the line and invite scrutiny. Nevertheless, in their capacity as coworkers, these professors have the duty to preach. Under such circumstances, "social conflicts" in varying forms effectively push individuals to pursue the free expression of religion as well as their demands for faith.[14] It is understandable that churches pay special attention to events concerning Christian groups. As a matter of fact, JM coworkers often include churches and coreligionists under "oppression" elsewhere in their prayers, along with the city and the nation.

Necessities of everyday life, large and small, also drive individuals to religious groups, including the need for assistance in times of hardship and illnesses, or the desire for friendship and camaraderie. JM Church helps raise funds for congregants in need. For instance, recently, a female congregant from Shanghai was distressed by her son's illness. The church not only asked the congregation to pray for both mother and son, but it has also found other ways to provide aid.

Second, the founding members of an emergent, urban religious group determine its niche, which tends to create a high degree of tension within the group. JM Church's experience proves the validity of Propositions 80, 90, and 91. At its inception, JM Church was arguably a sect, a splinter group of a larger church. Mr. Lin compares a church to a cell following the natural course of division. Indeed, in the early days of JM's foundation, it only had a very small

---

14   Two of the university professors have been questioned by the university administration.

congregation precisely to avoid "free riders." The fact that JM has managed to maintain a steady stream of revenue from donations reflects the commitment of the core congregants.

This small congregation has generated much tension. Rather than creating a tense relationship with the external social environment, however, JM Church's high standard for the character and strength of faith of its own congregants has been the source of tension. Internal tension has caused discord among congregants, resulting in departures. Congregants left the church as a result of disagreements in two major areas: the style of ministry and the identity of the church. Mr. Lin recalls a couple that left JM Church. The husband grew up in the Three-Self church system. He was troubled by the intense criticism of the Three-Self Church expressed by other JM congregants. Mr. Lin also mentions another female preacher from Henan. Not only did she grow up in the Three-Self Church, but the Three-Self also sponsored her studies at a theological seminary. She was very devoted to the Three-Self Church and could not bear JM's harsh criticism of it.

Although JM does not agree with the Three-Self Church's close relationship with the state, it nevertheless acknowledges the authenticity of Three-Self ministers, as well as that of lay members. Lin says that the congregants of JM pray for Three-Self members, hoping for their liberation from institutional shackles. Lin is sympathetic with congregants of the Three-Self Church, saying that all Christians read the same Bible. He believes that the Bible's teaching about church-state relations remains unchanged, regardless of the Three-Self Church's official interpretation of biblical teachings. Moreover, those who left JM Church have eventually repaired their relationship with the congregation. As to JM's views toward evangelicals and Pentecostals, the church is receptive to Pentecostals who do not engage in extreme expressions of faith.

All of JM's current coworkers were baptized after they joined the congregation. Their sermons are representative of the church's current views on thoughts and behavior, and they also reflect the coworkers' high level of education. For example, Mr. Wei's sermons are logical and follow an interpretive arc. He starts by examining the text of the verses and moves on to demonstrating various erroneous interpretations. He then proceeds to introduce correct interpretations and responses, and he concludes with a call to action. His style appeals to better-educated congregants. The congregants with less formal education, however, find his sermons difficult to follow at times.

In addition to setting the right tone for high-level subjects such as love, hatred, morality, and charity, coworkers at JM Church also lay down rules regarding customary practices. A case in point is the first sermon that Wei gave after Spring Festival:

> Many customs and practices in traditional Chinese culture contradict our faith. We were indeed tested during Lunar New Year. Take superstitions in Chinese culture. We Chinese worship our ancestors, kowtowing to them and burning paper money for them. However, as God's chosen people, we should exercise caution during these secular holidays. Our faith teaches us that we only worship one God, which is our Lord Jesus Christ. To abide by the teachings of our faith strictly, we should not worship ancestors, kowtow, or burn paper money. We should be committed to living our faith in our culture and should endeavor to change our culture.

Clearly, this attitude toward the outside world inevitably creates tension with it.

Some of the JM congregants would say, in a tongue-in-cheek fashion, that church membership does not come with any perks; instead, they give to the church every month. Despite the need for investment on the part of the congregants, JM Church managed to maintain a critical mass, albeit small, while continuing to grow.

Third, an emergent urban church is constantly searching for its niche as it continues to scale up and as religious professionals join its operation. Proposition 81 explains the process of sect-to-church transformation. Although JM Church is currently in the early stage of this transformation, its search for a niche will accelerate once the congregation grows larger and it gradually professionalizes its clergy. For example, in the early days of JM's establishment, it catered to a niche audience—the university professors who were the majority of the congregation. There was a downside to a high concentration of university professors. For instance, Mr. Lin recalls that it took several university professors an entire afternoon to assemble a shelving system purchased online. Over time, the church has welcomed congregants from all walks of life—including entrepreneurs, white-collar workers, average (Nanjing) residents, and retirees—into the congregation. Not only has such development reduced the proportion of university professors in the church, but the congregation has also become more diverse.

Religious professionals have also contributed to the formation of a niche. As ordained ministers endeavor to grow the congregation, they tend to become moderating forces within a church. The preaching style of Pastor Li, whose sermons focus strictly on biblical stories, provides an example. He spoke of the birth of Jesus in a sermon delivered on Christmas Eve, entitled "The Message of Grace" (*endian xinxi* 恩典信息). He explained that most people in the world are ignorant of divine grace. The shepherds brought a message about the lasting glory of God, namely, that the omnipotent God can move nonbelievers. Li cited Mary, the mother of Jesus, as an example of humility and perseverance and encouraged the congregants to be patient bearers of the good news about God.

5   Challenges and Responses

As a new urban church, JM finds itself in an advantageous position, equipped with unique resources and a solid foundation for expansion. However, when compared with a typical well-established church, JM has yet to overcome several challenges.

First, the church needs regular full-time ministers. There is a general shortage of ministers in China. It is common that young urban churches do not have full-time ministers; some do not even have full-time coworkers, even though they do have the need for both. In its current state, JM congregants provide pastoral care for one another. Pastor Li, as well as some coworkers, has expressed concerns about the church's status quo. He recognizes that appointing the recently baptized as coworkers is not ideal. These congregants are too inexperienced in life and ministry alike to serve as coworkers. Li also prefers those congregants who are heads of Christian families to serve as coworkers, as their experience in household management may translate into effective management of church affairs. Furthermore, Li emphasizes that a qualified coworker needs to have a fulfilled life, "fully equipped to engage with diverse experiences and diverse opinions." Finally, Li recognizes that church governance needs to be better institutionalized. Currently, the church's growth is contingent upon the good moral and life examples set by its coworkers. Compared with similar churches, the current coworkers seem to be up for the task. At the top of the church's agenda for 2016 is the professional development of its coworkers. The church has invited pastors to give lectures. Some of the coworkers are preparing to study at theological seminaries in order to become full-time ministers.

Second, the church has yet to formulate a coherent system of theology. A confession of faith and guidance for ethical living are at the core of a church. Specifically, congregants look to the church for guidance and answers in a rapidly changing society. More than answers to questions about faith derived from theology, congregants need the church to relate theology to encounters and challenges in life. The development of a systematic, practical theology will not only address seekers' concerns, but it can also serve as the baseline for recruitment. Pastor Li explains that faith ought to address the various problems facing all segments of Chinese society, not merely matters of faith but also practical concerns. The university professors in the congregation are well equipped to address practical concerns. Pastor Li is optimistic about the contributions of the intellectuals in their fold. He thinks that intellectuals can leverage their research skills and find creative ways to adapt the Christian faith for Chinese culture while living the Christian truth to the full. This task is all the more pressing, considering the church has had to address social issues and problems at every Sunday service.

Third, the church needs to formalize its operating mechanism. To date, according to Pastor Li, JM Church does not have a standardized system to maintain membership. Without a system of membership management and retention, church membership has a greater tendency to fluctuate, especially when disagreements arise. Li is saddened whenever congregants leave and feels that he can only rely on God to hold the congregation together, particularly in a church whose core congregants are university professors, who are perceived to be "anti-communal." For the time being, as JM is a relatively small church, the rule of ethical and devout exemplars is still viable. As the congregation continues to grow in number, however, institutionalization is inevitable for all aspects of church governance, including its finances and daily operation. There are currently a number of models available online for JM. For instance, the operational model of Early Rain (*Qiuyu zhifu* 秋雨之福) Church in Chengdu is of interest to the coworkers.

Fourth, JM needs a clear legal status. Even though JM is no longer viewed as a "family" church, it is still considered a private meeting point by the government and is referred to as a "house church." The church's legal status has had little negative impact on its growth over time. Nevertheless, the risk of governmental suppression remains high as long as the church is not recognized as a social organization. The solution to this challenge is yet to be found. The newly issued "Regulations on Religious Affairs" (*Zongjiao shiwu guanli tiaoli* 宗教事务管理条例) may add further complications to the church's future development.

JM Church has persevered in spite of current and foreseeable challenges; the congregation continues to be inspired to spread the gospel. Not long ago, JM's coworkers gave a Christian fellowship for drug addicts a gift of a few guitars to offer some assistance. Looking ahead, Pastor Li is optimistic about JM's ministry. He recognizes the rational inclination of a church consisting mainly of highly educated people. Rationalism is a positive force, he thinks; without it, the congregation may develop mystical tendencies or even blend folk customs with Christian practices. On the other hand, he has observed that worship in rural churches is emotionally charged; the undereducated seem to be especially demonstrative of their love for the Lord. In Pastor Li's view, urban churches are responsible for the development of their rural counterparts, with whom they should share resources. He also thinks that urban churches should take up the pastoral care of migrant workers in cities. Charitable engagement may be a priority on JM's agenda in the foreseeable future.

6 Conclusion

JM Church is the prism through which I examined the rise of an emergent Christian church in a major Chinese city, how it found a niche, and the challenges it faces. I have observed the church's key characteristics, pattern of expansion, and tacit rules of operation. My study aims to encourage additional case studies to facilitate comparison and further research. As JM Church continues to grow, I will also continue my investigation. By way of conclusion, I wish to present some issues that transcend the direct experiences of a single church. Both religious and newly formed social organizations in a rapidly changing society may expect the following developments in the foreseeable future.

First, there is an increasing need for mutual understanding and collaboration between the academic and corporate worlds. In an educational environment of standardized tests, Chinese society cannot rely on either academics or entrepreneurs alone for successful modernization. A society-in-transformation requires not only the intellectual contributions of academics, but also the resources and pragmatism of entrepreneurs. A religious organization may be an appropriate arena for academics and entrepreneurs to learn about one another and work collaboratively. A successful collaboration of this kind may be instrumental to advancing both the quality and capacity of socioreligious groups in China.[15]

Second, religious groups continue to experiment with self-governance. Unlike corporations, the majority of newly emerged religious groups and social organizations are inexperienced in self-governance and management. Although they will inevitably encounter problems, they are also "learning by doing."

Finally, the dissemination of general religious knowledge is imperative, albeit challenging. The longevity of a religious organization is not achieved by the expression and practice of faith alone. It is equally important that a religious organization develop a coherent narrative about different denominations

---

15 In Nanjing and other cities alike, an increasing number of university professors, entrepreneurs, professionals, and white-collar workers have been active participants in book clubs, private nonprofit organizations, and cultural organizations, as well as religious groups.

within a religion and explain, with cohesion, various sets of relationships—among different religions, between religion and science, between religion and the law, and between traditional Chinese culture and the universality of a modern civilization. However, a religious organization alone cannot accomplish the universalization of religious education or general knowledge. It behooves educational institutions and individual educators alike to engage in the promotion of general education, religious and otherwise, to achieve the full realization of religious freedom as well as the separation of church and state.

Bibliography

Stark, Rodney, and Roger Finke. *Acts of Faith: Explaining the Human Side of Religion*. Berkeley: University of California Press, 2000. Translated by Yang Fenggang 杨凤岗 as *Xinyang de faze—jieshi zongjiao zhi ren de fangmian* 信仰的法则—解释宗教之人的方面. Beijing: Zhongguo renmin daxue chubanshe, 2004.

CHAPTER 9

The Tricolor Market in Yunnan

The Christian Life of the Hani

Jiang Shen and He Ling

Despite the state's regulation of religious markets in China, it appears that strict control is doing little to suppress the religious market.[1] As legal religious options are not satisfying the public's demand, believers resort to illicit and clandestine alternatives. This tendency may result in a thriving, albeit unregulated, religious market. Stringent regulation may also further complicate the religious market, hence increasing obstacles to the effective management of religious activities.

One limitation of Fenggang Yang's tricolor market analysis of religion in China is that it is drawn primarily from the religious experiences of the Han Chinese population. There are fifty-six ethnic groups in China, fifty-five of which are non-Han minorities. To what extent is the tricolor market model applicable to the study of the religious landscape in ethnic minority areas? What are the guiding principles of the local government's regulation of the religious market? What prompts the government to target religious organizations and their activities and impose stringent control over them? Is government action the sole cause of the emergence of three types of religious markets?

To answer these questions, we conducted field research in January of 2015 in two townships in Honghe County 红河县 in the Hani 哈尼 region of Yunnan. Christian activities are particularly prominent in these areas. Our primary research method is the case study, supplemented with surveys conducted via questionnaires. Taking the interplay between the Hani's Christian faith and traditional religious belief as the starting point, we examine the conditions of Christianity in the black and red markets. What are the constraints on Christianity? In what ways do the constraints affect the development of

---

[1] The authors are grateful for Professor Han Junxue of Yunnan Minzu University for his supervision as we completed this chapter. We also want to thank Yang Lin, Yang Jiaxin, Liu Haifei, and Liu Jiangyan for their assistance in the process of our research and writing. Finally, we would like to acknowledge our subjects and their enthusiastic cooperation that made our research possible.

Christianity? Finally, we will investigate the forces that drive Christianity from both the black and gray markets into the red market.

1   The Development of Christianity in the Honghe Hani Region

Several ethnic groups reside in the Honghe Hani and Yi Autonomous Prefecture in Yunnan, including Han, Yi, Dai, and Yao, with Hani being the majority. According to the 2017 census, this area includes 13 townships, 91 village committees, and 824 village communities, with a population of 340,600. Over 96 percent of the population belongs to an ethnic minority group; 79.5 percent of these people are Hani.[2] Three religious traditions are represented here: Buddhism, Christianity, and ethnic minority traditional religion. It is said that the entry of Christianity into Honghe began in 1976, when local farmers introduced the religion after returning from seasonal work out of town.

Historically speaking, minorities in Honghe have been believers in traditional religion. Christianity's appearance in the 1970s caused disruption in many places, which caused the local government to outlaw Christian churches in 1998. We selected two representative townships, which we will refer to as Lan and Bai, where we conducted field research on the conditions of Christianity among the Honghe Hani. Lan is a Hani majority township, with a small, non-Hani migrant population. Out of a population of about 26,000, roughly 1,000 are Christians, all of whom are Hani. Bai township also has a population of about 26,000, with Hani and Yi being the majority. There are about 200 Christians, of which 25 percent are Yi, and the rest are Hani. Whereas the Yi can communicate in the Hani language, the reverse is not true. Thus, Hani is the principal language of religious activities.

When Christianity first emerged in Honghe, it spread rapidly. Local authorities soon claimed that evangelists capitalized on the believers' low education level and lack of judgment. They used unorthodox tactics such as miracles, magic, or witchcraft to lure followers into their fold. They also defrauded believers. Moreover, divisions within Christian groups grew. The factionalization of Christian groups has created even more obstacles for the management of religious affairs, adding to the government's woes. Furthermore, in the villages where Christianity is active, certain Christians challenge the traditional authorities (chiefs) of stockade villages (*cunzhai* 村寨). They view the

---

2   See Honghe County People's Government Network, Honghe County profile, http://www.hhx .hh.gov.cn/hhgk/xqjj/201708/t20170807_47651.html (accessed August 20, 2019).

traditional Hani worship of Zhaishen 寨神, the patron god of the stockade village, as a "feudal superstition," characterizing it as idolatry or devil worship. They refuse to participate in communal activities and traditional rites, which is seen as a rejection of Hani identity.

Christians in this area further infuriate government officials because they often refuse to obey the law in the name of following God's commands. Such examples have increased in recent years, and officials have claimed that Christians are a disruptive force against the peaceful coexistence of ethnic groups. Even though Honghe, which is situated on the Sino-Vietnamese border, may not appear to have many places of worship, there is, in fact, a high level of religious activity. Additionally, the party and government leadership are concerned that an excess of Christian activity may be detrimental to the preservation and even survival of Hani cultural traditions. The local government began a decade-long project of suppressing Christian activities in 1993. Christian evangelists were arrested, promotional materials were burned, and believers were abused verbally and physically. The government wished to force Christians to abandon their beliefs in the hope of eradicating Christianity completely. Against the backdrop of state-sponsored persecution, these churches entered the black market.

Contrary to the government's expectation, suppression and prohibition failed to eradicate Christianity. Instead, these measures further damaged church-state relations and intensified the existing disagreements between Christians and believers in traditional religion. To mitigate the tension, the local government tried outreach programs to improve its engagement with the Christian community. For instance, the government adjusted its internal management methods, expanded infrastructure in minority farming villages, elevated the overall standard of living, and promoted ethnic unity. At the same time, the government took steps to legalize the Christian churches that met official guidelines. According to one local bureaucrat, an official announcement stated:

> The government supports all legitimate religious activities and grants Christian churches legal status, so long as they exert no negative impact on the education and economic development of the community. The authorities have conducted two inspections on Christian churches and encouraged church members to collaborate with the government. The formal recognition of the Christian community rests upon mutual understanding and mutual respect.[3]

---

3 Interview with staff of the Honghe Religious Bureau.

As the general suppression of Christian activities came to an end in 2003, church-state relations improved, and the tensions between Christians and practitioners of traditional religions eased. By then, Christianity had developed into two markets. On the one hand, in Bai township, the new improvement encouraged the Christian community to demand further legalization. Local officials decided that graduates from seminaries who were active in Bai township were well-versed in government policies regarding religious affairs. These individuals could help the township reach a higher level of development, and might even set an example for other communities. On the basis of this assessment, the government legalized all Christian churches in Bai township and stopped interfering with Christian activities. On the other hand, the situation in Lan township is quite different. Lan has a larger Christian population than Bai; however, due to its complicated relationship with other groups, it presented greater difficulty. In spite of the local Christians' aggressive demand for legalization, neither the local government nor the Three-Self Church agreed to grant these churches legal status. Not only did Christian religious sites remain illegal, but local officials further intervened in their activities from time to time.

It follows that Christians in Honghe exist in what Yang characterizes as the black, gray, and red markets. A close examination of the Christians' conditions in the three markets reveals how the development of Christianity unfolded in these ethnic minority areas. It will also help us determine the contributing factors to such conditions as well as potential solutions to local difficulties. Furthermore, this discussion will shed light on the various views of ethnic minorities on the development of Christianity in local areas and how the transformation of local Christianity from the black or gray market to the red market is promoted.

2   Christian Transition from Black to Red

2.1   *Christianity in the Black Market*

Christians in the black market find themselves on the polar opposite side of the government. They also have a hostile relationship with believers in traditional religion. In the context of the government's suppression and the rejection of nonbelievers, Christianity was once viewed as a cult.

From a historical perspective, we can see that local ethnic minorities have long been practitioners of traditional religion. The introduction of Christianity was, first of all, a major imposition on ethnic traditions and culture. Secondly, it challenged the core of the minority group identity, namely a collective sense of belonging centered on the village. Because the local government had insufficient experience in managing new religious groups, it expressed its ignorance in terms of hostility toward Christians, who were already the object of long-held prejudices. The decision to deny churches a legal status was unanimous.

The Christians' zeal and unethical recruitment tactics also left a negative impression. From the government's standpoint, Christianity was spreading among villagers who were poorly educated and largely ignorant of their adopted religion. Most officials thought that Christians could not articulate the identity of Jesus or what the Christian religion represents in general. Moreover, Christian evangelical activities were perceived as radical, verging on unethical. According to one local government official,

> Christian activities are scandalous. They hold clandestine meetings in people's homes, and they don't allow kids to go to school. Our investigation reveals that Christians hire nude dancers to perform in their so-called activities; they impersonate the incarnation of Jesus; some claim that they can fly, and others cluck like chickens or bark like dogs. It's such a disgrace. Yet others refuse to treat their illnesses. A man lost his wife to a disease and can no longer afford to marry again.

Reports such as this have convinced the government that Christians are ill-informed simpletons and easily manipulated. It is no wonder that the government holds Christianity in such disdain.[4]

The poor reputation of Christians, as well as preconceptions about Christianity and prejudices against it, led the local government to take extreme measures and to suppress or seek to ban Christianity. Certain officials even maintained that it is possible to eradicate Christianity altogether. According to these bureaucrats, this may take three to five years, maybe longer, and the implementation may have to consider the situations in neighboring communities.

Local officials in Lan township, in particular, were even more determined to ban Christianity. They resorted to extralegal and violent measures, including incarcerating Christian leaders and burning Christian literature. Devout and committed Christians, on the other hand, responded in kind by refusing to cooperate. In the end, the conflict continued to escalate to such a degree that some Christians have died in incarceration. A Christian named Li described the events thus:

---

4   The data in this paragraph comes from interviews with local government staff.

> They [the officials] were raiding everywhere. They took everything. Our farmland, pigs, oxen, chickens, tea, fruit trees, and palms trees were all confiscated. They took our property for their own with no intention of returning it. They didn't respect the freedom of religion, saying that we promote feudal superstitions. The harassment only stopped after 2002. In 1993, twenty-seven of us were forced to renounce our faith and were put into a public procession on the streets of Lan township. Afterward, they continued hitting and kicking us if we returned to our faith. They'd ask if we were still believers. They'd beat you if the answer was yes, and they wouldn't bat an eyelash if you were beaten to death. In 1994, one hundred goons came to arrest us. We were taken to one police station that night and transferred to jail the next day. We were released two years later. My two sons were arrested in 1998 for their belief in Jesus. My older son returned home after sixteen days in the Lan township jail. My younger son was taken to jail and was beaten to death after three or four months. They wouldn't even let us see the body unless we each paid 40 RMB (6 USD). I only saw his grave after the fact. Actually, they'd come for me. I feared for my life at the time and left for Kunming to make a meager living, away from home. In 1999, I snuck back home in the darkness of the night once and began to make regular trips in 2003. The last persecution was in 2002. This was actually the worst of all the raids, and all government officials took part except for the education department. About one hundred people descended on us; even those who verbally challenged the officials (like my daughter, a non-Christian) were tortured and abused.

In Bai township, fining Christians for their meetings was the primary form of deterrence. A Christian interviewee indicated,

> Previously, the town government and the Religious Affairs Bureau forbade us from celebrating Christmas and Easter. If caught, we would face fines. The government wanted to suppress the development of Christianity for fear of its influence on education. Christians engaging in illicit activities are fined according to the degree of the offence. For example, an elder and an assistant were both fined 200 RMB (31 USD); some others have been fined, too. The Bureau of Ethnic and Religious Affairs put the word out that they would "handle" Christians. We were not scared. Our Sunday services should continue because we were not breaking the law.

Uncooperative Christians faced draconian punishments. An incident that happened in the village committee seat of one village in Bai township in 2006 is a case in point. During the Dragon Festival, the village committee, together with villagers, forcefully seized one pig from each of the three Christian households.[5] Christians were also abused both physically and verbally in public and forced to join humiliating processions through the streets. Other measures of suppression and intimidation included the denial of welfare or withholding applications for important personal documents.

The relationship between Christians and believers in traditional religion was little better; each side was constantly at the other's throat. Christians, who are in the minority, shifted their focus to internal unity as a mechanism to resist external pressure. In Emile Durkheim's words, religion is the source of social cohesion and unity.[6] However, between two religious groups in a society can contribute to division rather than social solidarity. Just as Peter M. Blau has argued, augmented internal cohesion undermines social unity.[7]

Christians address one another as brothers and sisters. They offer mutual aid and emotional support, and for many believers, this is the religion's main appeal. As a Christian leader explained, "Although there are not as many of us (compared to believers in traditional religion), when our brothers and sisters are in need, we support them with money. What do believers in traditional religion do in the same situation? They don't help each other when someone is in trouble." Cohesion among congregants is a powerful unifying force, but strong internal solidarity can also further widen the distance between Christians and believers in traditional religion. We can observe the two groups' disagreements in everyday life. The Hani's traditional belief is part and parcel of their historical memory and lived experience. Christian converts stopped participating in traditional Hani festivals and communal activities of the stockade village. These traditional festivals, rituals, and ceremonies helped to consolidate village identity and differentiated the Hani from other ethnic groups.

The traditional dragon festival of the Hani is a ceremonial event that typically involves the entire stockade village community. In traditional Hani

---

5   For the Hani people, the Dragon Festival comes in two installments, one in the first lunar month and the other in the third lunar month. People hope for blessings and happiness in the first installment, and for prosperous crops in the second.
6   Emile Durkheim, *The Elementary Forms of Religious Life*, translated by Joseph Ward Swain (London: George Allen and Unwin, 1915); translated by Lin Zongjin and Peng Shouyi as *Zongjiao shenghuo de chuji xingshi* (Beijing: Zhongyang minzhu daxue chubanshe, 1999).
7   Peter M. Blau, *Exchange and Power in Social Life* (New York: John Wiley and Sons, 1964); translated by Li Guowu as *Shehui shenghuo zhongde jiaohuan yu quanli* (Beijing: Shangwu yinshu guan, 2013), 90–101.

society, all members of the village chip in and share the cost of the festival, because these activities aim to bring blessing and good fortune to all villagers. For Christians to extricate themselves from communal activities is tantamount to nonfulfillment of a core obligation. In the village chief's opinion,

> The Dragon Festival is a time-honored tradition. Those who refuse to participate may as well be expelled from our village. Even if the Christians decline to take part, we still expect them to contribute in one way or another. They can donate a chicken or 20 RMB (3 USD), for example. A committee consisting of the team leader, assistant leader, chief, and elders can determine the specific amount or kind. I don't like Christians because they don't participate in traditional celebrations. They go against the entire village when they refuse to take part in the dragon festival; they are effectively renouncing their membership in the village. When Christians refuse to contribute, we (the team leader, assistant leader, chief, and elders) have to take over their duties. We would first caution them about losing their place in the village, and there are many other villagers who would happily replace them. And then we would deal out punishments according to our custom.

Followers of traditional religion have come to sever their connections to Christians as well. They withhold aid, for example, when Christians need help with weddings or funerals. In the meantime, Christians are obstinate and hold their ground. Some even deliberately challenge taboos by demonstrating their faith instead of participating in common ceremonial activities during the Dragon Festival. The fact that neither side is willing to compromise in that regard only worsens the division. As a result, the government becomes even more convinced that the spread of Christianity exerts a negative impact on ethnic unity and social stability.

In the black market, relationships between church and state, Christians and believers in traditional religion, and Christianity and traditional religion are in a perpetual state of deadlock and embattlement. Conflict between religious groups also intensifies church-state friction. In this context, Christians are under attack, and Christian leaders endure persecution. They are arrested, exiled, and even killed. Christians also suffer from overt discrimination. Their access to social welfare is denied. They are fined for their faith, and possessions are confiscated. People openly mistreat Christians and harass them, both verbally and physically. Certain Christians renounce their faith, either permanently or temporarily, in the face of such insurmountable pressure. Churches are forcibly dissolved or shut down. Committed Christians have no choice but to go "underground." They meet for clandestine services and religious celebrations in the privacy of their own homes and keep their Christian identities a secret.

Rather than eradicating religious activities, draconian measures may result in a thriving black or gray religious market.[8] In the face of persecution, certain Christians have persevered, but not without considerable sacrifices. According to one devout Christian,

> People say that Christianity is not a Hani tradition, so Hani should not adopt the Christian faith. They use tradition as an excuse to force us to give up our faith and even threaten to cast us out of the village. The way I look at it, we'll leave if they don't want us here. We are not in the wrong. They say that our faith is illegal. It is legal to me. But they keep insisting that we have done something wrong; I can't do anything about what they want to think of us. I'll accept whatever they'll do to us.

2.2   The Prospect of a Red Market

The government's unwaveringly repressive approach in managing Christian activities has generated some results. According to officials, it is the government's responsibility to take administrative measures to resolve the tension between Christianity and traditional religion. Compared to earlier times, there are now fewer Christian churches, and believers meet in secret in their own homes, which is an illegal religious activity. Indeed, some Christians have renounced their faith as a result. One Christian preacher reported to us, "Our numbers reached a peak of six hundred believers between 1987 and 1989. About half of these left us in 1992 and 1993. There are fifty households in our village. At the peak of our activity, twenty households were Christian (about sixty to seventy people). Now there are only six Christian families (about thirty members)." All parties involved have paid a steep price for this outcome.

After realizing that it would be impossible to entirely suppress Christianity, the local government reevaluated its approaches. At the prefecture level, an official in charge of the administration of religious affairs expressed the opinion that Christian churches are in disarray. The prefectural Bureau of Religious Affairs denied legal status to churches in Lan township because they did not meet the requirements. (The requirements for approval are that the church or group has professional religious personnel, who must be formally trained

---

8 Fenggang Yang, "The Red, Black, and Gray Markets of Religion in China," *Sociological Quarterly* 47.1 (2006): 93–122; translated and abridged by Yang Fenggang as "Zhongguo zongjiao de sanse shichang," *Zhongguo renmin daxue xuebao* 6 (2006): 41–47.

and certified to preach.) Churches in Lan township ignored the government's guidelines and neglected to reform themselves. Other officials stated that the government supports legitimate religious activities, as long as they do not negatively affect the educational system and economic development. Government officials paid Lan township two visits to persuade churches there to comply with official policy, invoking mutual respect and understanding in the hopes of potential legalization. Adjustments in the government's attitude and outreach methods, as well as the implementation of new policies, all paved the way for the legalization of Christian churches.

As a state agency on the front line, the township administration is the primary enforcer of the prohibition of Christianity. Specifically, when faced with the staunch defiance of Christians in Lan township, local government officials still consider Christianity a divisive force within the village communities and a potential obstacle to the enforcement of other government policies, even though they have steered away from direct oppression and persecution. Indeed, conflicts arise in areas where Christians are present. For example, when there is a death in the family, the Christian members demand a Christian funeral and their non-Christian counterparts insist on a traditional Hani burial. A disagreement of this kind disrupts familial and communal harmony. Christian churches also interfere with young people's choices of life partners. Christians are not allowed to marry nonbelievers. This prohibition intrudes on the youth's freedom to marry. In certain places, Christians always band together and act as an organized group, giving a hint of exclusivity. Christians and non-Christians do not seem to be able to communicate with one another due to their different beliefs and life choices. With regard to education, children of Christian families are raised in the faith, which has an impact on their education. Families with two faiths have trouble maintaining peace at home. In short, Christianity not only brings disunity into the village, but it also adds an extra burden to the local government's existing responsibilities for social cohesion.

Although the local government has steered away from physically harming Christian church leaders and believers as a management strategy, officials still maintain that it is necessary to keep a tight grip on religious affairs. They continue to approach Christian believers as persons who need to be educated to change their thoughts. Their interactions with Christian leaders, however, focus on discipline and punishment. They claim they have to reeducate them as a group and teach them the appropriate concepts of law and policy. They need to learn that their Christian practices are outlawed and banned by the state. Christianity remains unrecognized and illegal in Lan township today. Some low-level officials still apply harsh measures to curb the development of Christianity, including surveillance and burning Christian scriptures and promotional literature. According to the prefecture's TSPM/CCC (Three-Self Patriotic Movement / China Christian Church), on November 30, 2008, an armed force stormed Yang's home and burned three copies of the Bible and more than fifty copies of devotional literature. On February 23, 2010, government officials burned ten hymnals, eight Bibles, fifty gospel CDs, and twenty gospel pamphlets in the Chen family's possession. On February 9, 2011, on the pretext of an inspection at Weisheng Road, eight officials stormed another Chen family (when only elderly members were home). The branch village office secretary, at the behest of the township secretary, tore up ten Bibles and hymnals in the Chen's possession and burned them in a fire pit, while destroying a blackboard and CDs. The Yang family suffered the same fate. Four Bibles and hymnals were burned, and the central scroll in the house, as well as a Christian-themed calendar, were also destroyed.[9]

Granted, the prefecture and county governments no longer exercise stringent, top-down control over Christians in Lan township. Nonetheless, as the division between Christians and other villagers has become irreparable, the hope of mending the relationship between the two groups remains slim. Christians in Lan township continue to demand legalization, which the local government continues to deny. Thus, the prefecture government cannot do anything to move the demands forward. Meanwhile, conflict between Christian leaders and village leaders has reached the boiling point. In the eyes of the Christians, their relationship with other villagers "is poor; everyone ignores us. No one wants to talk to us. We are like enemies to them."[10] The non-Christian villagers typically keep silent about Christian affairs. Christians dare not reveal their true identities, as public evangelization is strictly forbidden.

To be fair, governments at the prefecture and county levels have adjusted their attitudes toward religious affairs considerably. Specifically, they have created guidelines for the legalization of Christianity. These changes have paved the way for Christians to transition out of the black market into the red market. The problem with the Christian black market in Lan township is a combination of the intransigent attitude of the local government and the antagonism between Christians and non-Christians. The solution cannot be unilateral, but requires the mediation of the prefecture and county governments, as well as a willingness to compromise on the part of both local officials and the Christian community.

---

9   This information comes from interviews and a visit to the Yang family, and was later confirmed by TSPM officials.
10 Interview with a Christian in Lan township.

3 Christians in the Red Market

In Bai township, where Christian churches have been legalized, Christian and non-Christian villagers manage to maintain amicable ties, as both sides are willing to compromise with each other and make concessions. Both groups in Bai township take a tolerant and inclusive approach to the issue of religious belief. Some regard membership in a Christian church as a pastime, especially for the elderly. Many young villagers think that church activities get the elderly out of their homes and that singing and socializing is good for them. The people of the township also embrace diversity when they discuss the influence of religion on the unity of an ethnic group. At least 70% of the population think that religious difference has no impact on ethnic cohesion. In Lan township, where interreligious relations are problematic, only 21% share this opinion, and 75% of the Lan population consider religious difference either a factor or a major determinant of ethnic unity. On the subjects of religion and ethnic identity, residents of Bai township also reveal diverse views: 39% of them prioritize ethnic cohesion, 23% think that religious belief should take precedence, and another 23% value both equally. The same survey from Lan township shows that 57% of the population value ethnic cohesion more than religious belief, and 19% think that both religion and ethnic identity are equally important.[11]

Traditionally, weddings and funerals are among the most important household events in Chinese society. In the ethnic minority areas of the mountains of Yunnan, a stockade village typically consists of several clans bearing a few family names. There are cases where one clan makes up an entire stockade village. Whether the relationship between members of divergent religious beliefs is managed prudently has direct implications for the unity and division of a clan or even an entire village. The consequences of Christianity's impact on family relations, therefore, are a concern of the government. Indeed, the introduction of Christianity has generated discord within certain clans. In Bai township, Christian and non-Christian villagers realize the imperative of negotiation and compromise. Take, for example, the negotiation of funerary arrangements in a family with two religious beliefs. Family members usually defer to a dying elderly person's wishes for the funeral and simply follow instructions. In the event that the person has no particular preferences, the two parties negotiate with goodwill and compromise on a combination of Christian and traditional

---

11 This data is derived from a survey in which we asked about interreligious relations in Bai and Lan townships in Honghe in December 2015. We retrieved eighty-five valid questionnaires.

funerary rituals. A choir sings hymns, and a *beima* 贝玛 rite featuring traditional scriptures is performed. All villagers help out at the funeral regardless of their religious beliefs.

Christian churches in Bai township have transitioned into a red market. Christians and non-Christians alike participate in earnest in traditional festivities as well as communal activities of the stockade village. Christians, however, do not worship, kowtow, or kneel to traditional deities, nor do they partake of sacrificial offerings. Regardless, because Christians fulfill their duties as villagers by taking part in communal activities and contributing to their success both in kind and in cash, non-Christian villagers reciprocate and make no objections to Christian abstinence from traditional rituals of worship. Moreover, Christians proactively take up charitable work in the village and endeavor to be a force for good in the community. They take care of the elderly, especially those living on their own; they help maintain public hygiene in the village; and they raise funds for the medical needs of poor families. They are often the first to offer aid to villagers in need. According to one church member, "At first the nonbelievers harassed us out of ignorance. Over time, they have come to learn who we are by our good deeds. Their understanding of us makes a difference." These acts have changed the public perception of the Christian faith.

Public opinion about Christianity also affects the government's attitude toward the church. As Christians in Bai township get along well with other villagers, the government is willing to legalize churches and officially acknowledge their status. One official stated,

> The conflict between traditional religion and Christianity is rooted in their different customs and practices. Specifically, disagreements over funerary customs often lead to open conflict. However, Christians do show up in traditional ceremonies, even though they don't join in the rituals or kowtow. They refrain from killing and typically shy away from traditional Hani rituals. Over time, the village, as a whole, has developed a tacit understanding and acceptance of Christian behavior. Christian families generally follow their own customs, but the village keeps with Hani traditions for the most part.

Christians also think that their efforts have resulted in a positive relationship with other villagers:

> Although we don't take part in the dragon worship, we make monetary contributions and share some of the expenses of the ceremonies.

> We also make frequent donations. For example, we donated 6,000 RMB (approximately 925 USD) after the Sichuan earthquake, and we help with the repairs of bridges, roads, and ditches. We get along well with other villagers. We give each other a hand during the peak farming season. Help is usually requested through neighbors and relatives; religious belief is not a consideration. We and other [non-Christian] villagers are on friendly terms.

On the contrary, Christian churches in Lan township still exist in a black market. Not only does the government deny them legal status, but the local Three-Self church also refuses to recognize them. According to the elders of the Honghe Prefecture TSPM/CCC,

> The Christians in Lan township are in a difficult situation with serious internal factional rivalry. They boycott the tradition of dragon worship and refuse to share the cost of the ceremonies. They often quarrel with other villagers. The local government has to take action to defend the well-being of the villagers and discipline the Christians. They [Lan township] have the largest number of Christians, but they also cause the most trouble in the area.

A leading official of the county-level party administration stated, "Of course we legalize the Christian churches in Bai township, because their members are well behaved and get along with fellow villagers. Regardless of the number of Christians in Lan township, we will not grant them legal status. They have also given up on legalization."

Indeed, in a black market, Christianity is suppressed, churches are under strict scrutiny, preachers are persecuted, and Christians are subject to open hostility. Contrary to the discrimination and illegitimacy associated with the black market, Christians in the red market are generally accepted by society. Officials in Bai township have stated, "Christians and non-Christians in Bai township have never gotten into great conflict. We are the leaders; we treat and protect Christians equally, like any other villagers." Some villagers think that Christianity can offer certain people, especially the elderly, emotional support, which is a positive influence. In this case, faith is an absolutely private matter, and belief has truly become a commodity in the free market of religion. Believers can be open about their faith, and with the permission of the government, they have started raising funds to build a proper church.

4 Motivations for the Suppression of the Christian Faith

Regarding the regulation of religion, Fenggang Yang argues that no religion can exist without some kind of management and control.[12] It is important, however, to investigate the underlying reasons why the local government in an ethnic minority area restricts the development of Christianity. In other words, we should ask what contributes to the emergence of a Christian black market and the growth of a gray market. Answers to these questions may point toward solutions to Christians' illegal status that are of practical significance for the Christian transition out of a gray or even illicit black market into a red market.

4.1 *Preserving and Defending Traditional Culture*

As stated above, Lan township is a Hani township where Christianity is illegal. Research has shown that multiethnic areas tend to be more tolerant of outsider cultures, compared to areas with homogenous ethnic compositions and relatively intact traditional cultural roots. Such a cultural community is porous and less resistant to foreign cultural elements. We can find many such examples. For instance, Bingzhongluo 丙中洛 in northwestern Yunnan is a multiethnic area, home to the Nu, Tibetan, and Bai peoples. Traditional religion, Protestantism, and Catholicism coexist in this region. However, it is difficult for Christianity to break into Xishuangbanna 西双版纳, a center of Theravada Buddhism, and Dali 大理, a center of the Bai people's local religion.

A religious economy consists of all religious activities, including an existing or potential "market" of believers, one or more organizations to attract and retain believers, and the religious culture of an organization. Yunnan is an underdeveloped ethnic minority region. Yunnan sits on the geographical margins of Chinese culture and has historically suffered both economic and cultural poverty. The traditional religious culture developed in such conditions is incapable of resisting a world religion such as Christianity. In the face of a rapidly changing society, the backward traditional culture of an ethnic minority no longer satisfies the needs of the local population.

Lan township is a Hani community that embraces a singular and intact cultural tradition. Christianity is an outsider religion whose teachings and rules contradict Hani traditional religious culture. Christians worship only one God and believe themselves to be the children of God. These beliefs are incompatible with the Hani traditional belief in natural deities, ghosts, and spirits,

---

12   Fenggang Yang, "Red, Black, and Gray Markets."

as well as ancestor worship. The two cultures inevitably contradict and compete with each other. Moreover, such competition can also be understood as a defense mechanism on the part of traditional Hani religious culture against Christian culture. The inclination to resist a foreign culture is also evident in the collective effort of local government, ethnic minority officials, and ethnic minority villagers to preserve traditional culture. In practice, quite a few Christians dismiss traditional worship as devil worship, feudal superstition, or idolatry. Christianity teaches against idolatry, and converts no longer give offerings to ancestors, which is considered a betrayal of the tradition of filial piety. On the other hand, believers in Hani traditional religion view conversion to Christianity as a sign that Hani identity has been lost.

4.2   A "Cult" under the Cloak of Christianity

The government keeps a close watch on the spread of cults in ethnic minority areas. The suppression of cults is one of the most pressing tasks of government agencies and their civilian extensions (village self-governance). Its significance is evident in the abundance of literature about cults posted on the bulletin boards of every township government building, administrative village, and village community. During fieldwork, we have observed the same phenomenon at all levels of administrative units. The majority of flyers on bulletin boards call for the rejection of cults and caution against their harmful nature.

During our interviews, officials in the local administration of religious affairs denied the presence of cults in Honghe. They also swore that villagers wholeheartedly rejected cults. One official exclaimed, "There are no cults in Honghe, and the villagers are adamantly against the spread of cults. Some cult leaders recruit members in the name of Christianity and misrepresent the words of the Bible. Some preachers disseminate teachings and tenets contrary to Christian belief just to attract converts." According to He, who works in the rural work brigade, "I have learned that some [self-identified] Christian preachers misled students into thinking that their academic performance would improve as long as they believed in God." Such acts violate the state guideline that no individual should interfere with education in the name of religion. Local religious leaders have realized the problematic evangelizing methods of these preachers and have avoided contact with them. A pastor of the TSPM Committee revealed to us in an interview, "We refrain from inviting members of illegal churches to our activities, because their extremist messages and recruitment methods are deeply troubling."

We can conclude that the government's suspicion of Christian evangelization has prompted a black market and a thriving gray market. Beyond the government's distrust of Christians, however, lies its irregular recruitment methods, as well as an extreme and radical means of expansion. These irregularities render Christianity susceptible to the manipulation of cult members. It is understandable that the government exercises extra caution in its treatment of Christianity, a religion that not only has a bad name but is also easily mistaken for a cult.

4.3 Long-Standing Prejudices and the Infiltration of Foreign Religions

Situated between south Asia and Southeast Asia, Yunnan's geopolitical significance is quite crucial. In recent history, Western missionaries have targeted Yunnan, an area with a high concentration of ethnic minorities, as a major destination for evangelization. Specifically, the encouraging results of Protestant missions among ethnic minority groups on the margins of mainstream Chinese society put Yunnan on the radar of other churches and missionary organizations.[13] Thereafter, an increasing number of Christian missions flooded into Yunnan. The ethnic minority areas of southwest China were historically considered a frontier for missionaries, some of whom became well known for their contributions to the expansion of Protestant Christianity, including Samuel Pollard (Bo Geli 柏格理) and James Adam (Dang Juren 党居仁) among the Miao, and James O. Fraser (Fu Nengren 傅能仁) among the Lisu.

Admittedly, Christianity and its missions have found their place in the socioeconomic backwater of Yunnan, a marginalized and remote peripheral area of China. Ethnic minorities, on the whole, lived in a constant state of deprivation with no hope of satisfying basic needs.[14] Christian missions not only stimulated socioeconomic development in the area, but also helped change the rudimentary lifestyle of many ethnic minorities. In addition to evangelization, missionaries helped the Miao and Lisu people create writing systems. These efforts were instrumental in encouraging cultural development. Before the introduction of Christianity, the ethnic minority lifestyle involved little planning or economic thinking. "Saving for a rainy day" was an unfamiliar concept, conspicuous consumption was the norm, and the notion of hygiene was nonexistent.[15]

Conversion to Christianity also resulted in major changes in behavior and customs. Christian converts vowed to not kill livestock as a sacrifice for dragon worship. They also stopped turning their grain into alcohol. We have observed

---

13 Han Junxue, "Jindai Yunnan jidujiao, tianzhujiao de bianqian ji zouxiang," *Yunnan zongjiao yanjiu*, no. 23 (2000): 49–60.

14 Qian Ning, ed., *Jidujiao yu shaoshu minzu shehui wenhua bianqian* (Kunming: Yunnan daxue chubanshe, 1998), 81.

15 Han Junxue, *Jidujiao yu Yunnan shaoshu minzu* (Kunming: Yunnan renmin chubanshe, 2000), 5–60.

during our fieldwork that the vast majority of Christian families refrain from drinking, whereas it is customary for non-Christian families to consume alcohol with three daily meals. Drinking sessions often last for an hour or longer. The Hani are a hospitable people who take pride in their guests' enjoyment of their humble homemade liquor. It is quite normal to consume five or six glasses of white liquor at every sitting. Refraining from alcohol, in fact, has helped Christian families cut down on their expenses. Christianity has also contributed to ending the coresidence of humans and livestock in the same space. In our fieldwork site, villagers took advantage of the uneven terrain in the mountains to build multistory houses in which humans occupy the upper stories and livestock are kept on the lower level. This design prevents the mixing of humans and animals.

Despite the aforementioned benefits of Christianity, the religion nevertheless entered China along with imperialistic aggressions imposed on the Chinese people by Western powers. The expansion of Christianity went hand in hand with imperialistic encroachment on Chinese sovereignty.[16] This impressed upon the Chinese people that Christianity is a "foreign religion" and a tool of the aggressors. Many Chinese still have difficulty welcoming Christianity. An official we spoke with expressed similar sentiments: "Christianity belongs to Western countries and is foreign. It is not our tradition, and we don't want it. These [Hani] elders will not accept it, either."

Thanks to the assistance of Honghe officials, we have gained access to information relevant to the government's investigation into the outreach of Christian groups. A good number of Christian groups and overzealous individuals evangelize in the name of service. In particular, foreigners and Christian missionary groups alike engage in evangelism without official approval. For instance, Partners in Hope, an American organization, has worked with a local school to supply English teachers. Instead of following the lesson plans, these teachers in fact are spreading Christian messages in the classrooms. Partners in Hope members often surreptitiously promote the Christian faith in their interaction with students and other teachers. Another American Christian organization, Bless China International, launched missionary activities in Honghe in 1999. The organization opened a project office in Honghe to coordinate evangelical efforts on the pretext of offering training programs for teachers and doctors in the villages. Bless China International was expelled from the area as a result of a government investigation. Its personnel, however, allied

---

16   Qin Heping, *Jiduzongjiao zai xinan minzu diqu de chuanbo shi* (Chengdu: Sichuan minzu chubanshe, 2004), 401–412.

themselves with the local Three-Self Church system and, by volunteering, continued missionary work and established three churches without governmental approval. Moreover, starting in 1999, a Korean corporation, Jinmai Fudi 金麦福地财团, became involved in Christian evangelization. The corporation partnered with a local organization in outreach to the disabled population. They provided the disabled with complimentary services in beauty, hairstyling, and computer troubleshooting, all as vehicles for Christian evangelization. Finally, in 2007, ten Korean missionaries, claiming to be tourists in Honghe, established a Korean Christian Cheongju Nanxi Village Christian Church.[17]

We cannot deny that Christianity has indeed contributed to economic development and helped improve the overall standard of living for many ethnic minorities in Yunnan. However, it is equally important to recognize the imprint left by a complicated history of imperialistic aggression and the suffering this has caused. The current state of irregular preaching, defiance of law, and uncoordinated and unorthodox recruitment methods has hit a nerve with the government. The government takes management of religious affairs seriously, as it is perceived as a matter of upholding the rule of law and defending the frontier and ethnic minority areas against foreign intrusion, as well as elevating the education level of Christian converts in these areas.

5   Conclusion

Examining the interplay between religion and society in contemporary Chinese society against the backdrop of a religious network of exchange, we find that the sacred capital of organized religion is inseparable from the existing power structure.[18] Fenggang Yang has identified three religious markets in Chinese society based on the government's judgment on the legality of various religions. Compared with "legal" religions, "illicit" religions are bound to require more capital in order to properly provide goods and services.[19] All the same, no government would relinquish its control over the religious market. It is also incumbent on all parties involved to strive for ethnic unity and

---

17   This information was supplied by government agencies in Honghe Prefecture.
18   Li Xiangping and Yang Linxia, "Zongjiao, shehui yu quanli guanxi—'zongjiao shichang lun' de shehuixue jiedu," *Huadong shifan daxue xuebao (zhexue shehui kexue ban)* 43.5 (2011): 2.
19   Ruan Rongping, Zheng Fengtian, and Liu Li, "Zongjiao xinyang xuanze—yige xifang zongjiao jingjixue de wenxian shuli," *Shehui*, 2013.4: 193–224.

communal harmony as they endeavor to make the religious market friendlier for Christians, to the effect of reducing costs for them.

It is advisable that Christians adopt a sensible approach to their interaction with the government—improving communication while asserting their legitimate rights. Some Christians we spoke with expressed such sentiments: "We hope our leaders continue their efforts in serving the people. Christians desire peace and will endeavor to meet government guidelines that are compatible with the Bible. We truly hope that our church will be approved." Moreover, Christians are responsible for managing their relationship with believers in traditional religion to obtain the best outcome. Granted, faith is a personal matter, but individuals cannot exist in a communal vacuum. Individuals can claim freedom of religion, but they are also obligated to their community. Our study has shown that most of the villagers resent Christians for their failure to fulfill their obligations to the stockade village.

With regard to the government's stance on Christianity, it is important to recognize that the reception of Christianity in society is a fait accompli. The religion cannot be dismissed or eradicated with draconian measures of suppression. A religion has a life of its own, and it satisfies individuals' needs. Neglecting public demands in the name of the preservation of traditional culture does nothing to generate desired outcomes. We recommend that the government improve the training of its religious affairs personnel and enhance the instruction and guidance for religious elites. The training should also aim to cultivate an ability to recognize legitimate religious teachings and to distinguish a regular religious group from a cult. Furthermore, long-held prejudices should not influence the administration of religious affairs. An official agrees that

> We must stop burying our heads in the sand and face the music. We should examine the substance of the religious leaders' messages, grant permission to legitimate religious groups, and only scrutinize the smaller groups that seem problematic. The quality of religious professionals is critical; the uneven quality of preachers, the congregants' choices of pastors, and discrepancies in believers' interpretations of the scriptures can all cause discord. We need to build a team of religious professionals with proper training.

It is equally imperative that the purveyors of the Christian belief set their followers' "this-worldly fulfillment" as the ultimate goal of their activities. The messages of cordiality, respect, and love ought to be disseminated among believers to strengthen internal cohesion, but they should also serve as the guidelines for interaction with the broader village community. Religion is an aspect of life. Indeed, Christianity is a foreign religion that inevitably challenges some elements of ethnic minority cultural traditions. Nevertheless, for Christianity to be in a constant state of tension and animosity vis-à-vis local traditions does not serve the religious purveyors' objective, which is to lay down roots for Christianity in an ethnic minority area. Looking ahead, we suggest that compromise, proper management of intergroup relations, mutual respect, and communication would be the best policy.

Bibliography

Blau, Peter M. *Exchange and Power in Social Life*. New York: John Wiley, 1964. Translated by Li Guowu 李国武 as *Shehui shenghuo zhongde jiaohuan yu quanli* 社会生活中的交换与权力. Beijing: Shangwu yinshu guan, 2013.

Durkheim, Emile. *The Elementary Forms of Religious Life*. Translated by Joseph Ward Swain. London: George Allen and Unwin, 1915. Translated by Lin Zongjin 林宗锦 and Peng Shouyi 彭守义 as *Zongjiao shenghuo de chuji xingshi* 宗教生活的初级形式. Beijing: Zhongyang minzu daxue chubanshe, 1999.

Han Junxue 韩军学. *Jidujiao yu Yunnan shaoshu minzu* 基督教与云南少数民族. Kunming: Yunnan renmin chubanshe, 2000.

Han Junxue 韩军学. "Jindai Yunnan jidujiao, tianzhujiao de bianqian ji zouxiang" 近代云南基督教、天主教的变迁及走向. *Yunnan zongjiao yanjiu* 云南宗教研究. no. 23 (2000): 49–60.

Honghe County People's Government Network. Honghe County profile. http://www.hhx.hh.gov.cn/hhgk/xqjj/201708/t20170807_47651.html (accessed August 20, 2019).

Li Xiangping 李向平 and Yang Linxia 杨林霞. "Zongjiao, shehui yu quanli guanxi—'zongjiao shichang lun' de shehuixue jiedu" 宗教、社会与权力关系—"宗教市场论"的社会学解读. *Huadong shifan daxue xuebao (zhexue shehui kexue ban)* 华东师范大学学报（哲学社会科学版）43.5 (2011): 1–7.

Qian Ning 钱宁, ed. *Jidujiao yu shaoshu minzu shehui wenhua bianqian* 基督教与少数民族社会文化变迁. Kunming: Yunnan daixue chubanshe, 1998.

Qin Heping 秦和平. *Jiduzongjiao zai xinan minzu diqu de chuanbo shi* 基督宗教在西南民族地区的传播史. Chengdu: Sichuan minzu chubanshe, 2004.

Ruan Rongping 阮荣平, Zheng Fengtian 郑风田, and Liu Li 刘力. "Zongjiao xinyang xuanze—yige xifang zongjiao jingjixue de wenxian shuli" 宗教信仰选择—一个西方宗教经济学的文献梳理. *Shehui* 社会, 2013.4: 193–224.

Yang, Fenggang. "The Red, Black, and Gray Markets of Religion in China." *Sociological Quarterly* 47.1 (2006): 93–122. Translated and abridged by Yang Fenggang 杨凤岗 as "Zhongguo zongjiao de sanse shichang" 中国宗教的三色市场, *Zhongguo renmin daxuexuebao (shehui kexue ban)* 中国人民大学学报（社会科学版）. 2006.6: 41–47.

PART 3

Beyond Religious Regulation

CHAPTER 10

Between the Sacred and the Secular
Zhanjiang Daoshi and the Religious Economy

Yan Jun and Lin Weizhi

In the greater Zhanjiang 湛江 metro area of Guangdong, villagers refer to religious specialists who perform Daoist rituals for the community as *daoshi* 道师.[1] This chapter specifically focuses on those individuals who are *huoju daoshi* 火居道士. This class of priests consists of individuals who are married and have secular jobs.[2] Huoju Daoshi serve individuals and families, as well as temples in villages, by performing ceremonies to avert calamities or rituals of communal renewal.[3] Most priests in Zhanjiang reside in village communities, with their families and in their own homes, and are generally indistinguishable from any other villager. The vast majority have full-time employment unrelated to religious activities. Only on occasions such as festivals and funerals or for specific ritual needs are these priests invited to put on robes and bring instruments to perform rituals for clients. As individuals or as a troupe, they perform rituals and receive monetary compensation in a mutually agreed-upon amount or per convention.

Daoshi is a hereditary profession. Because Daoshi appeal to deities and intercede on behalf of their clients, locals believe that only the male descendants of families who have venerated and served celestial beings for generations are eligible to serve in this capacity. In addition to hereditary

---

1 Locals in Zhanjiang call these religious specialists *daoshi* 道师 and not *daoshi* 道士. There are two plausible explanations for this convention. First, the local dialect does not distinguish *shi* 师 and *shi* 士. The confusion of terms has been passed down over time, and the locals have simply adopted the former. Second, these priests are familiar figures in the village community and take part in the villagers' quotidian routines. Villagers call them *shifu* 师傅 (Master), which was adapted into Daoshi.

2 Daoshi in Zhanjiang identify with a specific school. They are not the Daoshi of the Quanzhen sect 全真派 (Complete Perfection) who reside in temples. Rather, they live in the world and are associated with the Zhengyi sect 正一派 (Orthodox Unity). As there are no Quanzhen Daoist temples in Zhanjiang, sectarian affiliation is not a consideration in interactions between local Daoshi and the average villager.

3 Li Xiangping and Li Siming, "Xinyang yu minjian quanwei de jiangou—minjian xinyang yishi zhuanjia yanjiu zongshu," *Shijie zongjiao wenhua*, 2012.3: 110–119.

succession, to qualify for the profession and operate independently, a successor must serve an apprenticeship of three to five years before he is officially recognized by both his peers and community members in an induction ceremony.

The relationship between Daoshi and their village community has undergone drastic changes over the past few decades. An "exchange of gifts" model has morphed into a "price tag" model of transaction. Concomitant with this transition is the emergence of a religious market that operates on the principle of rational economics. Daoshi and believers are the sectors of supply and demand in this market. Daoshi make a profit by providing traditional religious ritual commodities, and villagers "purchase" religious ceremonies performed by Daoshi to fulfill religious needs, as well as various other needs. Rather than the imagined "purity" of religious behavior, the religious practices of Daoshi and villagers alike reveal a blend of the secular and the sacred. As the state's ideological grip on the citizenry continues to loosen, villagers are experiencing an unprecedented degree of religious needs.

The complexity in the practices of Zhanjiang Daoshi reflects the mixed motivations and strategic actions on both the supply and demand sides in religious activities. Does this phenomenon challenge the conventional wisdom of religious market theories? If this is a viable challenge, in what way can we adapt the existing theories to interpret diverse religious experiences?

After presenting a literature review, we propose a model of the religious market that considers dual preferences/strategies and apply it to a case study. We set forth three propositions. First, the religious preferences of consumers in the ritual market are not static. Consumers experience a transition from nonexistent to insatiable demand, and this is a reversible process. Second, granted that consumers have developed an appetite for specific religious practices, their preferences and strategies to pursue these are by no means unitary. Rather, we can observe a secular-sacred dual equilibrium in religious behavior. Third, in the same vein as consumer behavior, the ritual providers also reveal a dualism in their religious preferences and practices.

1   Literature Review and Analytical Frameworks

1.1   *Religious Market Theories: From Adam Smith to Acts of Faith*
The earliest theorization of the religious market is attributed to Adam Smith, who argued that a priest is governed by rational self-interest, and his goal is

to maximize economic self-interest.⁴ The priest, as the primary producer of religious products, generates income from either the voluntary donations of believers or the financial support of the state.⁵ The varying sources of income strongly influence the behavior of the priest. If his primary income is derived from voluntary donations, a church or temple will endeavor to maintain and strengthen the faith of the congregants, motivate conversions, and incentivize donations. All of these efforts result in the offering of better and higher-quality religious products. Conversely, if a temple relies largely on state sponsorship, the drive for excellence diminishes due to the lack of incentives to maximize self-interest or to survive. The priest becomes complacent as a result. Moreover, as the priest is a rational agent who seeks to maximize profit, he may engage in unfair competition, such as maligning competitors, deceiving believers, or allying with political powers in the hopes of monopolizing the religious market.⁶

The U.S.-based religious sociologists Rodney Stark and Roger Finke have developed a model based on a modified hypothesis of rational economic behavior. This theory extends the parameters of the religious agent's rational decisions. Stark and Finke state:

> *Within the limits of their information and understanding, restricted by available options, guided by their preferences and tastes, humans attempt to make rational choices.* ... Because their choices are *guided by their preferences and tastes.* Preferences and tastes define what it is that the individual finds rewarding or unrewarding. ... It acknowledges our capacity to find rewards in our dreams, hopes, loves, and ideals.⁷

Moreover, whereas the focus of Smith's analysis is the priest, Stark and Finke incorporate believers as analytical subjects and thus establish a model that

---

4   Adam Smith, *An Inquiry into the Nature and Causes of the Wealth of Nations* (Chicago: University of Chicago Press, 1977 [1904]); translated by Guo Dali and Wang Yanan as *Guomin caifu de xingzhi he yuanyin de yanjiu* (Beijing: The Commercial Press, 1997), 2:345–348. See also Laurence R. Iannaccone, "The Consequences of Religious Market Structure: Adam Smith and the Economics of Religion," *Rationality and Society* 3 (1991): 156–176; Liu Zhengfeng, "Lun yadang simi de zongjiao shichang lilun—jianlun zongjiao guanzhi de jingji jichu," *Shijie zongjiao yanjiu*, 2012.5: 1–7.
5   Smith, *An Inquiry*, 2:345–348.
6   Ibid.
7   Rodney Stark and Roger Finke, *Acts of Faith: Explaining the Human Side of Religion* (Berkeley: University of California Press, 2000), translated by Yang Fenggang as *Xinyang de faze—jieshi zongjiao zhi ren de fangmian* (Beijing: Zhongguo renmin daxue chubanshe, 2004), 37–38. Italics in original.

takes into account both the supply and demand sides in a market economy. They maintain that the religious economy consists of all religious activities in society, including the existing and potential markets of believers, one or more organizations that attract or retain believers, and also the various religious cultures that these organizations create. In this religious market, believers are rational consumers who calculate benefits and costs, and religious organizations and groups are firms that provide religious products.[8] Stark and Finke's model is built upon the premise that the believer's religious demands (preferences) are relatively stable, and so are the niches in the religious market. The role that religious firms play in the market is malleable over time. They seek to change religious policies to attract individuals who have different religious demands and to occupy different niches. These changes, in turn, shape the religious market at the macro level and affect its subsequent transformations.[9]

Since the 1970s, religious market theoretical propositions have undergone systematic revisions, and yet they have invited criticism on multiple fronts. Some critics argue that the hypothesis of the rational agent in the study of religious behavior conflates instrumental rationality with value rationality. Critics have argued that the calculation of cost and benefit central to the theory of rational choice only takes instrumental rationality into account. Only in a completely secular environment is a rational choice of religion possible.[10] Other scholars have indicated that the cost-benefit analysis oversimplifies the complexity of social relations and the fundamentals of a civilization, and that it neglects to consider the human desire for the transcendental and the search for the meaning of life that are intrinsic to any religious system.[11] Yet other scholars, drawing from Bourdieu, argue that human social behavior is not the product of subjective and rational calculation. Rather, it is the outcome of the interplay among habits, habitus, agency, and structure.[12]

---

8   Rodney Stark, "From Church-Sect to Religious Economies," in *The Sacred in a Post-Secular Age*, ed. Phillip E. Hammond (Berkeley: University of California Press, 1985), 139–149; Stark and Finke, *Acts of Faith*.

9   Rodney Stark and Laurence R. Iannaccone, "A Supply-Side Reinterpretation of the 'Secularization' of Europe," *Journal for the Scientific Study of Religion* 33.3 (1994): 230–252; Stark and Finke, *Acts of Faith*.

10 Steve Bruce, "Religion and Rational Choice: A Critique of Economic Explanations of Religious Behavior," *Sociology of Religion* 54.2 (1993): 193–205.

11 Fan Lizhu, "Xifang zongjiao lilun xia Zhongguo zongjiao yanjiu de kunjing," *Nanjing daxue xuebao (zhexue, renwen kexue, shehui kexue ban)*, 2009.2: 92–101; Fan Lizhu, "Xiandai zongjiao shi lixing xuanze de ma? Zhiyi zongjiao de lixing xuanze yanjiu fanshi," *Shehui* 6.9 (2008): 90–109.

12 Roland Robertson, "The Economization of Religion? Reflections on the Promise and Limitations of the Economic Approach," *Social Compass* 39 (1992): 147–157.

The second line of critique holds that Stark and his coauthors overemphasize the decisive role of the supply side in the religious market. In this "supply-side economics," the assumption of unchanging religious preferences is questionable. It treats believers as passive recipients of religious products, and thus does not consider the decision-making capability of individual believers. It also overlooks the influence of religious demands on individuals' religious choices.[13] Other critics challenge the validity of supply-side analysis. For instance, Li Xiangping points out that the model of religious economy implies an analysis of supply and demand. A focus on supply-side analysis is simply the prioritization of the more active and dominant role of religious firms. In the Chinese case, however, religious resources are absorbed into the (political) power structure. In a lopsided supply-and-demand relationship, there is little, if anything, that the supply side can do to dictate the religious market in a meaningful way.[14]

The third major line of criticism points out Stark's oversimplification of the dynamics between religious regulation and religious vitality. Stark and Finke state, "To the degree that religious economies are unregulated and competitive, overall levels of religious participation will be high."[15] Nevertheless, we cannot find in empirical research any support for a positive correlation between religious pluralism and religious participation; that is, religious regulation does not necessarily lower the level of religious activities.[16] Regulation is not an effective measure to control religious participation, nor does it dampen believers' enthusiasm. Regulation only creates the red, gray, and black religious markets that further complicate the landscape.[17] Suppression (mild suppression at a minimum) does not necessarily curb the vitality of religion; rather, it

---

13   Carl L. Bankston, "Rationality, Choice, and the Religious Economy: Individual and Collective Rationality in Supply and Demand," *Review of Religious Research* 45.2 (December 2003): 155–171; Fenggang Yang, "Religion in China under Communism: A Shortage Economy Explanation," *Journal of Church and State* 51.1 (2010): 3–33.

14   Li Xiangping and Yang Linxia, "Zongjiao, shehui, yu quanli guanxi—'zongjiao shichang lun' de shehuixue jiedu," *Huadong shifan daxue xuebao (zhexue shihui kexue ban)* 43.5 (2001): 1–7.

15   Stark and Finke, *Acts of Faith*, 201.

16   Mark Chaves and Philip S. Gorski, "Religious Pluralism and Religious Participation," *Annual Review of Sociology* 27 (2001): 261–281.

17   Fenggang Yang, "The Red, Black, and Gray Markets of Religion in China," *Sociological Quarterly* 47.1 (2006): 93–122. Translated and abridged by Yang Fenggang 杨凤岗 as "Zhongguo zongjiao de sanse shichang," *Zhongguo renmin daxue xuebao (shehui kexue ban)* 6 (2006): 41–47.

may generate unintended consequences that encourage the development of marginalized religious groups.[18]

As far as religious actors are concerned, we consider the value rationality in religious behavior as one of the dimensions in rationale calculation. Extended utility function does not exclude the actor's consideration for feelings or values. Likewise, field effect and individuality are not mutually exclusive. Unless we can prove that human behavior is dictated by the field and not by individual consciousness, we have to assume that behavior conforming to the demands of the field is the outcome of a complicated and rational decision-making process. It follows that applying the hypothesis of rational decision-making to the analysis of religious behavior is a viable exercise.

The model of religious economy is generally embraced by scholars. Some deem it to have replaced the Eurocentric "old paradigm" that is rooted in the theory of secularization.[19] This model was packaged as "religious market theory" when it was introduced into China as a universally applicable "new paradigm."[20] Scholars such as Graeme Lang, Selina Ching Chan, and Lars Ragvald have examined the economics of temples in China from the perspective of market competition and treated temples as active players in the religious market.[21] In this framework, the alignment between the temples' promotional strategies and the believers' religious enthusiasm is indicative of the success or failure of the temples.

However, some scholars question whether a model of religious economy based on Western experience is a suitable interpretive tool for Chinese conditions. For one thing, the theory of religious economy effectively articulates the patterns of transformation of exclusive religious systems without taking into account their inclusive counterparts. This approach is problematic when applied to the multitude of inclusive religious systems as well as pluralistic religious affiliations that are prevalent in Asia.[22] Additionally, the religious

---

18 Lu Yunfeng, "Kunan yu zongjiao zengzhang: guanzhi de feiyuqi jieguo," *Shehui*, 2010.4: 200–216.
19 R. Stephen Warner, "Work in Progress toward a New Paradigm for the Sociological Study of Religion in the United States," *American Journal of Sociology* 98.5 (1993): 1044–1095.
20 Lin Qiaowei, "Yang Fenggang boshi tan zongjiao shehuixue de fanshi zhuanxing," *Zongjiaoxue yanjiu* 3 (2003): 140–141.
21 Graeme Lang, Chan Selina Ching, and Ragvald Lars, "Temples and the Religious Economy," *Interdisciplinary Journal of Research on Religion* 1 (2005): 1–27.
22 Lu Yunfeng, "Chaoyue jiduzongjiao shehuixue—jianlun zongjiao shichang lilun zai huaren shehui de shiyongxing wenti," *Shehuixue yanjiu*, 2008.5: 81–97; Liang Jingwen, Chen Qian, Luo Si, and Chen Ruigang, "Minjian simiao yu Zhongguo zongjiao jingji—dui zongjiao jingji lilun de tantao," *Shijie zongjiao wenhua*, 2010.2: 21–26; Huang Feijun, "Zongjiao

economy model focuses on institutions and participation in organized religion, leaving little room for noninstitutionalized religion and individualized practices.[23]

1.2 Malleable Dual Preferences and the "Generic Practice of Faith" Analytical Model

During our fieldwork, we observed that Daoshi have gradually begun to exhibit the characteristics of suppliers of ritual commodities. At the same time, when faced with divine powers, villagers have shifted from a fearful and respectable attitude toward a tendency to simply conform to customary practices. In the past, Daoist practices in Zhanjiang revealed the characteristics of a "dormant religious market," while today's practices seem to have taken on a more explicit and transactional character. This study adopts the analytical approach of religious market theory: we treat believers as consumers of religious commodities and the religious institution or religious specialists as the suppliers. The basic assumption of this approach is that believers and religious specialists exhibit "rational choice" behavior—that is, both the supply and demand sides seek to maximize utility and benefits. Our approach is different from Stark and Finke's, as the latter overlook the "secular" behavior of the "sacred" individuals who were at the core of Adam Smith's analysis, and therefore Stark and Finke's paradigm severs the connection between religious practices and generic practices of faith. We propose to modify the existing religious market theory and suggest a new, comprehensive analytical framework.

1.2.1 Believers (Consumers)

In their construction of the religious economy/market model, Stark and Finke specify that even though believers have distinctive and varying preferences, the demand for religion remains stable in the long run, and religious change is the outcome of changes on the supply side.[24] In other words, "religious firms" offer various commodities to attract as many believers as possible. Believers, in turn, wish to obtain the most satisfying religious product at as low a cost as possible. As conversions (shifts across or within religious traditions) are quite commonplace in real life, Stark and Finke assume an intrinsic hierarchy in the

---

jingji lilun de xiandu—yi Zhongguo Taiwan diqu zongjiao shijian weili," *Shijie zongjiao wenhua*, 2013.1: 22–28.

23 Li Xiangping and Chen Bin, "Xiangqianxing de gonggong zongjiao—chuantong Zhongguo de zhengjiao guanxi zhi shehuixue jiedu," *Shanghai daxue xuebao (shehui kexue ban)*, 2006.4: 83–89; Fenggang Yang, "Red, Black, and Gray Markets."

24 Stark and Finke, *Acts of Faith*, 193.

believers' religious preferences.[25] For instance, "highly stable" religious preferences refer to individuals' fundamental preference for religion, which is not swayed by religious commodities. The eventual religious choice is contingent upon preferences as well as many other factors, including secular considerations. Therefore, extended utility function is a viable tool of analysis when applying the religious market theory to case studies.

Our case study of Zhanjiang priests suggests that attributing a stable, fundamental preference for religion to all believers is not a solid premise for analysis. In fact, there is vast diversity within the body of believers who are passionate participants in Daoist rituals. Some of them deeply believe in the folk religion that Daoshi represent and expect that their participation in rituals in service to the sacred powers will be reciprocated. Some even allow religious texts to dictate their lives and destinies as well as those of their extended family members. There are also ostensibly devout believers who self-identify as atheists. They explain such contradictory behavior in terms of conformity to customs and societal expectations, bending to cultural traditions rather than religious teachings or personal preferences. Yet other believers reveal a high degree of self-awareness as secular consumers of rituals. These individuals, who have little or no attachment to the specific religious or cultural preferences of the wider community, either "do as others do" to avoid the stigma of nonconformity or have ulterior, secular or economic motives for their religious participation. The diversity of believers illuminates a fundamental issue: consumers of rituals may have compound (dual) fundamental preferences, and those in different religious markets exhibit varied as well as variously distributed preferences.[26]

Consumers of ritual commodities may stand at different points on a secular–sacred continuum, depending on their preferences. Those who stand closer to the sacred end have a greater tendency of displaying religious preferences (fundamental preferences), and they are Stark and Finke's main subjects. Those who stand closer to the secular end of the continuum may reveal fundamental preferences such as "mysticism," "internalized local regulations," and "small-group norms" to a lesser and lesser degree, with "instrumental-rational

---

25   Ibid., 114.
26   This pattern of distribution of preferences is at once related to and different from Stark and Finke's perception of stable market niches. Both propositions are based on the believers' varying religious needs. Yet, we argue that the preference is, at its core, a blend of secular and sacred elements, rather than a manifestation of the tension between sacred ideals and social norms.

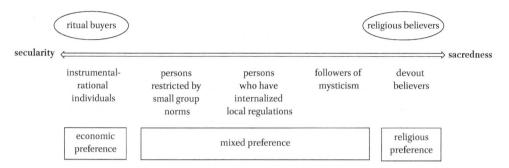

FIGURE 10.1   The secular–sacred continuum of religious consumers, an expansion of Stark and Finke's category of "believers" in their model of religious markets

individuals" marking the secular extreme of the continuum.[27] Over the course of the continuum, generic faith/belief transitions into religious belief. Namely, the transition from the left end to the right end in Figure 10.1 represents the emergence of the consciousness of a consumer of religious commodities (a believer). In fact, depending on the circumstances, a consumer may march from the secular in the direction of the sacred (for example, after a major life-altering event) or in the reverse direction (for instance, under the impact of governmental regulation or modernization). An individual may occupy different spaces on the continuum in different temporal contexts.

Individuals who stand firmly at either the secular or sacred end are extremely rare (they may be motivated by a singular preference such as unadulterated self-interest or the pursuit of holiness). The vast majority of consumers reveal varying degrees of the blending of dual preferences. Their purchasing behavior, it follows, is a means to fulfilling dual needs. It is worth noting that religious fundamental preferences are subject to change. As consumers interact with religious firms and make decisions about religious commodities, the internal balance between the two ends of the continuum is subject to change as well.

Contrary to the endogenous quality of this secular-sacred fundamental preference (possessing the endogenous quality does not preclude the possibility of change; it only makes the preferences stable), the consumer's decision-making can be swayed by external and structural (i.e., environmental) conditions. Therefore, the association between decision and preference is unstable. On the one hand, consumers with varying preferences may arrive at similar

---

27   These individuals are not motivated by internalized norms or peer pressure but by profit alone.

decisions. An ultra-secular consumer, for instance, may not care about the sacred nature of rituals, but he or she may exhibit an enthusiasm for high-quality rituals in order to satisfy the expectations of the immediate community. On the other hand, consumers with shared preferences may make divergent decisions. For example, consumers who have the same degree of sacred preferences may exhibit varying degrees of interest in rituals depending on their respective social status or educational level.

1.2.2   Ecclesiastics or Religious Organizations (Suppliers)

Stark and Finke do not explicitly discuss the preferences of religious firms in *Acts of Faith*. However, they view suppliers as the main drivers of change in the religions market.[28] A growth-minded religious firm, they explain, actively engages in product development and dissemination to attract believers. By the same token, a disengaged religious firm ends up withdrawing from the market due to a lack of innovative energy. We infer from that position that the classical religious market theory operates on the assumption of an underlying hierarchy of supplier preferences. The supplier of religious products possesses a singular and relatively stable fundamental preference (namely, to increase the influence of religion and the number of believers), and secular factors are integral in the decision-making process.[29]

Taking the reform and opening up of the early 1980s as a major watershed in the development of the religious market in China, the "marketization" of Zhanjiang Daoshi offers ample counterevidence against the above assumptions. Daoshi have the dual identity of religious specialists and members of the village community. Their interaction with villagers can be described as "gift exchange." Despite their economic gain, Daoshi have taken pride in their reputation and their sacred status as "guardians" of the community. As the market economy continues to flourish, secular preferences in the form of economic gain have taken a stronger hold on the Daoshi community, turning Daoshi from figurative suppliers of religious commodities into literal sellers of rituals. The expansion of the influence of religion is no longer a singular and stable preference. Expanding the believer base has become a means to foster revenue growth. Some Daoshi even self-identify as atheists.

It follows that the suppliers of ritual products can be differentiated along the secular-sacred continuum. The providers who stand closer to the sacred

---

28   Stark and Finke, *Acts of Faith*, 193.
29   There are plenty of interesting examples in this area. For instance, churches possess and manage large amounts of assets. Yet, they claim that the wealth accumulated is meant for investing in religious activities in the future rather than for the pursuit of profit.

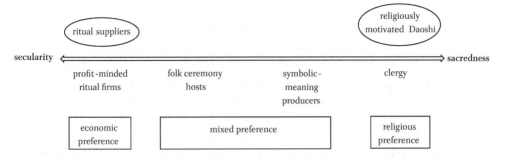

FIGURE 10.2 The secular–sacred continuum of religious providers, an expansion of Stark and Finke's category of "suppliers" in their model of religious economies/markets

end are more likely to be religiously motivated suppliers (they are the subjects of Stark and Finke). Those who stand closer to the secular end of the continuum are likely to be middle-of-the-road "symbolic-meaning producers" or "folk ceremony hosts." Those standing at the secular end would be the solely profit-minded "ritual firms." The suppliers who stand in the midsection of the continuum reveal various combinations of the dual secular-sacred preferences.[30] In each combination, sacred preferences are manifested by the spread of religious teachings or agendas determined by religious tenets. Secular preferences, on the other hand, are manifested by interest in nonreligious benefits, including economic, social, and cultural capital. Moreover, the sacred end of the continuum also illustrates the transition from generic faith/belief into religious belief. The movement from left to right in Figure 10.2 demonstrates the supplier's growth in self-consciousness.

As in the case of the consumer, preference is not the sole determining factor in the supplier's decision-making. The supplier, likewise, takes the broader environment (the composition of the believers, as well as institutional and structural factors) into consideration. Suppliers who share similar preferences do not necessarily adopt similar strategies, and those with divergent preferences may arrive at similar conclusions. Take a profit-minded supplier of religious commodities, for example. When faced with a consumer body that has low sacred (religious) preferences in an environment with considerable socioeconomic disparity, the supplier may not be motivated to promote the sacredness of rituals or may not be interested in the number of believers. Instead, the supplier may target a specific group of consumers with high economic values. By the same token, when the consumer body largely consists of devout believers and

---

[30] Arguably, the two preferences are irreplaceable for certain suppliers. They also have a bottom line for each preference. The same applies to consumers' behavior.

experiences relatively little socioeconomic disparity, the supplier may adopt a policy as a ritual firm would—a strategy that prioritizes the dissemination of the sacredness of religion and the expansion of the consumer body.

This line of thought deviates from Stark and Finke's analysis of religious firms in three respects. First, their interpretive model does not concern the divergent sacred preferences of the ritual suppliers, which excludes those standing on the left end of the continuum from the analysis. Second, in their examination of religious firms, Stark and Finke neglect the specificities and internal compositions of their preferences. They overlook the fact that the religious firms possess dual or even multiple preferences. Third, Stark and Finke conflate the preferences and decisions of the religious firms (including the average ritual providers). Sacred/religious preferences can be satisfied by other means than growing the number of believers, and it is possible that any decision to expand the believer base is the product of secular preferences.

1.3 From Religion to the Generic Faith/Belief Market Analytical Model

Both the supply and demand sides in Stark and Finke's analytical model lean on the sacred end of the continuum, i.e., the religious market. They further develop a market transition model that is predicated upon this assumption, as well as a series of propositions.[31] Our approach extends Stark and Finke's religious market model to the examination of generic faith/belief without sacrificing the cohesion of Stark and Finke's interpretive framework.

On both the supply and demand sides, the secular-sacred preferences varies in different social contexts. Suppliers may face consumer decisions in the form of conversion or reaffiliation. They may also witness the evolution of consumers' religious preferences, be they a newly emerging, unprecedented preference or a progression from weak to strong preferences. Consumers, likewise, may be exposed to a variety of recruitment strategies motivated by sacred/religious goals, while witnessing the decay or purification of religious organizations. These ostensibly random and arbitrary developments seem to follow an identifiable pattern of gradual transition. A case in point is the revival of religion in rural China after the reform and opening up. There was not a sudden surge of religious activities after a period of suppression and dormancy. Instead, we can observe an intensification of sacredness that has journeyed through intermediary phases such as folk religion.[32]

---

31 Stark and Finke, *Acts of Faith*, 193.
32 On closer examination, we may discover that it is impossible to overcome this middle ground. One may even have to backtrack in the transition. This is the effect of the constant negotiation between modernizing forces and the pursuit of sacredness.

This process of transformation is closely associated with the social changes that took place in China during the mid-twentieth century. The situation in China is different from the United States and in the Western world generally, in that the latter has never experienced a religious vacuum caused by a state ideology. Chinese idiosyncrasies render this particular kind of religious market a blind spot in classical theories.[33] Scholars who emphasize the impact of government regulation argue that a market of free competition—the basic assumption of religious market theory—does not exist in China, as both the supply and demand sides are integrated into the existing (political) power structure. However, a rejection of religious market theories as such may not be beneficial to our endeavor to establish a new interpretive model. We ask the following questions: Faced with varying degrees and conditions of regulation, what are the patterns of movement, for both the supply and demand sides, along the continuum? Once the two sides have identified their preferences, how will each determine its corresponding strategies? Finally, in what ways will these strategies affect the market in general? These questions align closely with the parameters of a dual-preference analysis.

Analysis of secular-sacred dual preferences helps bridge the gap between religious market theories and the theory of secularization. The theory of secularization competes directly with market theories. It draws conclusions from the Western experience, stating that modernization inevitably results in religious pluralism, which provides the conditions for a market. In this market environment, religious institutions become venues of transaction, religion becomes a commodity, and a large amount of religious activities come under the dictates of market economic principles. Pluralism leads to competition, which motivates churches to modify their theological tenets and create new products tailored to market demands.

2   Overview of the Case Study

We conducted fieldwork in Zhanjiang, Guangdong, which encompasses several villages in Xiashan 霞山 and Mazhang 麻章 districts, including Nanshan 南山, Xiatianzai 下田仔, Shitou 石头, Baoman 宝满, and Xiling 西岭. These villages were chosen because, first of all, the Daoshi who reside in them have established solid

---

[33]   This is the rationale for our references to consumers of rituals and ritual/sacred commodities, instead of believers and religious products.

social networks and professional connections. They have become the most prominent Daoshi in the area and have practically monopolized the local ritual market. These villages border Zhanjiang's urban center as well as the harbor. Daoshi and villagers alike are directly affected by urbanization and modernization in terms of their thoughts and behavior. Such influence is revealed in the divergent and pluralistic pursuits of sacred or secular preferences. This is an ideal subject for an analysis of the complex behavioral patterns in the religious economy.

The main subject of this study is the Daoshi company centered on Wubo 武伯, the current president of the Daoist Association in Zhanjiang. We interviewed Daoshi and believers alike and participated in religious activities conducted by Daoshi. Our study focuses especially on the ways in which Zhanjiang Daoshi manage their ritual businesses and interact with believers in both the religious and economic realms.

In the early 1980s, Wubo, together with a few other young men from Daoshi households, started his apprenticeship under the tutelage of an elderly Daoshi in Nanliu 南柳 village. This group of Daoshi formed the first network of a new generation of Daoshi in Zhanjiang after the reform and opening up of China. Wubo's senior family members were skillful at preserving their trade during the Cultural Revolution. Consequently, Wubo has access to a corpus of major Daoist rites and has become the only Daoshi in the younger generation who knows how to perform major rituals of purification (*zhaishi* 斋事). He started a company in his hometown of Nanliu. For the efficient division of labor, a company requires at least eight members. Wubo's fellow apprentices, Zhubo 珠伯, Aibo 矮伯, and Qiangshu 强叔, were recruited. As the business continued to expand, Wubo further recruited a Daoshi friend, Chengshu 程叔, into the company and accepted a few disciples from both within and outside of the village. The first highly specialized Daoshi company to be established during the reform and opening up thus emerged in Zhanjiang. The second generation of Daoshi began to join the company from 2000 onward, making the company the largest Huoju Daoshi troupe in greater Zhanjiang. Figure 10.3 indicates the personal connections among three generations of Daoshi who belong to this company. Rectangles represent Daoshi and apprentices with strong connections to the founder, Wubo, while ovals indicate those with weaker connections. The dark gray shading for Biaoye 彪爷 distinguishes him as growing up before 1949, light gray shading marks persons from the generation that grew up between 1949 and the reform era (late 1970s), and unshaded shapes indicate the most recent generation of Daoshi and apprentices, who grew up in the reform era.

Members of this company (they operate as both independent entities and members of a troupe) dominate the ritual market in the surrounding urban and rural areas. Wubo is by far the central and most influential figure. He has established steady sources of revenue throughout Guangdong, and at one

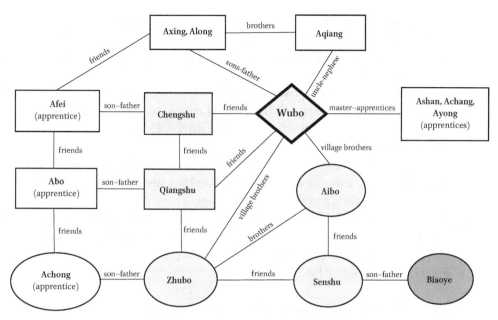

FIGURE 10.3   Personal connections among three generations of Daoshi in Zhanjiang

point his business extended to other Chinese provinces and even beyond China's borders. Below are the core members of the company:

1. Wubo (b. 1960): head of household of the most prominent Huoju Daoshi family in Nanshan village; current president of the Daoist Association, Zhanjiang
2. Zhubo (b. 1955): Huoju Daoshi in Nanshan; member of Wubo's Daoshi company
3. Aibo (b. 1956): Huoju Daoshi in Xiatianzai; member of Wubo's Daoshi company
4. Qiangshu (b. 1963): Huoju Daoshi in Baoman; member of Wubo's Daoshi company
5. Senshu (b. 1965): Huoju Daoshi in Shitou; an independent agent aspiring to form a company

3   From "Guardians of the Village" to "Providers of Ritual Commodities"

Prior to the reform and opening up, Daoshi in Zhanjiang regarded themselves as the guardians of the village community. Believers in the village provided Daoshi with economic support for the latter's apprenticeship and induction.

To reciprocate, Daoshi offered villagers semi-complimentary religious ritual services. Since the 1980s, as the overall standard of living has risen and traditional culture in the broadest sense has been restored, villagers have also been more eager to invest more in ritual services. As a result, Daoshi income has also increased. A set of unspoken and yet binding rules regarding fees for ritual services began to take shape, in the place of the convention of gift exchange. Daoshi have gradually reoriented toward the market and taken on the identity of the supplier of ritual commodities.

Although Daoshi outlooks and practices have become commercialized, they have maintained a degree of reverence for and submission to the sacredness of rituals. Thus, their preferences and strategic action reveal a secular-sacred hybridism. In what follows, we examine the profession of Daoshi in this context and analyze Daoshi's fee structure, business development, and the types of ritual products offered, as well as their concerns for reputation, benefit preference, and views on religion.

3.1 The Commercialization of the Daoshi Profession

The fee structure and services offered best illuminate the commercialization and market orientation of the Daoshi profession. Convention has it that a Daoshi does not demand monetary compensation in specific amounts for his ritual performances. Villagers typically chip in and offer the Daoshi a cash gift for his services. The specific amount of the gift is determined by both customary practice and the villagers' abilities. Villagers may, alternatively, gift some of the sacrificial offerings to the Daoshi as compensation for his service. In the 1980s, a Daoshi typically received four or five RMB (less than one USD) for a funerary rite. At the turn of this century, the going fee for such a ritual was around 100 RMB (over 12 USD), which was comparable to the previous cost when relative income levels are taken into account. As the preparation for rituals usually cost a significant amount, Daoshi typically did not profit from the ritual services. They held the belief that ritual services ought to be voluntary and that performing a full ritual ceremony was "doing good for the villagers." Because of this, it was common for Daoshi to derive income from another job.

However, as income from ritual services has surged exponentially since 2000, the Daoshi compensation scheme has shifted from "no charge" to "nonnegotiable." Clients have also begun to break with convention and ask Daoshi about their fees for services rendered, even though the unspoken rules would discourage this. Upon receiving an inquiry, a Daoshi will quote a fee, taking into account both convention and the scope of the service. The client typically refrains from negotiating the price, as believers usually consider rituals performed for the family to be priceless and think that bargaining disrespects the gods.

Daoshi, as "guardians," tend to provide their services in their villages of residence. The Daoshi living in neighboring villages are either fellow apprentices or business partners. They also respect one another's effective spheres of influence and refuse to break a tacit code of conduct. In the event that a Daoshi is invited to serve an out-of-village client, he would seek permission from the local Daoshi before taking the request. Likewise, out of consideration for either personal relationships or convenience, villagers tend to invite local Daoshi to satisfy their ritual needs. When both the demand and supply sides are bound by interpersonal connections, Daoshi business operations are stable and well-defined.

Changes have started to occur, however. Daoshi have begun to expand their territories, resulting in fierce competition. For one thing, the accelerated mobility of modern society has altered the structure of rural communities. The strong ties in villages are dissolving, and villagers are gaining greater liberty in appropriating weak ties (cost or quality) in their search for better, more qualified Daoshi. Likewise, as income from ritual services has increased, Daoshi have also become more motivated to solicit business or even seek dominance in the field. In villages where the profession of Daoshi has died out due to strict regulation, competition among individual Daoshi or companies of Daoshi has surfaced, operating in a new, profit-driven landscape that is a drastic departure from the established conventions in traditional village communities. In fact, we can observe the sprouting of divisive forces within the successful Daoshi company under discussion here.

3.2 *The Commercialization of Rituals*

Daoshi services touch all aspects of village life. From weddings to funerals, from overcoming mundane mishaps, like a missing chicken or a sick pig, to celebrating major family and clan events, such as blessing an ancestral hall or laying the foundation for one, Daoshi are involved in believers' entire life cycles. And yet, a significant number of traditional rituals have been sidelined in the modern Daoshi's repertoire. What have risen in an unprecedented manner are demands closely associated with the market economy.

Generally speaking, the main services that Zhanjiang Daoshi provide include *qingzhai* 清斋 for temples, *youzhai* 幽斋 at funerals,[34] *yinhun* 引魂 (summoning of souls), contracts for dealings with the gods and spirits, prayers

---

34   *Qingzhai* is a ritual for the living, such as the consecration of statues of deities or rituals of blessing performed at major festivals or on feast days. *Youzhai* is the ritual for the dead performed at a funeral. The latter is rather complex and requires the service of a Daoshi troupe.

for blessings and fulfilling vows, and selecting names for children. The most sought-after ritual in recent years is the "contract of sale" (买卖券).[35] This is analogous to a title deed but is used for symbolic transactions with the deities on behalf of both the living and the dead. There are two prevalent forms for contracts of sale in Zhanjiang. One is *yinqi* 阴契, a contract of sale for a burial site. The other is *yangqi* 阳契, a contract of sale for the construction of a house, temple, or ancestral hall. These contracts are drawn up using standard printed forms. Below is an example of the content of a *yangqi* contract of sale.

> Mr. A, resident of Zhanjiang, Guangdong, the People's Republic of China, purchases the property and land of Mr. A's predecessor for the construction of a private residence, and hereby makes a contract with the spirits of the ancestors in the presence of the celestial patrons of the property. All parties present are in agreement on the purchase price of 3,500 RMB [540 USD], paid in full on the ___ day of this month.
>
> With the celestial patrons of the property bearing witness, Mr. A and his predecessor Mr. B enter a legal agreement. This contract of sale affirms a voluntary transaction. Any revocation of the agreement will incur divine retribution.
>
> Scribe: Luo Yin
> Agent: Dongfang tudi
> Cashier: Mr. C
> Witness: Mr. D
>
> With reverence,
> Spiritual petition written in *shengcidong* 圣慈洞 style submitted to heavenly order, on ___ day ___ month ___ year
>
> Also present: Priest E
> Witnessed by: Altar master Kanghuang zhenjun

The rationale for the ritual of the contract of sale is this: in addition to completing the transfer of property ownership in the here and now, it is imperative to reach a parallel agreement with the spirits and deities in charge of the property. A sacred contract detailing the sacred land ownership is signed

---

[35] This is also known as *maidi quan* 买地券 in other regions of China. See Chen Jinguo, "'Maidi quan' xisu de kaoxianxue yanjiu—mintai diqu de shili," *Minsu yanjiu*, 2008.1: 129–164.

to avoid disputes in the future. A Daoshi plays the role of arbiter or supervisor in a worldly transaction and facilitates the communication between men and gods or men and spirits. Because villagers have expanded their geographic reach of property ownership and the varieties of property that can be held has increased, the ritual of contract of sale has also been extended to other aspects of commercial activities and is not limited to the places that supernatural powers normally inhabit (real property). Considering questions of property rights, it is possible that the contract of sale resorts to sacred powers to make up for the inadequacy of a worldly contract. Viewed as an innovation, the contract of sale is nothing less than an effective strategy that Daoshi have appropriated to expand their businesses. Our fieldwork did not generate sufficient information regarding the history of the contract of sale. Nevertheless, its practice, application, and function in everyday life suggest that this ritual mixes religious belief and market interests.

3.3 *Pluralistic Preferences of Daoshi: Economic Gain, Worldly Reputation, and Religious Belief*

Between the sacred and secular ends of the spectrum, Daoshi preferences range from economic gain, worldly reputation, and religious belief. Economic gain and worldly reputation are not isolated variables; rather, they are intertwined and exert influence over each other. Economic gain for Daoshi is contingent upon the volume of business. Factors that affect a Daoshi's reputation include his moral character, professional qualifications, and the effectiveness of ritual performances. Specifically, moral character concerns a Daoshi's personal conduct and ethics, which reflects his standing and social connections in a village community. Professional qualifications are objective indicators, such as a Daoshi's ranking, professional history, and his level of education and learning. A Daoshi's reputation rests directly on his effectiveness in ritual performances. Spectators at rituals make instantaneous, subjective judgments upon witnessing the flow of a Daoshi's chanting and his eloquence and rhythm, as well as his facial expressions and bodily movements.

Preferences vary widely in different temporal contexts and under different personal circumstances. Indeed, they reflect the drastic changes in contemporary China. In an era when ritual performances incurred little economic gain, Daoshi were primarily motivated by contact with the sacred in rituals and by the level of authority that accompanied a good reputation in a rural community. The ranking of a Daoshi implied comparable supernatural power and sacredness. Thus, Daoshi were eager to achieve a higher ranking as a form of self-fulfillment. Moreover, high-ranking Daoshi were more capable of resolving wide-ranging and complicated matters for villagers than their average counterparts, which also helped strengthen their reputation in the community. Reputation was the source of Daoshi authority in rural communities.[36] A Daoshi can increase his economic gain exponentially by strategically elevating his reputation or even by manufacturing a good reputation. The fundamental principle of the Daoshi profession is to strike a delicate balance between the cost of acquiring reputation and the satisfaction of consumers.

Daoshi views on religion have changed along with the commercialization of their practices. Many have begun to abandon day jobs and perform rituals full-time, which is a departure from the conventional practices of Huoju Daoshi. The religious significance of the altar has diminished as a result, and the Daoshi profession is moving toward the secular end of the continuum. Villagers of an older generation have remarked that Daoshi used to take rituals seriously, showing the appropriate reverence, and that they viewed their ecclesiastical status as the ultimate personal, as well as familial, honor. Although Daoshi have secularized and standardized the ritual process, they have not completely abandoned their deference to the sacred in everyday life, nor have they forgotten their core values. Some of the business-savvy Daoshi continue to believe, as one informant related to us, that "it is important to be reverent before the gods; regardless of your position or power, one must be diligent and cautious with their words when kneeling in front of the gods."

To be sure, room remains for the negotiation between professionalization and sacredness, as the prospects of economic gain in the lucrative ritual market are directly challenging certain taboos. The Daoist tradition forbids Daoshi from setting eyes on the remains of the deceased, as it is believed that the negative forces surrounding the cadaver cancel out the Daoshi's spiritual power. However, the state's reform of funerary practices requires the immediate cremation of the deceased in a mortuary. Contact with the dead is inevitable in a mortuary or a funeral home, and thus Daoshi have avoided the mortuary market despite the numerous business opportunities it offers.

Farmers living on the immediate outskirts of cities have come to replace Daoshi, providing simple and yet costly rituals for the dead in the service of surviving family members. Daoshi are ambivalent about this development. On the one hand, they accuse the amateurs of fraud and deception. As one Daoshi explained, "Playing the cymbals for a couple of hours is not how you complete the full set of rites, let alone do it right." On the other hand, quite a few Daoshi desire to break into a market that remains taboo and thus closed to professional Daoshi. To overcome the taboo, Daoshi have proposed two expedient strategies. The first is to perform the rite for the dead in a different space than the crematorium.

---

36   Li Xiangping and Li Siming, "Xinyang yu minjian quanwei de jiangou."

Daoshi would lead the surviving family members as they carried the ashes of the deceased back home and then perform the traditional rites. The ashes would then be buried or brought back to the mortuary afterward. The second is to carve out a designated space in the mortuary where Daoshi can perform rituals while safely isolated from the dead. This proposal has yet to be put into practice.

3.4   Beyond the Market: The Establishment of Political Legitimacy

Wubo and his associates' remarks indicate new developments in the relationship between Zhanjiang Daoshi and the state's official policy. Indeed, traditional culture has gradually been restored since the reform and opening up. In the early 1990s, however, the state had not granted full liberty to folk religious activities; it repeatedly issued orders to demolish local ancestral halls and clear out statues of deities, and it banned religious activities outside of the confines of temples.[37] The practices of Daoshi were not exempt. Wubo once reminisced that, in 1985, the secretary of the Municipal Political and Legal Affairs Commission accused him of promoting superstition and launched several investigations against him. He managed to evade the investigations through the influence of personal connections. In the 1990s, there were still some constraints, but the situation has much improved since 2005. Afterward, the provincial government in Guangdong pushed for cities to form religious associations, and the Zhanjiang Daoist Association was created in 2011. Wubo was the most prominent and influential figure among the local Daoshi and was elected president of the association in 2013.

Formalization was Wubo's goal. As president, he pushed for construction projects, efficient personnel management, and the reform of traditions. Through these initiatives, Wubo hoped to remove the stigma of "feudal superstition" from Daoshi and demand political legitimacy for his profession. First, the association plans to build a new Zhengyi temple on the outskirts of Zhanjiang.[38] The funds will be raised from government subsidies and through corporate as well as private sponsorships. The new temple will serve as the venue for rituals and religious instruction. But the officers of the association also believe that a regular religious site will be invested with the necessary symbolic significance. Specifically, they believe that a religious group based on a formal temple will appear legitimate to the government. Second, the association plans to create a registry of all Daoshi in the municipality of Zhanjiang and recruit them to join the association.

---

37   Zhu Haibin, "Minjian xinyang—Zhongguo zui zhongyao de zongjiao chuantong," *Jianghan luntan*, 2009.3: 68–74; Gu Guanfu and Long Feijun, "Yiwei Shanghai chengpai daoshi de koushushi—Gu Guanfu daozhang fangtan lu," *Shilin*, 2010.1: 94–99.
38   On the Zhengyi sect, see n. 2 above.

Membership for the hitherto unorganized Daoshi suggests legitimacy, and the association facilitates networking opportunities and partnerships. All members are required to pay an annual fee.[39] Finally, the association hopes to reform the induction process by introducing a dual certifying procedure, combining the bestowal of the Daoist register (*lu* 箓) and an official seal (*yin* 印).

Traditionally, an aspiring Daoshi in Zhanjiang would receive a stamp of approval after he successfully performed a major ritual, symbolizing his induction into the profession. The Chinese Daoist Association follows a different procedure: it fills out a limited quantity of applications on behalf of Daoshi for enrollment in the official registries of temples throughout the country (such as Longhu Shan 龙虎山 in Jiangxi). Although the customary stamp of approval is sufficient to legitimize Daoshi practices locally, Wubo remains concerned about the obstacles that confront Daoshi outside of Zhanjiang.[40] That is why Wubo not only invested a handsome sum of 200,000 RMB (over 30,000 USD) in his eldest son's induction—his first ritual performance—but, through connections, he also helped his son acquire official approval. Wubo is convinced that this is an inevitable path for all Daoshi in Zhanjiang.

The thriving ritual market directs the market orientation of the Daoshi fee structure. Additionally, the business is branching out of Daoshi home villages into neighboring communities. As Daoshi compete for business and adopt varying strategies, their status as guardians of the village has gradually given way to the role of suppliers of ritual commodities. The Daoshi's own reverence for the sacred has diminished, but the rules guiding their belief have not been completely replaced by instrumental, economic considerations. Rather, their everyday practices reveal a blend of religious as well as economic considerations, along with the pursuit of political legitimacy.

4   From "Sponsor of Religion" to "Buyer of Ritual Commodities": The Secularization of Believers

Similar to the transformation of Daoshi attitudes to the sacred, the villagers' outlooks on religion have also been desacralized. The worship of ancestors and

---

39   We are unable to provide details about membership fees. It is said that it costs regular members 700 RMB (about 100 USD) annually. Council members and higher-ranking officers would pay an even higher fee.
40   Interestingly, Wubo was unable to name the specific obstacles. He spoke in generic terms, stating that only those Daoshi endowed with official recognition could practice with legitimacy.

local spirits or deities used to be the primary form of folk belief in Zhanjiang. Daoshi were the celebrants of communal sacrificial ceremonies and took part in major events in the villagers' life cycles. Villagers were the major fundraisers and sponsors of Daoshi induction ceremonies. They have long assumed the role of sponsors of religion.

In the modern era, the spread of scientific reasoning, new political movements after the foundation of the PRC, and education informed by new ideologies have all considerably impacted the beliefs and religious practices of villagers. What believers used to consider as natural in their religious views has gradually given way to secularization, inching toward the positions of "mysticism" or "internalized local customs." The social structure has undergone drastic change following reform and opening up, and high mobility has accelerated the disintegration of traditional rural village communities. Believers have become less homogenous; the identity of "consumer of ritual commodities" has emerged, grown, and finally replaced the previous positions. For the majority of ritual consumers, a hybrid secular-sacred preference now dominates their purchasing behavior. The trajectory that believers of Zhanjiang Daoshi have followed illustrates vividly the complexity of these altered religious preferences in the past three decades.

4.1 *From "Gift Exchange" to the Consumption of Rituals*
In parallel with the transformation of the Daoshi fee structure as a ritual market came into being, villagers have transitioned from "gift exchange" to purchasing rituals. In the days when the village community was the center of life, villagers collectively sponsored the Daoshi induction ceremonies, essentially placing a deposit toward future ritual consumption. Thereafter, as members of the community, villagers would be entitled to reap the benefit of any blessing that Daoshi garnered on behalf of the entire village. When individuals or households hired Daoshi for ritual services, villagers typically prepared a "red envelope" (in cash or in kind), whose specific monetary value was determined by convention and ability, as a token of gratitude. The significance of the red envelope did not rest on its monetary value, but on the intangible value it represented.

As the ritual market has matured, villagers have come to embrace their roles as consumers of ritual commodities. Their attitudes have also become increasingly mixed and ambivalent. Paradoxically, stimulated by the general revival of traditional culture, villagers embraced their roles as believers, and a revival of religion followed. This can be seen as a return to sacredness. At the same time, believers have chosen the most secular of all means to fulfill their sacred needs, that is, transactions in the market. The blend of religious and market orientations is revealed, first and foremost, in the villagers' "no bargaining" principle. For fear of divine retribution, villagers dare not treat dealings with Daoshi as typical market transactions. As one interviewee explained:

> We dare not bargain with Daoshi because of our deference to the dead. The deceased deserve our respect, and we cannot live with the disappointment of our deceased family members. Money is no object when it comes to serving the dead. There is no negotiation in the Daoshi profession. We pay however much a Daoshi quotes. We do this out of respect and reverence for the deceased. If you overpaid, the Daoshi would not refund you. For example, say the market price is 10,000 RMB (1,500 USD), but you paid 20,000, the Daoshi will not refund you the extra 10,000. The more ethical Daoshi would tell you not to overpay.

The hybrid considerations are also revealed in the bidding process. Although villagers typically avoid negotiating with Daoshi, they find ways to weigh costs against benefits. Villagers typically learn and compare prices through their social networks. They look for the best person to perform the ritual, at a fee that falls into an acceptable price range. According to one villager:

> We have a general idea of the fees that Daoshi of different qualities charge. The better Daoshi charge more; the difference can amount to several thousand RMB. But if you go for the more expensive Daoshi, you must be prepared to pay a high price. Those who have little clue as to who to invite will consult with more savvy family members and friends. We take recommendations and compare prices and quality of service.

4.2 Oscillating between the Sacred and the Secular

The coexistence of sacred ends and secular means is as paradoxical as the villagers' newly recovered religious consciousness. The revival of religion does not propel the villagers from extreme secularism (atheism) straight into sacredness. Instead, villagers find themselves constantly swaying from one end to another, demonstrating a complex hybridism.

The villagers' attitudes toward ritual conventions and traditions are shaped more by customs than by specific Daoist teachings. Villagers in Zhanjiang, following custom, worship deities on the first and fifteenth days of the lunar calendar as well as on various feast days. Daoshi normally preside over these rituals (and they charge for the service), but most villagers consider these rituals as sacred and yet integral parts of daily life. As one villager explained, they are also mindful of the economic implications.

> I am not confident that these rituals are useful, but I feel uneasy not having them. These rituals don't take up much time and are usually finished in half a day. The offerings for the gods like chicken and pork don't cost us much, and we eat the offerings after the ceremonies anyways. That's why I don't mind going along with the tradition.

As for rituals concerning very specific, personal needs, we can observe a type of consumer whose sacred preferences can be satisfied by a mediocre level of service. The fact that these consumers repeatedly purchase ritual products indicates their religious demand. And yet the low importance placed on quality suggests that their needs are not driven solely by religious motivations.[41] For example, as the following quote suggests, some villagers do not prioritize the ranking and quality of Daoshi when choosing one to perform a ritual.

> I never thought of inviting a higher-ranking Daoshi to perform the ceremonies. Going through the motions is sufficient. I don't really believe in these things [spirits, ghosts, blessings, etc.]; there's no need to make the rituals more complicated than they should be. My thinking is that I'll pay for the services to get some peace of mind. I can't be bothered to shop around and hire a better Daoshi. I don't even consider the better ones.

All the same, when the villagers are faced with rituals of significance, their corresponding behavior reveals a greater degree of "sacredness." Some even resort to the rituals of multiple religious systems to fulfill the demand for sacredness. One villager, for instance, was not fully confident of the effectiveness of rituals. Nevertheless, it was of paramount importance to him that the soul of his late father should rest in his home, and he treated every step of the ritual process with the utmost reverence.

> The effects of rituals are not immediate, but I certainly feel much more at peace having performed the rituals. My father died in a hospital more than twenty years ago. I sought advice from a wise woman a while back, and she said that my father's soul did not return home and become a patron god. So, I hired a Daoshi to summon his soul at his grave. Afterward I asked for the wise woman's advice again, and she said that my father had

---

41 The low standard of quality is not due to any external constraints. Rather, it is the consumer's conscious decision, made after weighing prices and the level of demand.

returned home and that he had received all my offerings. A huge weight was lifted off my shoulders.

4.3 Structural Factors of the Villagers' Shifts in Religious Preferences

The rapid growth in the demand for rituals since the 1980s suggests that the vast majority of villagers have experienced an unprecedented revival of religious preferences. A key structural factor behind this change was the loosening of state control over religion. The Chinese state implemented harsh religious policies after 1949, as Communist ideology regarded most forms of folk religion as feudal superstition that needed to be eradicated. The combined forces of social discipline and political propaganda have had a profound impact on village attitudes toward religion. The immediate consequences were noticeable differences in religious preferences as well as different patterns of changing religious preferences across generations.

The villagers who came of age before the founding of the PRC regarded Daoshi as sacred. Despite decades of mass political movements and indoctrination through education, their deep-rooted beliefs or reverence for religion die hard. Some elderly villagers recall that the village never ceased hosting rituals and ceremonies even under the harshest suppression—these events simply moved underground. Many large-scale rituals had to be simplified or abandoned completely. All the same, simpler and smaller-scale rituals continued to be clandestinely performed, in the darkness of the night and in villagers' homes.

Those who grew up after the founding of the PRC are of a completely different mindset. The Maoist educational regime firmly instilled the atheist concept. Worldly political ideals and the cult of leadership filled the vacuum left by religion. As the Cultural Revolution came to an end, the ultra-left ideology waned and religious preferences resurfaced. As villagers recall their personal transformation with regard to the concept of religion, some subconsciously erase the distinction between secular notions and belief in the sacred (i.e., religion).[42] Such conflation, however, casts a spotlight on the continuum of belief, as seen in the response of one villager we interviewed.

> When Chairman Mao was in power, I didn't believe in spirits, so I was not afraid of ghosts as a kid. You could make me spend the night in the

---

42   We submit that the concept of religion needs to encompass a greater variety of practices and forms, although not all forms of belief ought to be considered religion. When all forms of belief are designated as religion, the concept is rendered meaningless.

graveyard; I wouldn't be scared. Chairman Mao was all powerful; he could ward off all types of supernatural beings. After Chairman Mao's passing, I read in the *Yangcheng Evening News* (*Yangcheng wanbao* 羊城晚报) that witches would dance in the Forbidden City when the weather changed, and the sound of galloping could be heard. Scientists were sending satellites into space but couldn't explain these phenomena. They are superstition and indeed mysterious. Now that I am thinking of it, I wouldn't dare to spend the night in the graveyard.

To summarize, the villagers have shifted from nurturers to consumers of rituals. Such a transformation reveals a secularization of faith that has not followed a linear trajectory. Highly market-oriented behavior is intertwined with considerations for the "sacred," paving a zig-zagged path, without clear signposts, toward religious revival. The loosening of religious regulations as well as the restoration of religious preferences has granted individuals greater liberty. However, with such liberty, believers are stripping faith off the altar in everyday practice and have reconstructed religion based on the logic of market economics that dominates contemporary Chinese society. The outcome is a one-of-a-kind folk religion.

5 Conclusion

In *Religion in Chinese Society,* C. K. Yang states that in the broadest sense, religion represents a continuum. On one end of the continuum is a highly emotionally charged atheism that aspires to an eternity-like state. On the other end there are "theistic belief systems with ultimate values fully symbolized in supernatural entities and supported by patterns of worship and organization."[43] Various forms of Chinese folk belief, the Daoshi in Zhanjiang included, are religion in the broadest sense. The religious market theory, as a major analytical paradigm of contemporary sociological studies, ought to transcend the "regionalism" of its birthplace, the West. This study has presented the evolution of the religious market theory, as well as its resilience, in the context of fieldwork. With an examination of the preferences and strategies on both the supply and demand

---

43 C. K. Yang, *Religion in Chinese Society: A Study of Contemporary Social Functions of Religion and Some of Their Historical Factors* (Berkeley: University of California, 1961), 26; translated by Fan Lizhu as *Zhongguo shehui zhong de zongjiao* (Shanghai: Shanghai renmin chubanshe, 2007), 39.

sides, our study seeks to strengthen the foundation of the market analysis paradigm through understanding micro-level behaviors. Moreover, our endeavor may expand the parameters within which the paradigm operates. This is the first objective of the present case study.

Our second, and more important, objective is to explore the analytical paradigms employed to investigate cultural phenomena (as represented by religion) in economic sociology. Robert Wuthnow compares the classical and the modified paradigms in his "New Directions in the Study of Religion and Economic Life."[44] He observes that the former approaches the religious economy from the perspective of rationality and the market, while the latter emphasizes the social meaning of practices in the religious economy. We agree with Wuthnow that an analytical perspective anchored in the social meaning of religious-economic behavior indeed complements and supports the existing religious market model. If religion can be understood as a set of norms regulating human society, the core questions for individuals to consider would be: "Can one reach a dual equilibrium by balancing interests and norms? Under what circumstances would the dual equilibrium fail?"[45] In other words, a religious market theory built upon an examination of preferences remains viable and compelling.

Bibliography

Bankston, Carl L. "Rationality, Choice, and the Religious Economy: Individual and Collective Rationality in Supply and Demand." *Review of Religious Research* 45.2 (December 2003): 155–171.

Bruce, Steve. "Religion and Rational Choice: A Critique of Economic Explanations of Religious Behavior." *Sociology of Religion* 54.2 (1993): 193–205.

Chaves, Mark, and Philip S. Gorski. "Religious Pluralism and Religious Participation." *Annual Review of Sociology* 27 (2001): 261–281.

Chen Jinguo 陈进国. "'Maidi quan' xisu de kaoxianxue yanjiu—mintai diqu de shili" "买地券"习俗的考现学研究—闽台地区的事例. *Minsu yanjiu* 民俗研究. 2008.1: 129–164.

---

44 Robert Wuthnow, "New Directions in the Study of Religion and Economic Life," in *The Handbook of Economic Sociology*, 2nd ed., ed. Neil Smelser and Richard Swedberg (Princeton: Princeton University Press, 2005), 603–626; translated by Luo Jiaojiang and Zhang Yonghong as "Zongjiao yu jingji shenghuo yanjiu de xin fangxiang," in *Jingji shehuixue shouce* (Beijing: Huaxia chubanshe, 2009), 674–700.

45 Liu Shiding, *Jingjixue de jingji shehuixue?*, paper presented at Beijing University (2014).

Fan Lizhu 范丽珠. "Xiandai zongjiao shi lixing xuanze de ma? Zhiyi zongjiao de lixing xuanze yanjiu fanshi" 现代宗教是理性选择的吗？质疑宗教的理性选择研究范式. *Shehui* 社会 28.6 (2008): 90–109.

Fan Lizhu 范丽珠. "Xifang zongjiao lilun xia Zhongguo zongjiao yanjiu de kunjing" 西方宗教理论下中国宗教研究的困境. *Nanjing daxue xuebao (zhexue, renwen kexue, shehui kexue ban)* 南京大学学报（哲学、人文科学、社会科学版）. 2009.2: 92–101.

Gu Guanfu 顾冠福 and Long Feijun 龙飞俊. "Yiwei Shanghai chengpai daoshi de koushushi—Gu Guanfu daozhang fangtan lu" 一位上海城派道士的口述史—顾冠福道长访谈录. *Shilin* 石林, 2010.1: 94–99.

Huang Feijun 黄飞君. "Zongjiao jingji lilun de xiandu—yi Zhongguo Taiwan diqu zongjiao shijian weili" 宗教经济理论的限度—以中国台湾地区宗教实践为例. *Shijie zongjiao wenhua* 世界宗教文化, 2013.1: 22–28.

Iannaccone, Laurence R. "The Consequences of Religious Market Structure: Adam Smith and the Economics of Religion." *Rationality and Society* 3 (1991): 156–176.

Lang, Graeme, Chan Selina Ching, and Ragvald Lars. "Temples and the Religious Economy." *Interdisciplinary Journal of Research on Religion* 1 (2005): 1–27.

Li Xiangping 李向平 and Li Siming 李思明. "Xinyang yu minjian quanwei de jiangou—minjian xinyang yishi zhuanjia yanjiu zongshu" 信仰与民间权威的建构—民间信仰仪式专家研究综述. *Shijie zongjiao wenhua* 世界宗教文化. 2012.3: 110–119.

Li Xiangping 李向平 and Chen Bin 陈彬. "Xiangqianxing de gonggong zongjiao—chuantong Zhongguo de zhengjiao guanxi zhi shehuixue jiedu" 镶嵌型的公共宗教—传统中国的政教关系之社会学解读. *Shanghai daxue xuebao (shehui kexue ban)* 上海大学学报（社会科学版）. 2006.4: 83–89.

Li Xiangping 李向平 and Yang Linxia 杨林霞. "Zongjiao, shehui yu quanli guanxi—'zongjiao shichang lun' de shehuixue jiedu" 宗教、社会与权力关系—"宗教市场论"的社会学解读. *Huadong shifan daxue xuebao (zhexue shehui kexue ban)* 华东师范大学学报（哲学社会科学版） 43.5 (2011): 1–7.

Liang Jingwen 梁景文, Chen Qian 陈蒨, Luo Si 罗斯, and Chen Ruigang 陈锐钢. "Minjian simiao yu Zhongguo zongjiao jingji—dui zongjiao jingji lilun de tantao" 民间寺庙与中国宗教经济—对宗教经济理论的探讨. *Shijie zongjiao wenhua* 世界宗教文化. 2010.2: 21–26.

Lin Qiaowei 林巧薇. "Yang Fenggang boshi tan zongjiao shehuixue de fanshi zhuanxing" 杨凤岗博士谈宗教社会学的范式转型. *Zongjiaoxue yanjiu* 宗教学研究. 2003.3: 140–141.

Liu Shiding 刘世定. "Jingjixue de jingji shehuixue?" 经济学的经济社会学? Paper presented at Beijing University, 2014.

Liu Zhengfeng 刘正峰. "Lun yadang simi de zongjiao shichang lilun—jianlun zongjiao guanzhi de jingji jichu" 论亚当·斯密的宗教市场理论—兼论宗教管制的经济基础. *Shijie zongjiao yanjiu* 世界宗教研究. 2012.5: 1–7.

Lu Yunfeng 卢云峰. "Chaoyue jiduzongjiao shehuixue—jianlun zongjiao shichang lilun zai huaren shehui de shiyongxing wenti" 超越基督宗教社会学—兼论宗教市场理论在华人社会的适用性问题. *Shehuixue yanjiu* 社会学研究. 2008.5: 81–97.

Lu Yunfeng 卢云峰. "Kunan yu zongjiao zengzhang: guanzhi de feiyuqi houguo" 苦难与宗教增长：管制的非预期后果. *Shehui* 社会. 2010.4: 200–216.

Robertson, Roland. "The Economization of Religion? Reflections on the Promise and Limitations of the Economic Approach." *Social Compass* 39 (1992): 147–157.

Smith, Adam. *An Inquiry into the Nature and Causes of the Wealth of Nations*. Edited by Edwin Cannan. London: Methuen, 1904. Repr., Chicago: University of Chicago Press, 1977. Translated by Guo Dali 郭大力 and Wang Yanan 王亚楠 as *Guomin caifu de xingzhi he yuanyi de yanjiu* 国民财富的形制和原因的研究. Beijing: The Commercial Press, 1997.

Stark, Rodney. "From Church-Sect to Religious Economies." In *The Sacred in a Post-Secular Age*, edited by Phillip E. Hammond, 139–149. Berkeley: University of California Press, 1985.

Stark, Rodney, and Roger Finke. *Acts of Faith: Explaining the Human Side of Religion*. Berkeley: University of California Press, 2000. Translated by Yang Fenggang 杨凤岗 as *Xinyang de faze—jieshi zongjiao zhi ren de fangmian* 信仰的法则—解释宗教之人的方面. Beijing: Zhongguo renmin daxue chubanshe, 2004.

Stark, Rodney, and Laurence R. Iannaccone. "A Supply-Side Reinterpretation of the 'Secularization' of Europe." *Journal for the Scientific Study of Religion* 33.3 (1994): 230–252.

Warner, R. Stephen. "Work in Progress toward a New Paradigm for the Sociological Study of Religion in the United States." *American Journal of Sociology* 98.5 (1993): 1044–1095.

Wuthnow, Robert. "New Directions in the Study of Religion and Economic Life." In *The Handbook of Economic Sociology*, 2nd ed., edited by Neil Smelser and Richard Swedberg, 603–626. Princeton: Princeton University Press, 2010. Translated by Luo Jiaojiang 罗教讲 and Zhang Yonghong 张永宏 as "Zongjiao yu jingji shenghuo yanjiu de xin fangxiang" 宗教与经济生活研究的新方向, in *Jingji shehuixue shouce* 经济社会学手册. 674–700. Beijing: Huaxia chubanshe, 2009.

Yang, C. K. (杨庆堃). *Religion in Chinese Society: A Study of Contemporary Social Functions of Religion and Some of Their Historical Factors*. Berkeley: University of California Press, 1961. Translated by Fan Lizhu 范丽珠 as *Zhongguo shehui zhong de zongjiao* 中国社会中的宗教. Shanghai: Shanghai renmin chubanshe, 2007.

Yang, Fenggang. "The Red, Black, and Gray Markets of Religion in China." *Sociological Quarterly* 47.1 (2006): 93–122. Translated and abridged by Yang Fenggang 杨凤岗 as "Zhongguo zongjiao de sanse shichang" 中国宗教的三色市场, *Zhongguo renmin daxue xuebao (shehui kexue ban)* 中国人民大学学报（社会科学版）. 2006.6: 41–47.

Yang, Fenggang. "Religion in China under Communism: A Shortage Economy Explanation." *Journal of Church and State* 51.1 (2010): 3–33.

Zhu Haibin 朱海滨. "Minjian xinyang—Zhongguo zui zhongyao de zongjiao chuantong" 民间信仰—中国最重要的宗教传统. *Jianghan luntan* 江汉论坛. 2009.3: 68–74.

CHAPTER 11

Urbanization and the Transformation of Migrant Worker Churches

A Case Study of Mount of Olives Church in Beijing

YUAN Hao

1   Urbanization and Migrant Worker Churches

Scholarship on Protestant Christianity in rural China has centered on topics such as church-state relations, Christian identity, causes of the spread of Protestant Christianity, and the dynamics between Christianity and folk religion.[1] In the past four decades, China's pursuit of modernization has necessitated the policy of reform and opening up, as well as the acceleration of urbanization, both of which went hand in hand with the rise of Christianity in the countryside. Although urbanization and the rise of Christianity in rural areas are parallel developments in contemporary China, the interplay between the two processes of social change has not received sufficient scholarly attention. As a critical aspect of social change in China, urbanization has a significant impact on the development of rural Christianity. This study will examine the interplay between urbanization and migrant worker churches.

Studies on the mutual influence between urbanization and migrant worker churches are few and far between. Duan Qi 段琦 offers an overview of the impact of urbanization on Protestant Christianity in China.[2] Huang Jianbo 黄剑波 examines the rise of migrant worker churches and the workers' motivations for conversion in a case study of the Yingshang Fellowship 颍上团队 in

---

1   See Ying Fuk-tsang, *Dangdai Zhongguo zhengjiao guanxi* (Hong Kong: The Alliance Bible Seminary, 1999); Jason Kindopp and Carol Lee Hamrin, *God and Caesar in China: Policy Implications of Church-State Tensions* (Washington, DC: Brookings Institution Press, 2004); Fenggang Yang, "The Red, Black, and Gray Markets of Religion in China," *Sociological Quarterly* 47.1 (2006): 93–122; Lap-yan Kung, "The Emergence of Exchange Politics in China and Its Implications for Church-State Relations," *Religion, State and Society* 38.1 (2010): 9–28.
2   Duan Qi, "2011 nian Zhongguo jidujiao zhuyao shijian ji chengshihua dui jiaohui de yingxiang," in *Zhongguo zongjiao baogao (2012)*, ed. Jin Ze and Qiu Yonghui (Beijing: Shehui kexue wenxian chubanshe, 2012), 64–104.

Anhui, and I have also elaborated on the concept of urbanization in China.[3] I identify three insufficiencies in the current scholarly understanding of the topics in question. First, researchers have taken the collectivity of Christians as the primary unit of analysis but neglected church organization as a valid unit of analysis. Second, whereas the impact of urbanization on the formation of migrant worker churches has been well researched, the response of the latter to urbanization remains understudied. Third, although broad surveys of migrant worker churches do exist, there are relatively few case studies of individual churches at the micro level.

Through an analysis of the Mount of Olives Church in Beijing, this chapter examines the interplay between migrant worker churches and the process of urbanization, focusing specifically on the transformation of the churches as well as their responses to the consequences of urbanization. I ask the following questions: What caused the rise of migrant worker churches in Beijing? How do these churches operate on a daily basis? What are the distinctive characteristics of urbanization in China? What changes and challenges does urbanization bring to migrant worker churches? How do migrant worker churches respond to the impact of urbanization? And what type of community of faith is a migrant worker church?

2 Research Design and Methodology

2.1 *Theoretical Framework*

My analysis of the interaction between the church organization and social change is inspired by congregational studies. Proposed by American religious sociologist Nancy Ammerman, congregational studies, as an interpretive framework, focuses on three aspects of a church: resources, structure of authority, and culture.[4]

In the framework of congregational studies, there are three types of resources: material resources, human resources, and organizational networks. Material resources include, primarily, the congregants (i.e., the size of the congregation, the socioeconomic status of the congregants, and the amount of their donations) and church property (such as the physical meeting places).

---

3 Huang Jianbo, *Dushili de xiangcun jiaohui—Zhongguo chengshihua yu mingong jidujiao* (Hong Kong: Logos and Pneuma Press, 2012); Yuan Hao, "Tingbujian de shengyin: Guanyu Zhongguo jidujiao chengshi mingong jiaohui de yanjiu," *Daofeng*, no. 39 (2013): 337–353.

4 Nancy T. Ammerman, *Congregation and Community* (New Brunswick, NJ: Rutgers University Press, 1997), 48–62.

A church's human resources refer to the professional staff, the clergy, and the laity. These are the factors that may have positive or negative implications for a church, which are also potential indicators of the vitality of a congregation.

Structure of authority refers to the decision-making process in a church—how decisions are made, and who takes part in the decision-making process. Some churches do not belong to any denomination and can make decisions independently. Others may be part of a larger denominational organization, whose decision-making processes are to varying degrees dictated by the denomination's leadership. Pastors, deacons, and the laity all contribute to decision-making.

Finally, examining a church from the perspective of its congregational culture will shed additional light on its practices, rituals, organizational development, and the orientation of new congregants. Moreover, the architectural style and interior design of a church are also worthy of investigation. All the above factors contribute to a particular congregational culture. As a congregation consists of a wide variety of individual believers, congregants play a role in fostering the distinctive character, traits, and tone of a church, namely, congregational culture. Specific congregational cultures often serve as the source for individual congregants' sense of identity.

In short, congregational studies synthesizes structuralism, organizational theory, and contextualism and serves as a viable analytical framework for the interplay between congregational organization and social change. I will examine the impact of urbanization on migrant worker churches, as well as the churches' responses, with respect to resources, culture, and the structure of authority.

A dynamic process arises when a migrant worker church reacts to urbanization and transforms itself. Ferdinand Tönnies's and Robert D. Putnam's theorizations may provide useful references for the changes that migrant worker churches underwent prior to their full transformation. Examining the transition from a traditional society into a modern one, Tönnies has identified two ideal types of social organizations: community and society. The former, community, takes shape on the basis of shared values and lived experience and is realized in organically formed groupings (such as families and clans). The core of human relationships in a community is comprised of sentiments. The basic forms of communities are consanguine, geographical, and religious.[5] Since the implementation of reform and opening up, migrant worker churches in Beijing

---

5 Ferdinand Tönnies, *Community and Civil Society*, ed. Jose Harris; trans. Margaret Hollis (Cambridge: Cambridge University Press, 2001), 26–27.

have been undergoing a transition to modernity. Tönnies's model provides an apt interpretive framework in this context.

The characteristics of a civic community, according to Putnam, include civic engagement, political equality, solidarity, trust, and tolerance, as well as social structures of cooperation.[6] I would argue that Putnam's characteristics of a civic community parallel Ammerman's tripartite analytical framework of congregational resources, culture, and authority. Thus, Putnam's dimensions of a civic community can be examined alongside Ammerman's tripartite framework.

2.2 Key Concepts

A migrant worker Christian is a peasant Christian who has left the rural area and currently lives and works in a city. A migrant worker church is made up of such Christians.[7]

Urbanization is the process of demographic movement into a city, while the city is experiencing rapid economic development, along with the growth of administrative bodies, expansion of political organizations, and advances in transportation.[8] Not only do the economy, society, and demography experience unprecedented change, but the way of life, behavioral pattern, and culture also change during urbanization. In this process, urban space continues to expand to the extent of overtaking rural and farming areas. Urbanization also designates a way of life and the culture of a city.

I chose Beijing as the fieldwork site for the following reasons. First, Beijing is the center of the Chinese political structure, culture, and economy. Second, urbanization is readily observable in Beijing. Behind the façade of rapid urbanization and modernization, Beijing has continued to exhibit the defining features of a traditional society in transition. Beijing can be viewed as a microcosm of urbanization in China. Finally, migrant worker churches in Beijing have experienced rapid growth. When I conducted fieldwork between 2010 and 2015, I managed to observe and take part in the activities of eleven migrant worker churches by snowball sampling. I interviewed more than twenty church leaders and lay congregants and collected materials amounting to more than

---

6   Robert Putnam, *Making Democracy Work: Civic Tradition in Modern Italy* (Princeton: Princeton University Press, 1993), 86–91.
7   Huang Jianbo, *Dushili de xiangcun jiaohui*, 18.
8   For more on urbanization, see John Friedmann, *The Prospect of Cities* (Minneapolis: University of Minnesota Press, 2002), 3–4; Gino Germani, *The Sociology of Modernization: Studies on Its Historical and Theoretical Aspects with Special Regard to the Latin American Case* (New Brunswick: Transaction, 1981), 52–54.

200,000 Chinese characters in interview transcripts. My interviews were conducted with a combination of semi-structured and structured questions.

3   Urbanization in Beijing

Armed with the definition of urbanization, as well as statistical data, we can begin to paint a general picture of Beijing's urbanization and examine it from four different angles: population, the expansion of the municipality, urban culture, and way of life.

The urban population has ballooned in recent years. Migrants from the provinces are the main addition to the population of Beijing, and rural migrants claim a large percentage of this growth. According to the sixth general census survey, Beijing had 19,612,000 permanent residents at the end of 2010.[9] In 2010, the number of migrant workers reached 5,000,000, amounting to nearly 25% percent of Beijing's population. Although migrant workers come from all over the country, Hebei, Henan, Shandong, and Anhui provinces are the main suppliers.[10]

The area of the municipality of Beijing continues to expand. Thanks to both the stimulation of the market and the state's initiatives, Beijing, since the 1990s, has rapidly urbanized. The city has expanded at a rate of 30 km² annually, from 346 km² in 1981 to 1,209 km² in 2005, to 1,400 km² in the present day. As urbanization continues, villages in the urban area and the farming communities on the outskirts of the city are gradually being absorbed into the municipality and turned into residential, commercial, or industrial districts.

There is also much diversity in culture and lifestyle in the city. Large numbers of migrants from the provinces have flooded into Beijing since the reform and opening up. The numerous regional cultures that have entered Beijing along with migrants have also reshaped the culture and ways of life of the city itself. Rural migrants from the provinces have formed communities based on geographical and familial connections, such as "Henan village" or "Anhui village," with "Zhejiang village" being the best known of all. The province-based communities have maintained the cultures and customs of home. Similar

---

9   Beijingshi diliuci quanguo renkou pucha lingdao xiaozu bangongshi, "Beijingshi diliuci quanguo renkou pucha zhuyao shuju qingkuang," http://www.bjstats.gov.cn/tjsj/tjgb/rpgb/201511/t20151124_327785.html (accessed August 20, 2019).

10   Beijingshi diliuci renkou pucha bangongshi (北京市第六次人口普查办公室). "Beijing changzhu wailai renkou laiyuan fenxi," https://wenku.baidu.com/view/a99c9bd7240c844769eaeefb.html (accessed August 20, 2019).

patterns of cultural isolation have been observed among Italian communities in Boston in the United States by Herbert Gans in 1982, as well as among the African-American population in Washington, DC, in Elliot Liebow's 1967 study.[11] The process of urbanization has reached an equilibrium in the majority of advanced Western countries, where diverse social and ethnic groups have managed to coexist in a multicultural environment. The rapid urbanization and modernization in Beijing are accompanied by extensive projects of demolition and reconstruction, which have not only negatively affected province-based communities but in many cases have also caused them to disintegrate. Without fixed geographic locations to sustain the traditional cultures and ways of life that these province-based communities represent, communities often find themselves on the verge of collapse.

The household registration system is an institutionalized means of population management. This system prevents migrant workers from establishing residency in a city, resulting in the loss of the full rights of citizenship. Migrant workers' basic rights as a citizen and access to social welfare services are also compromised. Consequently, migrant workers become "marginalized" people in a city.[12] A migrant worker's marginalized status is revealed in both socioeconomic status and cultural identity. Being marginalized makes it difficult for migrant workers to assimilate into urban life. It is equally difficult for Beijing migrant workers to readjust to the rural way of life when they eventually return home.

4 Migrant Worker Churches in Beijing

The migrant worker church, as one of the many types of Christian congregations in Chinese cities, is a product of recent socioeconomic and political developments. There were only two types of Protestant churches in Beijing prior to the 1990s: the Protestant Three-Self Church and house churches. Economic reform introduced market forces into the economy, and urbanization accelerated in the late 1990s. As the center of national politics, economic activities, and cultural life, Beijing was one of the first places to feel the impact of this massive wave of structural change. More varieties of Protestant churches emerged in Beijing as a result, including migrant worker churches, Wenzhouren Church

---

11   Herbert Gans, *The Urban Villagers* (New York: Free Press, 1982); Elliot Liebow, *Tally's Corner* (Boston: Little Brown, 1967).
12   Huang Jianbo, "Zhongguo chengzhen mingong de zongjiao shenghuo," *Ershiyi shiji*, no. 109 (2008): 104.

温州人教会, the independent Bridges International (*Haigui tuanqi* 海归团契), and campus fellowships. What follows is an overview of the formation, rise, and growth of migrant worker churches.

4.1 *Forming Migrant Worker Churches*

Migrant worker churches emerged in Beijing in the 1990s, with Christians from rural Henan and Anhui being the core members. To understand the formation of migrant worker churches, we cannot overlook the trend of population movements in China since the 1980s.[13] Broad structural changes such as the Protestant revival in rural areas, the internal division of the urban religious market, and the establishment of a market economy have all paved the way for the rise of migrant worker churches with political opportunities and resources.

Protestant Christianity in the countryside began to regain its vitality at the end of the Cultural Revolution, and the revival continued into the late 1990s. Specifically, Protestant Christianity has experienced remarkable growth in Jiangsu, Shandong, Anhui, and Henan, which some have dubbed the "Jesus nest" (*Yesu wo* 耶稣窝).[14] Moreover, the religious markets in urban and rural areas have undergone divergent developments, because the state takes different approaches to managing religious affairs in the urban and rural districts. The increasingly diverse and open lifestyle of the city offers religious groups greater opportunities for growth. Since state control is less effective in both the rural-urban borderland and urban villages, weak state control has carved out a gray area favorable for the formation of migrant worker churches. Finally, the rapid development of a market economy in cities has also generated numerous employment opportunities for the migrant population.

4.2 *Establishment and Growth of Churches*

Urbanization draws the rural population from the provinces into Beijing. Relevant literature has indicated that Christian migrant workers have not only joined the Three-Self Church to continue a religious life, but they have also organized prayer groups, means of communication, and other religious practices. A rudimentary congregation tends to develop into a meeting place or a

---

13 Chinese scholarship typically characterizes the migration of the rural population into cities as a population movement. International scholars have referred to the same phenomenon as migration. I adopt the latter concept in the analysis that follows.

14 Tony Lambert, *China's Christian Millions* (Oxford: Monarch, 2006), 85–98; Nanlai Cao, *Constructing China's Jerusalem: Christians, Power, and Place in Contemporary Wenzhou* (Stanford, CA: Stanford University Press, 2010), 1–4.

church, especially when religious professionals get involved in the organizational efforts with the support of province-based churches.

Migrant worker churches were founded in rapid succession in the late 1990s, thanks to the support of the China Gospel Fellowship (*Zhonghua fuyin tuanqi* 中华福音团契), Chinese for Christ Church (*Huaren guizhu jiaohui* 华人归主教会), and Yingshang Fellowship (*Yinshang tuandui* 颍上团队). They have grown at a striking speed in Beijing since 2000. For instance, Yingshang Fellowship and the China Gospel Fellowship established several dozen churches in Beijing in the span of a few years, totaling more than one thousand congregants. Two factors have contributed to the rapid growth and expansion of migrant worker churches.

First, church membership never stops growing. As the Chinese government aggressively pushes for urbanization, cities continue to attract the rural population, including Christians from farming villages. The migrant population serves as the engine of growth for migrant worker congregations. Mount of Olives Church, as a migrant worker church, has established twenty-six branch churches with a total of two thousand congregants since its founding in 1999. However, its expansion has relied on consolidating Christian migrant workers throughout the city rather than any concerted effort of targeted recruitment.

Second, churches experience cycles of division and renewal. One of the consequences of Beijing's continuing urbanization and urban expansion is the demolition of villages within the urban area as well as the removal of farming communities on the outskirts of the city. Changes in social conditions have also caused the split and dispersion of migrant worker congregations. As the urban landscape changes, churches respond by redistributing congregants into regional divisions based on street addresses. Religious professionals take part in the activities of regional divisions and recruit new members in the localities, through whom new churches are established, one after another. This pattern of division and reproduction precisely describes the expansion of Mount of Olives.

5 Overview of Mount of Olives Church

Beijing has witnessed the development of migrant worker churches out of the outgrowth of rural churches since the 1990s. The Mount of Olives Church is representative of a migrant worker church in an urban area. This section will examine the church's foundation, internal organization, and core messages.

5.1 *Foundation*

The China Gospel Fellowship established itself in rural China and began dispatching missionaries into cities to preach to migrant workers in the late 1990s. In 1999, a Christian couple from rural Henan started preaching in Beijing. They quickly realized that the target of their evangelization had to be migrant workers, due to their unfamiliarity with urban culture. Migrant workers in Beijing tend to concentrate in areas with lower costs of living, such as villages within an urban area or on the outskirts of the city, and form pockets of migrant communities throughout the city. The missionary couple made their way into these migrant communities to preach and establish churches. Before long, churches were established one after another throughout Beijing. In the span of a decade, the church gained nearly two thousand members, the majority of whom are migrants from Henan. Evangelism and recruitment have primarily relied on interpersonal networks made up of fellow townsmen, neighbors, or relatives.

5.2 *Organization*

The vast majority of migrant-worker congregants come from rural farming communities in the provinces. In Beijing, they tend to suffer from long work hours, low income, and poor living conditions. Migrant workers are literally foreigners in the city. Without residency and full citizenship, they are unable to assimilate into mainstream society and lack a sense of belonging in both the city and most urban churches. We can also observe internal stratification based on socioeconomic status among the congregants of migrant worker churches. Some of those who came early to Beijing, when market competition was not as fierce as it has now become, managed to fare extremely well. For instance, a few congregants became millionaires by running a recycling business. These select few are now volunteers at Mount of Olives Church, responsible for making major decisions on church affairs.

Regarding the governance of the church, Mount of Olives has adopted a rotation system. Preachers serve for three to four years at a time and step down at the end of their term. Pastor Liu is in charge of their assignments. Take Dianchang 靛厂 church, for example. Twelve preachers and volunteers form the core of this church. The preachers select the most enthusiastic and better-educated congregants to serve as coworkers. However, coworkers do not participate in the governance of the church; they only assist in the church's operation. As coworkers are not selected by the congregants, their involvement in church affairs is largely dependent upon preachers' personal preferences and leadership styles.

The church is not well organized. Churches with large congregations are equipped with few internal fellowships or groups, and the functions and roles of their current members are also ill-defined. Currently, leaders and assistant leaders are appointed to each subgroup. Yet those in leadership positions are unaware of their specific duties and functions, and they are unable to carry out their responsibilities as a result. Subgroups are usually maintained by the personal connections between the leaders and group members.

Taking into consideration the sizes of the congregations and the types of locations, three churches in Dongsanqi 东三旗, Dianchang, and Mingjia 名佳 stand out among more than twenty churches. They appear to be the most typical congregations in the Mount of Olives Church system and handle a great deal of church affairs.

The Dongsanqi church has the largest congregation of all three. The church has now relocated to a unit in the Tiantong Yuan 天通苑 residential building. When it was first founded in 2002, it was one of the largest and earliest congregations in the Mount of Olives Church system. The congregation was established in Dongsanqi village in northern Beijing, holding services and meetings in a rented residential compound. The church had a chief pastor, a dozen or so volunteers, and over two hundred congregants. According to the preachers' records, 80 percent of the congregants are from Gushi County 固始县 in Henan. Most of them are employed in the waste recycling sector in Beijing, which has become one of the key industries that supports the city's sanitation system.

The Dianchang church is a midsize congregation. After eight or nine relocations, it has finally found a home in a rented commercial property in a residential district in southern Beijing. Founded in 2005, the congregation now has more than one hundred members, with one full-time preacher, twelve volunteers, and four subgroups. Most of the congregants are also from Gushi. A preacher attempted to move the congregation into a residential building in 2009 to no avail. A new preacher made another attempt in 2012. Finally, in 2013, the church merged two branches into one and relocated once again. With the assistance of a congregant who was a real-estate agent, the church was able to move into a fairly spacious unit in a residential building.

The Mingjia church is the smallest of the three, located in a rented residential property in a residential district in northern Beijing. In 2009, residents at Mingjia Garden 名佳花园 who were attending the Dongsanqi church created a Mingjia group; later on, they moved the group to Mingjia Garden and rented a unit as a meeting place. Now this meeting place has become a church, situated in Mingjia Garden in northern Beijing. It is a neighborhood church whose congregants are predominantly residents of the community. It has one full-time preacher and thirty to forty congregants.

6 The Church's Response to the Resources Crisis: From Displacement to Resettlement

The two major challenges faced by migrant churches are suitable sites for churches and retaining members. These issues are connected. A typical outcome of the relocation of a church is the internal division into several subgroups. On the one hand, such division is conducive to rebuilding the church by recruiting new migrant workers into the renewed congregation. On the other hand, the relocation of a church inevitably leaves a number of congregants behind. The cycle of removal, loss of congregants, and recruitment of new members, together with the irregular employment of most migrant workers, all contribute to the fluctuation of church membership. Migrant worker churches as well as their congregants find themselves constantly moving. Urban expansion has resulted in the removal of urban villages and the elimination of the urban-rural borderland from the urban landscape. Because migrant worker churches settle in these areas, they are often forced to seek new meeting places. The Dianchang church, for example, has relocated six or seven times since its foundation in 2005. The congregation has met in residential houses, warehouses, restaurants, and even a public park. A preacher has remarked that all the preachers have become "experts in house-hunting" over the years, due to the nonstop series of demolitions and relocations.

In its foundational period, the Mount of Olives Church merely reacted to external changes. As soon as the construction company's bulldozers rode into the village, the church picked up and moved. In 2005, the Beijing parish, to which Mount of Olives Church belongs, started to encourage churches in the parish to lay down roots in the city and advocated for congregational restructuring. The Beijing parish's new approach to expansion inspired Mount of Olives Church to seek new ways of tackling the resources crisis. Below I will give three examples to illustrate the different strategies that coworkers adopted when addressing these problems.

6.1 *The Dianchang Church: From a Cottage in a Village to an Urban Apartment*

Founded in 2005, the Dianchang church has undergone several relocations, and every preacher has attempted a reform. In 2009, Preacher Hu coordinated the relocation from a cottage in a village to a unit in a residential building in Nansan Huan 南三环. The new church did not even last a month. Residents in the building filed complaints about the church with both the property management office and the neighborhood committee, complaining that the singing on Sunday mornings generated too much noise and disturbed the neighbors. Pressured from many sides, the church had to move out of the building and return to the cottage for Sunday services.

Preacher Yuan assumed his duty in 2012 and proposed to relocate the church to a residential building. In Yuan's assessment, relocation from the cottage to a residential building was only the first step of church reform. Moving the church to a residential building would prevent frequent relocations, which would in turn provide a sense of stability for growth and a physical foundation for future reorganization of the church. In addition, a church in a residential building serves as a base for evangelism and could draw residents in the community to the church. Yuan has been an advocate for reform; he has envisioned a local church consisting of primarily university students and residents in the neighborhood. Some coworkers were vehemently opposed to his proposal because the rent in a residential building would be higher and because migrant workers tend to leave a congregation after two to three years. Eventually, the church once again was forced to move due to an impending demolition project. The church lost a third of the congregation (about forty members) after the relocation, including those financially better-off congregants who had been active participants. Departures like this illuminate the differences in opinion among congregants regarding the restructuring and reform of the church.

6.2 The Mingjia Church: From a Neighborhood Group to a Neighborhood Church

When commenting on the transformation of the Dianchang church, Pastor Liu presented a perspective different from Yuan's:

> In my opinion, church reform should proceed in phases. For example, our church consists primarily of migrant workers, but about 10 percent of the congregants are residents in the community. We have endeavored to hold on to the 10 percent of the congregation to lay down roots in the community. With a solid base, we feel more optimistic about the future development of the church.[15]

---

15 Interview with Pastor Liu of the Mount of Olives Church, Beijing, August 2012.

The establishment of the Mingjia church was precisely the outcome that Liu had envisioned.

The Dongsanqi church had a congregation of about two hundred, and a small number of them were residents of Mingjia Garden. In 2009, Liu decided to start a neighborhood church and proceeded with renting a unit in Mingjia Garden. A preacher was appointed to the ministry, and Christian residents of the community were invited to attend services. The church also went on to cultivate a relationship with the neighborhood residents' committee. This approach to building a neighborhood church has generated positive outcomes. In the span of three to four years, the church has gained forty congregants, and twenty of them have been regular attendees. Even though the church is not officially registered with the municipality, church leadership encourages congregants to give back to the community by cleaning the neighborhood regularly and giving out gifts on major holidays, for example. The congregation is also on friendly terms with the residents as well as the neighborhood residents' committee members, which has secured the church a space for evangelization in the neighborhood. The success of the Mingjia church is built upon the active involvement of Christians in the community. These congregants have not only helped alleviate potential tension between the church and the community, but they have also bridged cultural differences as well as facilitated the church's assimilation into the neighborhood. Encouraged by the success of the Mingjia church, Pastor Liu sent a group of congregants from the Dongsanqi church to form a group in Tiantong Yuan in order to lay down roots for a church there.

6.3   The Dongsanqi Church: Purchasing Property for a Headquarters

Pastor Liu has a grand vision for Mount of Olives Church. He wishes to raise funds to establish a proper church and turn it into a headquarters in the service of branch churches. His plan is to fundraise church-wide and then purchase a piece of property near Dongsanqi church. This property will serve as the headquarters for the entire church system; it will not only provide a permanent place of worship but also offer theological training to satisfy the needs of branch churches.

Not all preachers share Pastor Liu's vision. During the debate over Liu's proposal, some were opposed to it, citing the repercussions of the open-air worship of Shouwang Church 守望教会. The opponents insisted that building a church could be construed as an attempt to openly institutionalize the church, which runs the unnecessary risk of inviting governmental scrutiny. Moreover, considering the high price of real estate in the city and the limited financial strength of the congregants, the church would not be able to raise sufficient funds to purchase a property that was sizable enough to hold services, let alone serve as a center for theological training. Nevertheless, as the chief pastor, Liu disregarded the opposing opinions, raised funds church-wide, purchased a unit in a residential building in Tiantong Yuan, and positioned it as the headquarters of Mount of Olives.

To summarize, migrant worker churches have endeavored to address the real estate crisis, mainly by relocating from cottages to residential buildings. Although congregations have found ways to meet the challenge posed by urbanization on the space front, they have continued to encounter new challenges after relocating.

7 Urbanization and the Church's Cultural Crisis

The multifaceted process of urbanization incurs more than changes in physical space. More importantly, it causes tensions in the cultural realm and necessitates adjustments in lifestyle. As Mount of Olives Church had to adjust to different spatial arrangements, it was simultaneously facing a genuine clash between congregational and neighborhood cultures.

The migrant worker churches that have settled in residential buildings have had to cope with even greater and more complicated difficulties in two areas specifically: migrant workers do not share the same code of conduct or the same level of public-mindedness with their new host communities. Congregants of one church in a residential building provided much feedback to their preacher shortly after the relocation. Pastor Liu summarized the congregants' concerns in an interview, stating that the migrant workers felt very much constrained by the rules against littering and the shoes-off requirement while indoors. When the church moved into Tianyue Community 天悦社区, the congregants were required to apply for key cards and use the cards for every entry. Not even two months into the relocation, congregants had trickled away, complaining that they felt uneasy and constrained. Compared to the environment of a residential building, a village in an urban area is less sanitary and less orderly—congregants could stand up and get a drink of water at will, and they could speak at a higher volume without disturbing others. The congregants brought these habits to their new meeting places.

8 The Church's Response to the Cultural Crisis: Formulating a Code of Conduct through Rational Thinking

Preacher Yuan of Mount of Olives Church realizes the importance of proper conduct and public-mindedness in relation to the church's continuous expansion and growth. A minority of the congregants share their preacher's opinion, viewing institutionalization as essential to the well-being of their church. However, they also acknowledge the difficulty of implementing a code of conduct among Christian migrant workers. According to congregant Wei Man 卫满,

> We would love the church to be well-organized; there would be no order without proper rules and sound guiding principles. We should conduct matters with rules and guidelines. But it is difficult to achieve that goal. For example, we have started requiring congregants to give prior notification before giving a testimony. Those who wish to give testimonies must sign up with their preacher or a coworker. Signing up doesn't guarantee a spot for testimony on the following Tuesday; there is usually a wait for a few weeks before one can give testimony, and no walk-ins are allowed. Before we implemented this rule, once the preacher had finished the sermon and welcomed newcomers, everyone would scramble to give testimonies, which often caused lots of commotion.[16]

Granted that there is much room for migrant worker churches to improve their rules of conduct and public awareness, they have effected some positive changes. A case in point is the new rule for testimony-giving after Sunday service at the Dianchang church. When the Dianchang church first started encouraging testimonies, there were no fixed rules. Any congregant who wished to give testimony would simply walk up to the altar, crowding the space. At times, the congregants would start side conversations before someone could finish giving a testimony. Additionally, many testimony-givers spoke in dialect, which caused resentment in the congregation. To improve the congregants' experiences, the preacher began to require congregants to sign up for a spot before giving testimonies. They were also required to have prepared speeches so that, when it came time to speak, they would not be overcome by stage fright. Finally, congregants were required to give testimony in Mandarin to help the rest of the congregation understand the speakers. These new rules have been effective in encouraging congregants to learn to speak Mandarin, be orderly, and follow the rules.

Communal activities hosted by migrant worker churches also help cultivate proper conduct and public awareness. Mount of Olives Church hosts a training session at a spacious church once every month on a Saturday. Typically, each

---

16 Interview with congregant Wei Man of the Dianchang church, Beijing, May 2012.

session draws over one hundred attendants. Congregants prepare and serve lunch for the event, and the attendants share a meal in the church courtyard. I took part in one of the training sessions in June 2011 and observed the congregants' behavior at lunchtime. The one hundred or so congregants made two lines, quietly and orderly awaiting their turn to be served by the coworkers. That scene is a stark contrast to the typical disorderly way of life in rural areas, which suggests that migrant workers have adopted some of the habits of urban life.

8.1   *A Faith Based on Reason*

Individuals living on the margins of a city are the Mount of Olives Church's target recruits. In the early days of the church's foundation, its spirituality focused on exorcism and spiritual healing. This approach revealed the influence of Pentecostalism, which arose along with the general revival of Protestant Christianity in rural China in the 1980s. The Pentecostalism, fundamentalism, and personalized faith of migrant worker churches are at odds with urbanization and the urban lifestyle. As urbanization is part and parcel of the process of modernization, the cultural norms of a modern, urban life present a challenge to migrant-worker culture. In *The Social System*, Talcott Parsons argues that a modern society represents a secular culture, one that is, in Max Weber's term, "disenchanted."[17] Exorcism and spiritual healing in the Pentecostal fashion have limited appeal in the secular society of a city. Urban Christians are more inclined to take a rational and intellectual approach to their faith. A case in point is the popularity of Christian bookstores in cities as well as the wide circulation of Christian publications among urban Christians.[18] The rapid pace of life in a city, along with urbanization, has compelled religious leaders to pay special attention to current events, rather than focusing solely on matters concerning the religious community. Additionally, the abundance of new media as well as new means of disseminating information have also widened the perspectives of better-off congregants possessing greater socioeconomic capital and encouraged them to engage with social issues.

---

17   Talcott Parsons, *The Social System* (Abingdon, UK: Routledge, 1991), 182–198.

18   Since Protestant Christianity has begun to flourish in Chinese cities in the 1990s, an increasing number of university students, intellectuals, and professionals have started attending church services. A new cultural phenomenon resulted: Christians have started to get involved in the writing and publication industries, as well as social services. In Beijing, for example, several Christian bookstores have opened. Books for China (Chenguang shudian 晨光书店) is one of the most prominent Christian bookstores and frequently hosts public lectures on scholarly and cultural topics.

Mount of Olives has, in many ways, transplanted a rural culture to an urban environment. It is a rural church in an urban area that has perpetuated rural culture. All the same, the church cannot avoid adapting to the lifestyle of a modern city, in terms of pastoral care, the governance of the church, and methods of evangelization. As a carrier of rural culture, Mount of Olives Church nonetheless has endeavored to modernize itself.

A younger generation of preachers question the Pentecostal style of evangelization. Even though these young preachers come from the countryside, they are educated and have lived in cities. Their urban sensibilities and habits of rational thinking keep them at arm's length from the church's Pentecostalism; some even openly question it. In fact, these younger preachers identify strongly with cities and are open to full assimilation into the urban life. One preacher shared his hopes and visions for the future:

> Even though I have lived in Beijing for several years, I feel financially strained because of my low income. And I still don't feel that I fit in after all these years. My children returned to Beijing after a short period of time back in our hometown. You know, life in a farming village [is far from ideal]. ... Although we are not well-off, we have the advantage of a better education and can enjoy the lifestyle of a city. I don't want my children to grow up in the countryside, nor do I wish for my parents to help raise my children. My parents hold outdated ideas.[19]

This preacher has revealed his aspirations for a life in the big city, as well as his struggles with the realities of urban life. His expectations for his children's education also indicate that a younger generation of preachers prefer to live in a city with their offspring, shedding the identities of rural villagers and adopting those of city folk.

9   The Church's Authority Crisis and Responses

Christianity in rural China is barely institutionalized and typically adheres to Christian primitivism.[20] As migrant worker churches model their operations after rural churches, Mount of Olives Church has never instituted any by-laws or codes of conduct. The operation of the church has relied on customary

---

19   Interview with preacher Yuan of the Mount of Olives Church, Beijing, May 2012.
20   Leung Ka-lun, *Gaige kaifang yilai de Zhongguo nongcun jiaohui* (Hong Kong: The Alliance Bible Seminary, 1999), 147–153.

practices, experience, or the initiatives of pastors and preachers. The church's founder, Pastor Liu, has leveraged his spiritual authority and charisma to direct the church's development and operation. His leadership is based on charismatic authority. However, urbanization and the urban lifestyle have challenged the barely institutionalized and personality-centered governance model on three major fronts: the continuous expansion of the church, the vitality of urban organizations and the bureaucratization within social organizations, and younger congregants' challenges to traditional church authority.

The continuous expansion of migrant worker churches is an immediate outcome of urbanization. In 2008, the Mount of Olives Church increased the number of its meeting places to twenty-five, which significantly enlarged the church. From Shahe 沙河 in Beiliu Huan 北六环 in the north to Dahongmen 大红门 in Nansi Huan 南四环 in the south, Mount of Olives has established churches in all five districts of Beijing. No longer is Pastor Liu able to conduct his ministry and visit every single church as he used to during the foundational period of Mount of Olives. Moreover, the increase in the number of churches has also increased the amount of administrative tasks. Pastor Liu is unable to attend to all matters personally. It has become clear that urbanization has forced the church organization to further its specialization and professionalization.[21] However, in the case of a church, specialization and professionalization effectively undermine the authority of the chief pastor. The chief pastor of Mount of Olives Church has responded by appointing additional preachers to branch churches so that every two to three meeting places share a preacher. He has also reached an agreement with the coworkers that he would hand over some governing authority to the preachers at local churches.

The rationalization and bureaucratization of urban organizations provides an organizational model for migrant worker churches. Cities have undergone a widespread social organizational revolution since the reform and opening up, in which a variety of social organizations have emerged and subsequently thrived.[22] These organizations have reached a high degree of institutionalization and bureaucratic standardization. In this context, Christian migrant workers are temporary residents in a city, and rejection—in employment, daily life,

---

21 Ronald Johnstone, *Religion in Society: A Sociology of Religion*, 8th ed. (Abingdon, UK: Routledge, 2006); translated by Yuan Yayu and Zhong Yuying as *Shehui zhong de zongjiao–yizhong zongjiao shehuixue* (Chengdu: Sichuan renmin chubanshe, 2012), 78–80.

22 He Jianyu and Wang Shaoguang, "Zhongguoshi de shetuan geming—dui shetuan quanjingtu de dingliang miaoshu," in *Zhongguo gongmin shehui lanpishu*, ed. Gao Bingzhong and Yuan Ruijun (Beijing: Beijing daxue chubanshe, 2008), 161.

and interpersonal relationships—seems to be the status quo of their lives.[23] The religious elites of migrant worker churches tend to have better social networks and interpersonal connections, and it is through these elites that the impact of urban social organizations on migrant worker churches manifests itself. For example, some of the preachers at Mount of Olives Church migrated from Henan to big cities such as Guangzhou and Beijing to work or to continue their education after they graduated from middle school. They are very much integrated into the urban way of life. Moreover, emerging urban churches have provided a model for the institutionalization of churches in general, as they are far more developed in organizational aspects and can help stimulate the organizational transformation of migrant worker churches.[24]

Emergent urban churches directly assist migrant worker churches in the latter's attempts at institutionalizing church governance at a time when urbanization has pushed rural churches on the outskirts of Beijing into office buildings. Leaders of one church who have foreseen the inevitable social and organizational change are also the leaders who have pushed for reform. They drafted the creed of the church, its codes of conduct, and its by-laws. This church has further received the support of another emergent urban church.[25]

A younger generation of congregants is challenging the authority of the church. Urbanization brings new members to migrant worker churches, especially an increasing number of youth. These young congregants tend to be better educated, less constrained by traditional norms, and fit into urban life much more easily than their older counterparts. Moreover, they have a different perception of authority. My interaction with the youth fellowship at the Mount of Olives Church has revealed that the younger generation is dissatisfied with the church's status quo. They are eager for greater involvement in church affairs, and they desire to affect change in certain aspects of the church's operation. Furthermore, they are outspoken about ideas for change, and when the church leadership refuses their proposals, they may even leave the congregation. The youth's challenge has effectively stimulated changes within the church.

---

23 Li Qiang, ed., *Zhongguo shehui bianqian sanshi nian* (Beijing: Social Sciences Academic Press), 120–127.
24 He Zhe, *Chengshizhong de linggong: yike zhishi fenzi jiqi jiating jiaohui de fazhan shilu* (Hong Kong: Mingfeng chuban, 2009), 139–143.
25 The church has received assistance from a pastor at the Shouwang Church, who has been a member of Shouwang's governing committee since 2010, as it has continued to transition into an urban church.

10 Conclusion

This chapter examined the rise, growth, and transformation of migrant worker churches in the context of urbanization, as well as the social change that urbanization has sparked in contemporary China. I have also addressed the ways in which migrant worker churches have responded to the impact of urbanization, especially to the crises that these churches have faced. Along the lines of congregational studies, I have argued that the different consequences of urbanization impact migrant worker churches in different ways at different levels, ranging from the material resources crisis to the cultural crisis at a deeper level. These two crises combined have also led to a crisis of authority. As urbanization has affected and reshaped migrant worker churches, the churches have also been alerted by these challenges and formulated responses to them. In the end, migrant worker churches address these crises by seeking different physical spaces for meetings, reforming codes of conduct and public awareness, and cultivating a life of faith based on reason. The shattering of a paternalistic style of governance in favor of a disciplined and democratic structure of authority was accomplished with much difficult internal negotiation and compromise. The transition into a fully democratic way of governance remains a work-in-progress.

Mount of Olives Church is a typical migrant worker church. The urban culture of Beijing has significantly altered its access to resources, its congregational culture, and its structure of authority. Reform-minded leaders have taken the initiative and led the congregation in its negotiation with changes incurred by urbanization. They have relocated the congregations to residential buildings and recruited members of urban neighborhoods. They have endeavored to institutionalize the governance of the church and undermined some of the church leaders' absolute authority. They have also gradually replaced Pentecostalism with more rational approaches to the Christian faith.

The case study of Mount of Olives Church has shown that a migrant worker church has provided a space in which reform-minded congregants as well as church leaders could implement change. They have been able to instill concepts of civic participation and introduce codes of proper conduct. Pentecostalism no longer monopolizes the practices of faith; instead, rationalism and self-reflection have become the preferred approach to pastoral care. No longer do congregants focus myopically on church affairs; some congregants have begun to appreciate the well-being of other social groups and to pay attention to greater societal concerns. All of these indicate that the community of faith is gradually embracing a modern and public-minded outlook.

Bibliography

Ammerman, Nancy T. *Congregation and Community*. New Brunswick, NJ: Rutgers University Press, 1997.

Beijingshi diliuci quanguo renkou pucha lingdao xiaozu bangongshi 北京市第六次全国人口普查领导小组办公室. "Beijingshi diliuci quanguo renkou pucha zhuyao shuju qingkuang" 北京市2010年第六次全国人民普查主要数据情况. http://www.bjstats.gov.cn/tjsj/tjgb/rpgb/201511/t20151124_327785.html.

Beijingshi diliuci renkou pucha bangongshi 北京市第六次人口普查办公室. "Beijing changzhu wailai renkou laiyuan fenxi." https://wenku.baidu.com/view/a99c9bd7240c844769eaeefb.html (accessed August 20, 2019).

Cao, Nanlai. *Constructing China's Jerusalem: Christians, Power, and Place in Contemporary Wenzhou*. Stanford, CA: Stanford University Press, 2010.

Duan Qi 段琦. "2011 nian Zhongguo jidujiao zhuyao shijian ji chengshihua dui jiaohui de yingxiang" 2011年中国基督教主要事件及城市化对教会的影响. In *Zhongguo zongjiao baogao (2012)* 中国宗教报告（2012）, edited by Jin Ze 金泽 and Qiu Yonghui 邱永辉, 64–104. Beijing: Shehui kexue wenxian chubanshe, 2012.

Friedmann, John. *The Prospect of Cities*. Minneapolis: University of Minnesota Press, 2002.

Gans, Herbert. *The Urban Villagers*. New York: Free Press, 1982.

Germani, Gino. *The Sociology of Modernization: Studies on Its Historical and Theoretical Aspects with Special Regard to the Latin American Case*. New Brunswick, NJ: Transaction, 1981.

He Jianyu 何建宇 and Wang Shaoguang 王绍光. "Zhongguoshi de shetuan geming—dui shetuan quanjingtu de dingliang miaoshu" 中国式的社团革命—对社团全景图的定量描述. In *Zhongguo gongmin shehui lanpishu* 中国公民社会发展蓝皮书. edited by Gao Bingzhong 高丙中 and Yuan Ruijun 袁瑞军, 133–156. Beijing: Beijing daxue chubanshe, 2008.

He Zhe 何哲. *Chengshizhong de linggong: yike zhishi fenzi yiqi jiating jiaohui de fazhan shilu* 城市中的灵宫：一个知识分子及其家庭教会的发展实录. Hong Kong: Mingfeng chuban, 2009.

Huang Jianbo 黄剑波. *Dushili de xiangcun jiaohui—Zhongguo chengshihua yu mingong jidujiao* 都市里的乡村教会—中国城市化与民工基督教. Hong Kong: Logos and Pneuma Press, 2012.

Huang Jianbo 黄剑波. "Zhongguo chengzhen mingong de zongjiao shenghuo" 中国城镇民工的宗教生活. *Ershiyi shiji* 二十一世纪. no. 109 (2008): 104–110.

Johnstone, Ronald. *Religion in Society: A Sociology of Religion*. 8th ed. Abingdon, UK: Routledge, 2016. Translated by Yuan Yayu 袁亚愚 and Zhong Yuying 钟玉英 as *Shehui zhong de zongjiao-yizhong zongjiao shehuixue* 社会中的宗教——一种宗教社会学. Chengdu: Sichuan renmin chubanshe, 2012.

Kindopp, Jason, and Carol Lee Hamrin. *God and Caesar in China: Policy Implications of Church-State Tensions*. Washington, DC: Brookings Institution Press, 2004.

Kung, Lap-Yan. "The Emergence of Exchange Politics in China and Its Implications for Church-State Relations." *Religion, State and Society* 38.1 (2010): 9–28.

Lambert, Tony. *China's Christian Millions*. Oxford: Monarch, 2006.

Leung Ka-lun 梁家麟. *Gaige kaifang yilai de Zhongguo nongcun jiaohui* 改革开放以来的中国农村教会. Hong Kong: The Alliance Bible Seminary, 1999.

Li Qiang 李强, ed. *Zhongguo shehui bianqian sanshi nian* 中国社会变迁 30年. Beijing: Social Sciences Academic Press, 2008.

Parsons, Talcott. *The Social System*. Abingdon, UK: Routledge, 1991.

Putnam, Robert. *Making Democracy Work: Civic Tradition in Modern Italy*. Princeton: Princeton University Press, 1993.

Tönnies, Ferdinand. *Community and Civil Society*. Edited by Jose Harris. Translated by Margaret Hollis. Cambridge: Cambridge University Press, 2001.

Yang, Fenggang. "The Red, Black, and Gray Markets of Religion in China." *Sociological Quarterly* 47.1 (2006): 93–122.

Ying Fuk-tsang 邢福增. *Dangdai Zhongguo zhengjiao guanxi* 当代中国政教关系. Hong Kong: The Alliance Bible Seminary, 1999. Repr., Hong Kong: China Alliance Press, 2005.

Yuan Hao 袁浩. "Tingbujian de shengyin: Guanyu Zhongguo jidujiao chengshi mingong jiaohui de yanjiu" 听不见的声音：关于中国基督教城市民工教会的研究. *Daofeng* 道风. no. 39 (2013): 337–353.

CHAPTER 12

Modern Individuals in Imagined Communities
An Anthropological Examination of Artist Churches in Songzhuang, Beijing

Hu Mengyin

Rural churches in urban areas in China have quickly become a common phenomenon across the country.[1] As urbanization progresses, and as the immigrant populations grow, especially in cities such as Beijing, Shanghai, and Guangzhou, the characteristics of rural churches, as well as their internal composition, also continue to evolve. On the one hand, many of the so-called immigrants in cities are now second- or even third-generation peasant-laborers. Their status has transformed from migrant laborers to permanent urban residents. The most pressing issue they face is the scarcity of living space, rather than their assimilation into urban life. The competition for space is a factor of modern life and not necessarily a consequence of discrimination against a specific group. On the other hand, the intensification of the division of labor, i.e., the heightened specialization of labor, has resulted in a tendency to classify social groups in cities by occupation. At the same time, there is a lack of a community to foster a common sense of belonging. These conditions of contemporary urban life have led to the formation of many Protestant churches with a focus on a specific profession. The emergence of artist churches in Songzhuang 宋庄, the newly established arts industry park in Beijing's Tongzhou District 通州区, is a case in point.

From the founders of the churches to subsequent leaders and congregants, all members of these churches are painters who live in Songzhuang. Congregants take their identity as artists very seriously, and churches of varying sizes have formed communities of some sort. A notable characteristic of these artist churches is a shared concept of homogeneity. Homogeneity refers to a state of unanimity. Once unanimity is breached, a church falls apart. Like some other districts of Beijing, Songzhuang has witnessed a revival and rapid development of religious belief in the past two decades. However, both local and foreign churches have been unable to expand; rather, they

---

[1] Huang Jianbo, *Dushili de xiangcun jiaohui—Zhongguo chengshihua yu minkong jidujiao* (Hong Kong: Logos and Pneuma Press, 2012). Also see chapter 11 by Yuan Hao in this volume.

have been trapped in a cycle of expansion and division. Whenever a church reaches a critical mass, it immediately breaks up into smaller units. This is the main contributing factor to the multiplicity of churches of varying sizes in Songzhuang.

The wider scholarly discussion of rural churches in urban areas is helpful when examining the artist churches in Songzhuang. As Songzhuang has developed into an "artist village," its churches have attempted to fashion themselves as part of traditional villages. Members of these artist churches are also residents of the Songzhuang artist village. They have experienced the effects of capitalism, which have shrunk their living space. That is, the "village in a city" is on the brink of dissolution. Although the artist churches are not complete transmutations of villages or replacements for them, they nevertheless offer release and assistance to their members as they cope with the fierce competition for space. These churches gather and consolidate the unattached individuals in a large city and shape them into one cohesive entity. As the discussion of rural churches in urban areas continues, it is important to examine the social context in which these churches operate. This examination will help us, first, to more accurately articulate the characteristics of these artist churches, and second, to gain a better understanding of the relationship between the individual and the community.

This chapter is an anthropological study based on on-site interviews with artists in Songzhuang. In what follows, I will examine the tension between the modernized individual and the community—in this case, the artist churches. Specifically, I take the cases of two different churches to demonstrate divergent approaches to fostering a community. One church encourages its members to become fully developed individuals, and the other stresses the homogeneity of the community. The concepts of community and the ways it is imagined are derived from Charles Taylor's *Modern Social Imaginaries*.[2] Taylor indicates that social imaginaries are first formulated by social elites, who then disseminate these concepts to the rest of society. Eventually, elite social imaginaries become norms and come to be perceived as timeless. Regarding the two churches in question, their respective leaders are instrumental in shaping notions of community and even dictate the characteristics of their churches. A discussion of the tension between individuals and their community also contributes to an understanding of the multiple small-scale and internally divided churches of Songzhuang. Furthermore, the divergent approaches taken by the

---

2   Charles Taylor, *Modern Social Imaginaries* (Durham, NC: Duke University Press, 2003); translated by Lin Manhong as *Xiandai shehui xiangxiang* (Shanghai: Yilin Chubanshe, 2014).

two churches under discussion may shed light on the effects of contemporary social conditions, as well as oppressive capitalism, on the individual.

1 The Cross in the Artist Village

Today, Songzhuang has many names—"Original Art District," "Chinese Soho," or "Culture Factory," to mention a few. But it is most commonly known as the "artist village." Currently, at least 6,000 artists live in Songzhuang; the number may reach 10,000 when nonresident artists are included. Songzhuang also attracts large numbers of art students, visual and action artists, poets, writers, and musicians. Altogether, Songzhuang hosts up to 20,000 artists of all kinds. This is not the population of a village. The town of Songzhuang consists of 47 administrative villages and 100,000 registered residents. It falls under the jurisdiction of Tongzhou, Beijing, and borders Shunyi District 顺义区 to the north and Chaoyang District 朝阳区 to the west. The heart of the artist village was originally Xiaobao village 小堡村 of Songzhuang. As several large art museums and art districts have gradually taken over Xiaobao village, great numbers of artists have also relocated to the village's peripheries. The Songzhuang government's efforts in developing the cultural industry have made Xiaobao village an artistic landmark of Songzhuang. However, governmental support is not the only factor contributing to the village's rise to fame. The earliest artists-in-residence, including Huang Yongyu 黄永玉, Li Xianting 栗宪庭, and Fang Lijun 方力钧, have all played an important part. The name "artist village" is, moreover, inspired by its previous incarnation—the artist village in Yuanmingyuan 圆明园.

Li Xianting is representative of some of the earliest artists in Songzhuang, who are directly connected to the artists of Yuanmingyuan. As government pressure on some artists increased, the artist village in Yuanmingyuan was forced to close. This was a major factor in many villagers moving to Songzhuang. Low real-estate prices, together with the atmosphere of the countryside, made Songzhuang an appealing retreat from the outside world. The affordable housing, large spans of space, remoteness from the city center, and inaccessibility of Songzhuang all satisfied the desire for an idyllic lifestyle. However, admirers followed famous artists like Li Xianting and Huang Yongyu into Songzhuang. Before long, a "painter village" based in Xiaobao village came into shape.

The villagers of Xiaobao were not prepared for the sudden emergence of the painter village in Songzhuang. Apart from selling their old houses to these newcomers, villagers took no interest in either the painters or their paintings. From 1994, when Huang Yongyu first moved to Songzhuang, until 2000, an average of twenty-five artists moved to Songzhuang each year.[3] This pushed the artist population to about two hundred by the start of the new millennium. Between 2001 and 2004, the artist population increased even more rapidly, adding about one hundred new residents annually. The influx of artists also resulted in tension with the villagers. Although the artists clearly were not welcome, an artist community in Songzhuang was nevertheless firmly established by 2005. As the resident artists continued to attract families and friends into the village, both the villagers and the village administration took steps to address the problems caused by overpopulation. On the one hand, villagers took the new residents to court over property rights. On the other hand, they made an effort to help the artists assimilate into the village community. For example, new restaurants began to pop up near art studios. Some villagers even took an interest in painting and became "indigenous" artists. The government's attitude toward all this shifted over time. Early on in 1994 and 1995, the local government was very suspicious of the newly established artist village. But it remained neutral during the argument over property rights between the villagers and artists, and in 2004, the newly appointed Party secretary, Hu Jiebao 胡介报, recruited Li Xianting to assist in planning the transformation of Songzhuang into a cultural establishment.

Both Xiaobao village and Songzhuang thrived in the wake of these policies. Art museums, galleries, and studios appeared in rapid succession. More and more artists moved into the village to open galleries or studios. Collaborations with international artists also increased. The Songzhuang Culture and Art Festival generates over a million RMB annually in sales of artwork.[4] The "culture sets up the stage for the economy to put on a show" strategy is thoroughly exemplified in the fashioning and promotion of Songzhuang. However, even though the cultural industry has significantly boosted local economic growth, the producers of the cultural industry—the artists—have continued to hover over the poverty line. Only about 10 percent of the artists in Songzhuang make a living wage by creating art alone.[5] The average cost of living for artists in Songzhuang, and in Xiaobao in particular, is about 60,000 RMB per year. The majority of the artists can barely satisfy their basic needs by selling their art. In fact, it is common for members of several of the churches in Songzhuang to

---

3 Kong Jianhua, "Beijingshi Songzhuang yuanchuang yishu jijuqu fazhan zai yanjiu," *Beijing shehui kexue*, 2007.3: 22.
4 Lin Jinglu, "Zhongguo Songzhuang huajiacun diaoyan yu fazhan baogao," *Wenyi lilun yu piping*, 2013.3: 75.
5 Ibid., 73.

receive assistance from family members or other congregants. Churches have become a safety net for these artists.

Protestant Christianity began gaining a foothold in Songzhuang around 2000, primarily among the artist community. Evangelical activities began in 1998. The earliest preachers, as well as congregants, were all Christian converts. Artist Zhang, baptized in November of 2000, claims that he was the very first Christian in Songzhuang.[6] Immediately after his baptism, Zhang began preaching with fellow Christians and remained actively involved in evangelism for a year. The first congregation consisted of five or six painters. Each of their paths to conversion was different, and they only started attending a church after relocating to Songzhuang. Zhang explained to me that his home was the first church.

In many ways, Zhang's personal journey parallels the development of churches in Songzhuang. Most of the current church leaders have been, at one point or another, members of Zhang's congregation; they converted as a result of the initial evangelical efforts. As Artist Li explains, "At first these people formed a church, which then brought in more congregants. The original church no longer exists, but many early members have established their own churches." Evangelical efforts in the early 2000s did not result in significant growth in church membership, nor did it contribute to the increase in the number of churches. Nevertheless, the first church has expanded from less than ten to nearly fifty congregants, holding small-group meetings and fellowships during the week. The earliest group of Christians sowed the seeds for the subsequent spread of Christianity in Songzhuang.

The first Christians all agreed that evangelization was a pressing task. They not only introduced the Christian faith to other artists through everyday social interaction, but they also endeavored to convert family members. Some even travelled to Henan to receive proselytizing training in order to preach more effectively back in Songzhuang. By 2006, six or seven churches had been established in Songzhuang. Among these, a pair of sisters who ran an art supply business headed two churches, and the rest could claim the first Christians among their congregants. Lin and Wang are both congregants of the first church, and now they are leaders of new churches. According to them, the expansion of churches in Songzhuang after 2006 has much to do with the entry of external churches.

---

6   Pseudonyms are used throughout this chapter. It is difficult to verify Zhang's claim. However, he is undoubtedly the first baptized Christian among the earliest Christians to congregate in Songzhuang.

The Christian population enjoyed notable growth after 2006. As the churches grew larger in scale, their numbers were also on the rise. In addition to the Protestant Three-Self Church, Songzhuang now has a few dozen churches. According to Lin's estimate, there are over one hundred churches in the area, and congregations range in size from twenty to thirty members to just a few. Although Lin and Wang were among the earliest churchgoers, they know little about many of the current churches. In their view, the diversity of the church scene is caused by the influx of external churches.

The so-called external churches are not all of the same variety. They are churches from other parts of Beijing, Henan, or Inner Mongolia, and some are even from Korea. The ever-increasing outsider population in Songzhuang has also become diverse. Besides the northward migrants who first moved to the artist village, there are now art students in universities, as well as professionals in the cultural and creative industries, who came to Songzhuang for work and stayed. Newcomers who were already churchgoers in their universities or places of work have now joined churches in Songzhuang. Some organize small-group meetings that later develop into fellowships.

Some external churches were started by preachers sent into Songzhuang. For example, Wang noted that a woman from a church in Chaoyang district heads a large church of about fifty members. Compared to other churches in Beijing, provincial churches, such as those from Henan and Inner Mongolia, are very active in their recruitment efforts. Lin's church has gotten into a conflict with one of the Henan churches over poaching members, for instance. A Korean church generously supports missionary activities in Songzhuang. Not only do the missionaries organize communal activities, but they also offer monetary incentives, such as gifts or financial assistance, to attract potential churchgoers. These recruitment tactics were successful at first. A Christian with firsthand experience finds the Korean church lively and their activities appealing, especially the Christmas concerts. After a while, however, these tactics haven fallen flat. Although the Korean church boasted one hundred congregants in the first two years of its activities, it was unable to retain its membership. The group of Korean missionaries ended up leaving Songzhuang.

The expansion of Christian activities in Songzhuang should not be treated as an isolated phenomenon. In the decade between 2001 and 2010, Protestant Christianity not only experienced a revival but also grew rapidly, both in Beijing and in China as a whole. Viewed in this context, the expansion of Protestantism in Songzhuang is not an exception. The growth in the numbers of churches elsewhere in Beijing and the influx of provincial churches in Songzhuang are both quite understandable. What is exceptional about the development of

Christianity in Songzhuang is that, whereas large-scale churches are few and far between, there are numerous small, active churches. The most populous church is the Three-Self church, with about one hundred members. Any non-Three-Self churches with a congregation of fifty members are considered large. Most churches have between twelve and twenty members.[7] That is to say, the expansion of Christianity in Songzhuang is reflected in the increase in both the number of Christians and the number of churches, while large churches remain an exception.

As Wang explains it, this phenomenon can be attributed to the high mobility of the Songzhuang population. Artists in residence are in fact the minority population in Songzhuang, while artists who want to try their luck keep flooding in. They tend to stay for a few months, attempting to sell their paintings, and leave when they fail to establish a business. Wang has devoted several months at a time trying to recruit newcomers to his church, but they would leave the church when they could not make it in Songzhuang. Their faith would leave with them. The core members of Wang's church are permanent residents in Songzhuang; about one-third of them are artists, and the rest are employees of companies in the cultural industry nearby. At every Sunday service that I have attended, I have observed about thirty in attendance, among whom many are painters, poets, and musicians. But regulars have been few. Commenting on my observation, Wang said that his church is more like an inn that receives travelers and visitors—the friends and acquaintances of the artists—than the house of the Lord.

Lin has a different take on the matter. He thinks that the entry of external churches is disrupting the cohesion of local churches. Division is so common that one can find three or four churches in one alley. Lin perceives that these external churches fail to appreciate the local circumstances and the artists' inclinations. Their attempt to recruit members from existing local churches has had the opposite effect and most artists have turned away from external churches. At the same time, aggressive recruitment has also inspired new or different ideas among the congregants, stirring up internal friction within churches. The history of the first church repeats itself: the local churches lack fellowship and organization, and any disagreement can tear a church apart. It appears that whenever an external church comes in, it disrupts the status quo and causes existing churches to split from within.

---

7   For example, Lin's church has twenty-two members, and there are sixteen in Wang's church.

2   Cycles of Division

It seems that Songzhuang churches have never broken out of the cycle of division. The first congregation, of which Zhang was a member, ended in a schism. Zhang played a significant role in this splintering. In the early days of this church, members participated in Sunday services and small-group Bible study sessions during the week. Pastoral care was not provided at all. After the initial year of passionate devotion, Zhang began asking questions about the Christian faith, to which none of his fellow congregants were able to provide satisfactory answers. The only instruction Zhang received was to follow the guidance of the Bible. Dissatisfied with the responses, Zhang decided to leave the congregation. His departure led to a serious debate among fellow congregants over his behavior. The debate between two camps caused an irreparable split within the church.

Similar patterns of division have been commonplace ever since this first schism. Disagreements among individuals result in groups holding opposing opinions, which usually end up with an internal realignment of alliances. The Christian artist community revealed its personality traits soon after Protestant churches first entered Songzhuang. On the one hand, artists highly value individuality. They are not shy about expressing personal opinions and expect to be treated as fully developed individuals. On the other hand, the Christian artist community does not seem to value cohesion. The artists are not troubled by the formation and dissolution of the congregations. In Zhang's experience, his congregation met regularly for a year or so, but there was never a definitive leader of the fellowship. Therefore, when disagreements arose, those members on the same side of an issue tended to band together, and the congregation became factionalized.

Lin's and Wang's remarks, as well as the example of Zhang, all point to the fact that division is an uncomfortable situation that churches in Songzhuang have to tackle. Every church seems destined to split up after a period of growth. This was the case with the first church, as well as the many churches today. In the case of Zhang, when a shared understanding within the church is no longer intact, individuals seek those who agree with them and form cliques. Lin also observes that when certain members of a church begin to accept new and different ideas, they challenge the conventional practices of the church, which unavoidably causes rifts. Lin's church has undergone several waves of division, one of which was propelled by the desire of congregants for a different preaching style. Certain congregants, through contact with members of a different church, discovered a more appealing method of preaching. Accordingly, they asked Lin to make adjustments to his pastoral style. When he failed to adopt a different approach, the discontented congregants left his church. Wang, one of the first members of the earliest church, feels helpless, saying, "The quarrels continued and then the church just fell apart." Thus, when discord arises among congregants, or, when a common goal is no longer shared, congregants tend to band with those who are in agreement rather than attempting to reconcile with one another. This tendency is a typical behavioral pattern of many Christians in Songzhuang, who for one reason or another have decided to leave their current church, and who start attending a different church or stop going to church all together. In Songzhuang, almost every conflict within a church becomes a public, communal event. Nearly every congregant has an opinion and bands with others who take a similar stance. Thus, rifts in churches often end with the exodus of a group of congregants.

Thus far, my examination of churches in Songzhuang reveals many personality traits of Christian artists, including their disorganized nature. These traits, however, are not sufficient explanations for the persistence of the cycle of division. Nevertheless, such behaviors make the discord among Christian artists all the more noticeable. That division is the norm and not the exception may in fact be an unintended consequence of the artists' pursuit of homogeneity or unity. At first glance, churches in Songzhuang can be described as charismatic organizations. Their first congregants have all become leaders in subsequently established churches. Considering the history of churches in Songzhuang, it is understandable that strong personalities attract followers. In reality, the status quo of perpetual disunity reflects an underlying desire for and emphasis on a shared identity among Christians in Songzhuang. For one church member to openly challenge the leader is more than a disagreement between two individuals. It is a sign of the weakening of a collective sense of identity. Although such a sense of identity is not necessarily Christian in nature, the church is nevertheless a community by definition, and thus the sense of identity is church-based.

It is difficult to pinpoint the aforementioned sense of identity because church members cannot fully articulate it in specific terms. For some, identity is based on the concept of artistic creation, arguing that "the purpose of Christian art is to represent society." At a material level, the question of whether a given painting should be for sale also reveals a particular conception of art. Under normal circumstances, the issue of identity rarely comes up. The question of identity only becomes apparent when a particular problem presents itself.

It is noteworthy that Christian artists in Songzhuang are eager to establish a new sense of identity almost as soon as the existing one collapses. Compromise is a rarity. As soon as discord is out in the open, congregants are divided into opposing camps. That is, when friction is apparent and when the existing unity is broken, not only do the defiant members and leaders seek to shape a new sense of collective identity, but everyone else in the church also feels compelled to redefine the community based on a renewed sense of homogeneity. The desperate need for identity is not the inclination of any single individual. It seems to be a state of mind common to all Christian artists in Songzhuang.

Earlier, I examined the case of Zhang and argued that, on the one hand, the Christian artists in Songzhuang highly value individuality. They demonstrate this value in both the expression and the legitimacy of this individuality. On the other hand, these artists are disorganized, and their churches are lacking in both leadership and cohesion. My discussion in the previous pages has demonstrated that Christian artists are neither absolute individualists nor indifferent about church organization. Rather, they exhibit a strong desire for pure homogeneity. When conflicts arise, instead of compromising for the sake of congregational unity, the Christian artists tend to retreat to even smaller groups to find commonality. It is important to note that the sense of identity is not an abstract or ideological construct. At every occasion of disagreement, members choose sides based on practical concerns. Therefore, the search for a common sense of identity is by no means metaphysical; it is, rather, fully rooted in the individuals' specific circumstances and pragmatic considerations. An appreciation for the Christian artists' pursuit for homogeneity is instrumental to a deeper understanding of the underlying reasons for the perpetual disunity within churches in the last decade or so, as well as the current state of a multiplicity of small churches in Songzhuang.

When disagreements arise, the Christian artists' insistence on homogeneity explains their unwillingness to compromise for the sake of the integrity of the community. As a consequence, churches in Songzhuang are trapped in a perpetual cycle of expansion and division. In recent years, these churches have come to fashion themselves as village communities, very much like traditional rural communities. This is to say, churches have come to rely on the existing social network as a stabilizing force. By promoting an identity akin to that of a village community and by embracing the diversity of church members, churches seek to shift individual artists' focus from homogeneity to the consolidation of congregational cohesion. Nevertheless, the former approach toward homogeneity does not prevent churches from falling into the trap of cyclical division. The latter approach makes the development of a church overly dependent on personal connections. Specifically, the suspicious attitude toward new members has an even greater impact on a congregation's well-being. In that regard, Songzhuang is representative of the tension between an imagined community and the individuals in it. Similar cases can be found in most contemporary Chinese cities.

3   The Village and the Individual in an Urban Environment

Painters, sculptors, and dealers started flooding into Songzhuang in the 1990s. The official policy for the establishment of Songzhuang as a center for the cultural industry was confirmed in 2004. Starting in 2005, Songzhuang has hosted a Culture and Art Festival every year, attracting both domestic and foreign capital investments into the town. Songzhuang has also been populated by a growing number of cultural and creative industries, in addition to galleries and art museums. An artist village has thus taken shape on the main square of Xiaobao. Moreover, the residential population of Songzhuang continues to grow beyond the artist community. The original painter village has now developed into an artist village with a wider range of permanent residents. But for the original artists in residence, Songzhuang's development into an artist village has stripped them of the freedom that it originally offered. As large amounts of capital continue to pour into Songzhuang to the extent of monopolizing the art market, Songzhuang's initial openness has given way to exclusiveness, as perceived by the "grassroots" artists. Today, 90 percent of the painters are excluded from the art market, without access to this new artist village.

Most of the artists who attend Songzhuang's churches are among the excluded 90 percent. In fact, more and more Christian artists have relocated to the peripheries of Xiaobao. Since congregations typically meet at the homes of church leaders or members, churches migrate along with the population to nearby villages. We can observe exclusiveness in these churches. Their acceptance of new members and rejection of external churches parallels the formation of traditional Han Chinese rural village communities. In a way, churches in Songzhuang, just like the painter village itself, exemplify a village community.

The painter village that first came about near Yuanmingyuan existed as a traditional rural community in a large city. As opposed to the artistic establishments in the artist village in today's Songzhuang, the painter village around Yuanmingyuan was not defined by physical structures or geographical boundaries. A cluster of artists formed the village, which was built upon interpersonal relationships and formed a social hierarchy comprising a "mayor," the "gentry," and commoners. Just like traditional Chinese villages, the Yuanmingyuan painter village resisted and challenged the power exercised by the state (formerly the imperial authority). Direct challenges to the state eventually ended with defeat. The painter village in Songzhuang, on the other hand, has chosen to negotiate and collaborate with the state. For example, artists like Li Xianting take on the role of a "gentleman" and negotiate with the local government. Interpersonal connections among artists have replaced ties of blood and locality in this particular "natural village," which makes it difficult to demarcate a physical community or locate the source of a common identity. Moreover, the "gentry" in Songzhuang are by no means the political or legal equivalents of the "gentlemen" in traditional rural communities. As Songzhuang continues to expand, the original members of the painter village have gradually been excluded from the new artist village. The "gentlemen" have also lost the little influence they used to exert on the local government. Nevertheless, the traditional-style village has not disappeared. It has morphed into groups of varying sizes, migrated into the peripheral villages, and persisted as an imagined community. The Christian church is a type of imagined community.

Christian churches in Songzhuang are different from other artist communities in one respect. Although interpersonal relationships remain the foundation of the churches' expansion, they are able to nourish a common sense of identity by drawing clear boundaries for their members. These churches are, however, quite exclusive with self-imposed segregation. Wang related to me that members of his church all enjoy close personal ties to one another. He has personally examined every single member to ensure their "trustworthiness." In the past couple of years, many have reached out to him and expressed interest in attending his church. He has rejected some and referred others, including some newly arrived artists who are curious about the Christian faith, to the Three-Self Church. Those whom Wang has welcomed into his congregation have to participate in the fellowship for one year before receiving baptism. Wang does not accept Christians who have been baptized in other churches.

Wang's personal experience suggests that in its formative period, local Protestant churches in Songzhuang took evangelism very seriously. Even after the first schism, Christian artists were eager to establish new churches and continue to recruit new members. It is in this context that Lin complains about "external churches" that often "poach from our flock." The recruitment effort in Wang's church has now become a particularly rigorous process. On the other hand, Lin continues to welcome seekers and baptized Christians alike to his church, and yet the Sunday service is viewed as a public space for socialization as much as a religious gathering. The same can be observed in Wang's church. The Sunday service is a socializing event for regular congregants and nonmember Christian artists alike, even though the recruitment process remains strict.

One finds striking similarities when comparing Christian socialization with similar behaviors in a traditional Chinese village community. Exclusion of outsiders is commonplace, but cyclical public events are rarely affected. Villages coordinate celebratory feasts and open their gates to outsiders and visitors. Feasts are the exception, however. Villagers are generally conservative and closed-minded. It is extremely difficult for those from out of town to fit in and assume the identity of a villager. The outsider identity lingers for years, even for those who become associated with the village community by marriage. In the eyes of the churches in Songzhuang, only a rebirth through baptism grants a person legitimacy as a member of the community.

Newcomers are treated with suspicion primarily because their connection to existing members of a church is tenuous at best. In the case of a traditional rural community, an outsider is often treated with suspicion because he lacks social ties to the local community. The outsider is not connected to the villagers by either blood or geography, and thus has no basis for an identity. It is necessary, therefore, for an individual to anchor himself to a social network of relationships in a traditional Chinese society. Only after finding his place in the community would this individual be able to realize his life goals. For a rootless individual without a social network to break into a new community is challenging, as his identity is unknown and the foundation on which he builds a life is weak. Such an individual easily adds volatility to the community. This volatility affects the sense of security of other members of the community and could disrupt communal harmony under specific circumstances. Marriage is the primary means through which an outsider finds a place in the local web of social relationships, even though he may still be marginalized.

As the newcomer gradually establishes himself in society as a parent and the head of a household, he also accumulates social capital and builds his own network, moving along the threads of the social fabric from the periphery toward the center. The same process can be observed in the churches in Songzhuang. To regular congregants, itinerant churchgoers and Christians baptized in other churches add instability to the existing social network. New members of this kind often cause anxiety and concern in a church and could become scapegoats at times of internal friction (although the correlation between new membership and scapegoating is unsubstantiated). For example, Lin attributes the several waves of split in his church to the negative influence of external churches on his fellow congregants. Even though members of external churches remain outside of local churches, their presence nonetheless is a disruptive force that exerts a negative impact on existing social relationships.

As churches in Songzhuang endeavor to maintain a social network similar to that of a traditional rural community, they also come to promote "the church" as a broader concept rather than simply a place of worship. This new emphasis on the concept of a community, just like the caution exercised in accepting new members, is motivated by the concern for potential division from within. This renewed focus on cultivating a sense of identity is not a pursuit of homogeneity among Christian artists, an effort that I have discussed in the previous pages. It is, rather, a notion of community very much akin to a village identity in traditional Chinese society, in which one finds clearly defined boundaries, as well as a personal sense of identity derived from the network of social relationships.

A sense of belonging developed as such does not prioritize individuality, nor does it support individual expression or the pursuit for individual legitimacy. In fact, church leaders promote a village identity, with which they intend to replace the Christian artists' sense of homogeneity centered on individuality. Since the village identity is grounded in a solid social network, it has a greater potential for defending a church's integrity when disagreements arise. There are plenty of biblical references to a notion of village identity, and yet, in practice, a village identity is realized in the web of social and interpersonal connections. In the event of a "village identity crisis," therefore, socio-personal relationships can serve as a defense mechanism against division within a church. The earlier sense of homogeneity is not rooted in social connections but in considerations for individuality. At a time of discord, there are few stabilizing forces holding a church together.

The two expressions of identity are built on different foundations. A village identity is derived from a collective sense of belonging, whereas a homogenous identity is based on expressions of individuality and individual legitimacy. Interestingly, as churches attempt to prioritize the former type of identity over the latter, they are not met with significant resistance. For one thing, a village community is a familiar concept and thus is well received by church members. For another, as churches become increasingly diverse, homogeneity becomes a less realistic goal. Even many Christian artists have given up on attempting to achieve homogeneity in their congregations. Take Wang's church, which differs from the earliest congregations of painters in that its regular members work in the arts industry but are not predominantly artists. They are employees of cultural media companies, sales people in arts-and-crafts shops, singers, and owners of clothing stores. Besides Wang himself, only three other congregants are painters as traditionally defined. Another example is Lin's church. The majority of the congregants are artists, including sculptors and musicians; painters make up less than half of all the artists in the congregation. This composition renders homogeneity unrealistic. Lin and Wang both observe that disagreements within churches have shifted in the past two years, from the early attention to individual points of view to the more recent debate over pastoral care and development. For instance, there has been an ongoing discussion about appointing a pastor-in-residence in Lin's church, which suggests that internal friction now threatens the organization of the church. In that way, a village identity has not only superseded the pursuit for a homogeneous identity, but it has also become a stabilizing force that sustains a church as a village community.

The majority of Songzhuang's church members are among the 90 percent who live at the subsistence level. At a time when the socioeconomic gap continues to widen, the departure of church members from Xiaobao for its peripheries also marks a geographical divide. Christian churches in Songzhuang cannot avoid tackling the hardships in the artists' livelihoods. All church members are burdened by the travails of life, and the church can no longer provide a refuge from material troubles. Church leaders and congregants alike are equally pressured by financial difficulties, and their faith and practice as Christians cannot help but be affected. Belief and practice are precisely the most discussed topics among church members. In addition to poverty, artistic expression and the artists' desires for recognition are also causes for concern. The sudden boom of an artist square in Xiaobao, in the eyes of the artists, signifies the might of capitalism. As the artists are confronted with this symbol, they also face a dilemma: they at once disdain the commercialization of the arts trade and are impressed by the power of capital. Such ambivalence leaves the artists in a constant state of anxiety, as they find themselves in limbo. Faith, to them, provides a sense of certainty. This certainty represents the aforementioned two types of identity. One is the desire for homogeneity as an outlet for the anxiety about individual expression and legitimacy. The other, village identity, helps relieve worries about everyday life.

Undoubtedly, churches in Songzhuang provide daily necessities for their members. The expenditure records of Lin's church include line items of monthly assistance payments to the congregants. That churches actively promote Sunday services as open networking platforms benefits congregants in a pragmatic way. The church has become a major venue for art exhibitions or for connecting with industry representatives. At the same time, the church as a traditional village is well received by the congregants. The hometown atmosphere of such a church offers Christian artists a sense of security in times of hardship. They view their shared Christian identity as an "intrinsic connection." Even though churches remain relatively closed off to outsiders, as congregants interact with the outside world, they still share a common Christian identity vis-à-vis non-Christians or Christians in other churches. In their perceptions, the village identity forged by the church and the Christian identity of an individual operate on different playing fields. The church-as-a-village is not a real village community. It is imagined as a traditional rural community, and yet it is not a space in which members carry out mundane daily routines.

Indeed, Christian identity is demonstrated in everyday interactions, which reveal the characteristics of both the village identity and the homogeneous identity. As Christians, artists in Songzhuang make assumptions about interpersonal relationships—namely, that they feel closer to fellow Christians and distant from non-Christians. They also set expectations for themselves as individuals in their interactions with other Christian artists. For instance, they expect fellow Christian artists to resonate with their artistic self-expressions from the Christian perspective.

Assumptions made based on a shared Christian identity are as elusive as an idealized "Christian" or "Christianity." A case in point is Lin's grievances against Christian entrepreneurs. Lin has had the idea of inviting Christian entrepreneurs to take part in the social hours after Sunday services. He expects these entrepreneurs to be as interested in art collection as their non-Christian counterparts. Works of Christian artists, it follows, ought to appeal to Christian entrepreneurs more strongly than other types of art. It turns out that most Christian entrepreneurs are disinterested in Christian art; they are, rather, attracted to the works of renowned artists. I attended an exhibition in April 2014 in which paintings of Lin and other church members were on display, along with the works of Christian artists from outside of Songzhuang. Lin's church was the exhibition hall, where I met far fewer Christian entrepreneurs than representatives of the cultural industry and galleries. One of the participating artists, Zhou, remarked that such an attendance pattern was common. The works of Christian artists are indistinguishable from those currently found on the art market in Songzhuang, nor are they produced with specific consumers in mind. Lin indicated that Christian entrepreneurs show little interest in spiritual subject matters, with which he is very disappointed. It frustrates him that Christian entrepreneurs appear to favor "worldly" art. On the flip side, Lin is concerned that the creations of Christian artists, including his own works, may not be sufficiently "spiritual," and thus they fail to represent the life of Jesus in their art.

In sharp contrast to Lin's experience, Wang has entered his works into exhibitions in churches in Korea, where paintings by Christian artists are well received. More and more Songzhuang Christian painters are beginning to put their works on display in Korea. These exhibitions are not held every year, but they typically take place in the summer and winter. Since 2010, participation in exhibitions in Korea has become increasingly common. At the same time, Christian artists continue to send their works to non-Christian-themed exhibitions, but their sales rates remain low. According to Zhang, the success of Christian-themed exhibitions is indicative of the strength of Christianity in Korea, as evidenced by the high sales rates of paintings and other types of works of art. Korean Christians are very enthusiastic about purchasing paintings with Christian subject matter. In China, however, not even a large space for the art trade, such as Songzhuang, has reached the expected level of development.

Lin's perspective indicates the expectations that come with a "Christian" identity. Christian entrepreneurs are expected to favor Christian art over worldly art on the basis of their Christian fellowship or spirituality. This also suggests that Christian artists define and identify themselves as Christians through the prism of a spiritual-versus-worldly binary in their everyday dealings. I observe a correlation between Christian artists' self-identity and their own marginalization in a capitalist economy. Membership in a spiritual community aside, the fact of the matter is that Christian artists in Songzhuang are reluctantly marginalized and branded, in both geographical terms and in the cultural industry. To improve their status, the artists must seek a new social identity, and the categorizations of "Christian" and "non-Christian" help reassign their place in society. Under this framework, Christian entrepreneurs and artists belong to the same category, in which the marginalizing effects of capitalism are not a consideration. However, since such categorization is predicated upon the artists' preconception of "Christian" identity, real-life experiences are often proven to be contradictory. Christian entrepreneurs would rather invest heavily in the works of renowned artists than purchase Christian art, or they would offer much lower prices for Christian art than expected. In spite of this unequal treatment, Christian artists in Songzhuang persist in their self-refashioning. They rationalize the gap between expectation and reality. They argue that their art fails to appeal to Christian entrepreneurs because it is not sufficiently spiritual by the standard of "worldly" art. This realization thus prompts Christian artists in Songzhuang to reflect upon their own creative process, especially the spiritual aspects of it. Artistic introspection is easier said than done, however. What exactly is Christian art? This question continues to puzzle church leaders and congregants alike.

4   Conclusion

An examination of churches in Songzhuang must situate these within the development of the area as a "culture industry town." The Christian artists in Songzhuang are also residents who happen to be artists. They are usually poor, hovering just above the poverty line. Such hardship can be attributed to both their geographical marginalization and the tight art market. In addition to the continuous expansion of the artistic buildings and spaces in Xiaobao, the Christian artists of Songzhuang also struggle in the megacity of Beijing.

Church members in Songzhuang are at once Christians, artists, and northward migrants. They are accustomed to the stress of urban life, which has been a constant in the lives of many.

Changes came to Songzhuang after the expansion-and-division cycle had repeated itself for nearly ten years. By then, churches had come to resemble traditional Chinese rural communities. Just like the artist village in Songzhuang or even the earlier painter village in Yuanmingyuan, churches have become village communities reconstructed in cities. In the fashion of traditional rural communities, these churches have maintained their integrity by relying on a close-knit web of interpersonal connections. Instead of an individual-centered homogenous identity, churches conceived as natural villages rely on a community-based village identity. A village identity is rooted in a network of social connections that supersedes and replaces a homogeneous identity.

In the same way that a rural community is predicated upon locality and blood ties, churches construct the notion of "the church" on the foundation of intimate social relationships among congregants. A sense of belonging and certainty brought about by a village identity, in the meantime, helps moderate the anxiety incurred by the loss of a homogenous identity and the decline of individual self-legitimization. Furthermore, cultivating a sense of belonging and certainty seems to offer a more effective solution than individualistic self-legitimization to a conundrum—namely, that the artists are marginalized in the capitalism of the cultural industry centered in Xiaobao. Churches, as village communities and social organizations, fashion themselves as solutions to their congregants' socioeconomic problems in an adverse, highly capitalist environment. A church is effective in helping people cope with adversities because it has a clearly defined and internally coherent social organization. This fact has been deeply impressed upon Christian artists.

This imagined community appears more real than the community in Songzhuang, as if it were a defensive tower that resists the impact of capitalism and urban pressures on space. Despite the churches' emphasis on a collective village identity, individuals have not fully forged a collective whole. Rather, individual identity now is fixated on the notion of "Christian." "What is a Christian?" "What kind of Christian am I?" The search for answers to these questions, in a way, is the extension of the search for a homogeneous identity. That is, although an individual may have a strong sense of communal identity, the essence of an individual identity remains intact; a sand tower is still built with individual grains of sand. A church perceived as and fashioned after a traditional village remains a conceptual entity. It does not radically transform an individual qua individual, and the imagined social network does not have practical implications for real-life problems. The recreation of a rural community in the form of a church in a big city should be more aptly viewed as a symbolic act and not a construction of a community. This question deserves further investigation beyond an examination of churches as traditional villages in a big city.

The two churches under discussion, to which Lin and Wang respectively belong, are representative of rural churches in urban areas. Lin concluded our interview by saying that the church has a plan to build a team of trained professionals who will engage in pastoral care and intellectual development. The development of a professional pastoral team also signals specialization in the church. The duties of every coworker will be clearly defined in the church bylaws that are currently in the making. In Lin's opinion, the church is a "community" only when it can appeal to the expectations and senses of identity of every individual member. The other church, under Wang's leadership, on the other hand, has transformed into a typical "rural community in an urban area." Membership remains stable and close-knit, with little fluctuation in headcount. The church leadership typically assumes multiple roles and responsibilities. There is no observable specialization of duties, and decisions are usually made by consensus. Church members demand a high degree of internal cohesion and unity, and a "community" is envisioned as such. These are two distinctive examples. Nevertheless, they are indicative of the wide variety of conceptualizations of a community, which may be rooted in different perceptions of a "modern society."

As for the artist churches in Songzhuang, neither a "church of professionals" nor a "rural church" is an appropriate conceptualization of my subjects. The artist churches in Songzhuang have developed and evolved in their very particular contexts and under very specific circumstances. What, then, is the broader significance of a study of one exceptional case? Songzhuang is exceptional in that few other places share the same circumstances of its formation and its subsequent development. The process of promoting Christianity among artists in Songzhuang can be said to be quite eventful. With regard to my thesis, however, Songzhuang can arguably be seen as a microcosm of small towns under the impact of urbanization and capitalism. The artists in Songzhuang are also representative of a generation of Chinese who are caught between urban and rural areas and between affluence and poverty. Under the veneer of the artists' conviction of and passion for their vocation is a host of emotionally charged reflections on the nation, society, and history. Although introspective, they feel simultaneously confused, indignant, disheartened, and even hopeless. Furthermore, the development of Christianity in Songzhuang parallels the broader changes in society. In the final analysis, stories of the Christian artists and their churches reveal the tension between faith and practice and between individuals and community. They provide clarity as we seek a deeper understanding of contemporary Chinese society and Christians, as well as Christians in Chinese society.

Bibliography

Huang Jianbo 黄剑波. *Dushili de xiangcun jiaohui—Zhongguo chengshihua yu mingong jidujiao* 都市里的乡村教会—中国城市化与民工基督教. Hong Kong: Logos and Pneuma Press, 2012.

KONG Jianhua 孔建华. "Beijingshi Songzhuang yuanchuang yishu jijuqu fazhan zai yanjiu" 北京宋庄原创艺术集聚区发展再研究. *Beijing shehui kexue* 北京社会科学. 2007.3: 21–26.

Lin Jinglu 林京路. "Zhongguo Songzhuang huajiacun diaoyan yu fazhan baogao" 中国宋庄画家村调研与发展报告. *Wenyi lilun yu piping* 文艺理论与批评. 2013.3: 71–75.

Taylor, Charles. *Modern Social Imaginaries*. Durham, NC: Duke University Press, 2003. Translated by Lin Manhong 林曼红 as *Xiandai shehui xiangxiang* 现代社会想象. Shanghai: Yilin chubanshe, 2014.

CHAPTER 13

Choosing between God's Will and the Law

A Study of Chinese Christians' Dilemma over Fertility Desires and Behaviors

WANG Ling

1   Introduction

Religion, as one of the major determinants of fertility desires and behaviors, has increasingly attracted the attention of researchers. In China, the one-child policy that has been strictly enforced for four decades further complicates the impact of religious beliefs on fertility desires and behaviors. Since the 1990s, Chinese researchers have generated an abundance of economic and sociological studies about the fertility desires of the general population. These studies have focused on specific social groups, such as women in rural areas, the migrant population, various ethnic groups, the urban population, and youth. However, little research has been done regarding the correlation between religious belief and fertility. Research on fertility desires and behaviors of Chinese Christians is nearly nonexistent in the study of Chinese religion and sociology. In 2017, Li Feng 李峰 published a study on the impact of religious belief on fertility desires. Li drew upon the 2010 data derived from the Chinese General Social Survey (CGSS) and concluded that religious teachings indeed directly influence individuals' fertility desires. Specifically, Christians reveal a greater desire for fertility than both non-Christians and believers of folk religions.[1]

There is considerable international scholarship on the impact of religious belief on fertility. The religiosity hypothesis maintains that the teachings of certain religious groups have a direct impact on their believers. The social characteristics hypothesis denies a direct correlation between religiosity and fertility behavior. Instead, it proposes that the socioeconomic status of believers is the fundamental driver of reproductive decisions. The minority group status hypothesis indicates that members of a minority religious group tend to

---

1 Li Feng, "Zongjiao xinyang yingxiang shengyu yiyuan ma? Jiyu CGSS2010 nian shuju de fenxi." *Shijie zongjiao yanjiu*, 2017.3: 18–34.

impose regulations on their own fertility behavior to the benefit of the group's overall well-being.

Although some scholars are not inclined to accept the religiosity hypothesis, the broader scholarship on this topic suggests that the effects of religious beliefs on fertility desire and behavior are significant. For example, Kevin McQuillan compares the fertility rates of three different religious groups and concludes that religious beliefs shape reproduction in three ways. First, a religion clearly articulates rules regarding reproductive behavior. Second, a religious organization has the capability and means to enforce these rules. Third, specific religious beliefs form the core of an individual's identity. Furthermore, the more devout an individual is, the more likely it is that religious teachings will shape the individual's attitude toward reproduction.[2]

Applying this theoretical framework to examine a house church in Beijing, which I will call Grace Church, I seek to better understand the fertility desires and behaviors of Chinese Christians. I observed Grace Church over an extended period of time, during which I conducted interviews with the congregants, facilitated several panel discussions, and conducted surveys on WeChat. My study generated a peculiar outcome: the congregants of Grace Church demonstrate a much higher fertility desire than the national average, and yet their fertility rate is significantly lower than the national average.

This raises a series of questions: What could have caused such an unusual discrepancy between fertility desire and fertility behavior? What are the determinants? In what ways does the one-child policy, which many view as contradictory to Christian teachings on reproduction, affect individual Christians' fertility behaviors? Moreover, the Chinese government ended the one-child policy and implemented the universal two-child policy nationwide on January 1, 2016. How did Chinese Christians respond to this policy change? How differently did they react to it compared to other groups? How has their specific reaction been translated into fertility behaviors? This chapter answers the above questions by examining the members of Grace Church and seeking to understand the attitudes toward abortion among church leaders and congregants, as well as faith-based anti-abortion activities.

---

[2] Kevin McQuillan, "When Does Religion Influence Fertility?" *Population and Development Review* 30.1 (2004): 25–56.

2 The Discrepancy between Fertility Desire and Fertility Behavior

2.1 *An Overview of Grace Church*

Grace Church is a house church located in the municipality of Beijing. Among the 107 regular congregants (children excluded), 86 are baptized Christians, and the rest are unbaptized blood relatives. My subjects are the 86 baptized congregants. Women form the majority (68.6%) of the congregation, and the vast majority of them are in their early to mid-adulthood. Members born in the 1970s and 1980s make up 68.9% of the congregation.

The current church leadership consists of Pastor Rao[3] and her husband, along with two other couples. The six-member board of coworkers makes decisions about church affairs collectively. Pastor Rao is the head of the coworkers. The congregation is divided into eight small groups; each is headed by a group leader and meets periodically. In addition to the Sunday service, the congregants gather for discipleship training, prayer meetings, and pre-evangelism groups during the week. On the whole, the connection among church members is loose at best. Over half of the congregants only attend Sunday services.

Grace Church has never declared its denomination. According to some coworkers, it is nondenominational. However, considering its theological leanings, certain core members of the staff identify Grace Church with the more conservative branch of evangelical churches. The church has little contact with outside groups. The pastor and coworkers of the church typically deliver Sunday sermons. In more recent years, however, the church has invited an increasing number of guest speakers.

2.2 *An Unusual Discrepancy: Higher Fertility Desires vs. Lower Fertility Rates*

My interviews with members of Grace Church reveal a divergence between fertility desires and fertility behaviors. Fertility desire refers to individuals' views, attitudes, and inclinations toward reproduction. It is reflected in the intention to have children, the number of children desired, the sex of the children desired, and the timing of births.[4] Fertility desire may not be fully realized in actual reproductive behavior for a number of reasons. The former president of the Population Association of America, S. P. Morgan, indicates that factors

---

[3] Pseudonyms are used throughout this chapter.
[4] Gu Baochang, "Shengyu yiyuan shengyu xingwei he shengyu shuiping," *Renkou yanjiu* 35.2 (2011): 43–59.

such as the tempo effect, infecundity, and competition play a role in keeping the birth rate far below the level of fertility desire.[5]

Population studies have indicated a discrepancy between fertility desires and behaviors in developed and developing countries alike.[6] All the same, the divergence exhibited in Grace Church is even more striking. Though the relatively small number in our sample of Grace Church couples makes this description more anecdotal than scientific, it is relevant to note that the couples' fertility desires were higher than the national average and their birth rate lower than the national average.

Concerning fertility desire, a survey of twenty-eight congregants of Grace Church, aged between 27 and 53 years old (i.e., born between 1963 and 1989), shows that their ideal number of children is 2.37. Official statistics indicate that the ideal number of children for the population in the Huabei 华北 region is 1.94.[7] In a press release announcing the implementation of the two-child fertility policy, issued by the Beijing Municipal Commission of Population and Family Planning on July 8, 2014, officials state that the fertility desire of women of childbearing age in Beijing is only 1.3 children. In this regard, the ideal number of children for the congregants of Grace Church exceeds those of the Huabei population and the residents of Beijing by 0.43 and 1.07 respectively.

As to fertility behavior, the number of existing children is an important measure of fertility rates in demography. This number refers to the cumulative number of legitimate and illegitimate children, adopted children, and dependent stepchildren. My survey shows that Grace Church members born in the 1960s have an average of one child, and those born in the 1970s have an average of 1.06 children. (Due to late marriage and late childbearing, those born in the 1980s have an average of only 0.18 children. This is considered an aberration and is not included in my comparative study.)

According to the China Family Panel Study conducted by Beijing University in 2010, women in their thirties had an average of 1.5 children (CFPS 2010). The higher one's age, the greater the number of children. For example, women who

---

5 S. P. Morgan, "Is Low Fertility a Twenty-First-Century Demographic Crisis?" *Demography* 40.4 (2003): 589–603.
6 Alicia Adsera, "An Economic Analysis of the Gap between Desired and Actual Fertility: The Case of Spain," *Review of Economics of the Household* 4:1 (2006): 75–95; Yang Juhua, "Yiyuan yu xingwei de beili: fada guojia shengyu yiyuan yu shengyu xingwei yanjiu shuping ji dui Zhongguo de qishi," *Xuehai*, 2008.1: 16–22.
7 Chinese Academy of Social Sciences, *Shehui lanpi shu: 2016 nian Zhongguo shehui xingshi fenxi yu yuce* (Beijing: Shehui kexue wenxian chubanshe, 2015).

are in the 54-year-old age bracket have an average of two children.[8] It is clear that the number of children of Grace Church members born in the 1960s and 1970s is far lower than that of women in their respective age groups.

Another set of statistical data further corroborates the gap between the fertility rate of Grace Church and the national fertility rate. According to the estimate of Wang Guangzhou 王广州, a research fellow at the Institute of Population and Labor Economics, about 20 percent of the permanent residents of Beijing have excess children. Among the twenty couples in Grace Church, only one has exceeded the official limit, which represents 5 percent of the married population in the church. (All twenty husbands and wives are baptized. I have excluded those couples in which only one member is baptized.)

2.3 Grace Church's Exceptional Enthusiasm for the Universal Two-Child Policy

China's two-child policy began on January 1, 2016. From this date, the government permitted married couples to have two children. More than a year after the policy's implementation, the response of the general population was lukewarm at best, contrary to the government's expectation. A survey conducted by the All-China Women's Federation in 2016 shows that 53.3% of families were not interested in having a second child. The level of disinterest exceeded 60% in urban areas.[9] Tencent News (Tengxun xinwen 腾讯新闻) conducted a survey of 100,000 users, and the result was similar: only 31.4% of the participants planned to have a second child.

The total number of live births in 2016 also indicates that the general population is less than enthusiastic about the two-child policy. According to data published by the National Bureau of Statistics, there were 17,860,000 births in 2016. This was 1,310,000 more than the number of births in 2015, but it still fell far short of the estimate of the Commission of Population and Family Planning.[10]

All the same, members of Grace Church are exceedingly enthusiastic about the universal two-child policy. By the end of July 2017, among the twenty-one women of childbearing age (i.e., adults under 49 years old) who had already

---

8 Wang Guangzhou, "Zhongguo laonianren qinzi shuliang yu jiegou jisuanji fangzhen fenxi," *Zhongguo renkou kexue* 34.3 (2014): 2–16.

9 See the December 22, 2016, report by Zhonghua quanguo funu lianhe hui, *Shishi quanmian lianghai zhengce dui jiating jiaoyu de yingxiang*.

10 Demographer Yao Meixiong 姚美雄 argued that the universal two-child policy was apparently not well received. See her article "Ba quanmian guli shengyu dingwei xin jiben guoce henyou biyao," *China Reform* (*Zhongguo gaige luntan*), February 28, 2017.

had one child, seven had had a second child, one was pregnant, two were trying to become pregnant, and one was still making up her mind. Ten women were firmly against having a second child. Some of them were concerned about their age: nine of them were more than 40 years old, and six were around 45 years old. They did indicate that they would consider trying for a second child if they were younger. Others were concerned about their own health conditions and the financial strains of childrearing. In total, 47.6% of the twenty-one women of childbearing age were planning to have a second child. Those who had had a second child and those expecting made up 33.3% of the group. This proportion far exceeds the general population's desire to have a second child. A coworker at Grace Church was very excited about the population growth:

> In the past, we would be lucky to add one child a year to the congregation. Now there are six or seven at once, and they are all second children. The children lighten us up!

The abovementioned statistical data illustrate the unusual divergence between the fertility desire and fertility behavior of the congregants of Grace Church. They demonstrate a greater fertility desire than that of the general population. Additionally, according to Li Feng's study, the fertility intentions of Christians are on average 2.13 children, as opposed to the 1.72 for nonbelievers. These numbers indicate that not only is the fertility desire of the Grace congregation greater than that of other demographic groups, but it is also higher than that of other Christians.

3   The Distinction between God's Will and Governmental Authority

The discrepancy between the fertility desire and reproductive behavior of the congregants of Grace Church raises additional questions. Why do they demonstrate a higher degree of fertility desire than other groups? In the interviews and surveys conducted with nearly forty congregants at Grace Church, I have discovered that religious belief is a critical determinant of both the congregants' above-average fertility desires and below-average fertility behaviors. Generally speaking, Christian teachings encourage the congregants' fertility desires. At the same time, religious belief is a major motivator for the congregants to impose constraints on and regulate their own fertility behaviors. The end result is the congregants' willing compliance with the laws and regulations of the state, which leads to a fertility rate that is far lower than the national average.

3.1 *Distinguishing between Attitudes toward Reproduction and Fertility Desires*

The distinctive attitudes toward reproduction held by the congregants of Grace Church have a direct impact on their desire to reproduce. The attitude toward reproduction refers to individuals' ideas and decisions about reproduction in specific social, economic, and cultural contexts. In China, four decades of the strict enforcement of the one-child policy, as well as the promotion of related ideas, such as "over-population is a burden on the nation" or "over-population causes intense competition for resources," have fundamentally altered the Chinese attitude toward reproduction. The traditional concepts of "offspring bring blessings" or "raising children to provide for old age" no longer carry much weight. Family planning is certainly the prevailing attitude toward reproduction.

My interviews with some residents of Beijing of childbearing age reveal that the notion of "continuing one's bloodline" has been lost among those born in the 1980s and 1990s. The younger generation values personal happiness and individual fulfillment. Childrearing is perceived as time- and capital-intensive labor.

The congregants of Grace Church, however, do not share the same sentiment. In fact, 80 percent of my interviewees share the belief that "children are a gift of Jesus" and "being fruitful and multiplying is God's blessing." Mrs. Deng, a congregant who is currently planning for a second child, expressed her attitude toward reproduction in terms of her religious belief:

> If I were not a Christian, I would probably not desire a second child. A second child is a considerable demand on my efforts and adds to my financial burden. [To have a second child] would be asking for trouble. My friends agree with me. They encourage me to put the money and efforts into caring for myself, updating my wardrobe, traveling, or just enjoying life. But I believe that a child is a gift from God. It is priceless, and I am willing to do anything for it.

Similarly, Mrs. Fan thinks that children are far more valuable than money or other kinds of rewards:

> I believe that children are God's blessing. In the Bible, God promises Abraham offspring—countless offspring just like the sand on the beach—not money or other kinds of rewards. That tells me that children are precious in the eyes of God.

An attitude toward reproduction based on biblical teachings directly shapes the fertility desires of the congregants of Grace Church. This influence is clearly reflected in their fertility intentions and number of births.

The ideal number of children for Mrs. Hu is three. She indicates that she has never wanted children to care for her in old age. She also said:

> I learned from a news report that the birth rate in the Muslim world is quite high, which leads to rapid population growth. This is quite alarming. If our birth rate continues to be low, our population growth will suffer. I am always moved whenever guest preachers encourage young Christians to have more children so that they can expand the kingdom of God. It is a shame that the two-child policy came too late for me. I am getting old. I may not be able to have more children.

The effect of reproduction on expanding the religious landscape is apparent to coworker Lin, who has only one child. Born in the 1960s, she is past childbearing age and has given up hope for a second child.

> Christians should follow God's will and have many children. The book of Genesis makes it clear: be fruitful and increase in number. If we don't have more children, Muslims will fill the earth. I am useless in that department, though. Now I can only hope for grandchildren.

In addition to faith, congregants of Grace Church also desire more children because they would like to give their only child a companion. They are also concerned that a single child will be overburdened by the requirement to care for aging parents. Some simply prefer a big family. An online survey of 100,000 participants by Tencent News in early 2016 lists three major motivations for a second child: to give children a wholesome childhood, to distribute the burden of caring for aging parents, and to reduce the risk of losing the only child. Comparing these motivators with the attitudes of Grace Church congregants, it is clear that religious belief exercises considerable influence on the congregants' fertility desires.

3.2   *Family Planning as a Red Line*

High fertility desire does not necessarily translate into comparable fertility behavior. Research has shown that factors such as cultural differences, state of the economy, and employment status all contribute to the disparity between the two. This is especially noticeable in China due to its former one-child policy. Prior to the promulgation of the universal two-child policy in 2016, the one-child policy was imposed on the general population.

The one-child policy was first enacted in the 1970s and was implemented throughout China incrementally. In the words of an open letter on population control issued on September 25, 1980, by Central Party authorities to Party members throughout the country, the objectives of the one-child policy were to "curb the pace of population growth" and "facilitate the realization of the four modernizations in Socialism." Both the open letter and the subsequent "Law of the People's Republic of China on Population and Family Planning" included distinctive language that "encouraged one married couple to have only one child." The official attitude of the Chinese government was to advocate for voluntary family planning. In reality, however, the one-child policy has been forcibly imposed upon the population nationwide, for understandable reasons. The one-child policy went against the fertility desires of the general population, however, and its implementation was met with various forms of resistance. The Chinese government developed four measures to enforce the policy.[11]

1. The government implemented a one-vote-down system at all levels of governmental agencies. The one-vote-down system was a punitive mechanism that denied merits and even demoted or dismissed government officials in a leadership role who failed to comply with the one-child policy. This measure made the enforcement of the one-child policy, as well as the penalization of its violation, an absolute priority of every governmental agency.

2. The state imposed a "social maintenance fee" on families with excess births, on the grounds that they placed an undue burden on public resources. The social maintenance fee required violators to pay additional fines. Provincial governments had the authority to set the amount of the penalty. Typically, the fee was quite high, in some cases up to ten times the average annual income of the local population. In certain cases, the fee was adjusted based on the violator's income level.[12] In 2014, the renowned film director Zhang Yimou 张艺谋 was fined 7.48 million RMB (1.15 million USD) for violating the one-child policy. This scandal also brought about a debate over such penalties, with many arguing that this system favors the rich, for they can afford to pay an obscene amount

---

11   Liang Zhongtang, *Zhongguo jihua shengyu zhengce shilun* (Beijing: Zhongguo fazhan chubanshe, 2014), 374–377.

12   Zhan Zhongle, *Gongmin shengyu quan yu shehui fuyangfei zhidu yanjiu* (Beijing: Falü chubanshe, 2011), 160–165.

in fines. These social maintenance fees have placed extreme financial burdens on middle- and lower-income families. On the whole, these penalties have been effective in curbing the fertility desires of ordinary families.
3. Additional children could result in loss of employment or expulsion from the Party. In addition to paying a social maintenance fee, violators may also lose their Party membership or even their jobs. This is a particularly harsh punishment for employees of government agencies, state-owned industries, and state-run corporations.
4. The government would deny registration of residence for excess children. In the event that a family fails to pay the social maintenance fee, the local law enforcement can deny residency for the extra child. The consequences of such a denial may be severe, with the unregistered child labeled a *heihu* 黑戶, who has no legal status. Such a person would lack access to all sorts of social services, including education. A 2015 survey conducted by an associate research fellow at the Academy of Macroeconomic Research of the National Development and Reform Commission, Wan Haiyuan 万海远, counts approximately 13,000,000 *heihu* all over China. Among these, over half are excess children who were denied residency.

The media has reported other ways that the one-child policy was enforced, such as forced abortions. A woman by the name of Feng Jianmei in Shaanxi, for example, was forced to terminate her pregnancy in the seventh month. Her family was also required to attend family planning education lessons. Draconian enforcement mechanisms, together with governmental propaganda, have created a negative perception of the violation of the one-child policy. All of these are deterrents for the fertility desires of the general population.

As residents of Beijing, the congregants of Grace Church are equally affected by the aforementioned deterrents. Nevertheless, that does not fully explain the congregation's below-average fertility rates. One may infer that Christian teachings elevate the congregants' fertility desires. Thus, despite the deterrence of the one-child policy, the expression of the congregants' high fertility desires ought to be a fertility rate equal to or greater than the national average. However, the birth rate at Grace is considerably lower than the national average. What other factors are at play here?

3.3 *Obedience to the Guidance and Will of the Authorities*

My interviews revealed a number of factors that discourage fertility desire, including the legal prohibition (the one-child policy), the overwhelming demand on time and effort, considerations of health, and financial situation. An additional factor that affects Grace Church congregants' fertility desires is religious teaching. Several congregants believe strongly that Christians should obey the government's family planning policy and support its enforcement. In particular, Mrs. Cao is especially opposed to excess births: "A Christian's duty is to be obedient to the authorities. If the government puts a limit on reproduction, I will of course comply with state policy. It reflects poorly on the congregation when our members violate the one-child policy."

Congregant Wang shares that sentiment, saying that Christians are first and foremost members of society and are obligated to obey the law. The one-child policy, as the law of the land, is sanctioned by God despite its unreasonable demands. It is a Christian duty to submit to the higher powers. Coworker Lin used to share the above perspectives. But now she regrets that congregants did not attempt to have more children.

> I didn't used to give the one-child policy any thought. The government had its reasons to limit childbirths. Now as I think back on it, I find this policy contradictory to God's will. I know that members of some other churches have two or three children in a family. Our congregants are obedient subjects and almost never violate the law. Our church teaches us well that we should submit to the higher powers.

"Submission to higher powers" is taken straight out of the Bible: "Let everyone be subject to the governing authorities, for there is no authority except that which God has established. The authorities that exist have been established by God. Consequently, whoever rebels against the authority is rebelling against what God has instituted, and those who do so will bring judgment on themselves" (Romans 13:1–2).

During interviews, the congregants revealed that sermons in their church put great emphasis on "submission to higher powers." Congregants are encouraged to consider the reputation of the church and to be able to give proper Christian testimonies by obeying the authorities. Such instruction has a direct impact on the reproductive behaviors of the congregants. They proactively suppress their fertility desires. They are even willing to resort to abortion in the event of an accidental pregnancy in order to comply with the one-child policy. For this reason, even though the congregants' fertility desire is as high as 2.37 children, far exceeding the average of 1.3 children desired by women of childbearing age in Beijing, their effective fertility rate falls far below the national average.

My interviews and surveys also indicate that the divergence between the congregants' fertility desires and actual behaviors reflects another dilemma. It is the conflict between the Christian teaching of "be fruitful and multiply" and the government's one-child policy. Under most circumstances, the push and pull between the two ends may result in reproductive behaviors other than what has been observed in Grace Church. Nonetheless, because the congregants obey the teaching of "submission to higher powers," their fertility behavior ends up favoring the government's stance. The consequence is strikingly low fertility.

Of McQuillan's three conditions in which religious beliefs affect fertility, the congregants of Grace Church meet the first condition, i.e., that Christian teachings take a firm stance on the topic of procreation. But the second condition is missing. Namely, the church has neither the ability nor the means to demand that its congregants carry out these teachings. Instead, the church's emphasis on submission to higher powers effectively suppressed the congregants' higher-than-normal fertility desires. In this way, Christian belief acts as a disincentive rather than a motivator with respect to a positive fertility rate. The third condition, that the more devout an individual is, the greater a motivator religious belief is, will be addressed in the following section.

4 Darkness in the Sanctuary: Abortions in Grace Church

Congregants with one child had been wary of accidental pregnancies prior to the promulgation of the universal two-child policy. Accidental pregnancies put congregants in a bind. One the one hand, carrying the pregnancy to term was a violation of the law, and thus an act of disobedience against the authorities. On the other hand, the alternative, abortion, also put Christians in an impossible position. My study of Grace Church shows that several women who became pregnant by accident sought abortion with the knowledge of church leaders. In these cases, congregants chose to submit to governmental authority.

4.1 *The Pervasiveness of Abortion*

Four decades of strict enforcement of the one-child policy have created a top-heavy demographic structure, as the population is rapidly aging and the population of young people is relatively small. A side effect is the pervasiveness of abortion. According to the annual reports of the Commission of Population and Family Planning since 1971, there have been nearly 400,000,000 cases of abortion registered with the state's Population and Family Planning agencies. That is the equivalent of about 10,000,000 cases per year. The total number of abortions would be even more striking if we were to take into account unregistered abortions and the myriad instances of medical abortion.

In the span of three years, between 2008 and 2010, there were at least three cases of abortion in Grace Church. All of them took place after the parties concerned had consulted with church leaders.

4.1.1   Case 1

Mrs. Meng got pregnant by accident in 2008. At the time, she and her husband already had one child. They debated whether they should keep the second child. Meng was concerned about her health conditions and the family's finances. At the same time, the couple feared the consequences of violating "submission to higher powers." Distressed, they decided to consult with one of the church leaders, Mrs. Liu. Meng recalled their conversation as follows:

> The first thing she said to me was, "Do you have a target number of children in mind?" I said no. Then I told her that if the child is the cup that God has passed onto me, I will drink from it without hesitation. I mean, the prospect of one more child and the travail and the stress that come with it all frighten me, but I am willing to endure them if the child is God's command. To that she said, "How can you be certain that this child is a cup from God? You are pregnant because your birth control failed. When Jesus prayed at Gethsemane, the cup he spoke of referred to the cross. He took the cup to fulfil the kingdom of God. Your situation is far from that." Her response upset me deeply. Then she asked how long I had been pregnant. I said about forty or fifty days. She replied, "You'd better hurry." Enough said. I knew what I had to do.

Meng's husband was overwhelmed with regret as he reminisced:

> We had just become Christians at the time and were naïve. We took the church leaders' words as the word of God, and we just followed the instruction. They made it clear that we could not violate the law. Christians cannot disobey the state's policy. I deeply regret it. If I could go back in time, I would defend my child with my life. No one would have been able to change my mind.

4.1.2   Case 2

Mrs. Pan became pregnant by accident in 2010. She had always wanted a second child but never acted on it in light of the strict one-child policy. Her husband, a non-Christian, did not want a second child for fear of the financial strain of raising two children in Beijing, as well as the repercussions of violating state policy. He asked her to terminate the pregnancy. In addition, he was an employee of a state-run corporation at the time and might lose his job for an excess birth. Pan went to church leader Mrs. Liu in a state of distress.

> She asked if the pregnancy was unplanned. I said yes, it was an accident. She said, "How could you two be so careless?" I felt that she was accusing me of failing at birth control, which was very hurtful. Afterward Pastor Rao also said that I should come to a consensus with my husband because having a second child is a family decision. At the time I was not only pressured to submit to higher powers, but I also felt compelled to submit to my husband. Pressures from both sides crushed me like a mountain.

4.1.3   Case 3

In 2010, Mr. Qiu's wife got pregnant with their second child, even though she had an IUD. Qiu was worried that the IUD would affect the fetus's development, and he consulted with Pastor Rao.

> I recall that she didn't give clear instructions as to whether we should get an abortion. She said that the well-being of a new life is in God's hands. But I wavered; I couldn't bring myself to entrust the matter to God. I was so concerned about the fetus's health that I couldn't cope with the stress. Then I asked my wife to get an abortion.

Although the three cases vary from one another, we can see that the parties involved sought guidance from church leaders when they were distressed and indecisive. The end result for all three was an abortion. It is clear that the church leaders' words carried considerable weight in their decisions. The only couple that had an excess birth, however, took a different route when they discovered the unplanned pregnancy.

4.1.4   Case 4

In 2015, Mr. Wei's wife got pregnant unexpectedly. Instead of notifying the church leaders, Wei and his wife made a personal decision to keep the child.

> We weren't faring well financially. Our one child had put enough [financial] strain on us already. We'd never thought of having a second child. My wife was in tears when we discovered the unplanned pregnancy. I said to her that life is precious. We must keep this child and treat it just like we did our first one. I kept the whole thing from the church. I wanted to follow God's guidance and wouldn't allow anyone's judgement to negatively affect my wife. By law, we ought not to have the second child. The

Bible teaches that we should carry it to term. What we did was against the law, but it conforms to God's will. There are man-made laws and there are God's laws, and the latter is a higher power than the former. God's laws supersede man-made laws.

When we compare the three cases of abortion and the case of Wei, we can see that decisions were made on the grounds of the individuals' personal attitudes toward abortion and their respective interpretations of religious teachings. There were differences in their responses even though they are members of the same congregation under the guidance of the same leaders. This observation by no means suggests that Wei is more devout than the others. Nevertheless, Wei seems to conform more closely to Christian teachings so far as the matter of abortion is concerned.

These cases also corroborate McQuillan's three conditions regarding the influence of religious beliefs on reproduction. When the first two conditions are constant (the same Christian teachings and the same congregation), the level of devotion determines the influence of religious teachings on fertility behavior. The first three congregants all chose abortion, whereas Wei, the fourth case, decided to keep the second child. He and his wife are therefore the only couple in the congregation who have an excess child.

4.2 *Christians' Attitudes toward Abortion*

Although Christian denominations are not unified in their attitudes toward abortion, most do share the notion that God shapes a fetus in his image and that abortion is a form of killing. A great many biblical verses also affirm the value of life. Take Psalm 139:13, for example: "For you created my inmost being; you knit me together in my mother's womb."

There seems to be no consensus about abortion among the congregants and leaders of Grace Church. When I interviewed the church leader, Pastor Rao, in late 2015, she indicated that Christian churches have yet to decide whether a fetus younger than three months old should be considered human. When she was interviewed again in February of 2016, she took a different position. She maintained that when both parties in a couple are Christian, the couple ought to carry an unplanned pregnancy to term, because the fetus is a life.

Several congregants have indicated that the issue of abortion has never come up in Sunday sermons or during any other meetings. Mrs. Meng, the subject of Case 1, is very upset by her ignorance about abortion. "Back then I didn't think of a fetus as a human. I only thought of it as a cluster of cells, not a life, and didn't really have feelings for it. After that, I learned more about abortion and read books about it. I felt very sad when I saw a tiny little lump of soft fetus that a unit leader brought back from a church in the U.S."

My survey of a few other house churches and the Three-Self churches in Beijing also suggests that Christians have varying degrees of knowledge about abortion. Indeed, certain pastors maintain that abortion goes against Christian teachings. But in the event that congregants get pregnant by accident and run the risk of violating the one-child policy, pastors typically acquiesce to or even encourage abortions. It is also common for churches to ignore the issue of abortion at Sunday services and other church meetings. With the exception of Early Rain Church (Qiuyu Zhifu 秋雨之福教会) in Chengdu, which issued a formal statement against abortion in 2016, the vast majority of churches in China are silent about the pervasiveness of abortion.

4.3 The Rise of an Anti-abortion Ministry in Grace Church

Most churches in the United States are staunchly anti-abortion, in sharp contrast to the Chinese churches' general silence on the issue of abortion, on the one hand, and on the other hand their negligence in providing information about abortion to their congregants. In addition to anti-abortion advocacy, many American churches also support pregnancy help centers as an attempt to reduce the incidences of abortion. According to the director of PassionLife in the United States, John Ensor, there are nearly 3,000 church-based pregnancy help centers throughout the country, providing pregnancy crisis intervention services to pregnant women free of charge.[13] These help centers have been effective in the prevention of abortions. According to data derived from the United States Census Bureau, in 1991, the total population of the United States was 253 million, with a total of 1.6 million abortion cases. The U.S. population in 2015 was 320 million, and the cases of abortion were 800,000. Whereas the total U.S. population has enjoyed steady growth, the number of abortions has been reduced by half over a twenty-five-year span. In Ensor's opinion, church-led pregnancy crisis intervention has been instrumental to the decline of abortion.

Notably, an anti-abortion mission has emerged within Grace Church and other Chinese churches alike. At Grace Church, congregants who have had abortions are forming an anti-abortion group and beginning to engage in anti-abortion advocacy within the congregation. They also collaborate with other churches and offer assistance to pregnant women in crisis. My research has also indicated that anti-abortion ministries are starting to emerge in churches

---

13 Personal conversation with John Ensor, May 2017.

outside of Beijing, such as those in Shaanxi, Sichuan, Anhui, and Guizhou, among other provinces.

5 Conclusion

My study of the fertility desire and reproductive behavior of the congregants at Grace Church leads to the following conclusions. First, Christian belief has a positive impact on congregants' fertility desires. During my interviews, congregants indicated that faith has a positive influence on their fertility desires, with 80 percent of the congregation believing that faith has influenced their desire to reproduce. This conclusion is consistent with the outcome of the CGSS 2010 survey on the correlation between religious belief and fertility desire. Li Feng's analysis of the CGSS data also indicates that there is a direct correlation between religious teachings and individuals' fertility desires. Believers generally have a greater desire to reproduce than nonbelievers, and Christians, in particular, show a greater fertility desire than believers of Chinese folk religion.

Second, under the dictate of "submission to higher powers," congregants of Grace Church are especially susceptible to the state's one-child policy. They exhibit a greater tendency to self-regulate and to comply with the government's guidelines. This inclination is clearly observable in the discrepancy between the fertility desires and reproductive behaviors of the congregants. Driven by religious belief, the congregants exhibit a level of fertility desire higher than the national average. Nevertheless, their actual reproductive rate is considerably lower than the national average. Only one in twenty couples had an excess birth, which puts the congregation at a much lower excess rate than that of the permanent residents in Beijing (approximately one in five couples).

The congregants of Grace Church responded promptly to the universal two-child policy, as they had to the one-child policy. During the first nineteen months of the policy's implementation, seven out of the twenty-one women of childbearing age who had already had one child gave birth to a second child. The percentage of second births far exceeds the national average. The change in family planning policy effectively released the shackles on the congregants' fertility desires. The result was a greatly increased birth rate.

Third, the church's guidance plays a critical role in determining how religious belief may influence reproductive decisions. The three cases of abortion in Grace Church demonstrate that instructions of the church (or lack thereof), the leaders' attitudes, and other congregants' reproductive behaviors all have a direct impact on fertility behavior. My interviews reveal that the congregation never openly discusses teachings relevant to birth control or reproduction. Leaders and coworkers of the church have, however, expressed the command to obey the law, and by extension, a prohibition on excess births. They also emphasize "submission to higher powers" and comply with the one-child policy by example. All of these factors negatively impact the fertility rate of the congregation.

Fourth, the more devout and Bible-oriented an individual is, the greater the degree to which Christian belief is a determinant for her (or his) fertility behavior. The comparison of the three abortion cases and the sole excess birth case substantiate this.

There are at least three topics that merit future research. First of all, my study focuses on a single church. It is worth discussing to what degree Grace Church is representative of house churches in Chinese cities. Do other churches share Grace Church's higher-than-average fertility desire? In a society in which low fertility desire is the status quo, would people of childbearing age, especially those born in the 1980s and 1990s, share the same enthusiasm about procreation as the congregants of Grace Church? And how representative is Grace Church's lower-than-average fertility rate?

Despite the church leaders' silence and complicity concerning the issue of abortion, which is the case in most house churches (including Grace Church) and Three-Self churches, an increasing number of churches are taking a different approach. Pastors and congregants alike, especially those in house churches, are increasingly inclined to encourage church members not to have abortions rather than complying with state laws when deciding whether to continue a pregnancy. In a good number of churches in Beijing, it is not uncommon to find congregants with two or three children—some pastors have two children. For these reasons, it is unclear whether Grace Church is a representative case.

Second, many factors contribute to the level of fertility desire, and religious belief is only one. Socioeconomic variables such as income level, education level, female employment, and the preference for sons should all be taken into consideration. To what degree do these nonreligious factors affect the above-average fertility desires of the congregants of Grace Church? And given the relatively higher-than-average fertility desire among Christians, the fertility rate of the Christian community may also be elevated to a level that far exceeds the national average, especially after the promulgation of the universal two-child policy. The rise of anti-abortion ministries in churches may also suppress the abortion rate and further increase the birth rate among Christians.

Bibliography

Adsera, Alicia. "An Economic Analysis of the Gap between Desired and Actual Fertility: The Case of Spain." *Review of Economics of the Household* 4.1 (2006): 75–95.

Chinese Academy of Social Sciences. *Shehui lanpi shu: 2016 nian Zhongguo shehui xingshi fenxi yu yuce* 社会蓝皮书：2016年中国社会形势分析与预测. Beijing: Shehui kexue wenxian chubanshe, 2015.

Gu Baochang 顾宝昌. "Shengyu yiyuan shengyu xingwei he shengyu shuiping" 生育意愿、生育行为和生育水平. *Renkou yanjiu* 人口研究 35.2 (2011): 43–59.

Li Feng 李峰. "Zongjiao xinyang yingxiang shengyu yiyuan ma? Jiyu CGSS2010 nian shuju de fenxi" 宗教信仰影响生育意愿吗？基于 CGSS2010 年数据的分析. *Shijie zongjiao yanjiu* 世界宗教研究. 2017.3: 18–34.

Liang Zhongtang 梁中堂. *Zhongguo jihua shengyu zhengce shilun* 中国计划生育政策史论. Beijing: Zhongguo fazhan chubanshe, 2014.

McQuillan, Kevin. "When Does Religion Influence Fertility?" *Population and Development Review* 30.1 (2004): 25–56.

Morgan, S. P. "Is Low Fertility a Twenty-First-Century Demographic Crisis?" *Demography* 40.4 (2003): 589–603.

Wang Guangzhou 王广州. "Zhongguo laonianren qinzi shuliang yu jiegou jisuanji fangzhen fenxi" 中国老年人亲子数量与结构计算机仿真分析. *Zhongguo renkou kexue* 中国人口科学 34.3 (2014): 2–16.

Yang Juhua 杨菊华. "Yiyuan yu xingwei de beili: fada guojia shengyu yiyuan yu shengyu xingwei yanjiu shuping ji dui Zhongguo de qishi" 意愿与行为的背离：发达国家生育意愿与生育行为研究述评及对中国的启示. *Xuehai* 学海. 2008.1: 16–22.

Yao Meixiong 姚美雄. "Ba quanmian guli shengyu dingwei xin jiben guoce henyou biyao" 把全面鼓励生育定为新基本国策很有必要. *China Reform* (*Zhongguo gaige luntan* 中国改革论坛). February 28, 2017.

Zhan Zhongle 湛中乐. *Gongmin shengyu quan yu shehui fuyangfei zhidu yanjiu* 公民生育权与社会抚养费制度研究. Beijing: Falü chubanshe, 2011.

Zhonghua quanguo funu lianhe hui 中华全国妇女联合会. *Shishi quanmian lianghai zhengce dui jiating jiaoyu de yingxiang* 实施全面两孩政策对家庭教育的影响. December 22, 2016.

CHAPTER 14

Online Religious Communities in a WeChat Age
From Public Accounts to Megagroups

Yan LIU

1   Introduction

Over the past few years, China has witnessed a nationwide crackdown on Christianity. When President Xi Jinping took power in 2012, the Chinese government adopted different measures to put religious organizations under government control. On September 9, 2016, China's Supreme Court, Supreme People's Procuratorate, and the Ministry of Public Security issued the "Provisions on Several Issues Concerning the Collection, Extraction, Examination, and Judgment of Electronic Data in Criminal Cases." This document claims that information from mobile text, email, online social groups, and other network application services can be extracted as evidence in court trials. Under these regulations, which went into effect in October 2016, the religious freedom of Chinese people is significantly limited.

On September 7, 2017, the Chinese central government released the draft of the "Revised Regulations on Religious Affairs," which went into force on February 1, 2018.[1] New articles and content were added to the original regulations to stress the Party's leadership over religious groups, religious spaces and land use, religious activities and education, religious publications, and online information release. According to the revised regulations, the government is the final arbiter of the legal status of religious groups and religious space; no individuals or groups can manifest their faith in a nondesignated place without the consent of the government. The gathering of Christians in fellowship at home or in any other public space is illegal. Individuals and groups are not allowed to attend overseas religious training, conferences, or gatherings without government approval. With the revised regulations, the government's religious administration enlarges its administrative domain while shouldering fewer responsibilities.[2]

---

1   State Council of PRC, "The Revised Regulations on Religious Affairs," August 26, 2017, http://www.gov.cn/zhengce/content/2017-09/07/content_5223282.htm (accessed August 20, 2019).
2   Yang Fenggang, "The Final Version and Draft Version of the 'Religious Affairs Regulations,'" CareerEngine, September 10, 2017, https://posts.careerengine.us/p/59b4a5e5a6a1de190ea0368e (accessed August 20, 2019).

According to the *International Religious Freedom Report 2017*, released by the U.S. State Department in May 2018, cases of religious adherents who died in detention and the abuse, jailing, and torture of followers of both registered and unregistered groups continued in China.[3] It seems that a new round of persecution has come again, raising questions about the future of Christianity in China.[4] Some leaders of house churches worry that there could be a new round of repression against Christian house churches in China.[5] Will government restriction work to keep religious groups in the private sphere? What role will social media play under these circumstances?

According to the tricolor model of religious markets, suppressive regulation may provoke the growth of the gray market, which includes "all religious and spiritual organizations, practitioners, believers, and religious activities."[6] Based on the triple-market religious model, this chapter argues that with the development of Internet technologies, the religious gray market in China is expanding quickly in diverse forms and contents. Specifically, this chapter looks at the creation and sharing of Christian (Protestant) content on WeChat, the most popular messaging app used in China. The complexity of the religious phenomena of the Internet community makes it harder for the government to define legal and illegal religious activities. The deprivation of freedom of thought and of speech will provoke greater mass demand for political liberty and religious freedom. Thus, for a variety of reasons, a new era of religious flourishing may be coexisting with the "religious winter."

First, new Internet technologies and cell phones will enable religious resources to become more visible, accessible, and available through mobile phones; thus, the Christian faith is growing from a personal religion to a more public religion on a mobile media platform.

The second reason for the new flourishing of religion is related to how religious messages spread on WeChat. When information is blocked on WeChat

---

3 Richard Finney, "Religious Repression Ramps Up in China, Myanmar: Report," *Radio Free Asia*, May 29, 2018, https://www.rfa.org/english/news/china/religious-05292018165236.html (accessed August 20, 2019).
4 Katie Mansfield, "China Launches 'Religious Winter' in Bid to Destroy Christianity in Fierce Crackdown." Express.com.uk, September 30, 2017, http://www.express.co.uk/news/world/715834/China-Christians-launches-religious-winter-bid-destroy-Christianity (accessed August 20, 2019).
5 Matthew Carney, "Chinese Communist Party Readies Crackdown on Christianity," Mobile ABC News, October 8, 2016, http://mobile.abc.net.au/news/2016-10-08/chinese-communist-partys-crackdown-on-religion/7912140?pfmredir=sm (accessed August 20, 2019).
6 Fenggang Yang, "The Red, Black, and Gray Markets of Religion in China," *Sociological Quarterly*, 47.1 (2006): 93–122.

public accounts or web links, people can transfer it to images, PDF documents, or even voice or video messages, and thus the same content can still be circulated among WeChat friends or friend circles. Even if the information disappears from the WeChat platform, it is often released and broadcast on other platforms before the Internet police can block or delete it. The crackdown on some public accounts and the blockage of different voices will reveal to the public the extent to which they have been deprived of information freedom. The more information is deleted or blocked from mobile sources, the more curious people will be. WeChat users can still see the titles of deleted articles, and they can still search for the titles and access those articles online. This makes the blockage of information difficult.

Third, a variety of functions of the WeChat platform enable new forms of knowledge transmission and creation. Social groups are using the WeChat platform to broadcast news and lectures. The formation of megagroups on the WeChat platform reinforces fast broadcasting of ideas and a common cultural awareness among group members. Supported by the government as a tool of economic and technological development, WeChat is becoming a great platform for the exchange of political thoughts and cultural views. Because it is tied up with countless economic and political interests, it will be impossible for the government to control this huge vessel of information by blocking the whole WeChat platform. Through the accumulation of knowledge, capital, and human relationships on the platform, WeChat will help reshape people's view of the world.

Finally, the mobile platform will enable followers of different religions from around the world to form communities with similar values and allow them to work together for the same cause and a shared agenda. The WeChat platform will play an even greater role in shaping Chinese people's awareness of human rights and will facilitate the development of civil society with social groups of common values and beliefs.

2 Data and Methodology

This research includes information from WeChat research reports, Christian WeChat public accounts, WeChat megagroups, smaller groups, and individual WeChat conversations. The information collected from Christian WeChat public accounts includes general background, mission statements, and the titles and contents of articles released in public accounts. The intercommunication data of the released WeChat articles and their readers were studied as well. Based on my observation of megagroup activities on the WeChat platform for six months, I have extracted the characteristics of such groups and how they are formed.

2.1 Advantages of the WeChat Platform

2.1.1 Easy Accessibility

Free services, easy accessibility, and the multimedia information transmission function are the top three reasons users choose WeChat.[7] WeChat has become one of the most popular mobile apps in the world since Tencent released it in 2011. About 80 to 90 percent of cell phone users in mainland China use WeChat or QQ mobile apps.[8] By August 2016, WeChat had a total user population of 700 million around the world,[9] and about 90 percent of the users were located in mainland China.[10]

2.1.2 Lower Threshold for We-Media

Compared with traditional publishers and presses in mainland China, the WeChat platform gives more freedom to Chinese people regarding the promotion of news and ideas, even though it is under heavy governmental Internet restriction and surveillance. News released from journals, newspapers, and traditional publishers must go through several levels of censorship. However, news and ideas on the WeChat platform are usually released and broadcasted to other platforms before the Internet police can block or delete them.

The threshold for news release has been minimized on the WeChat platform. To apply for a personal WeChat public account, one needs only a verified name, personal identification number, bank account, and cell number. To apply for an organizational account, one needs only the name of the organization, the code of the institution, an identification number, and the cell number of the person who manages the account. The WeChat number is connected to the bank account of the manager or the organization.

---

7   Kuang Wenbo, "Zhongguo weixin fazhan de lianghua yanjiu," *Guoji xinwenjie*, 2014.5: 147–156.
8   Chinese Internet Network Information Center (CNNIC), "The 2015 Annual Report of the Social Media Application Users' Behavior" 2015 年中国社交应用用户行为研究报告. April 2016, http://www.cnnic.net.cn/hlwfzyj/hlwxzbg/sqbg/201712/P020180103485975797840.pdf (accessed August 20, 2019).
9   Peter Weber, "China Has an Amazing Smartphone Super-app. You May Not Want the West to Replicate it," *The Week*, August 10, 2016, http://theweek.com/speedreads/642014/china-amazing-smartphone-superapp-may-not-want-west-replicate (accessed August 20, 2019).
10 Tencent Research Institute, "The 2015 Annual Report on the Economic and Social Influence of WeChat" 2015 年微信社会经济影响力研究报. March 2016, http://www.199it.com/archives/452179.html (accessed August 20, 2019).

When applying for a WeChat public account, applicants can choose a subscription account, service account, or enterprise account depending on their needs. A subscription account supports the release of a single message every day and is the option most widely adopted by individual and group media applicants. A service account is designed for enterprises and companies to provide service inquiries, and it will allow the account owner to release four messages—usually commercial—every month. An enterprise account is mainly used for internal communications of companies and social groups.

2.1.3 Organically Forging Strong Ties

According to the Chinese Internet Network Information Center's (CNNIC) 2015 annual report, people's motivations for using WeChat include: "to promote interaction and emotional bonds between friends" (80.3%), "to learn about the hottest news" (50.2%), "to get knowledge useful for my life and work" (49.1%), and "to learn about things in which I am interested" (45.8%). Compared with two other social media platforms used in China, Weibo and Momo, users of WeChat form stronger ties in the virtual community.[11]

The information exchanged among users on WeChat enjoys a higher level of privacy and security. Wang Xiaobo and Gu Xiaotong explain how the technical design of WeChat enables "the free flow of information within the context of heavy Internet policing and surveillance in the People's Republic of China."[12] They conclude that the three functions unique to the WeChat app—Moments, Friends' Circle, and Share To—ensure the privacy and security of information disseminated via the platform. With those functions, the "free dissemination of information and public involvement through social media" is also ensured.[13] Thus, technology, design, and social context interact to promote the possibility of social innovation.

Kuang Wenbo compared the characteristics, functions, and perceived accessibility and trustworthiness of WeChat and other media such as Weibo, newspapers, broadcasts, and TV in China.[14] He found that the credibility of WeChat is the highest among all. Compared with a weak-tie media platform like Weibo, the strong-tie social media WeChat platform promotes the trustworthiness of information through person-to-person transmission and provides a platform

---

11   Chinese Internet Network Information Center, "2015 Annual Report," 38–39.
12   Wang Xiaobo and Gu Xiaotong, "The Communication Design of WeChat: Ideological as Well as Technical Aspects of Social Media," *Communication Design Quarterly Review* 4.1 (2016): 23–35.
13   Ibid., 23.
14   Kuang, "Zhongguo weixin fazhan de lianghua yanjiu."

for people to share their opinions with a wider audience. The hold-to-talk voice messaging, instant video talks, one-to-many text and voice messaging, and photo/video sharing functions greatly cater to users' needs and enrich the forms of information released from the WeChat platform.

2.2 Religious Public Accounts on WeChat

According to the CNNIC 2015 report, the WeChat public account, similar to a blog function on the WeChat platform, has become one of the major WeChat services.[15] Around 58% of WeChat users read posts from a WeChat public account.[16] In 2015, the number of WeChat public accounts exceeded 10 million, with 11.2% of these accounts belonging to governments at different levels or NGOs.[17] The number of government WeChat public accounts exceeded 83,000 in August 2015.[18] Although none of the reports mention religious public accounts, it cannot be denied that a significant amount of religious public accounts are also active on the WeChat platform. These reports neglected the religious accounts partly because the number of religious public accounts is comparatively lower than that of mainstream and recreational WeChat public accounts. The government's strict control over religious activity in public is another reason.

There are individual public accounts like "Wang Yi's Microphone" and "Christ Today." There are WeChat public accounts belonging to certain groups of people, such as fellowships, churches, or religious organizations like IJingjie or Living Rock. There are WeChat public accounts attached to Christian news websites like *Christian Times* and *Behold*. There are also WeChat public accounts attached to government-recognized Christian journals and electronic journals like *Tian Feng* 天风. Besides these well-known public accounts, many religious WeChat public accounts from different social backgrounds are created every day.

Compared with other types of public accounts, the religious public statements may be smaller in number. However, they attract a significant number of readers, and their readers are increasing day by day. The most popular religious public accounts usually win their readers through high quality and effective interactivity. Most of the religious public accounts keep the comment and praise function open to readers. Readers can often see the comments of other readers at the end of an article and add their own comments. Different

---

15 Chinese Internet Network Information Center, "2015 Annual Report."
16 Ibid., 28–29.
17 Tencent Research Institute, "2015 Annual Report."
18 Ibid., 47.

public accounts serve diverse groups of people. For example, "OC Behold" and "OC Overseas Campus" aim to serve young Christians and students, and their WeChat public accounts are attached to Christian news websites. With growing numbers of followers, the rise of many Christian public accounts opens the possibility for new networks.

"Jingjie" 经解, which was started in February 2013, was China's first nonprofit WeChat public account focusing on Christian faith. The editors are a group of religious media professionals with a deep concern for public issues. This account aims to meet people's spiritual needs and to restore the element of faith in news events and figures. I collected data from the WeChat public account "Ijingjie," the successor to the "Jingjie" public account, at the beginning of December 2016. In the thirty days of November 2016, "IJingjie" released 27 articles. Some of the articles were combined with a small video of a Bible story at the top of the pages. The average number of clicks received by each of the 27 articles in November was 19,742 per article; the average number of praises (or "thumbs up") was 217 for each article, and the average number of comments per article was 29. With a click of the "reward" key at the end of the article, readers could also make a small financial donation. The donation could be of any amount between 1 and 256 yuan, and each original article received an average of 117 donations.

By December 5, the article "America's Future Does Not Depend on the President—The Christian Voice of 'Revive Us'" (November 7) had won the highest number of clicks among the 27 articles released in November, totaling 63,652 clicks. An article that discussed how the Christian faith helped to bring back a family, "Our Marriage Resurrected after the Ninth Year of Divorce" (November 18), was second with 47,533 clicks. In third place was an article about Chinese badminton Olympic champion Lin Dan's recent scandal: "Can People Stick to the Bottom Line on Their Own? On Lin Dan's Derailment during His Wife's Pregnancy" (November 21). From the following table of the top three articles and the responses they attracted on Ijingjie, we see that the interaction between readers and writers is very active (Table 14.1). Some of the comments of readers won hundreds of praises.

"Wang Yi's Microphone" is a WeChat public account named after the well-known pastor of Early Rain Church in Chengdu. By early October, the average number of clicks received by the 15 articles he released in September 2016 was about 5,800, and the average number of praises per article was 90. By December 5, the article "Surplus Grace" (November 24) had won the highest number of clicks among the articles released in November, with 18,379. The article "How Can Christians Identify Heresies?" (November 1) had a click rate of 16,166. In third place was the article "Will Revolution Happen in China Again?" (November

TABLE 14.1 Responses to the top three articles released on "Ijingjie" in November 2016 as of December 5, 2016, with average responses to all articles released by the account in November 2016

	Clicks per article	Praises per article	Comments per article	Donations per article
1. "America's Future"	63,652	448	38	210
2. "Our Marriage Resurrected"	57,052	688	98	270
3. "On Lin Dan's Derailment"	47,533	534	32	120
Average of 27 articles released in November 2016	19,742	217	29	117

15). The average number of clicks received by each of the 15 articles released in November was 7,631, and the average number of praises and comments per article were 125 and 25 respectively (see Table 14.2). Note that the average number of clicks received by Wang Yi's articles increased from around 5,800 in September to 7,631 in November. However, the public account "Wang Yi's Microphone" was shut down in October 2017. Although Wang had set up a new public account, "Messages from the Heavenly Kingdom" (*Tianguo weikan* 天国微刊), by the end of October 2017, it did not survive into 2018. On February 5, 2018, Wang started a new WeChat public account named "Autumn of the Heavenly Kingdom."

Zhao Yi analyzed the integration of traditional paper media with the WeChat platform using the example of the *Yangzi Evening News* (*Yangzi wanbao* 扬子晚报) WeChat public account.[19] He concluded that the public account is characterized by its combination of flexible and interactive information exchange. Bai Bo proved that among well-educated people, information quality is far more important than the recreational aspect in attracting more users to a specific WeChat account.[20] The data from the Christian public WeChat accounts mentioned above also support Zhao's and Bai's conclusions.

---

19   Zhao Yi, "Cong weixin gongzhonghao kan chuantong meiti de xin fazhan: Yi *yangziwanbao* weixin gongzhonghao weili," *Chuanmei*, 2014.5: 36–39.
20   Bai Bo, "Gaoxiao tushuguan weixin yonghu jieshou xingwei yanjiu: Jiyu jishu jieshou moxing" (Jilin University, master's thesis, 2015), 49–55.

TABLE 14.2 Responses to the top three articles released on "Wang Yi's Microphone" in November 2016 as of December 5, 2016, with average responses to all articles released by the account in November 2016

	Clicks per article	Praises per article	Comments per article	Donations per article
1. "Surplus Grace"	18,379	353	44	Not shown
2. "How Can Christians Identify Heresies?"	16,166	146	44	Not shown
3. "Will Revolution Happen in China Again?"	14,372	253	55	Not shown
Average of 15 articles released in November 2016	7,631	125	25	—

Most of the Christian WeChat public accounts are easily recognized by their visual elements and their content. Images of the cross, the Bible, light, and Jesus are frequently used as the background of an article. The most common types of articles include personal faith testimonies, spiritual practices, everyday Bible verses, hymns, and sermons. The terms and concepts of Christianity are frequently used in the articles. The world and people's lives are interpreted through the lens of the Bible. Articles on family, education, marriage, and career are always popular with readers.

Take the WeChat public account "Christian Times" as an example. It calls itself a network gospel ministry, and its mission is to spread the gospel. It also claims that it is trans-denominational and will not be affiliated with any group or church organization. Its mission is to become a platform or a bridge between churches, society, government, and believers, and to build the kingdom of God. The WeChat account "Christian Times" is linked to the website of *Christian Times*, with columns on the church, service, theology, society, family, life, and business. *Christian Times* presents rich and profound content to meet the needs of Christians' spiritual lives. According to the statement of *Christian Times*, content is the soul of a website, and the content of a Christian website should be taken from the church and used in the church.

As its mission statement explains, *Christian Times* records the history of the various churches under the leadership of God; it records the acts of Christians and their institutions in all spheres of society to witness the grace of God. In September 2016, the WeChat public account "Christian Times" released a total of 182 articles, averaging five to seven articles every day. On each day's table of contents, there are reflections on current religious issues, faith testimonies, Christian hymns or poems, gospel messages, sermons, or Bible stories. "Christian Times" does not only release personal faith testimonies. Within that month, it released seven articles about the life of preachers in rural and urban areas, twelve articles on church services and church management, and three articles about religious services across national borders.

Christian WeChat public accounts respond to social issues in different ways. Articles on hot topics typically attract more readers. However, texts on political issues may lead to the blockage of articles or even the shutdown of the WeChat public account. The faith communities supporting the public accounts are usually vague in their legal identity: some of them belong to the traditional gray market. Even if they belong to the government-supported red market, they cannot ensure that every word released on the public account is not on the government's forbidden list.

Setting up a new WeChat public account is the common practice of those who encounter a shutdown. "IJingjie" was recovered after a twenty-day shutdown of "Jingjie" by an official WeChat administrator. "Wang Yi's Microphone" was set up after the public account of Wang Yi's church, the "Early Rain WeChat Journal," had been shut down.

A range of responses from authorities are directed at religious WeChat public accounts depending on the content of their posts, or of the comments left beneath them by users. Different accounts roughly correspond to the tricolor religious market model outlined by Fenggang Yang.[21] In the "black" category would be "Wang Yi's Microphone," which on September 22, 2016, released an article titled "24 Citizens' Proposal for the Interpretation of Articles 36 and 89 of the Constitution." It argues that the "Revised Regulations on Religious Affairs" violates the constitution, and that the comment solicitation process of the "Revised Regulations" should be terminated immediately. When you click on the link to the article page, however, you are directed to a page that displays the message, "This content cannot be viewed. Users have complained that it violates relevant laws, regulations or policies." However, if you are interested in

---

21 Fenggang Yang, "Red, Black, and Gray Markets."

this article, you can enter the name of this article in a search engine and easily find it on various websites.

"Christian Times," which could be considered in the gray market, released an article titled "The Legislative Affairs Office of the State Council Promulgated a Public Notice on the Revised Draft of the Regulations on Religious Affairs" on September 8, 2016. By early October, it had received over 9,300 clicks. On September 9, 2016, "Christian Times" released an article named "What Are the Differences between the Revised Religious Affairs Ordinance (Draft) and the 2004 Regulations on Religious Affairs?" This article compared in detail the clauses in the two versions of regulations but did not comment on the differences. On September 24, "Christian Times" released an article titled "The Revised Regulations on Religious Affairs (Draft)—Views and Analysis of Some Religious Scholars and Pastors of House Churches." This article made both positive and negative comments on the "Regulations" and questioned the ambiguity, reasonability, and feasibility of the "Regulations."

Another faith-based WeChat public account, "Cedar Leadership," was started by scholar Zhao Xiao, a typical "red market" Christian. He released two articles by Feng Xuewei, the general director of the former State Council Legislative Affairs Office, on October 10 and November 15, 2016. The titles of the articles were "Several Principles of Establishing Religious Affairs Legislation by Drawing on the Historical Development of Religious Freedom" and "Comments and Suggestions on the Draft of the Revised Regulations on Religious Affairs." Compared with the article blocked in "Wang Yi's Microphone," these two articles expressed a similar stand. They expressed an opinion contradictory to the mainline media and advocated for religious freedom with professional legislative analysis and historical facts.

From the above examples, we see that different WeChat public accounts may be considered as red, black, or gray by the government. It is common for WeChat public accounts from the black market to be censored or shut down. The voices of the "gray market" religious leaders and populace may also be blocked or deleted by WeChat administrators, but less frequently. In comparison, the voices of people with higher social status or more official positions enjoy higher tolerance from the government, and they can talk about some sensitive issues that others cannot.

3   The Megagroup: A Comprehensive Platform

While a church with more than 2,000 attendees can be considered a megachurch, many WeChat megagroups have 10,000–20,000 members or even more. This is possible despite the limits on group size built into WeChat. Tencent Technology, the designer of WeChat, set a 500-member limit to the number of people in a WeChat group, and individuals who join a group with over 100 people are required to go through real-name verification and to link their personal bank account to their WeChat account.

Given these restrictions, how can a WeChat group reach the level of tens of thousands of people? Let us examine how a megagroup is formed. A WeChat group can easily be established through the invitation function of the WeChat app. The host of the group simply chooses a person from his contacts and initiates a conversation; the host can keep on inviting people to join this conversation until the number of people in this group reaches the limit of five hundred. But there is no limit to the number of groups that a host can create. Therefore, a host can reach tens of thousands of people by forming more and more groups.

How does a host integrate many individual groups into a megagroup? The technologies offered by the WeChat platform and some information technology enterprises provide the means to do so. The WeChat app enables individuals to send point-to-point and point-to-group information in the form of a voice message, video, image, or text. The host of the megagroup can use broadcasting equipment or software to send a message in any of these forms to all of the groups at the same time. The information the host sends out will be automatically received and stored on the receiver's phone. People who receive the message can read or listen to the message anytime. In this sense, the WeChat app enables a phone to become a portable information storage device.

The receiver of the message can ignore the host's message or respond with comments, questions, or relevant information in the receiver's own WeChat group or in a private conversation. The host can further interact with members of different groups in a WeChat group or private conversation and share the conversations with all the other groups. A host will usually share discussions of the most frequently asked questions and hot topics with all his groups. Thus, a hot topic can involve hundreds of people in a discussion and generate new knowledge. After several rounds of discussion and debate, a common understanding or value can be reached within the WeChat megagroup arranged by the host.

3.1   *Characteristics of Megagroups*
There are a number of important components necessary to sustain a megagroup. This section will go over some of these core elements, using one of the WeChat megagroups, which I will call "Thoughts," as an example.

3.1.1 Clear Mission

The megagroup "Thoughts" consists of forty subgroups and about a dozen affiliated groups. The subgroups are automatically enlarged by the invitation function, which randomly sends out invitations to other WeChat users, and the affiliated groups mainly focus on some specific fields such as history, culture, international politics, economics and finance, market analysis, new industry analysis, or investment. The megagroup accumulated a total of 28,000 people in its subgroups and affiliated groups within two years.

The introduction to the megagroup contains a very clear statement of its mission and cultural characteristics:

> We are Chinese descendants from around the world. We use the same language and share the same heritage of Chinese culture. Through the Internet, we connect across the oceans. We learn the facts of Chinese history and culture here, and we explore the future path of Chinese civilization. The Internet brings us together; it enables us to exchange ideas and enlightens us with a broader cultural rationality. The persistent collision of thoughts here will surely bring about personal enlightenment and insight and awaken our consciousness and self-confidence. Once this consensus is formed, and the power of the social groups is cultivated, this nation will surely present a grand new ideological enlightenment. Before this, we need to learn to think, using the essence of human civilization, and to guide future change with an inner conscience. This introduction of the megagroup encourages people with open minds to work together with people of similar ideas and to change the current system.

3.1.2 Clear Vision

This megagroup has a clear vision for future development. It plans to develop a large or mid-sized Internet community with unique cultural values. To achieve a scale effect, the megagroup aims to reach two million to five million people. In the first stage of the megagroup's development, it focused on the cultivation of a study group on the WeChat platform, and it will gradually expand its services to include tourism, family and marriage, immigration and studying abroad, business logistics, and the promotion of new products. To create an online community with both social and economic values, the host is planning to set up a media platform both inside and outside mainland China with steady financial support.

3.1.3 Content-Oriented Study

Within the past two years, this megagroup has invited some well-known scholars, experts, and pastors at home and abroad to give lectures on the WeChat platform. Each lecture is simultaneously broadcasted to all the subgroups of the megagroups, and three lectures are broadcasted every week on average. These lectures provide a systematic analysis of the hot topics of politics, economics, and culture in the world and in China.

Under the initiative of group members, this WeChat community started a series of book-reading activities. Some classic books are recited and recorded, and the voice messages of the books were broadcasted to the megagroup. The most popular titles include *Two Treaties of Government*, *The Spirit of Law*, *The Wealth of Nations*, *The Protestant Ethic and the Spirit of Capitalism*, the Declaration of Independence, *The Road to Serfdom*, *The Principles of Economics*, *Investment Theory*, and *Social Science and Statistical Analysis*. The host of the megagroup has declared that the lectures and book reading activities stimulated individuals' innovation and thinking. Whether adults or students, their way of thinking, knowledge structure, and openness to new ideas are significantly improved.

3.1.4 Charismatic Leader

The host of this megagroup is a Christian and an expert in macroeconomics with a doctoral degree in economics. He releases his comments on current affairs, macroeconomics, and cultural and religious topics on a daily or weekly basis. Most often, his message is initially broadcasted to the megagroup in the form of a voice message; the voice message is later transformed into a text message and shared within the subgroups of the megagroup.

The host has established a good relationship with scholars, activists, merchants, and freelance writers at home and abroad. He introduces every invited lecturer to the audiences in the subgroups. He comments on every lecture, analyzes different opinions and theoretical traditions, and makes claims that can hardly be found in mainstream media. He advocates common sense, democracy, civil society, and freedom, and he bitterly criticizes the totalitarian government and the distorted official history. Therefore, the impression he gives to the members of the megagroup is that he is knowledgeable, righteous, and conscientious.

3.1.5 Sustained Financial Support

To support the broadcast of information in different forms, the megagroup releases donation notices to every subgroup and encourages its members to donate. Although some people will donate a small amount of money from time to time, and some people never donate, all of them are equally welcome. The names of those who have donated money are posted on the group space almost every week. The donations usually range from 5 to 3,000 yuan. Donors may also choose to remain anonymous.

The megagroup has also instituted a membership system. The annual membership fee is 50,000 yuan or more for honorary members, 2,800 yuan or more for senior members, 1,000 yuan for ordinary members, and 220 yuan for access to lectures and book readings. Honorary members are invited to participate in high-level community gatherings of experts and elites and to join the community counselor committee. The host offers to senior members and ordinary members a comprehensive analysis of political, economic, and financial situations, as well as new industry and investment around the globe.

3.1.6   A Small Team and Various Broadcasting Technologies

At present, a very small team is supporting the whole project. There are only two core members who contact the whole WeChat group: the host and the administrator. The original content created by the team is comprised of the host's comments on various topics in the form of voice messages and texts and the administrator's oral reading of some classic books. The manager periodically sends messages to all WeChat group members to ask for comments and solicit donations.

The fast development of WeChat technology, the rich functions of various software, and the existence of other online platforms compatible with WeChat are the key elements that enable a small team to manage the entire megagroup. Qianliao, WeChat Information Exporter, and Himalaya FM are some of the most frequently used voice services in the megagroup.

In addition to the regular broadcasting of voice messages in the megagroup, the platform Qianliao literally "a thousand talks"—is frequently used in the WeChat megagroup. The administrator releases information to the megagroup about lectures, including the speaker, the exact title, and the time, to be delivered via the Qianliao platform. Members interested in the topic can listen to the lecture for a small fee, usually ranging from 5 to 50 yuan. The member simply scans the QR code of the lecture and completes the payment. The member can either listen to the live broadcast of the lecture and communicate with the lecturer directly through Qianliao or access the lecture anytime after the live broadcast.

The Qianliao platform is also convenient for the lecturer, who simply needs to download a Qianliao app and record a voice message with it. The lecturer can promote the lecture by sharing it with different groups and receive payments. Anyone who has something to say can use the Qianliao app as a personal radio station to share a message; through this technology, different values and ideas enter people's lives and help shape new thoughts. It is almost impossible for common government censorship techniques to work on this private broadcast station.

The first broadcast of a lecture in the megagroup always consists of a series of fragmentary voice messages. On the WeChat service, a single voice message cannot exceed sixty seconds. Therefore, a sixty-minute lecture will need to be sent to each member in at least sixty pieces. Although the WeChat app enables many pieces of information to be played automatically without pause, the playback of the lecture could be interrupted by other apps or functions on the phone. Due to the time delay between sending and receiving messages, the fragments of a lecture could be received out of order. To solve this problem, the host and the manager turn the fragmented voice message into an MP3 audio file via WeChat Voice Exporter. The reconstructed lecture is usually sent again to the megagroup for the convenience of all. The message may also be stored online for the group members to download, or it could be stored on the Himalaya FM platform, where it can be listened to at any time.

4 An Interactive Culture and Value Platform

4.1 Ambiguity: Is the Megagroup Cultural or Religious?

Although the main purpose of the "Thoughts" megagroup is to explore the correct direction for the development of national culture, lectures broadcast to the megagroup often feature comparisons of different religions and their influence on Chinese culture. The lectures covering religious topics include "The Relationship between Western Civilization and Christian Culture," "Will Christian Culture Bring us Democracy?" "A Conversation between Confucius's *Analects* and the Bible," "The Life Philosophy of Laozi," "Laozi's Realm of Life: Return Good for Evil," and "The 'Democratic' Thoughts of Laozi." Some lecturers clearly express their identity as Christian, and some of them strongly express their love of traditional Chinese culture. The lectures often arouse heated discussion in the subgroups. Questions posed by members after the talk are immediately forwarded to the lecturer, who will usually answer questions on the spot in the form of a voice or text message. This discussion will be simulcast to all the subgroups.

Among the books promoted and read in the megagroup, there are some that focus on traditional values, such as *The Canon of the Way* and *The Analects of Confucius*. The Bible is the most frequently discussed book in the megagroup.

The megagroup includes an affiliated WeChat group named "Knowing Jesus," which has about one hundred members. The lectures and book-reading activities of the megagroup are also promoted in this affiliated group. The links and content shared here are mostly from public accounts with religious themes. The members of the affiliated group also share videos and voice messages from their churches.

4.2   Interactivity: Questioning and Answering

The megagroup is a very active online community. The host and group manager introduces lecturers and sends voice messages containing comments on current issues or quotations from classic books almost every day. Faith, justice, culture, conscience, and human rights are the themes most frequently mentioned in the lectures and conversations. The most frequently discussed questions include the following: Do Chinese people need faith? What is faith? Can Christian culture save China? Can we find confidence in our traditional culture?

Discussions after reading activities are always heated in the megagroup. After the group manager read Locke's *Two Treaties of the Government* to the megagroup, one of the group members left a message in a subgroup space: "I am very surprised to see that Locke mentioned the Bible and Adam so many times in his book. I just cannot understand why he talked about Adam and God so often in a book on government. I am very curious about the Bible, and I feel the urgent need to read the Bible and to figure out what Locke is talking about." A group member responded to him on WeChat immediately, "I strongly support your decision to read the Bible. You will never regret it!"

Whenever anyone asked questions about the Bible or Christianity, there was almost always someone in the group who responded. From the language used in the answers, it is not difficult to discern that there are many Christians in the megagroups. Some of them even use biblical words and phrases as the names of their WeChat accounts, for example, "The way, the truth, and the life," "Serve the kingdom of the Lord," and "Immanuel." Some of these members are in mainland China, and some of them are overseas Chinese. A Chinese Christian from the United States even shared photographs of scenes of worship in his church to support his claim that the fundamentalist Christian Church is pious and meek.

Sometimes debates among the group members are heated. Some of them are staunch followers of traditional Chinese culture. They consider Christianity to be a very dangerous religion that could drive Chinese people into betraying their traditions. They post links to articles and recordings of conversations that refute the Christians and their bad behavior. The Christians in the group, on the other hand, tend to take every opportunity to link current topics of discussion to Christian culture and try to transmit the message of the gospel to other group members. Once a Christian leaves a message about the gospel on the WeChat group chat space, other Christians will step up with more information.

4.3　*Individuals, Public Accounts, and Groups*

On the WeChat platform, individual users, public accounts, groups, and megagroups form incredibly complex webs and sub-webs. Information from individuals, public accounts, and groups is transmitted quickly over space and time. In a megagroup, concepts and ideas are discussed, evaluated, combined with other concepts, accepted, or renewed. Comparatively isolated social groups are thus reconnected and reorganized.

If we consider the articles criticizing the new religious regulations on WeChat public accounts to be an open call for religious freedom, then the release of messages from religious WeChat public accounts and discussions of religious topics among individuals, groups, and megagroups on WeChat could be described as the practice of religious freedom. WeChat technologies enable the transmission of knowledge to happen under any circumstances, and the transmission of the gospel is no longer confined to a specific time, space, or group. WeChat links people around the world together and enables them to work together for similar values and pursuits.

During the comment solicitation process of the revised draft of the "Regulations on Religious Affairs" in 2017, Chinese Christians around the world received a 6,689-word letter via WeChat, email, or other point-to-point social media. The title of the letter was "To Cry out Aloud for the Freedom of Faith: A Fasting Prayer of Twenty-One Days." The letter, composed of twenty-one parts, prescribed the content of prayers offered on each day of the twenty-one-day program.

The letter invited Chinese Christians from around the world to pray for the churches' right to hold religious gatherings at home and on legal property, to own property and maintain religious personnel, and to evangelize overseas. The letter encourages Christians to pray for the legalization of seminaries and community services in China, the formation of legal aid groups to stand up for the church, the unity of the church, and the courage of church leaders, Christians, and students in seminaries. The letter also encouraged Christians to pray for state leaders, the State Council, the deputy of the National People's Congress, the religious bureaus, the neighborhood committees, the national security police, and the owners of gathering places. Finally, the letter invited Christians to pray for the authority and kingdom of the Lord. Although the regulations were approved according to the Chinese government's plan, the adversity experienced by Chinese Christians put Christian members of house churches around the world in the same boat and urged them to work together.

With the help of modern information technology, Chinese Christians are contacting each other and working together for the same agenda.

Yan Ling argues that if we view media as a subsystem of society, any change within the subsystem will influence other subsystems in society and thus provoke an adjustment of the social structure.[22] Although media is no more than an instrument of communication, it has taken on an organic existence as people's source of information and spiritual life, making it an indispensable part of peoples' lives. On WeChat, the transmitter and receiver of information are equal in status. People with similar values and preferences are able to contact each other through comments on the articles released on WeChat public accounts, "Friend Circle" links, and group conversations. This has made the establishment of more intimate ties with people on WeChat more readily possible.

4.4 Reproducibility: Restriction and Reshuffling

Different elements deeply rooted in the system of the social economy contribute to the organic integration of the WeChat ecosystem.[23] The suppression of certain spheres of this WeChat ecosystem might cause a series of reactions from different social groups. According to Fenggang Yang,

> Heavy regulation cannot effectively reduce religion. It can only complicate the religious market by pushing religious organizations and believers into the black and gray markets. Under heavy regulation, the gray market is not only huge, but it is also volatile, providing a fertile ground for NRMs [new religious movements]. For regulators and regulation enforcers, the gray market means an unmanageable state of religious affairs.[24]

With the deletion and blockage of WeChat articles and information, the government's restrictions on people's basic human rights—the right to exercise free thought and free speech, to practice religion, and to gather together—are more visible to the public than ever before. Government censorship on WeChat exposes users to the fact that the suppression of dissidents is commonplace. By attracting the attention of more individuals, government censorship provokes a greater awareness of human rights among the masses.

---

22 Yan Ling, "Weixin: meijiahua shengcun de xin wuzhong," *Xiandai chuanbo*, 2016.2: 140–143.
23 Tencent Research Institute, "2015 Annual Report."
24 Fenggang Yang, "Red, Black, and Gray Markets."

On November 29, 2016, many WeChat groups, such as "Thought Salon," "Walking in the Rain and Hardship," "Road to Constitutionalism," "Consensus," and "Toward the Republic," were shut down for engaging in discussions on freedom and democracy. Many famous scholars' WeChat accounts were blocked from transmitting messages, and some WeChat lecture groups were also closed. One of the subgroups of the WeChat megagroup "Thoughts" and one of the megagroup administrator's personal WeChat accounts were shut down as well.

The reason for this government action was that after the death of Fidel Castro on November 25, many websites discussed the event and compared Cuba's social institutions with those of China.[25] In response, the owner of the WeChat account "Walking in the Rain and Hardship" released a notice to group members, informing them that a new group with a new name would be created, and that group members could withdraw from the original one and invite more friends to join the new group.

Qiao Long references scholars in a discussion of how the Internet is—or is not—controlled in China. One of these scholars, Wang Jiangsong, argues that words cannot be completely controlled unless the authorities cut off the Internet:

> [The WeChat group] can be rebuilt or even multiplied. The original host can withdraw from a group, and everyone else in that group can be the new host. Everyone can build new groups and gather the original group of people together and continue to do what they have been doing before. Therefore, the Internet society poses a challenge to the traditional political system: coercive regulation does not work unless you cut off the whole Internet.[26]

Chen Yongmiao argues that control over public speech has always been restricted in China. From BBS, blogs, and Weibo (a microblogging service similar to Twitter) to WeChat, the government's control on media increased in step with the upgrade of information technologies.[27] With each new round of upgraded products, more and more people are joining the democratic movement. Many hosts of WeChat groups have established more groups where

---

25   Qiao Long, "Reyi kasiteluo zhi si duibi xianxing tizhi duoge zhongguo weixin qun zao guanbi," *Radio Free Asia*, November 29, 2016, http://www.rfa.org/mandarin/yataibaodao/meiti/ql1-11292016104848.html (accessed August 20, 2019).
26   Ibid.
27   Ibid.

they can store their contacts in case of a sudden interruption of service. The shutdown, reestablishment, and flourishing of some WeChat religious public accounts, as well as the closing and expanding of some WeChat groups, have proved this. The vitality of these WeChat accounts and groups provides a glimpse of a future online civil society that will hasten the formation of a practical civil society.

According to Seva Gunitsky, China's WeChat is rapidly becoming "both a source of active citizen participation and a tool for non-democratic governments."[28] Under an authoritarian government, China is seemingly drifting away from the global trend toward democracy. However, WeChat has reshuffled the ecological order of media.[29] It influences people's modes of expression and action and gradually changes people's cognition of self, others, and the social environment.

5   Conclusion

The easy accessibility of WeChat functions and services has created a great opportunity for social change and cultural renewal among Chinese people. The shutdown, rebuilding, and development of religious public accounts reveal Christian communities' vitality under government restrictions. The formation and expansion of WeChat megagroups forge a great potential for the spread of culture, thoughts, values, and faith reformation. Christian individuals and groups have adroitly capitalized on such new technology to spread religious messages and connect like-minded individuals. The use of WeChat, and particularly of WeChat groups, has enabled actors to expand the gray market of religion in China.

In the WeChat age, individual accounts, public accounts, and megagroups form a large network. The interactive comment function offered by WeChat connects strangers and opens a channel to other public web platforms. Individual discourse can enter the public platform through the "forward" and "share" functions. Thus, an acquaintance-oriented interactive evaluation system develops into a stranger-oriented public evaluation system that equips the user's self-cognition system with various value standards. In the WeChat ecological system, social and political forces exert equal influence. The competition, mutation, evolution, and symbiosis of these forces will further promote

---

28   Seva Gunitsky, "Corrupting the Cyber-commons: Social Media as a Tool of Autocratic Stability," *Perspectives on Politics* 13.1 (2015): 42.
29   Yan Ling, "Weixin."

the development of WeChat, and they may also further promote religious ideas, interaction, and practices.

The religious gray market is developing and renewed day by day. Although users may not directly express their cultural and religious identity, the interactivity among them cradles the future scalability of a huge Internet community of faith. The reproducibility of a faith community and online civil society, despite heavy restrictions by the government, has ushered the idea of human rights and democracy into Chinese society. However, it is not clear whether these ideas will change the current authoritarian political order.

Bibliography

Bai Bo 白波. "Gaoxiao tushuguan weixin yonghu jieshou xingwei yanjiu: Jiyu jishu jieshou moxing" 高校图书馆微信用户接受行为研究—基于技术接受模型. Jilin University, master's thesis. 2015.

Carney, Matthew. "Chinese Communist Party Readies Crackdown on Christianity." Mobile ABC News, October 8, 2016. http://mobile.abc.net.au/news/2016-10-08/chinese-communist-partys-crackdown-on-religion/7912140?pfmredir=sm (accessed August 20, 2019).

Chinese Internet Network Information Center (CNNIC). "The 2015 Annual Report of the Social Media Application Users' Behavior" 2015年中国社交应用用户行为研究报告. April 2016. http://www.cnnic.net.cn/hlwfzyj/hlwxzbg/sqbg/201712/P020180103485975797840.pdf (accessed August 20, 2019).

Finney, Richard. "Religious Repression Ramps Up in China, Myanmar: Report." *Radio Free Asia*, May 29, 2018. https://www.rfa.org/english/news/china/religious-05292018165236.html (accessed August 20, 2019).

Gunitsky, Seva. "Corrupting the Cyber-commons: Social Media as a Tool of Autocratic Stability." *Perspectives on Politics* 13.1 (2015): 42–54.

Kuang Wenbo 匡文波. "Zhongguo weixin fazhan de lianghua yanjiu" 中国微信发展的量化研究. *Guoji xinwenjie* 国际新闻界. 2014.5: 147–156.

Mansfield, Katie. "China Launches 'Religious Winter' in Bid to Destroy Christianity in Fierce Crackdown." Express.com.uk. Sept 30, 2017. http://www.express.co.uk/news/world/715834/China-Christians-launches-religious-winter-bid-destroy-Christianity (accessed August 20, 2019).

Qiao Long 乔龙. "Reyi kasiteluo zhi si duibi xianxing tizhi duoge zhongguo weixin qun zao guanbi," 热议卡斯特罗之死对比现行体制 多个中国微信群遭关闭. *Radio Free Asia*, November 29, 2016. http://www.rfa.org/mandarin/yataibaodao/meiti/ql1-11292016104848.html (accessed August 20, 2019).

State Council of PRC 中华人民共和国国务院. "The Revised Regulations on Religious Affairs" 宗教事务条例. August 26, 2017. http://www.gov.cn/zhengce/content/2017-09/07/content_5223282.htm (accessed August 20, 2019).

Tencent Research Institute. "The 2015 Annual Report on the Economic and Social Influence of WeChat" 2015年微信社会经济影响力研究报. March 2016. http://www.199it.com/archives/452179.html (accessed August 20, 2019).

Wang Xiaobo and Gu Xiaotong. "The Communication Design of WeChat: Ideological as Well as Technical Aspects of Social Media." *Communication Design Quarterly Review* 4.1 (2016): 23–35.

Weber, Peter. "China Has an Amazing Smartphone Super-app. You May Not Want the West to Replicate It." *The Week*, August 10, 2016. http://theweek.com/speedreads/642014/china-amazing-smartphone-superapp-may-not-want-west-replicate (accessed August 20, 2019).

Yan Ling 严玲. "Weixin: meijiahua shengcun de xin wuzhong" 微信：媒介化生存的新物种. *Xiandai chuanbo* 现代传播, 2016.2: 140–143.

Yang Fenggang 杨凤岗. "The Final Version and Draft Version of the 'Religious Affairs Regulations'" 《宗教事务条例》颁布版和送审稿文本对照. CareerEngine, September 10, 2017. https://posts.careerengine.us/p/59b4a5e5a6a1de190ea0368e (accessed August 20, 2019).

Yang, Fenggang. "The Red, Black, and Gray Markets of Religion in China." *Sociological Quarterly* 47.1 (2006): 93–122.

Zhao Yi 赵亿. "Cong weixin gongzhonghao kan chuantong meiti de xin fazhan: Yi *Yangzi wanbao* weixin gongzhonghao wei li" 从微信公众号看传统媒体的新发展——以《扬子晚报》微信公众号为例. *Chuanmei* 传媒. 2014.5: 36–39.

Conclusion: Whence and Whither Religious Markets in China

Fenggang YANG

This chapter not only concludes this volume of case studies of religious groups in the changing religious markets in China, but it also offers, for the first time, responses to major criticisms of religious market theories as they have been applied to China. Since its introduction fifteen years ago, the tricolor market theory, along with the broader economic approach to the study of religion, has met with acceptance, rejection, and criticism. The acceptance varies from appreciative to enthusiastic; the rejection is due to distaste for economic terms and market principles; scholarly criticisms are, as usual, measured and analytical, but also evince some misreadings or misunderstandings, which may not be rare for any new theory. Up to now I have not responded to criticisms directly but have rather continued to develop the theory through my books and theory-driven empirical studies. In this epilogue, however, it seems apt to recount the developmental process of this theory, discuss representative reactions to it in China and beyond, its usefulness for the ethnographic studies in this book, and offer some suggestions for going forward.

My discussion here will focus on major criticisms and reactions that have been formally published in Chinese inside China, which are available to Western scholars through the library-subscribed digital database of Chinese publications. I will not respond to criticisms that might have appeared in China's publications with restricted circulation that outsiders normally do not have access. In books and journal articles published in the West, there have been, as well, a fair amount of comments and criticisms of the religious market theory in general and my tri-color market theory in particular, with which I have engaged directly or indirectly through multiple research projects and publications, and thus it is not necessary to discuss much in this chapter.

1   The Bumpy Path of a New Theory

At the time of writing, the world has been under the coronavirus pandemic for almost six months. The first pandemic of this century was SARS in 2003, which forced me to stay put in the college town of West Lafayette, Indiana, instead of traveling to China for planned research and lecturing. I used the unexpected

CONCLUSION: WHENCE & WHITHER RELIGIOUS MARKETS IN CHINA 323

chunk of time to translate *Acts of Faith* into Chinese.[1] I did it both to introduce the latest development in the sociology of religion to Chinese academia and for my own purpose of gaining a thorough understanding of every word of the book, which systematically articulates a theory distilled from numerous empirical studies.

Up to that point, I had not been part of the school of religious economies or rational choice theories in my own studies of religion. My sociological training was primarily under the mentorship of Dean R. Hoge (1937–2008), a prominent sociologist of religion who studied Catholics and mainline Protestants in the United States and was open to various theories. During my graduate and postdoctoral years, I conducted research on immigrant religion in the U.S. within the framework of projects directed by R. Stephen Warner and Helen Rose Ebaugh.[2] Both are eminent sociologists of religion who, broadly speaking, fall into the new paradigm in the sociology of religion, yet not within the school of religious economies or rational choice theories. In fact, it was Warner who first heralded the new paradigm in the sociology of religion,[3] but he has repeatedly contended that this new paradigm includes multiple theories. Rodney Stark, Roger Finke, and their associates have developed what they themselves have called "supply-side theories of religious economies"; other scholars have constructed distinct theories, such as the "subculture identity theory,"[4] to explain why religious vitality persists in society instead of declining in tandem with modernization, as theorized by Peter Berger and others.[5]

Honestly speaking, my initial reaction to the so-called rational choice theory of religion was distaste for its seeming sacrilege. How could one compare

---

1 Rodney Stark and Roger Finke, *Acts of Faith: Explaining the Human Side of Religion* (Berkeley: University of California Press, 2000); translated by Yang Fenggang as *Xinyang de faze—jieshi zongjiao zhi ren de fangmian* (Beijing: Zhongguo renmin daxue chubanshe, 2004).

2 See R. Stephen Warner and Judith G. Wittner, eds., *Gatherings in Diaspora: Religious Communities and the New Immigration* (Philadelphia: Temple University Press, 1998); Helen Rose Ebaugh and Janet S. Chafetz, eds., *Religion and the New Immigrants: Continuities and Adaptations in Immigrant Congregations* (Walnut Creek, CA: AltaMira, 2000); Helen Rose Ebaugh and Janet S. Chafetz, eds., *Religions across Borders: Transnational Religious Networks* (Walnut Creek, CA: AltaMira, 2002).

3 R. Stephen Warner, "Work in Progress toward a New Paradigm for the Sociological Study of Religion in the United States," *American Journal of Sociology* 98.5 (1993): 1044–1093.

4 Christian Smith, *American Evangelicalism: Embattled and Thriving* (Chicago: University of Chicago Press, 1998).

5 Peter L. Berger, *The Sacred Canopy: Elements of a Sociological Theory of Religion* (Garden City, NY: Doubleday, 1967); Peter L. Berger, *A Rumor of Angels: Modern Society and the Rediscovery of the Supernatural* (Garden City, NY: Doubleday, 1969).

the sacred to the profane and consider religious faith to be based on rational calculation? However, when I recovered my academic detachment and applied the theory to various religious phenomena around me, the economic approach appeared sharp and effective. Failure to detach is not uncommon in academia, but it often frustrates life inside as well as outside academia. This reminds me of a popular Chinese comedian's crosstalk (相声) about a physician who ruined a banquet he hosted because he couldn't help but explain the dishes to the guests using anatomical terms for the various organs and cuts of meat. The ability to detach oneself from the objects and subjects of study is a basic requirement for social scientific research.

Therefore, upon the publication of *Acts of Faith* in 2000, I adopted it as one of the textbooks for my sociology of religion courses in the United States.[6] I also lectured on it, together with other works in the new paradigm, at a number of universities in various parts of China.[7] Before I undertook my translation of the book in 2003, I encouraged some graduate students in sociology to translate the book into Chinese, but the religious, economic, and sociological terms proved to be too new and challenging for them. The Chinese edition of the book was published in early 2004, in time for the first Summer Institute for the Social Scientific Study of Religion held at Renmin University, which I co-organized. The Summer Institute became an annual event consisting of two weeks of lectures by well-known social scientists of religion from the United States or Europe; each year the participants included several dozens of Chinese graduate students and young scholars from various universities throughout China.[8]

In the process of translating the book, I began to theorize about the religious reality in China and made the first presentation of some rough ideas at the

---

6 In those years, I taught "The Sociology of Religion" at the University of Southern Maine and "Religion in America" at Purdue University.

7 At Sichuan University, I discussed the paradigm shift in the sociology of religion in an interview that was published in the *Journal of Religious Studies*. See Lin Qiaowei, "Yang Fenggang boshi tan zongjiao shehuixue de fanshi zhuanxing," *Zongjiaoxue yanjiu*, 2003.3: 140–141.

8 Prominent scholars of various theoretical schools who gave series of lectures included Eileen Barker, Dean Hoge, Roger Finke, Gordon Melton, Steve Warner, Grace Davie, Nancy Ammerman, Jose Casanova, Jay Demerath, Roberto Cipriani, Giuseppe Giordan, Richard Madsen, and Robert Weller. Some Chinese and Western scholars gave one or two single talks, such as Fang Litian, Zhuo Xinping, He Guanghu, Gao Shining, Li Xiangping, Hei-yuan Chiu, Katherine Meyer, David Palmer, Joe Tamney, Patricia Wittberg, Fuk-tsang Ying, and Min Zhou, among others. My key operating partner was Wei Dedong, a scholar of Buddhist philosophy by training who had been dragged into the sociology of religion. Several of the interpreters of lectures have become scholars in full bloom, including Nanlai Cao, Anning Hu, Anna Sun, Yuting Wang, and Jiexia Zhai (Autry).

2003 annual meeting of the Society for the Scientific Study of Religion, under the title "Religions in Communist China: Open, Black, and Gray Markets in a Shortage Economy." The feedback from friends and participants of the annual meeting was mixed and perplexing. It became apparent that the presentation included too many theoretical concepts that needed clarification, and that it was necessary to include much more basic information of religions in China to provide context for the argument. I would have to write a book or break the study into multiple pieces. Because I was a pre-tenure assistant professor at a research university in the United States, the faculty suggested that I prioritize publishing journal articles over writing a book.

Yet I already knew that theoretical articles on religion in China would face high hurdles in the submission and review process. I had just experienced a negative encounter with a major journal whose editor rejected my first article on religion in China. The rejection of this manuscript was based on a single review that claimed that the author must not know the field of religion in China at all, even though I was actually part of the emerging discipline of religious studies in the 1980s—first as a graduate student at Nankai University, where I wrote my thesis in the philosophy of religion, then at Renmin University of China, where I was one of two faculty members in the newly formed division of religious studies within the department of philosophy. That article was eventually published in another journal,[9] but the experience left me scarred. Therefore, I anticipated that my new manuscripts would probably be reviewed by scholars who disliked theorizing religion in economic terms, or who were knowledgeable in either Chinese society or in religion, but not both. In sum, theorizing on religion in China in economic terms was a risky undertaking for a junior scholar, but my thoughts on those concepts and phenomena were too exhilarating to be contained.

I decided to work on the triple-market article first, because the typology of different markets should be less difficult to explain or understand than the shortage economy or oligopoly, even though, logically speaking, the triple religious markets follow from the shortage economy of religion, which follows from the religious oligopoly. Based on feedback from Chinese and American scholars, I changed the initial label of "open market" to "red market" because it is a market that is not really open or free, but rather constrained and tainted with the "red" Communist ideology; also, the phrase "tricolor market" (*sanse shichang* 三色市场) sounds snappier in Chinese. After careful revisions and

---

9 Fenggang Yang, "Between Secularist Ideology and Desecularizing Reality: The Birth and Growth of Religious Research in Communist China," *Sociology of Religion* 65.2 (2004): 101–119.

refinements following two rounds of reviews and rejections by top sociological journals, this article was eventually accepted by *The Sociological Quarterly*, which is commonly regarded as a top second-tier general sociological journal.[10] Many scholars believed that the top-tier sociological journals were unfavorable toward studies of religion, which was reflective of the discipline in general. Although the American Sociological Association was founded in 1905, it was not until 1994 that a section on the sociology of religion was formed. The top journals had not published anything on religion in China, and the pool of reviewers for such a topic was limited at the time. There were several active sociologists of Chinese society, but decades of secularist education had resulted in an obvious deficit of knowledge of religion. As an indication of that deficit, the Chinese General Social Survey did not include a single question on religion in its early rounds. This was not due to a lack of religion in Chinese society but to a lack of knowledge and appreciation of religion among the Chinese sociologists who were trained in China's atheist educational system. Things have changed somewhat in recent years.

As further signs of academic acceptance of my theorizing of religion in China, the tricolor article won the 2006 Distinguished Article Award of the American Sociological Association Section on the Sociology of Religion. The publication of this article helped to ensure that I received early promotion to associate professorship with tenure in that year. Meanwhile, colleagues at Renmin University helped to publish an abbreviated Chinese version in the *Journal of Renmin University of China*.[11] Two years later, a full translation of the article was published in the *Journal of China Agriculture University*.[12] In hindsight, there was substantial academic freedom in China at that time, which decreased in the years that followed.

While the triple market manuscript was under review, I took some time to delve into the literature of economics, especially the writings of János Kornai, a Hungarian economist who developed the "economics of shortage" to explain socialist economies in the Communist states.[13] This literature was introduced to China in the late 1980s and made a strong impression on me. Thanks to the

---

10 Fenggang Yang, "The Red, Black, and Gray Markets of Religion in China," *Sociological Quarterly* 47.1 (2006): 93–122.

11 Yang Fenggang, "Zhongguo zongjiao de sanse shichang," *Zhongguo renmin daxue xuebao*, 2006.6: 41–47.

12 Yang Fenggang, "Zhongguo zongjiao de sanse shichang," trans. Yang Jianghua, *Zhongguo nongye daxue xuebao (shehui kexue ban)*, 2008.4: 93–112.

13 János Kornai, *Economics of Shortage* (Amsterdam: North-Holland, 1980) (the Chinese translation was published in 1986); János Kornai, *The Socialist System: The Political Economy of Communism* (Oxford: Oxford University Press, 1992).

reforms toward a market economy, China's material wealth of goods and services moved out of chronic shortage in the late 1990s, but religion has remained under the ideology-based policy that was formulated in the 1950s and reinforced in the reform era. It took four more years before my shortage economy and oligopoly articles were published in journals, because the obstacles of the review process mentioned above remained in place in Western academia.[14] By then, I had been promoted to full professorship because I had a substantial number of other publications besides this set of articles on religious markets.

Scholarly feedback made me believe that it was necessary to pull the fragmented and scattered pieces together in order to present an overall picture of the religious situation in Communist-ruled China. In a book-length treatment, under the title *Religion in China: Survival and Revival under Communist Rule*, I had more space for describing ideological and policy contexts and discussing conceptual and theoretical tools. The publisher eagerly released this book in 2011, in advance of the 2012 copyright date.[15]

A whole is more than the sum of its parts. The book led to remarkable reactions. First, some of the most active scholars in the sociology of religion joined an "author-meets-critics" panel at the 2012 annual meeting of the Society for the Scientific Study of Religion, and this event attracted a sizeable audience. Second, many major journals published reviews of the book, including *New York Review of Books, American Journal of Sociology, Social Forces, Contemporary Sociology, European Journal of Sociology, Journal of the Scientific Study of Religion, Sociology of Religion: A Quarterly Review, Journal of Asian Studies, Journal of Church and State, Journal of Contemporary Religion, Journal of Chinese Religions, Religion and Society in Central and Eastern Europe*, and the French journal *Archives de sciences sociales des religions*, among others.[16] All

---

[14] Fenggang Yang, "Religion in China under Communism: A Shortage Economy Explanation," *The Journal of Church and State* 52.1 (2010): 3–33; Fenggang Yang, "Oligopoly Dynamics: Consequences of Religious Regulation," *Social Compass* 57.2 (2010): 194–205.

[15] Fenggang Yang, *Religion in China: Survival and Revival under Communist Rule* (New York: Oxford University Press, 2012).

[16] The reviews of the book *Religion in China: Survival and Revival under Communist Rule* include (in alphabetical order of authors' last names): Andrew Stuart Abel, *Sociology of Religion* 73.2 (2012): 228–230; Gene Cooper, *Contemporary Sociology* 42.1 (2013): 122–124; Helen Rose Ebaugh, *Journal for the Scientific Study of Religion* 52.2 (2013): 448–449; Vincent Goossaert, *Archives de sciences sociales des religions* 160 (October–December 2012): 304–305; Ian Johnson, *New York Review of Books*, 58.20 (2011): 55–58; Eric Yang Liu, *Sociological Forum* 28.2 (2013): 419–422; Richard Madsen, *Journal of Asian Studies* 71.4 (2012): 1126–1127; Brian J. Nichols, *Religious Studies Review* 39.3 (2013): 198; James V. Spickard, *Journal of Contemporary Religion* 29.1 (2014): 162–164; Bryan S. Turner, *European Journal of Sociology / Archives Européennes de Sociologie / Europäisches Archiv*

but one praised the book while offering some criticism of the type commonly seen in scholarly reviews and to which authors usually do not respond. The one exceptional negative review will be discussed in a later section. Third, the book has been translated into Korean and Italian and will soon be published in a Chinese translation,[17] reaching readers beyond Anglophone academia. Finally, in the following year, I was totally surprised by my nomination and then successful election as the President of the Society for the Scientific Study of Religion. This is the primary scholarly association that I have attended regularly since my years of graduate studies, and I was the first non-white person elected to that position since the founding of the society in 1949.[18]

2   Scholarly Reactions to the Theory in China

The first decade of the twenty-first century was an exciting time for the introduction of the social scientific study of religion to China. First, a number of classic books in the sociology of religion were translated and published in China.[19] Second, the publication of the Chinese versions of *Acts of Faith* and some other books by Rodney Stark and his associates stimulated further theoretical discussions.[20] Third, the lectures by renowned scholars at the annual

---

für Soziologie 53.3 (2012): 338–342; Carsten T. Vala, *Social Forces* 93.2 (2014): e54; Martin King Whyte, *American Journal of Sociology* 118.1 (2012): 240–242; Franklin J. Woo, *China Review International* 18.4 (2011): 549–554; Xinzhong Yao, *Journal of Chinese Religions* 40 (2012): 155–157; Anthony C. Yu, *Journal of Church and State* 54.3 (2012): 459–462; Siniša Zrinščak, *Religion and Society in Central and Eastern Europe* 6.1 (2013): 75–77.

17   Korean edition: 중국의 종교: 공산 통치하에서의 생존과 부흥, translated by Song Jae-ryong and Yoo Kwang-suk (Seoul: Dasan Publishing Co., 2017); Italian edition: *La religione nella Cina comunista: Dalla sopravvivenza al risveglio*, translated by Emanuela Claudia Del Re, published by Franco Angeli, 2020; Chinese edition, 宗教在中國：黨治下的存活與復興, (forthcoming).

18   See Elaine Howard Ecklund, "Diversifying the Social Scientific Study of Religion: The Next 70 Years," *Journal for the Scientific Study of Religion* 59.1 (2020): 5–17; Fenggang Yang's presidential address, "Exceptionalism or Chinamerica: Measuring Religious Change in the Globalizing World Today," *Journal for the Scientific Study of Religion* 55.1 (2016): 7–22.

19   Gao Shining of the Chinese Academy of Social Sciences was a champion who translated books, published articles, and organized translation series of books. See Gao Shining, "Zongjiao shehuixue yanjiu zai zhongguo dalu de fazhan," *Shanghai daxue xuebao (shehui kexue ban)*, 2007.3: 96–99; Li Huawei, "Zongjiao shehuixue zai zhongguo dalu de fazhan lichen," in *Zhongguo shehui kexueyuan shijie zongjiao yanjiusuo wushinian fazhan licheng, 1964–2014*, ed. Institute of World Religions, Chinese Academy of Social Sciences (Beijing: China Social Sciences Press, 2014).

20   For example, Rodney Stark, *The Rise of Christianity* (Princeton, NJ: Princeton University Press, 1996) was published as *Jidujiao de xingqi*, translated by Huang Jianbo and Gao

Summer Institute and the presentations at the annual conference on the social scientific study of religion provided opportunities for face-to-face interactions with top scholars in the West. Finally, my lectures on the new paradigm in the sociology of religion at several universities, my presentations of the Chinese religious markets, and the empirical projects I directed or funded contributed to the rising tide of the social scientific study of religion.[21]

The religious market theories immediately attracted the attention of scholars and officials in China. Scholars' appreciation and enthusiasm was reflected in conference discussions, publications, and graduate theses. According to Wei Dedong 魏德东, a scholar of religious studies at Renmin University of China,

> The first printing of the Chinese edition of *Acts of Faith* had 5,000 copies, which were sold out quickly; a second printing was made in 2007. This is rare among books on theories of religion [in China]. More than ten book reviews have been published within a short few years. Numerous graduate theses applied this new theoretical model. A good number of research projects emerged. Actually, "religious market" has become a trendy term not only in academia but in religious, political, and media circles. ... After the Chinese edition [of "The Red, Black, and Gray Markets of Religion in China"] was published in the *Journal of Renmin University of China*, it not only had a significant influence on the sociology of religion in China but also attracted the attention of multiple government agencies.[22]

According to Zhang Zhigang 张志刚, a scholar of religious studies at Peking University,

> The publication of the Chinese edition of *Acts of Faith* in 2004 caused enthusiastic responses. Not only did "religious market" become a trendy

---

Mingui (Shanghai: Shanghai Guji Publishing House, 2005); Rodney Stark and William Sims Bainbridge, *The Future of Religion: Secularization, Revival, and Cult Formation* (Berkeley: University of California Press, 1985) was published as *Zongjiao de weilai*, translated by Gao Shining, Zhang Xiaomei, and Liu Dianli (Beijing: Renmin University of China, 2006).

21 See Huang Jianbo, "Ershinian lai zhongguo dalu jidujiao de jingyan yanjiu shuping," in *Jidujiao sixiang pinglun (di jiu juan)*, ed. Xu Zhiwei (Shanghai: Shanghai shiji chuban jituan, 2009), 345–366; Huang Jianbo and Mengyin Hu, "Trends and Reflections: A Review of Empirical Studies of Christianity in Mainland China," *Review of Religion and Chinese Society* 6.1 (2019): 45–70; Li Huawei, "Zongjiao Shehuixue."

22 Wei Dedong, "Zongjiao shehuixue de fanshi zhuanhuan jiqi yingxiang," *Renmin daxue xuebao*, 2010.3: 67–68.

term, but also many scholars tried to apply this new paradigm to study the present status of religion in China and published some stimulating theoretical explanations. For instance, Yang Fenggang published "Tricolor Markets of Religion in China," which received praise among sociologists of religion both in China and the United States.[23]

Indeed, after the tricolor market article was published, a faculty member of a provincial administration college, which is a training institution for party-state officials, made some remarks at the concluding session of the 2007 Summer Institute, held at Shanghai University. He said that some officials of the Religious Affairs Bureau and his colleagues held a study session (or multiple sessions) on the article. "We of course will always say that the tricolor market theory is wrong, but outside the study session, most of us admit that this is a powerful theory helpful for making sense of the complex religious situation in China." He explained that the officially stated position was that religious groups and activities were either legal or illegal and there was no such thing as a gray market.

The ambivalence of officials and official theoreticians reported by this person appears not to be limited to his province. Following some fieldwork trips to China, Richard Madsen, a renowned sociologist of religion who is also an expert on religion in China, wrote:

> As the evolution of grassroots religion in China grows more dynamic, the government must now decide which of the churning changes in religious life are orthodox and which are not. Scholars and officials concerned with religious affairs are adopting the Chinese-American sociologist Fenggang Yang's idea that there are "red" (legitimate), "black" (illegitimate), and "grey" markets for religion. The government's task is to sort the points of "grey" into clear-cut "red" and "black." Yet the "grey" market is so huge and diversified that this is very hard to do, and in any case, it would require a degree of expertise that is in short supply in China.[24]

The popularity of the tricolor theory can be tracked by searching for some keywords in the China National Knowledge Infrastructure (CNKI) database of journals and theses. The earliest mention of religious market theories and Rodney Stark appeared in an interview with me that appeared

---

23 Zhang Zhigang, "Dangdai zhongguo zongjiao guanxi yanjiu chuyi," *Beijing daxue xuebao (zhexue shehui kexue ban)* 48.2 (2011): 34.
24 Richard Madsen, "The Upsurge of Religion in China," *Journal of Democracy* 21.4 (2010): 67.

in *Religious Studies Journal* in 2003 (see Figure 15.1). After the publication of *Acts of Faith* in 2004, and especially after the publication of the tricolor market article in 2006, there was a steady increase of articles mentioning these keywords for several years. Between 2006 and 2019, 294 journal articles and theses mentioned both *sanse shichang* (tricolor market) and Yang Fenggang. A noticeable dip happened around 2015, then a dramatic drop in 2018. An uninformed reader might see a normal curve of the natural lifespan of theoretical terms, which usually come and go, but the dip and drop are actually due to increased censorship in the new era of Xi Jinping's rule, as I will explain below.

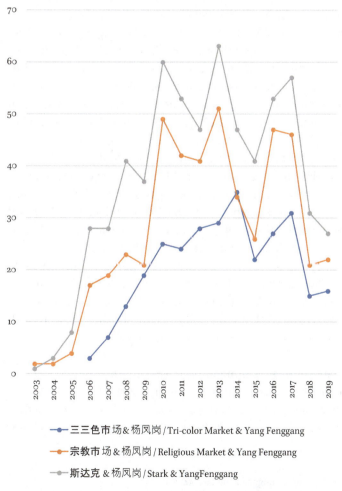

FIGURE 15.1   Number of articles and theses in CNKI with the keywords "Tricolor Market & Yang Fenggang," "Religious Market & Yang Fenggang," and "Stark & Yang Fenggang"

Several scholarly criticisms of the religious market theories began to be published in China in 2008. Many of the publications show confusion with respect to the terminology of various theoretical paradigms, theories, models, and approaches; I do not critique such confusions here, but readers should keep this in mind when reading some of the quotes below. I want to focus on the more substantial criticisms, which Zhang Zhigang summarized as follows:

> First, does this new theoretical paradigm have universal applicability? The religious market theory developed mainly through examining the religious situations of Europe and America. Can this kind of empirical research results explain the religious phenomena in countries or societies where "Christianity is not the mainstream"? Second, from the previous objection we may draw another question: The religious market theory is based on data mainly of institutionalized religious organizations and their activities "typically found in Christianity." Does this kind of research tendency ignore noninstitutionalized religions and their evolvements? Furthermore, the religious market theory emphasizes Western mainstream religious traditions and ignores various other religious phenomena. Does this mean that the recent sociology of religion in Europe and America is Christianity-centric, or to a large extent even has turned into the "Christian sociology of religion"? Third, as a religious economic model, the religious market theory postulates that religious change is mainly driven by the supply side. Does this explanation disregard the other two factors of the religious market, i.e., changes in religious demand and governmental regulation? Lastly, the religious market theory over-directly applies economic principles, especially market laws, to the study of religious phenomena, so that it disregards the sacred nature of religious traditions, reducing complicated religious faith to "commercialized rational choice." How many religious people can agree with such a simplified, even vulgarized, theoretical tendency?[25]

If these are accurate summaries of major criticisms in Chinese publications, they are merely repeating some of the criticisms of Rodney Stark and his associates that have been advanced by Western scholars, such as those raised by Stephen Sharot, whom Zhang quotes.[26] Zhang was familiar with my tricolor

---

25   Zhang Zhigang, "Dangdai zhongguo zongjiao," 34–35.
26   Stephen Sharot, "Beyond Christianity: A Critique of the Rational Choice Theory of Religion from a Weberian and Comparative Religions Perspective," *Sociology of Religion* 63.4 (2002): 427–454.

market article, as he indicated in a passage quoted earlier, but he failed to understand the contents and ignored the fact that my study has addressed most of these criticisms. My article demonstrates that the economic approach is applicable in China, although some substantial modifications are necessary. It particularly highlights the importance of the regulation factor and the demand-driven dynamics. Most religions in China are non-Christian and non-institutionalized. In fact, the major components of the gray market are folk religions that are "diffused" (to use C. K. Yang's term[27]) or embedded in other social institutions. Paradoxically, their seeming weakness in organization makes them difficult for the atheist party-state authorities to control and suppress. Overall, the criticisms mentioned by Zhang repeat existing criticisms of other religious market theories, whereas the tricolor market theory is a further development of earlier theoretical constructs.

Li Xiangping 李向平, a sociologist of religion at East China Normal University in Shanghai, understands well that the tricolor market theory of religion is a response to criticisms of the existing religious market theories and is a further development.

> Carefully examining the "tricolor markets" of religion in China, people should see that this theory has a kind of penetrating power [of explanation]. It has discovered that the acquisition and expression of legality is pivotal in the structure and construction of the religious markets in China. … The new paradigm of religious market theories provides a whole new perspective for the study of religious phenomena in contemporary China and has stimulated more scholars to engage in empirical research in the sociology of religion in China, so that they may collect rich data and facts and examine the applicability of the propositions of the religious market theories in Chinese contexts. Meanwhile, the religious market theories have also provided a beneficial reference point and opened a new path of thinking for Chinese authorities in their management of religious affairs and for religious organizations in their religious development.[28]

Following Li, Huang Haibo 黄海波, a junior sociologist of religion at the Shanghai Academy of Social Sciences, comments that my study has addressed the limitations of the existing economic approach.

---

27 C. K. Yang, *Religion in Chinese Society: A Study of Contemporary Functions of Religion and Some of Their Historical Factors* (Berkeley: University of California Press, 1961).
28 Li Xiangping and Yang Linxia, "Zongjiao, shehui yu quanli guanxi—'zongjiao shichanglun' de shehuixue jiedu," *Huadong shifan daxue xuebao (zhexue shehui kexue ban)* 43.5 (2011): 1–7.

In the English monograph *Religion in China* that came out later, Yang Fenggang has expanded and revised this framework of analysis and proposed to use "the political economic approach" to explore religious phenomena in contemporary China. By emphasizing that the Chinese religious economy is a "shortage economy," this research shows that the religious supply is under heavy regulation, religious demand is constantly changing, and religious regulation is ineffective due to the "invisible hand" of market forces or economic laws.[29]

Unfortunately, Huang otherwise simply repeats criticisms that had previously appeared in Chinese publications. Moreover, he disregards all the praise found in a long and in-depth review of my book by Zhang Wenjie 张文杰 and only mentions Zhang's quibbles about some remaining issues.[30]

Fan Lizhu 范丽珠, a scholar of religious studies at Fudan University, refuted the "rational choice" justification for focusing on instrumental rationality and disregarding value rationality and asserted that the "religious economy paradigm [sic]" was totally wrong. Fan further made a claim that applying this theory to the study of religion in China would be "dangerous," but she did not substantiate what the dangers were.[31] Yet her article cited my tricolor market article as an application of theory to the study of religion in China.

The "rational choice" criticism voiced by Fan and others is misguided at best. Stark and Finke have disclaimed this label in their writings and in an interview with Chinese scholars.[32] In *Acts of Faith*, Stark and Finke qualify the concept of rational choice with social and psychological conditions that could be acceptable to many social scientists. Proposition 1 states, "Within the limits of their information and understanding, restricted by available options, guided by their preferences and tastes, humans attempt to make rational choices." From this starting point, what Stark and Finke set out to do is to examine various religious phenomena as dependent variables. Of course, it is reasonable to ask where personal preferences and tastes come from, but it is also reasonable to say that this question is subject to other research and theorizing outside

---

29 Huang Haibo, "Zhongguo jingyan yu bentu lilun: jinnian lai zhongguo zongjiao shehuixue lilun redian," *Zongjiao shehuixue*, 2017.5: 8.

30 Zhang Wenjie, "Zhongguo zongjiao yanjiu de 'zhengzhi jingjixue' changshi: ping *Zhongguo de zongjiao*," *Shehui* 34.3 (2014): 205–229.

31 Fan Lizhu, "Xiandai zongjiao shi lixing de ma? Zhiyi zongjiao de lixing xuanze yanjiu fanshi," *Shehui* 28.6 (2008): 90–109.

32 Wei Dedong and Liu Yang, "Zongjiao yanjiu de renti lilun: Fang zongjiao shehuixuejia luodeni sidake," *Zhongguo minzubao*, October 7, 2008.

this theoretical system. It is undeniable that a majority of humans base their actions on rational reasoning, asking the question "Is it worth it?" when they make decisions. This is why social science makes it possible to discover common behavioral patterns without negating the particularities of individuals, groups, and societies. No one claims that one hundred percent of human behaviors can be explained in rational terms or by social science, which is part of the reason why we also need the humanities and arts. Moreover, it is incorrect to criticize Stark and Finke for focusing exclusively on instrumental rationality, as they have pointed out that for some people, salvation is far more valuable than their time, money, and even life in this world. Even some religious virtuosos have reasoned that their religious dedication is worth it; as Jesus says, "What good will it be for someone to gain the whole world, yet forfeit their soul? Or what can anyone give in exchange for their soul?"[33] Understandably, atheists will neither acknowledge nor accept such value rationality or the value of souls.

Lu Yunfeng 卢云峰, a sociologist of religion at Peking University, was probably the first Chinese scholar to criticize religious market theories on the grounds of their supposed Christianity-centric characteristics.[34] However, Lu once studied as a postdoctoral fellow under Rodney Stark at Baylor University, and he himself has applied this theory in his studies of Yiguandao in Taiwan and Falun Gong in China. Therefore, the Christianity-centric labeling in the title of Lu's article appeared to be ill-conceived, as I will discuss in the next section.

Also in 2008, Ji Zhe, a scholar in religious studies originally from China who is based in France, published an article in China that criticizes the "religious economies model [sic]" as one of three postsecular theories.[35] He points to the perceived problems of its individualistic methodology, its rationalistic assumption of economic persons, and its tendency to reduce social relations in religion to market relations. This characterization shows his misunderstanding or prejudice. Also, regarding this theory having "deeply West-U.S.-centric colors" (shenke de Xifang-Meiguo zhongxinlun secai 深刻的西方-美国中心论色彩) shows his nebulous thinking: is the theory U.S.-centric, Euro-centric, or West-centric? After all, as Ji admits in his article,

---

33 Matthew 16:26.
34 Lu Yunfeng, "Chaoyue jiduzongjiao shehuixue—jianlun zongjiao shichang lilun zai huaren shehui de shiyongxing wenti," *Shehuixue yanjiu*, 2008.5: 81–97.
35 Ji Zhe, "Ruhe chaoyue jingdian shisuhua lilun?—ping zongjiao shehuixue de san zhong houshisuhua lunshu," *Shehuixue yanjiu*, 2008.4: 55–75.

It is undeniable that this religious economies model is an easily operationalizable theory with powerful explanations. Indeed, this theory has shown dynamic vitality from the beginning and quickly led to many empirical studies inside and outside the United States that apply this model. In recent years, under the vigorous promotion by Professor Fenggang Yang of Purdue University in the U.S., the economic model, under the name of "religious market theories," was introduced to China as a universally applicable "new paradigm." Many Chinese scholars responded enthusiastically, even praising it as a "Copernican revolution" in the sociology of religion. The application and examination of this theory in Chinese society stimulated some excellent studies, such as those of Lu Yunfeng on the enterprise logic of analyzing Falun Gong organization and theoretical change, Yang Fenggang on the divided markets of religion according to the level of political regulation, and Li Xiangping on combining religious market theories and grasping the diffused characteristics of Chinese religions.[36]

However, Ji expresses his worries that the popularity of the "religious economies model" may cause Chinese academia to neglect other theories, particularly those that originated in Europe, especially "sociological questions and profound insights related to secularization theories." Why would any scholar have this kind of worry? In Western academia, it is hard to imagine a monopoly of any single theory or theoretical approach. Indeed, there are many American and European sociologists of religion who have conducted excellent studies of religion without engaging the economic approach, and I have invited some Western scholars of other theoretical orientations to the Summer Institutes.[37]

On various occasions in China, some anthropologists or sinologists, especially those based in Europe, who are either ethnic Chinese or non-Chinese, have verbally vented their dislikes of religious market theories with expressions more than polemic.[38] In contrast, some other Europe-based sociologists have offered meaningful and nuanced criticisms, as in the book *Religious America, Secular Europe? A Theme and Variations*.[39]

---

36 Ji, "Ruhe chaoyue," 59.
37 For a list of scholars who lectured at the Summer Institutes, see n. 9 above.
38 See, for example, Qu Jingdong, Lu Yunfeng, Liang Yongjia, et al., "You guan 'zongjiao shichang lilun' de yici yuanzhuo taolun," *Zhongguo yanjiu* 19.1 (2014): 208–227.
39 Peter Berger, Grace Davie, and Effie Fokas, *Religious America, Secular Europe? A Theme and Variation* (New York: Routledge, 2008). Unfortunately, a reading of this book by Lu Yunfeng seems to have missed the question mark in the title and the contents of the book itself. See Lu Yunfeng, "Weihe shi 'zongjiao meiguo, shisu ouzhou'?," *Dushu*,

3 Disciplinary Disgust and Ideological Repulsion

There has been a peculiar type of reaction to the religious market theories among some scholars. This peculiar type of reaction seems to have poisoned parts of Chinese academia, and for this reason, I offer a brief account of such expressed rejections.

Disciplinary dislike shows up in a review of my book by Anthony C. Yu (Yu Guofan 余國藩, 1938–2015), a scholar of religious studies and literature at the University of Chicago, whose best-known work is his translation of the Chinese classical novel *Journey to the West* (*Xiyouji* 西遊記). He published a book titled *State and Religion in China: Historical and Textual Perspectives*,[40] in which he tried to attribute the current regulation of religion to ancient China. I read it and cited it in my book but did not discuss it because of its lack of relevance to my study of contemporary China. Yu made three criticisms of my book: First, religious economy is an analogy that is no better than Marx's metaphor of religion as the opium of the people. Yu could not understand and rhetorically questioned why some people held on to religion in spite of its attempted eradication. "Second, his [Fenggang Yang's] market analogy also founders in charting religion's decline." Yu said religion had declined in Europe and the Americas, and he had not seen that the "market analogy can elucidate" any of this. It does not seem that he had read the extensive literature about religious vitality in the United States, as reviewed by Steve Warner in heralding the new paradigm, nor the numerous books by Rodney Stark and his associates since the 1980s, nor the publications by Peter Berger since the 1990s. Third, Yu was critical of my insistence on "empirical research" and claimed that "Yang dismisses 'armchair philosophers and theologians who read texts instead of observing human beings.'" Actually, I have always encouraged social science students to read and master philosophy and theology in order to do good social scientific research. What I did in this book was simply calling for more empirical studies of actual religious life in society.

Interestingly, among many book reviews, Chinese anthropologist Liang Yongjia (梁永佳) chose to cite only Anthony Yu in support of his own rejection of the religious market theories.[41] He also repeated the criticism offered

---

2016.3: 150–159. For a different reading of this book, see Yang Fenggang, "Zongjiao meiguo, shisu ouzhou de zhuti yu bianzou," *Dushu*, 2016.4: 159–168.

40 Anthony C. Yu, *State and Religion in China: Historical and Textual Perspectives* (Chicago: Open Court, 2005). Yu's review of *Religion in China* is published in *Journal of Church and State* 54.3 (2012): 459–462.

41 Liang Yongjia, "Zhongguo nongcun zongjiao fuxing yu 'zongjiao' de Zhongguo mingyun," *Shehui* 35.1 (2015): 161–183. As far as I could find, this is the only article in which Liang published a deliberate criticism of religious market theories.

by others that market theories are only suitable to explain Christianity and similarly exclusivist religions, which, as I have argued above, is simply not the case. In addition, in this article he appears to dislike the distinction between the sacred and the secular, God and Caesar, religion and magic, and so on. This is a manifestation of distinct features of a certain kind of anthropology that favors and romanticizes the undifferentiated primitive mind and tribal or local society over against modernity and the universality of humanity. This kind of anthropology, which inherits the imperialist and colonist tradition at the roots of the discipline, seeks exotic otherness to the West, a project that has been rightfully criticized as orientalism by Edward W. Said.[42] Unfortunately, some Chinese anthropologists have sought the exotic and unique otherness of Chinese traditions in contemporary society. Western anthropologists or sinologists engaged in this quest, at least partially, as a critique of Western modernity, and the over rationalization in early modern times. However, when Chinese anthropologists do this, they use the premodern to reject modernization and deny universal values and the universal nature of Chinese humanity. In an interesting twist, in line with the neo-leftist criticism of global capitalism, Liang says that free market competition in the religious sphere will only benefit the "big corporations," such as Christian denominations, and thus he calls for state intervention, even though the state is ruled by a Leninist party based on the ideology of Marxist atheism that has campaigned to eradicate Chinese cultural traditions for decades.

Following these criticisms by scholars, militant atheists launched their political assaults. In 2011, *Science and Atheism (Kexue yu wushenlun* 科学与无神论), the main magazine of the militant atheists, published a series of featured articles. The first one was titled "Religious Markets, Open to Whom?"[43] Hiding behind the penname Qiu Yue 秋月, this "Beijing scholar" opens the article with the perceived problem of the "house churches" that have become widespread throughout China and are particularly studied by the sociologists of religion. This "scholar" opposes the market principle of equal access. The editorial foreword to this issue attributes an "ulterior motive" to those who would introduce religious market theories to China:

> With the help of this kind of commodity [i.e., spiritual products], they have destroyed socialist Poland and destroyed the Soviet Union. Then the scholars of religion in that country [the U.S.] invented the "religious

---

42 Edward W. Said, *Orientalism* (New York: Vintage Books, 1979).
43 Qiu Yue, "Zongjiao shichang, dui shei kaifang?," *Kexue yu wushenlun*, 2011.2: 14–18.

market theories" to encourage people who strive for their state interests to market their religion as if they were marketing a commodity. It is understandable that one serves one's own master. It is not understandable why a Chinese scholar is also enthusiastic about the interests of theirs [i.e., American scholars].[44]

The second featured article, written under the penname Shen Zhang 沈璋 and titled "On the Selling Points of the 'Religious Market Theories' amid the 'Religious Cultures' in Mainland China," goes all out. It first introduces some basic terms and propositions of *Acts of Faith*, mixed with distorted interpretations and assertions, such as this one:

> The guiding notion of *Acts of Faith* is to disregard religion's accommodation to the social environment and its fusion with the cultural environment, albeit religion roaring out of the sky amid social turmoil, and seek religious revivals in the "clash of civilizations." Therefore, its biggest feature is to encourage religious exclusivity, break down the existing social order and cultural structure, and resist state constitutional principles rather than market laws.[45]

It goes on to attack the motives behind the Chinese translation:

> About the translator of this book, Mr. Yang Fenggang, we never learn about his citizenship: Is he a Chinese or American? We only know that he uses Renmin University of China as his base of activities, and his job is at Purdue University in the U.S. We do not know whether he is a Christian, but we know that he has spared no effort in promoting Christianity. He published the [Chinese version of the] book *Conversion, Assimilation, and Adhesive Identities* in 2008, which was recommended for "those contemporary Chinese who are seeking cultural identity to make reflections": should they be Chinese Christians or American Christians? Or "adhere" together, be everything and nothing whatsoever. These kinds of questions leave the reader puzzled about Mr. Yang's identity. Now people may come to the understanding through *Acts of Faith* that he is actually a trader in culture who sells foreign religious

---

44 "Juan shouyu: Ping 'zongjiao shichang,'" *Kexue yu wushenlun*, 2011.2: 1.
45 Shen Zhang, "Ye tan 'zongjiao shichanglun' jiqi zai zhongguo dalu 'zongjiao wenhua' zhong de maidian," *Kexue yu wushenlun*, 2011.3: 9.

products—what is popularly known as a second-hand profiteer or comprador of culture.[46]

The author further attacks the social scientific study of religion. I applied for and received some grants from the John Templeton Foundation and distributed as smaller grants to scholars to support their own social scientific studies of religions in China. After reviewing some of the supported projects, the author determines that the purpose of all these projects is to investigate the religious situation in China and collect religious information. The Summer Institutes, furthermore, were regarded as training classes in multi-level marketing. The author concludes,

> Mr. Yang Fenggang puts China's evil cults, underground churches, and legal churches into tricolor markets, which are taken straight from *Acts of Faith*. The effect is to bolster the evil cults, blaze a trail for the underground churches, and attack the legal churches. That is to say, he is not just making a profit as a second-hand profiteer.[47]

The magazine *Science and Atheism* was launched in 1999 during the campaign to eradicate Falun Gong. In the following decade, the militant atheists gathered their forces and resources through petitioning higher authorities. With the support of state funding, they have established a research center under the Institute of Marxism in the Chinese Academy of Social Sciences, held annual meetings, published a series of books, and regularly written petitions to the CCP Center calling for the Party to strengthen atheist education through schools and mass-media propaganda, prohibit CCP members from believing in religion or participating in religious activities, and launch anti-Christian and anti-Islamic campaigns by designating them as "foreign" religions. They have also criticized the national religious policy or its implementation for lapses in controlling religion and tried hard to derail academic studies of religion in general and of Christianity in particular.[48] In the new era under Xi Jinping, the militant atheists have prevailed in setting up a policy agenda, increased restrictions on religions, and increased censorship of scholarship on religion.

---

46   Ibid., 12.
47   Ibid., 13.
48   For more discussion of the rise of militant atheism in recent years, see Fenggang Yang, "Sinicization or Chinafication? Cultural Assimilation vs. Political Domestication of Christianity in China and Beyond," in *The Sinicization of Chinese Religions: From Above and Below*, ed. Richard Madsen (Leiden: Brill, 2021).

This is why we see the dip and drop of articles and theses mentioning religious market theories after 2012 (Figure 15.1).

Careful readers may see that some of the criticisms by scholars have provided the militant atheists with ammunition for their political attacks. Moreover, their assaults have not only polluted Chinese academia but also bolstered press censorship to such a degree that they may even have hindered some of the unfair critics in their own publication efforts. This should be a lesson for academicians who desire to attain or maintain a healthy academic environment.

4 Going Forward: Refine, Revise, or Replace

Since its initial formulation, the tricolor religious market theory has had a history of about fifteen years, during which religions and religious regulations in China have undergone many changes, some of which have been dramatic, such as a significant increase in restrictions on Christianity and Islam; the demolition of Christian churches, mosques, rooftop crosses, and crescents;[49] the subjugation of underground Catholic bishops, the outlawing of Protestant house churches, and the campaign for the Chinafication (*Zhongguohua* 中国化) of all religions.[50] Many friends and foes have asked: Is the tricolor market theory still valid? Should it be refined, revised, or replaced? How should we go forward in terms of empirical research and theoretical development? Because of space limitations, I can only offer very brief responses to such questions here.

First of all, the explanatory power of religious market theories in general has passed the test of time and survived many challenges. The tricolor market theory was developed primarily to explain the religious situation in contemporary China, where religion survived radical eradication during the Cultural Revolution and revived despite the imposition of restrictive regulations in the era of economic reform. As the theory predicted, more elaborate regulations would be devised to address the growing gray market of religion, but they would either prove to be unenforceable or would result in unexpected consequences.

---

49 See Fenggang Yang, "The Failure of the Campaign to Demolish Church Crosses in Zhejiang Province, 2013–2016," *Review of Religion and Chinese Society* 5.1 (2018): 5–25; Fuk-tsang Ying, "The Politics of Cross Demolition: A Religio-Political Analysis of the 'Three Rectifications and One Demolition' Campaign in Zhejiang Province," *Review of Religion and Chinese Society* 5.1 (2018): 43–75.
50 See Yang, "Sinicization or Chinafication?"

> Regulating these kinds of activities [in the gray market] requires more elaborative rules regarding legal boundaries, and in enforcing such rules, authorities must exert great care to delineate ambiguous boundaries or borderline zones. Meanwhile, religious suppliers and consumers can be very creative in responding to adverse rules, and thus it is almost impossible for authorities to regulate ambiguous exchanges and/or enforce such regulation.[51]

As Richard Madsen noted in a passage quoted earlier, the party-state has tried hard to force religious groups and activities in the gray market into either the red or black markets. However, the case studies in this edited volume show that this enforcement has encountered myriad difficulties due to varied local contexts and interactive dynamics. For example, Ke-hsien Huang's chapter examines the True Jesus Church (TJC), an indigenous Pentecostal sect with a long history that was suppressed in the 1950s to 1980s. In recent years, however, some of the TJC congregations in some areas have joined the local Protestant Three-Self Patriotic Movement Committees, thus moved from the black or gray market to the red market. Huang attributes this to a new generation of congregational leaders who are more informed of the logic of bureaucracy and adept at dealing with local officials. But, in other areas, TJC congregations remain in the gray market. In all places, TJC congregations try to preserve their distinctive denominational traditions, which is against certain regulations.

The chapter on Hani churches in Yunnan by Jiang and He shows that whether the churches become registered with the authorities or not has multiple factors, including the relationship between Christianity and local traditional religious beliefs, church-state relations in different localities, and the level of organization in evangelistic efforts by Christians in different areas. Hao Yuan's chapter examines the Society of Disciples (SD), which has been listed as one of the *xiejiao* (evil cults) by the authorities. Instead of taking an antagonistic approach to the party-state, however, some SD leaders have made attempts to negotiate with the local authorities, and their tactics have worked insofar as they are not actively suppressed by the party-state, unlike the Church of the Almighty God that has become a major target of crackdowns. Indeed, some churches in the red market chose to move to the gray market, as the chapter by Hui Li shows. In these cases, religious motivation, personality of church leaders, and their relations with local officials in charge of religious affairs are in play.

---

51 Fenggang Yang, "Red, Black, and Gray Markets," 97.

Deji Kong's chapter presents one of the most fascinating cases of the gray market religion: the Yunnan Ethnic Theme Park presents a church of Miao (Hmong) people as representing Miao ethnic culture, even though Christians remain a minority among the Miao people. The distinct choir singing of Miao Christians made it attractive for tourism, which is sanctioned by cultural experts and provincial officials. The theme park employs a clergyperson to station the church, and the church functions as an actual church for employees of various ethnic backgrounds, even though it is not considered a religious sites by the religious affairs bureau, thus not in the red market.

Not only are many Christian churches in the gray market. Hao Zhao tells the story of a folk religious temple dedicated to Caishen (God of Wealth) in a rural county of Sichuan. The temple managers refused to join either the Buddhist or Daoist association, and the temple is thus not recognized by the religious affairs bureau as a legally approved religious site. However, the temple established a senior citizens center on temple grounds, which provides some level of legitimacy or legality for the temple as a civic community. In Zhanjiang, Guangdong Province, Yan and Lin show folk religious priests as suppliers of religious services actively adapting to new social, political, and cultural environments. Cuicui Zhao's chapter presents a case of religious competition between a seaside Christian church and local folk religious adherents in Zhejiang Province. Although the church is in the red market, the folk religious adherents use folk religious beliefs to derail the construction of the church building and appeal to the local authorities for the legitimacy of the folk religion.

Yunze Xiao examines house churches in northern Jiangsu Province. While they are in the gray market, their organizational challenge is as much adapting to urbanization as to state suppression. Hao Yuan's chapter on migrant worker churches in Beijing show similar interactions between urbanization and organizational transformation of the church. In comparison, Zhipeng Zhang's case of a house church in the city of Nanjing, a niche church for certain college-educated urbanites, shows how some religious groups choose to remain small and flexible in the gray market. Mengyin Hu's case of arist churches are similarly niche churches in the gray market.

The gray market churches are not beyond the influence by the party-state. As Ling Wang shows, leaders of a house church in Beijing used to enforce the single-child policy by the party-state. As that policy was replaced with a two-child policy in 2016, a pro-life ministry began to sprout within this church and among many other house churches. Finally, Yan Liu presents glimpses of online Christian communities. Even though the party-state has tried hard to regulate religious messages on the internet, many WeChat groups have constantly adapted to evade censorship, persist, and flourish.

In response to the growth of gray market religious groups, the party-state implemented the Regulations of Religious Affairs in 2005. However, it soon became apparent that these were not uniformly enforced. Following several years of overhaul in the new era of Xi Jinping's rule, the party-state finally issued a revised and significantly expanded version of the "Regulations," which took effect in 2018. Since then, a number of specialized regulations, dealing with matters such as religious associations, religious venues and legal personhood, and religious academies (seminaries), have been released or are in the making. However, as predicted,

> Increased religious regulation will lead not to reduction of religion per se, but to a triple religious market. Although participation in formal religious organizations may decline, other forms of religiosity will persist and tend to increase. Moreover, given its ambiguous nature, a gray market in a heavily regulated society is likely to be large, volatile, and unsettled, making religious regulation an arduous task and impossible to enforce.[52]

Overall, religion remains in short supply, religious awakenings continue unabated, and religious seekers and followers keep turning and churning. Based on close or distant observations, we can see that many old and new religions such as Mormonism, Bahaism, Hinduism, Yiguandao, various Christian sects, and numerous spiritual cults springing from Chinese traditions have been active in China, either trying hard to move from the black market to the gray or from the gray market to the red, or enjoying their gray status. The new regulations have outlawed Christian house churches, driving them into the black market, but most of the house churches have remained active in new forms, even during the coronavirus pandemic, and some host energetic online gatherings with thousands of participants and promote evangelistic missions within and beyond China.

Second, the tricolor religious market theory certainly needs further refinement, development, and revisions. There are misunderstandings of certain concepts that require further clarification and articulation by appealing to reason, logic, and scientific principles. For example, some scholars still think that religious market theories are about the commercialization of religions, i.e., literally selling religious goods and ritual services for money. This confusion may be due to the fact that in China, "temple economy" is an established discipline that studies properties, taxation, and rituals performed for a fee in traditional temples.

---

52 Ibid., 99.

Also, commercialization has become a serious problem in many traditional temples in recent years. Not only are the prices of incense sticks or bell-ringing outrageously high, but they may also be purchased by businesspeople and presented to officials as bribes. Moreover, some sacred mountains with temple complexes have been repackaged as commercial companies to be listed on the stock market. However, religious market theories are not about commercialization of religious goods and services at all, but about religious supply, demand, and regulation, and the idea of the religious market is not merely an analogy or metaphor. Also, some scholars of Chinese traditional religions have misunderstood my definition and classification of religion as denigrating folk religions, which is simply not the case. My definition and classification are actually inclusive, broad, and justly affirmative of noninstitutionalized beliefs and practices. I have articulated my definition further in a new article, "The Definition of Religion for the Social Scientific Study of Religion in China and Beyond."[53]

Building on the initial tricolor religious market theory, I have developed the shortage economy and oligopoly theories in articles and books. Further theoretical construction can be done within the theoretical framework, such as answering questions like these: At the micro level, how can one measure or document religious awakening among individuals? Under what conditions do dormant religious needs turn into active demand in the market? At the meso level, what are the patterns of religious group dynamics in different markets? How do religious groups operate in the black market? How do religions compete in the red market? How do groups in the gray market self-position themselves and set up goals? At the macro level, how can the boundaries of different religious markets be demarcated? How can religious markets be quantified?

When the tricolor market theory was developed, quantitative data on religion in China were extremely limited. Moreover, "Creativity in evading regulations also makes it difficult for researchers to document and quantify the extent of gray-market religiosity."[54] Nevertheless, more and better quantitative data have become available, so that some quantitative studies have become possible. I have worked with my former PhD student, Anning Hu, and made the first quantitative studies of Chinese folk religion,[55] the major component of the

---

53   Fenggang Yang, "The Definition of Religion for the Social Scientific Study of Religion in China and Beyond," in *Concepts and Methods for the Study of Chinese Religions I: State of the Field and Disciplinary Approaches*, ed. André Laliberté and Stefania Travagnin (Berlin: De Gruyter, 2019), 23–44.
54   Fenggang Yang, "Red, Black, and Gray Markets," 97.
55   Fenggang Yang and Anning Hu, "Mapping Chinese Folk Religion in Mainland China and Taiwan," *Journal of the Scientific Study of Religion* 51.3 (2012): 506–522; Anning Hu and

gray market. This kind of study may have contributed to the documentation of religious change around the globe. For the first time, the Pew Research Center included "folk religion" on the same level as institutionalized religions in *The Future of World Religions: Population Growth Projections, 2010–2050*, which was released in 2015.[56] With more and better data, our research team has provided more historical, qualitative, and quantitative accounts of the tricolor religious market in the *Atlas of Religion in China: Social and Geographical Contexts*.[57] Much more can be done in this regard. However, we have also realized the limitations of existing measurements of religion and religiosity in social surveys. We have been working to experiment with new survey questions that may be better at capturing forms of religiosity and spirituality particularly prevalent in East Asian societies.[58]

Religion in China is often treated as a specific case within a larger theoretical construction; that is, a general theory based on some society is extended to China as an afterthought. The tricolor religious market is the first theory that has been constructed specifically to explain the situation of religion in China. But as a social science theory, it should have broader applicability. However, because of personal limitations of knowledge, time, and resources, it is impossible for myself or my research team to engage in studies of religion in many other societies. Meanwhile, it will take time for scholars in other societies who may become interested in the theory to apply it in their own research. As my book has been translated into Korean, Italian, Chinese, and Russian, some scholars in those societies have recently begun to take up the challenge. Additionally, scholars in the Czech Republic, Vietnam, and some other societies have indicated to me the probable applicability of the theory in explaining religious change in their own societies.

Third, is it necessary to replace the religious market theories with alternative theories? As a sociologist, following my mentor and role model Dean Hoge,

---

Fenggang Yang, "Trajectories of Folk Religion in Deregulated Taiwan: An Age-Period-Cohort Analysis," *Chinese Sociological Review* 46.3 (2014): 80–100.

56 Pew Research Center, *The Future of World Religions: Population Growth Projections, 2010–2050*, April 2, 2015, https://www.pewforum.org/2015/04/02/religious-projections-2010-2050/ (accessed December 30, 2015).

57 Fenggang Yang, *Atlas of Religion in China: Social and Geographical Contexts* (Leiden: Brill Academic Publishers, 2018).

58 Yang, "Exceptionalism or Chinamerica?"; Xiaozhao Y. Yang and Fenggang Yang, "Estimating Religious Populations with the Network Scale-Up Method: A Practical Alternative to Self-Report," *Journal for the Scientific Study of Religion* 56.4 (2017): 703–719; L. Luke Chao and Fenggang Yang, "Measuring Religiosity in a Religiously Diverse Society: The China Case," *Social Science Research* 74 (2018): 187–195.

I have always been open to alternative theories and approaches. However, social science as a collective enterprise is cumulative and should take solid steps based on empirical data and the logic of theoretical development. Some Chinese official theoreticians and scholars have countered the religious market theories with a so-called theory of the "lost balance of religious ecology" (*zongjiao shengtai shihenglun* 宗教生态失衡论).[59] Unfortunately, thus far, this has not become a social scientific theory, but remains an ideology-based strategic theory (*celun* 策论), offering justification for the party-state to suppress Christianity, Islam, and other so-called "foreign" religions (never mind that the Party itself is based on a foreign ideology). However, it is not totally impossible to develop a social scientific theory of religious ecologies. As a matter of fact, I myself explored it in an empirical study many years ago that is described in the article "More Than Evangelical and Ethnic: The Ecological Factor in Chinese Conversion to Christianity in the United States."[60] I have also applied the geographical approach to construct the religious landscape.[61] What eventually can be developed from these theoretical explorations remains unclear at the present time.

It is important to regard social scientific theories as tools for the purpose of knowing or explaining social reality. I have compared them to such tools as eyeglasses, because they help give a clearer vision of a complex reality.[62] As tools, however, their value depends on their usefulness in facilitating research and explanation, or helping people to understand reality. Social scientists ought not to idolize any theory or ideologize it. It is also important to remember that social reality is always more complex than any theory can capture. As Johann Wolfgang von Goethe says in Faust, "Grau, teurer Freund, ist alle Theorie und grün des Lebens goldner Baum" (All theory is gray, my friend, but forever green is the tree of life).

---

59 Duan Qi, "Zongjiao shengtai shiheng yu Zhongguo Jidujiao de fazhan," in *Dangdai Zhongguo minzu zongjiao wenti yanjiu, di 4 ji*, edited by Gansu Research Base Office of China United Front Work Theoretical Research Association's Ethnic and Religious Theories (Lanzhou: Gansu Ethnic Press, 2009), 137–149; Mou Zhongjian, "Zongjiao shengtai lun," *Shijie zongjiao wenhua*, 2012.1: 1–10; Li Xiangping, " 'Zongjiao shengtai' haishi 'quanli shengtai'—Cong dangdai Zhongguo de 'zongjiao shengtai lun' sichao tanqi," *Shanghai daxue xuebao* (*shehui kexue ban*), 2011.1: 124–140; Li Huawei, "Zongjiao shehuixue"; Huang Haibo, "Zhongguo jingyan yu bentu lilun."
60 Yuting Wang and Fenggang Yang, "More Than Evangelical and Ethnic: The Ecological Factor in Chinese Conversion to Christianity in the United States," *Sociology of Religion* 67.2 (2006): 179–192.
61 Fenggang Yang, "Studying Religions in Time and Space," *Asian Journal of Religion and Society* 4.2 (2016): 19–35; Fenggang Yang, *Atlas of Religion in China*.
62 Yang and Hu, "Mapping Chinese Folk Religion," 508.

Bibliography

Abel, Andrew Stuart. Review of *Religion in China: Survival and Revival under Communist Rule*, by Fenggang Yang. *Sociology of Religion* 73.2 (2012): 228–230.

Berger, Peter L. *A Rumor of Angels: Modern Society and the Rediscovery of the Supernatural*. Garden City, NY: Doubleday, 1969.

Berger, Peter L. *The Sacred Canopy: Elements of a Sociological Theory of Religion*. Garden City, NY: Doubleday, 1967.

Berger, Peter, Grace Davie, and Effie Fokas. *Religious America, Secular Europe? A Theme and Variation*. New York: Routledge, 2008.

Chao, Luke L., and Fenggang Yang. "Measuring Religiosity in a Religiously Diverse Society: The China Case." *Social Science Research* 74 (2018): 187–195.

Cooper, Gene. Review of *Religion in China: Survival and Revival under Communist Rule*, by Fenggang Yang. *Contemporary Sociology* 42.1 (2013): 122–124.

Duan Qi. "Zongjiao shengtai shiheng yu Zhongguo Jidujiao de fazhan" 宗教生态失衡与中国基督教的发展. In *Dangdai Zhongguo minzu zongjiao wenti yanjiu, di 4 ji* 当代中国民族宗教问题研究，第4辑. edited by Gansu Research Base Office of China United Front Work Theoretical Research Association's Ethnic and Religious Theories, 137–149. Lanzhou: Gansu Ethnic Press, 2009.

Ebaugh, Helen Rose. Review of *Religion in China: Survival and Revival under Communist Rule*, by Fenggang Yang. *Journal for the Scientific Study of Religion* 52.2 (2013): 448–449.

Ebaugh, Helen Rose, and Janet S. Chafetz, eds. *Religion and the New Immigrants: Continuities and Adaptations in Immigrant Congregations*. Walnut Creek, CA: AltaMira, 2000.

Ebaugh, Helen Rose, and Janet S. Chafetz, eds. *Religions across Borders: Transnational Religious Networks*. Walnut Creek, CA: AltaMira, 2002.

Ecklund, Elaine Howard. "Diversifying the Social Scientific Study of Religion: The Next 70 Years." *Journal for the Scientific Study of Religion* 59.1 (2020): 5–17.

Fan Lizhu 范丽珠. "Xiandai zongjiao shi lixing xuanze de ma? Zhiyi zongjiao de lixing xuanze yanjiu fanshi" 现代宗教是理性选择的吗？质疑宗教的理性选择研究范式. *Shehui* 社会 28.6 (2008): 90–109.

Gao Shining 高师宁. "Zongjiao shehuixue yanjiu zai zhongguo dalu de fazhan" 宗教社会学研究在中国大陆的发展. *Shanghai daxue xuebao (shehui kexue ban)* 上海大学学报（社会科学版）. 2007.3: 96–99.

Goossaert, Vincent. Review of *Religion in China: Survival and Revival under Communist Rule*, by Fenggang Yang. *Archives de sciences sociales des religions* 160 (October–December 2012): 304–305.

Hu, Anning, and Fenggang Yang. "Trajectories of Folk Religion in Deregulated Taiwan: An Age-Period-Cohort Analysis." *Chinese Sociological Review* 46.3 (2014): 80–100.

Huang Haibo 黄海波. "Zhongguo jingyan yu bentu lilun: jinnian lai zhongguo zongjiao shehuixue lilun redian" 中国经验与本土理论：近年来中国宗教社会学理论热点. *Zongjiao shehuixue* 宗教社会学 2017.5: 3–21.

Huang Jianbo 黄剑波. "Ershinian lai zhongguo dalu jidujiao de jingyan yanjiu shuping" 二十年来中国大陆基督教的经验研究述评. In *Jidujiao sixiang pinglun (di jiu juan)* 基督教思想评论（第9辑）. edited by Xu Zhiwei 许志伟, 345-366. Shanghai: Shanghai Shiji Publishing Corp., 2009.

Huang, Jianbo, and Mengyin Hu. "Trends and Reflections: A Review of Empirical Studies of Christianity in Mainland China." *Review of Religion and Chinese Society* 6.1 (2019): 45–70.

Ji Zhe 汲喆. "Ruhe chaoyue shisuhua lilun?—ping zongjiao shehuixue de sanzhong houshisuhua lunshu" 如何超越经典世俗化理论？—评宗教社会学的三种后世俗化论述. *Shehuixue yanjiu* 社会学研究. 2008.4: 55–75.

Johnson, Ian. Review of *Religion in China: Survival and Revival under Communist Rule*, by Fenggang Yang. *New York Review of Books* 58.20 (2011): 55–58.

"Juan shouyu: Ping 'zongjiao shichang'" 卷首语：评'宗教市场论'. *Kexue yu wushenlun* 科学与无神论. 2011.2: 1.

Kornai, János. *Economics of Shortage*. Amsterdam: North-Holland, 1980.

Kornai, János. *The Socialist System: The Political Economy of Communism*. Oxford: Oxford University Press, 1992.

Li Huawei 李华伟. "Zongjiao shehuixue zai zhongguo dalu de fazhan lichen" 宗教社会学在中国大陆的发展历程. In *Zhongguo shehui kexueyuan shijie zongjiao yanjiusuo wushinian fazhan licheng*, 1964–2014, 中国社会科学院世界宗教研究所五十年发展历程 1964–2014, edited by Institute of World Religions, Chinese Academy of Social Sciences, 61–74. Beijing: China Social Sciences Press, 2014.

Li Xiangping. "'Zongjiao shengtai' haishi 'quanli shengtai'—Cong dangdai Zhongguo de 'zongjiao shengtai lun' sichao tanqi" 宗教生态'还是'权力生态'—从当代中国的'宗教生态论'思潮谈起. *Shanghai daxue xuebao (shehui kexue ban)* 上海大学学报（社会科学版）. 2011.1: 124–140.

Li Xiangping 李向平 and Yang Linxia 杨林霞. "Zongjiao, shehui yu quanli guanxi—'zongjiao shichang lun' de shehuixue jiedu" 宗教、社会与权力关系—"宗教市场论"的社会学解读. *Huadong shifan daxue xuebao (zhexue shehui kexue ban)* 华东师范大学学报（哲学社会科学版）43.5 (2011): 1–7.

Liang Yongjia 梁永佳. "Zhongguo nongcun zongjiao fuxing yu 'zongjiao' de Zhongguo mingyun" 中国农村宗教复兴与"宗教"的中国命运. *Shehui* 社会 35.1 (2015): 161–183.

Lin Qiaowei 林巧薇. "Yang Fenggang boshi tan zongjiao shehuixue de fanshi zhuanxing" 杨凤岗博士谈宗教社会学的范式转型. *Zongjiaoxue yanjiu* 宗教学研究. 2003.3: 140–141.

Liu, Eric Yang. Review of *Religion in China: Survival and Revival under Communist Rule*, by Fenggang Yang. *Sociological Forum* 28.2 (2013): 419–422.

Lu Yunfeng 卢云峰. "Chaoyue jiduzongjiao shehuixue—jianlun zongjiao shichang lilun zai huaren shehui de shiyongxing wenti" 超越基督宗教社会学—兼论宗教市场理论在华人社会的适用性问题. *Shehuixue yanjiu* 社会学研究. 2008.5: 81–97.

Lu Yunfeng 卢云峰. "Weihe shi 'zongjiao meiguo, shisu ouzhou'?" 为何是'宗教美国, 世俗欧洲'? *Dushu* 读书. 2016.3: 150–159.

Madsen, Richard. Review of *Religion in China: Survival and Revival under Communist Rule*, by Fenggang Yang. *Journal of Asian Studies* 71.4 (2012): 1126–1127.

Madsen, Richard. "The Upsurge of Religion in China." *Journal of Democracy* 21.4 (2010): 58–71.

Mou Zhongjian. "Zongjiao shengtai lun" 宗教生态论. *Shijie zongjiao wenhua* 世界宗教文化, 2012 1: 1–10.

Nichols, Brian J. Review of *Religion in China: Survival and Revival under Communist Rule*, by Fenggang Yang. *Religious Studies Review* 39.3 (2013): 198.

Pew Research Center. *The Future of World Religions: Population Growth Projections, 2010–2050*. April 2, 2015. https://www.pewforum.org/2015/04/02/religious-projections-2010-2050/.

Qiu Yue 秋月. "Zongjiao shichang, dui shei kaifang?" 宗教市场，对谁开放? *Kexue yu wushenlun* 科学与无神论, 2011.2: 14–18.

Qu Jingdong 渠敬东, Lu Yunfeng 卢云峰, Liang Yongjia 梁永佳 et al. "You guan 'zongjiao shichang lilun' de yici yuanzhuo taolun" 有关'宗教市场理论'的一次圆桌讨论. *Zhongguo yanjiu* 中国研究 19.1 (2014): 208–227.

Said, Edward W. *Orientalism*. New York: Vintage Books, 1979.

Sharot, Stephen. "Beyond Christianity: A Critique of the Rational Choice Theory of Religion from a Weberian and Comparative Religions Perspective." *Sociology of Religion* 63.4 (2002): 427–454.

Shen Zhang 沈璋. "Ye tan 'zongjiao shichanglun' jiqi zai zhongguo dalu 'zongjiao wenhua' zhong de maidian" 也谈'宗教市场论'及其在中国大陆'宗教文化'中的卖点. *Kexue yu wushenlun* 科学与无神论. 2011.3: 5–13.

Smith, Christian. *American Evangelicalism: Embattled and Thriving*. Chicago: University of Chicago Press, 1998.

Spickard, James V. Review of *Religion in China: Survival and Revival under Communist Rule*, by Fenggang Yang. *Journal of Contemporary Religion* 29.1 (2014): 162–164.

Stark, Rodney. *The Rise of Christianity: A Sociologist Reconsiders History*. Princeton: Princeton University Press, 1996. Translated by Huang Jianbo 黄剑波 and Gao Mingui 高民贵 as *Jidujiao de xingqi: yige shehuixuejia dui lishi de zaisi* 基督教的兴起：一个社会学家对历史的再思. Shanghai: Shanghai guji chubanshe, 2005.

Stark, Rodney, and William Sims Bainbridge. *The Future of Religion: Secularization, Revival, and Cult Formation*. Berkeley: University of California Press, 1985. Translated by Gao Shining 高师宁, Zhang Xiaomei 张晓梅, and Liu Dianli 刘殿利 as *Zongjiao de weilai* 宗教的未来. Beijing: Renmin University of China, 2006.

Stark, Rodney, and Roger Finke. *Acts of Faith: Explaining the Human Side of Religion.* Berkeley: University of California Press, 2000. Translated by Yang Fenggang 杨凤岗 as *Xinyang de faze—jieshi zongjiao zhi ren de fangmian* 信仰的法则—解释宗教之人的方面. Beijing: Zhongguo renmin daxue chubanshe, 2004.

Turner, Bryan S. Review of *Religion in China: Survival and Revival under Communist Rule*, by Fenggang Yang. *European Journal of Sociology / Archives Européennes de Sociologie / Europäisches Archiv für Soziologie* 53.3 (2012): 338–342.

Vala, Carsten T. Review of *Religion in China: Survival and Revival under Communist Rule*, by Fenggang Yang. *Social Forces* 93.2 (2014): e54.

Wang, Yuting, and Fenggang Yang. "More Than Evangelical and Ethnic: The Ecological Factor in Chinese Conversion to Christianity in the United States." *Sociology of Religion* 67.2 (2006): 179–192.

Warner, R. Stephen. "Work in Progress toward a New Paradigm for the Sociological Study of Religion in the United States." *American Journal of Sociology* 98.5 (1993): 1044–1095.

Warner, R. Stephen, and Judith G. Wittner, eds. *Gatherings in Diaspora: Religious Communities and the New Immigration.* Philadelphia: Temple University Press, 1998.

Wei Dedong 魏德东. "Zongjiao shehuixue de fanshi zhuanhuan jiqi yingxiang" 宗教社会学的范式转换及其影响. *Renmin daxue xuebao* 人民大学学报. 2010.3: 61–69.

Wei Dedong 魏德东 and Liu Yang 刘洋. "Zongjiao yanjiu de renti lilun: Fang zongjiao shehuixuejia luodeni sidake" 宗教研究的人本理论：访宗教社会学家罗德尼·斯达克. *Zhongguo minzubao* 中国民族报. October 7, 2008.

Whyte, Martin King. Review of *Religion in China: Survival and Revival under Communist Rule*, by Fenggang Yang. *American Journal of Sociology* 118.1 (2012): 240–242.

Woo, Franklin J. Review of *Religion in China: Survival and Revival under Communist Rule*, by Fenggang Yang. *China Review International* 18.4 (2011): 549–554.

Yang, C. K. (杨庆堃). *Religion in Chinese Society: A Study of Contemporary Social Functions of Religion and Some of Their Historical Factors.* Berkeley: University of California Press, 1961.

Yang, Fenggang. *Atlas of Religion in China: Social and Geographical Contexts.* Leiden: Brill Academic Publishers, 2018.

Yang, Fenggang. "Between Secularist Ideology and Desecularizing Reality: The Birth and Growth of Religious Research in Communist China." *Sociology of Religion* 65.2 (2004): 101–119.

Yang, Fenggang. "The Definition of Religion for the Social Scientific Study of Religion in China and Beyond." In *Concepts and Methods for the Study of Chinese Religions I: State of the Field and Disciplinary Approaches*, edited by André Laliberté and Stefania Travagnin, 23–44. Berlin: De Gruyter, 2019.

Yang, Fenggang. "Exceptionalism or Chinamerica: Measuring Religious Change in the Globalizing World Today." *Journal for the Scientific Study of Religion* 55.1 (2016): 7–22.

Yang, Fenggang. "The Failure of the Campaign to Demolish Church Crosses in Zhejiang Province, 2013–2016." *Review of Religion and Chinese Society* 5.1 (2018): 5–25.

Yang, Fenggang. "Oligopoly Dynamics: Consequences of Religious Regulation." *Social Compass* 57.2 (2010): 194–205.

Yang, Fenggang. "The Red, Black, and Gray Markets of Religion in China." *Sociological Quarterly* 47.1 (2006): 93–122. Translated and abridged by Yang Fenggang 杨凤岗 as "Zhongguo zongjiao de sanse shichang" 中国宗教的三色市场, *Zhongguo renmin daxue xuebao (shehui kexue ban)* 中国人民大学学报（社会科学版）, 2006.6: 41–47. Also translated by Yang Jianghua 杨江华 as "Zhongguo zongjiao de sanse shichang" 中国宗教的三色市场, *Zhongguo nongye daxue xuebao (shehui kexue ban)* 中国农业大学学报（社会科学版）. 2008.4: 93–112.

Yang, Fenggang. *Religion in China: Survival and Revival under Communist Rule*. New York: Oxford University Press, 2012. Korean edition: 중국의 종교: 공산 통치하에서의 생존과 부흥. Translated by Song Jae-ryong and Yoo Kwang-suk. Seoul: Dasan Publishing Co., 2017. Italian edition: *La religione nella Cina comunista: Dalla sopravvivenza al risveglio*. Translated by Emanuela Claudia Del Re. Milan: Franco Angeli, 2020. Chinese edition: 宗教在中國：黨治下的存活與復興. Translated by Jiayin Hu, Jun Lu, Zhen Wang, and Yongguang Xue. Forthcoming.

Yang, Fenggang. "Religion in China under Communism: A Shortage Economy Explanation." *Journal of Church and State* 51.1 (2010): 3–33.

Yang, Fenggang. "Sinicization or Chinafication? Cultural Assimilation vs. Political Domestication of Christianity in China and Beyond." In *The Sinicization of Chinese Religions: From Above and Below*, edited by Richard Madsen. Leiden: Brill, forthcoming.

Yang, Fenggang. "Studying Religions in Time and Space." *Asian Journal of Religion and Society* 4.2 (2016): 19–35.

Yang Fenggang 杨凤岗. "Zongjiao meiguo, shisu ouzhou de zhuti yu bianzou" 宗教美国、世俗欧洲的主题与变奏. *Dushu* 读书, 2016.4: 159–168.

Yang, Fenggang, and Anning Hu. "Mapping Chinese Folk Religion in Mainland China and Taiwan." *Journal of the Scientific Study of Religion* 51.3 (2012): 506–522.

Yang, Xiaozhao Y., and Fenggang Yang. "Estimating Religious Populations with the Network Scale-Up Method: A Practical Alternative to Self-Report." *Journal for the Scientific Study of Religion* 56.4 (2017): 703–719.

Yao, Xinzhong. Review of *Religion in China: Survival and Revival under Communist Rule*, by Fenggang Yang. *Journal of Chinese Religions* 40 (2012): 155–157.

Ying, Fuk-tsang. "The Politics of Cross Demolition: A Religio-Political Analysis of the 'Three Rectifications and One Demolition' Campaign in Zhejiang Province." *Review of Religion and Chinese Society* 5.1 (2018): 43–75.

Yu, Anthony C. Review of *Religion in China: Survival and Revival under Communist Rule*, by Fenggang Yang. *Journal of Church and State* 54.3 (2012): 459–462.

Yu, Anthony C. *State and Religion in China: Historical and Textual Perspectives*. Chicago: Open Court, 2005.

Zhang Wenjie 张文杰. "Zhongguo zongjiao yanjiu de 'zhengzhi jingjixue' changshi: ping *Zhongguo de zongjiao*" 中国宗教研究的"政治经济学"尝试评《中国的宗教》. *Shehui* 社会34.3 (2014): 205–229.

Zhang Zhigang 张志刚. "Dangdai zhongguo zongjiao guanxi yanjiu chuyi" 当代中国宗教关系研究刍议. *Beijing daxue xuebao (zhexue shehui kexue ban)* 北京大学学报（哲学社会学版）. 48.2 (2011): 33–41.

Zrinščak, Siniša. Review of *Religion in China: Survival and Revival under Communist Rule*, by Fenggang Yang. *Religion and Society in Central and Eastern Europe* 6.1 (2013): 75–77.

Bibliography

Abel, Andrew Stuart. Review of *Religion in China: Survival and Revival under Communist Rule*, by Fenggang Yang. *Sociology of Religion* 73.2 (2012): 228–230.

Addison, James Thayer. "Chinese Ancestor-Worship and Protestant Christianity." *Journal of Religion* 5 (1925): 140–149.

Adsera, Alicia. "An Economic Analysis of the Gap between Desired and Actual Fertility: The Case of Spain." *Review of Economics of the Household* 4.1 (2006): 75–95.

Aikman, David. *Jesus in Beijing: How Christianity Is Transforming China and Changing the Global Balance of Power*. Washington, DC: Regnery; Lanham, MD: National Book Network, 2003.

Allès, Élisabeth, Leïla Chérif-Chebbi, and Constance-Hélène Halfon. "Chinese Islam: Unity and Fragmentation." *Religion, State and Society* 31.1 (2003): 7–35.

Ammerman, Nancy T. *Congregation and Community*. New Brunswick, NJ: Rutgers University Press, 1997.

"Anhong tianzhujiao jidujiao jiben qingkuang" 安红天主教基督教基本情况. Anhong Religious Affairs Bureau Records. Anhong: Anhong Religious Affairs Bureau, 2014.

Anonymous. "Defense Statement: En Hua, a Member of Anhong Church." *Chinese Law & Religion Monitor* 6.1 (2009): 45–52.

Anonymous. "Defense Statement: Wan Xian, a Member of Anhong Church." *Chinese Law & Religion Monitor* 6.1 (2009): 53–58.

Ashiwa, Yoshiko, and David L. Wank. *Making Religion, Making the State: The Politics of Religion in Modern China*. Stanford, CA: Stanford University Press, 2009.

Averill, Stephen C., ed. *Zhongguo dazhong zongjiao* 中国大众宗教. Translated by Cheng Zhongdan 陈仲丹. Nanjing: Jiangsu renmin chubanshe, 2006.

Bai Bo 白波. "Gaoxiao tushuguan weixin yonghu jieshou xingwei yanjiu: Jiyu jishu jieshou moxing" 高校图书馆微信用户接受行为研究—基于技术接受模型. Jilin University, master's thesis, 2015.

Bankston, Carl L. "Rationality, Choice, and the Religious Economy: Individual and Collective Rationality in Supply and Demand." *Review of Religious Research* 45.2 (December 2003): 155–171.

Barnett, Robert. "Symbols and Protest: The Iconography of Demonstrations." In *Resistance and Reform in Tibet*, edited by Robert Barnett and Shirin Akiiner, 238–258. London: Hurst & Company, 1994.

Bays, Daniel. "A Tradition of State Dominance." In *God and Caesar in China*, edited by Jason Kindopp and Carol Lee Hamrin, 25–39. Washington, DC: Brookings Institution Press, 2004.

Beijingshi diliuci quanguo renkou pucha lingdao xiaozu bangongshi 北京市第六次全国人口普查领导小组办公室. "Beijingshi diliuci quanguo renkou pucha zhuyao shuju qingkuang" 北京市2010年第六次全国人民普查主要数据情况. http://www.bjstats.gov.cn/tjsj/tjgb/rpgb/201511/t20151124_327785.html.

Beijingshi diliuci renkou pucha bangongshi 北京市第六次人口普查办公室. "Beijing changzhu wailai renkou laiyuan fenxi." https://wenku.baidu.com/view/a99c9bd7240c844769eaeefb.html (accessed August 20, 2019).

Berger, Peter. "Religion in Global Civil Society." In *Religion in Global Civil Society*, edited by Mark Juergensmeyer, 11–22. New York: Oxford University Press, 2005.

Berger, Peter L. *A Rumor of Angels: Modern Society and the Rediscovery of the Supernatural*. Garden City, NY: Doubleday, 1969.

Berger, Peter L. *The Sacred Canopy: Elements of a Sociological Theory of Religion*. Garden City, NY: Doubleday, 1967. Translated by Gao Shining 高师宁 as *Shensheng de weimu: zongjiao shehuixue lilun zhi yaosu* 神圣的帷幕：宗教社会学理论之要素. Shanghai: Shanghai renmin chubanshe, 1991.

Berger, Peter, Grace Davie, and Effie Fokas. *Religious America, Secular Europe? A Theme and Variation*. New York: Routledge, 2008.

Blau, Peter M. *Exchange and Power in Social Life*. New York: John Wiley, 1964. Translated by Li Guowu 李国武 as *Shehui shenghuo zhongde jiaohuan yu quanli* 社会生活中的交换与权力. Beijing: Shangwu yinshu guan, 2013.

Brown, G. Thompson. "Jidujiao zai Jiangsu Mingcheng diqu chuanjiao jianshi, 1884–1941" 基督教在江苏明城地区传教简史 (1884–1941). In *Mingcheng wenshi ziliao* 明城文史资料. vol. 31, translated by Yang Naizhuang 杨乃庄 and edited by Zhongguo renmin zhengzhi xieshang huiyi Jiangsu sheng Mingcheng weiyuanhui wenshi weiyuanhui 中国人民政治协商会议江苏省明成明城委员会文史委员会. Mingcheng, Jiangsu, China: Zhongguo renmin zhengzhi xieshang huiyi Jiangsu sheng Mingcheng weiyuanhui wenshi weiyuanhui, 2010.

Bruce, Steve. "Religion and Rational Choice: A Critique of Economic Explanations of Religious Behavior." *Sociology of Religion* 54.2 (1993): 193–205.

Cao, Nanlai. *Constructing China's Jerusalem: Christians, Power, and Place in Contemporary Wenzhou*. Stanford, CA: Stanford University Press, 2010.

Carney, Matthew. "Chinese Communist Party Readies Crackdown on Christianity." Mobile ABC News, October 8, 2016. http://mobile.abc.net.au/news/2016-10-08/chinese-communist-partys-crackdown-on-religion/7912140?pfmredir=sm (accessed August 20, 2019).

Chan Bing 陳彬. "Zongjiao yeyou shichang?—Luodeni Sidake de zongjiao shichang lilun pingshu" 宗教也有市場?—羅德尼·斯達克的宗教市場理論述評. *Daqing shifan xueyuan xuebo* 大庆师范学院学报. 2009.5: 45–50.

Chan, Cheris Shun-ching. "The Falun Gong in China: A Sociological Perspective." *China Quarterly* 179 (2004): 665–683.

Chao, Luke L., and Fenggang Yang. "Measuring Religiosity in a Religiously Diverse Society: The China Case." *Social Science Research* 74 (2018): 187–195.

Chau, Adam. *Miraculous Response: Doing Popular Religion in Contemporary China.* Stanford, CA: Stanford University Press, 2006.

Chau, Adam. "Modalities of Doing Religion and Ritual Polytropy: Evaluating the Religious Market Model from the Perspective of Chinese Religious History." *Religion* 41.4 (2011): 547–568.

Chau, Adam, ed. *Religion in Contemporary China: Revitalization and Innovation.* London: Routledge, 2011.

Chaves, Mark, and Philip S. Gorski. "Religious Pluralism and Religious Participation." *Annual Review of Sociology* 27 (2001): 261–281.

Chen Jinguo 陈进国. "'Maidi quan' xisu de kaoxianxue yanjiu—mintai diqu de shili" "买地券"习俗的考现学研究—闽台地区的事例. *Minsu yanjiu* 民俗研究, 2008.1: 129–164.

Chen Xiaoyi 陈晓毅. *Zhongguo shi zongjiao shengtai: qingyan zongjiao duoyang xing gean yanjiu* 中国式宗教生态：青岩宗教多样性个案研究. Beijing: Shehui kexue wenxian chubanshe, 2008.

Chinese Academy of Social Sciences. *Shehui lanpi shu: 2016 nian Zhongguo shehui xingshi fenxi yu yuce* 社会蓝皮书：2016年中国社会形势分析与预测. Beijing: Shehui kexue wenxian chubanshe, 2015.

Chinese Christian Rights Defense Lawyers Association. "Summary of the Seminar on the Anhong Church Case and Religious Freedom." *Chinese Law & Religion Monitor* 6.1 (2009): 101–120.

Chinese Internet Network Information Center (CNNIC). "The 2015 Annual Report of the Social Media Application Users' Behavior" 2015 年中国社交应用用户行为研究报告. April 2016. http://www.cnnic.net.cn/hlwfzyj/hlwxzbg/sqbg/201712/P020180103485975797840.pdf (accessed August 20, 2019).

Christensen, Erleen J. *In War and Famine: Missionaries in China's Honan Province in the 1940s.* Montreal: McGill-Queen's University Press, 2005.

"Concerning the Investigation and the Banning of the 'Shouter Sect' and Other Cultic Organizations and Their Situation and Suggestions for Action issued by Ministry of Public Security" 中共中央办公厅、国务院办公厅下发《关于转发〈公安部关于查禁取缔"呼喊派"等邪教组织的情况及工作意见〉的通知》. *Ting zi* 厅字 50 (1995).

Cooper, Gene. Review of *Religion in China: Survival and Revival under Communist Rule,* by Fenggang Yang. *Contemporary Sociology* 42.1 (2013): 122–124.

Deleuze, Gilles. *The Fold: Leibniz and the Baroque.* Minneapolis: University of Minnesota Press, 1993.

Deleuze, Gilles. *The Logic of Sense.* New York: Columbia University Press, 1990.

Dong Renda 东人达. *Dianqian chuanbian jidujiao chuanbo yanjiu* 滇黔川边基督教传播研究. Beijing: Renmin chubanshe, 2004.

Dou Zhiping 窦志萍. "Shehuizhuyi xin nongcun jianshe yu xiangcun lüyou xietiao fazhan yanjiu: Yi Fuminxian xiaoshuijingcun wei li" 社会主义新农村建设与乡村旅游协调发展研究——以富民县小水井村为例. *Kunming daxue xuebao* 昆明大学学报, 2007.2: 7–11.

Duan Qi 段琦. "2011 nian Zhongguo jidujiao zhuyao shijian ji chengshihua dui jiaohui de yingxiang" 2011年中国基督教主要事件及城市化对教会的影响. In *Zhongguo zongjiao baogao (2012)* 中国宗教报告（2012）, edited by Jin Ze 金泽 and Qiu Yonghui 邱永辉, 164–104. Beijing: Shehui kexue wenxian chubanshe, 2012.

Duan Qi. "Zongjiao shengtai shiheng yu Zhongguo Jidujiao de fazhan" 宗教生态失衡与中国基督教的发展. In *Dangdai Zhongguo minzu zongjiao wenti yanjiu, di 4 ji* 当代中国民族宗教问题研究，第4辑, edited by Gansu Research Base Office of China United Front Work Theoretical Research Association's Ethnic and Religious Theories, 137–149. Lanzhou: Gansu Ethnic Press, 2009.

Dunn, Emily C. "'Cult,' Church and the CCP: Introducing Eastern Lightning." *Modern China* 35.1 (2009): 96–119.

Dunn, Emily. *Lightning from the East: Heterodoxy and Christianity in Contemporary China*. Leiden: Brill, 2015.

Dunn, James D. G. *The Partings of the Ways between Christianity and Judaism and Their Significance for the Character of Christianity*. Grand Rapids, MI: Eerdmans, 1999. Translated by Yang Hui 杨慧 as *Fendao yangbiao: Jidujiao yu youtaijiao de fenli jiqi dui jidujiao texing de yiyi* 分道扬镳：基督教与犹太教的分离及其对基督教特性的意义. Hong Kong: Logos and Pneuma Press, 2015.

Durkheim, Emile. *The Elementary Forms of Religious Life*. Translated by Joseph Ward Swain. London: George Allen and Unwin, 1915. Translated by Lin Zongjin 林宗锦 and Peng Shouyi 彭守义 as *Zongjiao shenghuo de chuji xingshi* 宗教生活的初级形式. Beijing: Zhongyang minzu daxue chubanshe, 1999.

Ebaugh, Helen Rose. Review of *Religion in China: Survival and Revival under Communist Rule*, by Fenggang Yang. *Journal for the Scientific Study of Religion* 52.2 (2013): 448–449.

Ebaugh, Helen Rose, and Janet S. Chafetz, eds. *Religion and the New Immigrants: Continuities and Adaptations in Immigrant Congregations*. Walnut Creek, CA: AltaMira, 2000.

Ebaugh, Helen Rose, and Janet S. Chafetz, eds. *Religions across Borders: Transnational Religious Networks*. Walnut Creek, CA: AltaMira, 2002.

Ecklund, Elaine Howard. "Diversifying the Social Scientific Study of Religion: The Next 70 Years." *Journal for the Scientific Study of Religion* 59.1 (2020): 5–17.

Fan Lizhu 范丽珠. "Xiandai zongjiao shi lixing xuanze de ma? Zhiyi zongjiao de lixing xuanze yanjiu fanshi" 现代宗教是理性选择的吗？质疑宗教的理性选择研究范式. *Shehui* 社会. 28.6 (2008): 90–109.

BIBLIOGRAPHY

Fan Lizhu 范丽珠. "Xifang zongjiao lilun xia Zhongguo zongjiao yanjiu de kunjing" 西方宗教理论下中国宗教研究的困境. *Nanjing daxue xuebao (zhexue, renwen kexue, shehui kexue ban)* 南京大学学报（哲学、人文科学、社会科学版）. 2009.2: 92–101.

Finney, Richard. "Religious Repression Ramps Up in China, Myanmar: Report." *Radio Free Asia*, May 29, 2018. https://www.rfa.org/english/news/china/religious-05292018165236.html (accessed August 20, 2019).

Friedmann, John. *The Prospect of Cities*. Minneapolis: University of Minnesota Press, 2002.

Gans, Herbert. *The Urban Villagers*. New York: Free Press, 1982.

Gao Bingzhong 高丙中. "Zuowei feiwuzhi wenhua yichan yanjiu keti de minjian xinyang" 作为非物质文化遗产研究课题的民间信仰. *Jiangxi shehui kexue* 江西社会科学, 2007.3: 146–154.

Gao Jun 高俊. "Jiangsu feijidujiao yundong shimo" 江苏非基督教运动始末. *Puyang zhiye jishu xueyuan xuebao* 濮阳职业技术学院学报, 2014.4: 40–42.

Gao Jun 高俊. "Qingmo Jiangsu minjiao chongtu de qiluo" 清末江苏民教冲突的起落. *Anqing shifan xueyuan xuebao (shehui kexue ban)* 安庆师范学院学报（社会科学版）. 2014.6: 111–114.

Gao Shining 高师宁. "Zongjiao shehuixue yanjiu zai zhongguo dalu de fazhan" 宗教社会学研究在中国大陆的发展. *Shanghai daxue xuebao (shehui kexue ban)* 上海大学学报（社会科学版）. 2007.3: 96–99.

Germani, Gino. *The Sociology of Modernization: Studies on Its Historical and Theoretical Aspects with Special Regard to the Latin American Case*. New Brunswick, NJ: Transaction, 1981.

Gladney, Dru C. *Dislocating China: Muslims, Minorities, and Other Subaltern Subjects*. Chicago: University of Chicago Press, 2004.

Goossaert, Vincent. Review of *Religion in China: Survival and Revival under Communist Rule*, by Fenggang Yang. *Archives de sciences sociales des religions* 160 (October–December 2012): 304–305.

Goossaert, Vincent, and David Palmer. *The Religious Question in Modern China*. Chicago: University of Chicago Press, 2010.

Goforth, Rosalind. *Goforth of China*. Grand Rapids, MI: Zondervan, 1937.

Gu Baochang 顾宝昌. "Shengyu yiyuan shengyu xingwei he shengyu shuiping" 生育意愿、生育行为和生育水平. *Renkou yanjiu* 人口研究. 35.2 (2011): 43–59.

Gu Guanfu 顾冠福 and Long Feijun 龙飞俊. "Yiwei Shanghai chengpai daoshi de koushushi—Gu Guanfu daozhang fangtan lu" 一位上海城派道士的口述史—顾冠福道长访谈录. *Shilin* 石林, 2010.1: 94–99.

Gunitsky, Seva. "Corrupting the Cyber-commons: Social Media as a Tool of Autocratic Stability." *Perspectives on Politics* 13.1 (2015): 42–54.

Han Junxue 韩军学. *Jidujiao yu Yunnan shaoshu minzu* 基督教与云南少数民族. Kunming: Yunnan renmin chubanshe, 2000.

Han Junxue 韩军学. "Jindai Yunnan jidujiao, tianzhujiao de bianqian ji zouxiang" 近代云南基督教、天主教的变迁及走向. *Yunnan zongjiao yanjiu* 云南宗教研究. no. 23 (2000): 49–60.

Hattaway, Paul. *Henan: The Galilee of China*. Carlisle, UK: Piquant Editions, 2009.

He Jianyu 何建宇 and Wang Shaoguang 王绍光. "Zhongguoshi de shetuan geming—dui shetuan quanjingtu de dingliang miaoshu" 中国式的社团革命—对社团全景图的定量描述. In *Zhongguo gongmin shehui lanpishu* 中国公民社会发展蓝皮书. edited by Gao Bingzhong 高丙中 and Yuan Ruijun 袁瑞军, 133–156. Beijing: Beijing daxue chubanshe, 2008.

He Xuefeng 贺雪峰. "Lun Zhongguo nongcun de quyu chayi—cunzhuang shehui jiegou de shijiao" 论中国农村的区域差异—村庄社会结构的视角. *Kaifang shidai* 开放时代. 2012.10: 108–129.

He Zhe 何哲. *Chengshizhong de linggong: yike zhishi fenzi yiqi jiating jiaohui de fazhan shilu* 城市中的灵宫：一个知识分子及其家庭教会的发展实录. Hong Kong: Mingfeng chuban, 2009.

Honghe County People's Government Network. Honghe County profile. http://www.hhx.hh.gov.cn/hhgk/xqjj/201708/t20170807_47651.html (accessed August 20, 2019).

Hu, Anning, and Fenggang Yang. "Trajectories of Folk Religion in Deregulated Taiwan: An Age-Period-Cohort Analysis." *Chinese Sociological Review* 46.3 (2014): 80–100.

Hu, Jiayin. "Spirituality and Spiritual Practice: Is the Local Church Pentecostal?" In *Global Chinese Pentecostal and Charismatic Christianity*, edited by Fenggang Yang, Joy K. C. Tong, and Allan H. Anderson, 159–180. Leiden: Brill, 2017.

Huang Dianchi 黄殿墀, ed. *Mingcheng minzu zongjiao zhi* 明城民族宗教志. Mingcheng: Mingcheng shi minzu zongjiao shiwuju 明城市民族宗教事务局, 1991.

Huang Feijun 黄飞君. "Zongjiao jingji lilun de xiandu—yi Zhongguo Taiwan diqu zongjiao shijian weili" 宗教经济理论的限度—以中国台湾地区宗教实践为例. *Shijie zongjiao wenhua* 世界宗教文化, 2013.1: 22–28.

Huang Haibo 黄海波. "Zhongguo jingyan yu bentu lilun: jinnian lai zhongguo zongjiao shehuixue lilun redian" 中国经验与本土理论：近年来中国宗教社会学理论热点. *Zongjiao shehuixue* 宗教社会学 2017.5: 3–21.

Huang Jianbo 黄剑波. *Dushili de xiangcun jiaohui—Zhongguo chengshihua yu mingong jidujiao* 都市里的乡村教会—中国城市化与民工基督教. Hong Kong: Logos and Pneuma Press, 2012.

Huang Jianbo 黄剑波. "Ershinian lai zhongguo dalu jidujiao de jingyan yanjiu shuping" 二十年来中国大陆基督教的经验研究述评. In *Jidujiao sixiang pinglun (di jiu juan)* 基督教思想评论（第9辑）. edited by Xu Zhiwei 许志伟, 345–366. Shanghai: Shanghai Shiji Publishing Corp., 2009.

Huang Jianbo 黄剑波. "Zhongguo chengzhen mingong de zongjiao shenghuo" 中国城镇民工的宗教生活. *Ershiyi shiji* 二十一世纪. no. 109 (2008): 104–110.

Huang, Jianbo, and Mengyin Hu. "Trends and Reflections: A Review of Empirical Studies of Christianity in Mainland China." *Review of Religion and Chinese Society* 6.1 (2019): 45–70.

Huang Jingchun 黄景春. "Sanshi nianlai caishen xinyang jiqi yanjiu zhuangkuang gaishu" 30年来财神信仰及其研究状况概述. *Changjiang daxue xuebao (shehui kexue ban)* 长江大学学报（社会科学版）. 2008.6: 12–16.

Huang Jingchun 黄景春. "Shanghai jie caishen xisu de lishi yu xianzhuang yanjiu" 上海接财神习俗的历史与现状研究. *Minsu yanjiu* 民俗研究. 2010.3: 134–145.

Huang Yilong 黄一龙. *Liangtou She: Mingmo Qingchu diyidai tianzhujiaotu* 两头蛇：明末清初第一代天主教徒. Shanghai: Shanghai guji chubanshe, 2006.

Huang, Ke-hsien. "Dyadic Nexus Fighting Two-Front Battles: A Study of the Microlevel Process of the Official-Religion-State Relationship in China." *Journal for the Scientific Study of Religion* 53.4 (2014): 706–721.

Huang, Ke-hsien. "Sect-to-Church Movement in Globalization: Transforming Pentecostalism and Coastal Intermediaries in Contemporary China." *Journal for the Scientific Study of Religion* 55.2 (2016): 407–416.

Huaren jidujiaoshi renwu cidian 华人基督教史人物词典. http://bdcconline.net/zh-hans/stories/jia-yuming.

Hunter, Alan, and Kim-Kwong Chan. *Protestantism in Contemporary China*. Cambridge: Cambridge University Press, 1993.

Iannaccone, Laurence R. "The Consequences of Religious Market Structure: Adam Smith and the Economics of Religion." *Rationality and Society* 3 (1991): 156–176.

Ji Zhe 汲喆. "Ruhe chaoyue shisuhua lilun?—ping zongjiao shehuixue de sanzhong houshisuhua lunshu" 如何超越经典世俗化理论?—评宗教社会学的三种后世俗化论述. *Shehuixue yanjiu* 社会学研究. 2008.4: 55–75.

Jia Wei 贾薇 et al. "Fumin Xiaoshuijing jiangban qian? Shiren danyou miaozu 'tianlai zhisheng' congci yakou" 富民小水井村将搬迁？世人担忧苗族"天籁之声"从此哑口. *Kunming Daily* 昆明日报. March 23, 2009.

Jiangsu sheng shehui kexueyuan ketizu 江苏省社会科学院课题组. "Jiangsu sheng nongcun zongjiao zhuangkuang ji duice yanjiu" 江苏省农村宗教状况及对策研究. *Jiangsu sheng shehuizhuyi xueyuan xuebao* 江苏省社会主义学院学报. 2003.3: 7–10.

Jiayang Pingcuo 加央平措. "Guandi xinyang yu gesaer chongbai—yi Lasa pamari gesaer lakang wei zhongxin de taolun" 关帝信仰与格萨尔崇拜—以拉萨帕玛日格萨尔拉康为中心的讨论. *Zhongguo shehui kexue* 中国社会科学. 2010.2: 200–291.

Jing, Jun. *The Temple of Memories: History, Power and Morality in a Chinese Village*. Stanford, CA: Stanford University Press, 1996. Translated by Wu Fei 吴飞 as *Shentang jiyi: yige Zhongguo xiangcun de lishi, quanli yu daode* 神堂记忆：一个中国乡村的历史、权力与道德. Fuzhou: Fujian jiaoyu chubanshe, 2013.

Johnson, Benton. "On Church and Sect." *American Sociological Review* 28 (1963): 539–549.

Johnson, Ian. Review of *Religion in China: Survival and Revival under Communist Rule*, by Fenggang Yang. *New York Review of Books* 58.20 (2011): 55–58.

Johnstone, Ronald. *Religion in Society: A Sociology of Religion*. 8th ed. Abingdon, UK: Routledge, 2016. Translated by Yuan Yayu 袁亚愚 and Zhong Yuying 钟玉英 as *Shehui zhong de zongjiao–yizhong zongjiao shehuixue* 社会中的宗教——一种宗教社会学. Chengdu: Sichuan renmin chubanshe, 2012.

"Juan shouyu: Ping 'zongjiao shichang'" 卷首语：评'宗教市场论.' *Kexue yu wushenlun* 科学与无神论. 2011.2: 1.

Kang, Jie. *House Church Christianity in China: From Rural Preachers to City Pastors*. Cham, Switzerland: Palgrave, 2016.

Kindopp, Jason. "Fragmented Yet Defiant: Protestant Resilience under Chinese Communist Party Rule." In *God and Caesar in China*, edited by Jason Kindopp and Carol Lee Hamrin, 122–145. Washington, DC: Brookings Institution Press, 2004.

Kindopp, Jason, and Carol Lee Hamrin. *God and Caesar in China: Policy Implications of Church-State Tensions*. Washington, DC: Brookings Institution Press, 2004.

Kipnis, Andrew. "*Suzhi*: A Keyword Approach." *China Quarterly* 186 (2006): 295–313.

Koesel, Karrie J. *Religion and Authoritarianism: Cooperation, Conflict, and the Consequences*. New York: Cambridge University Press, 2014.

Kong Jianhua 孔建华. "Beijingshi Songzhuang yuanchuang yishu jijuqu fazhan zai yanjiu" 北京宋庄原创艺术集聚区发展再研究. *Beijing shehui kexue* 北京社会科学. 2007.3: 21–26.

Kornai, János. *Economics of Shortage*. Amsterdam: North-Holland, 1980.

Kornai, János. *The Socialist System: The Political Economy of Communism*. Oxford: Oxford University Press, 1992.

Kuang Wenbo 匡文波. "Zhongguo weixin fazhan de lianghua yanjiu" 中国微信发展的量化研究. *Guoji xinwenjie* 国际新闻界. 2014.5: 147–156.

Kung, Lap-Yan. "The Emergence of Exchange Politics in China and Its Implications for Church-State Relations." *Religion, State and Society* 38.1 (2010): 9–28.

Lagerwey, John. "Du caractère rationnel de la religion locale en Chine," *Bulletin de l'École française d'Extrême-Orient* 87.1 (2000): 301–315. Translated by Fan Lizhu 范丽珠 as "Zhongguo zongjiao dehe lixing" 中国宗教的合理性. In *Faguo hanxue (di 4 ji)* 法国汉学（第4辑）, 338–354. Beijing: Zhonghua shuju, 1999.

Lambert, Tony. *China's Christian Millions*. Oxford: Monarch, 2006.

Lambert, Tony. *The Resurrection of the Chinese Church*. Wheaton, IL: Harold Shaw, 1994.

Lang, Graeme, Chan Selina Ching, and Ragvald Lars. "Temples and the Religious Economy." *Interdisciplinary Journal of Research on Religion* 1 (2005): 1–27.

Leung, Beatrice. "China's Religious Freedom Policy: The Art of Managing Religious Activity." *China Quarterly* 184 (2005): 894–913.

Leung Ka-lun 梁家麟. *Gaige kaifang yilai de Zhongguo nongcun jiaohui* 改革开放以来的中国农村教会. Hong Kong: The Alliance Bible Seminary, 1999.

Li Feng 李峰. "Huidao shehui: dui dangqian zongjiao shehuixue yanjiu fanshi zhi fansi" 回到社会：对当前宗教社会学研究范式之反思, *Jianghai xuekan* 江海学刊. 2013.5: 95–100.

Li Feng 李峰. *Xiangcun jidujiao de zuzhi texing ji shehui jiegou xing weizhi—Huanan Y xian X zhen jidujiao jiaohui zuzhi yanjiu* 乡村基督教的组织特征及其社会结构性位秩—华南Y县X镇基督教教会组织研究. Shanghai: Fudan daxue chubanshe, 2005.

Li Feng 李峰. "Zongjiao xinyang yingxiang shengyu yiyuan ma? Jiyu CGSS2010 nian shuju de fenxi" 宗教信仰影响生育意愿吗？基于 CGSS2010 年数据的分析. *Shijie zongjiao yanjiu* 世界宗教研究. 2017.3: 18–34.

Li Huawei 李华伟. *Xiangcun jidutu yu rujia lunli—yuxi licun jiaohui gean yanjiu* 乡村基督徒与儒家伦理—豫西李村教会个案研究. Beijing: Shehui kexue wenxian chubanshe, 2013.

Li Huawei 李华伟. "Zongjiao shehuixue zai zhongguo dalu de fazhan lichen" 宗教社会学在中国大陆的发展历程. In *Zhongguo shehui kexueyuan shijie zongjiao yanjiusuo wushinian fazhan lichen*. 1964–2014, 中国社会科学院世界宗教研究所五十年发展历程 1964–2014, edited by Institute of World Religions, Chinese Academy of Social Sciences, 61–74. Beijing: China Social Sciences Press, 2014.

Li Qiang 李强, ed. *Zhongguo shehui bianqian sanshi nian* 中国社会变迁 30年. Beijing: Social Sciences Academic Press, 2008.

Li Xiangping 李向平. "Gongmin jidutu yu jidujiao de Zhongguohua wenti" 公民基督徒与基督教的中国化问题. *Wenhua zongheng* 文化纵横. 2014.8: 108 109.

Li Xiangping. "'Zongjiao shengtai' haishi 'quanli shengtai'—Cong dangdai Zhongguo de 'zongjiao shengtai lun' sichao tanqi" 宗教生态'还是'权力生态'—从当代中国的'宗教生态论'思潮谈起. *Shanghai daxue xuebao (shehui kexue ban)* 上海大学学报（社会科学版）. 2011.1: 124–140.

Li Xiangping 李向平 and Chen Bin 陈彬. "Xiangqianxing de gonggong zongjiao—chuantong Zhongguo de zhengjiao guanxi zhi shehuixue jiedu" 镶嵌型的公共宗教—传统中国的政教关系之社会学解读. *Shanghai daxue xuebao (shehui kexue ban)* 上海大学学报（社会科学版）. 2006.4: 83–89.

Li Xiangping 李向平 and Li Siming 李思明. "Xinyang yu minjian quanwei de jiangou—minjian xinyang yishi zhuanjia yanjiu zongshu" 信仰与民间权威的建构—民间信仰仪式专家研究综述. *Shijie zongjiao wenhua* 世界宗教文化. 2012.3: 110–119.

Li Xiangping 李向平 and Yang Linxia 杨林霞. "Zongjiao, shehui yu quanli guanxi—'zongjiao shichang lun' de shehuixue jiedu" 宗教、社会与权力关系—"宗教市场论"的社会学解读. *Huadong shifan daxue xuebao (zhexue shehui kexue ban)* 华东师范大学学报（哲学社会科学版）. 43.5 (2011): 1–7.

Li Xiaoguang 李小光. "Daojiao yu minjian caishen xinyang wenhua beijing zhi bijiao" 道教与民间财神信仰文化背景之比较. *Zongjiaoxue yanjiu* 宗教学研究. 1997.4: 117–120.

Lian, Xi. *Redeemed by Fire: The Rise of Popular Christianity in Modern China*. New Haven: Yale University Press, 2010.

Liang Jingwen 梁景文, Chen Qian 陈蒨, Luo Si 罗斯, and Chen Ruigang 陈锐钢. "Minjian simiao yu Zhongguo zongjiao jingji—dui zongjiao jingyi lilun de tantao" 民间寺庙与中国宗教经济—对宗教经济理论的探讨. *Shijie zongjiao wenhua* 世界宗教文化. 2010.2: 21–26.

Liang Yongjia 梁永佳. "'Diexie' de xiandu—yige Dali jieqing de difang yiyi yu feiyihua" "叠写"的限度—一个大理节庆的地方意义与非遗化. In *Zongjiao renleixue (disi ji)* 宗教人类学（第四辑）. edited by Jin Ze 金泽 and Chen Jinguo 陈进国, 127–143. Beijing: Shehui kexue wenxian chubanshe, 2013.

Liang Yongjia 梁永佳. "Zhongguo nongcun zongjiao fuxing yu 'zongjiao' de Zhongguo mingyun" 中国农村宗教复兴与"宗教"的中国命运. *Shehui* 社会 .35.1 (2015): 161–183.

Liang Zhongtang 梁中堂. *Zhongguo jihua shengyu zhengce shilun* 中国计划生育政策史论. Beijing: Zhongguo fazhan chubanshe, 2014.

Liebow, Elliot. *Tally's Corner*. Boston: Little Brown, 1967.

Lin Jinglu 林京路. "Zhongguo Songzhuang huajiacun diaoyan yu fazhan baogao" 中国宋庄画家村调研与发展报告. *Wenyi lilun yu piping* 文艺理论与批评, 2013.3: 71–75.

Lin Qiaowei 林巧薇. "Yang Fenggang boshi tan zongjiao shehuixue de fanshi zhuanxing" 杨凤岗博士谈宗教社会学的范式转型. *Zongjiaoxue yanjiu* 宗教学研究, 2003.3: 140–141.

Liu, Eric Yang. Review of *Religion in China: Survival and Revival under Communist Rule*, by Fenggang Yang. *Sociological Forum* 28.2 (2013): 419–422.

Liu, Jifeng, and Chris White. "Old Pastor and Local Bureaucrats: Recasting Church-State Relations in Contemporary China." *Modern China* 45.5 (2019): 564–590.

Liu Shiding 刘世定. "Jingjixue de jingji shehuixue?" 经济学的经济社会学? Paper presented at Beijing University, 2014.

Liu Yanwu 刘燕舞. "Mentuhui zai Hunan de chuanbo" 门徒会在湖南的传播. *Zhanlüe yu guanli* 战略与管理. 2009.8: 20–28.

Liu Yi. "Pentecostal-Style Christians in the 'Galilee of China.'" *Review of Religion and Chinese Society* 2 (2014): 156–172.

Liu Zhengfeng 刘正峰. "Lun yadang simi de zongjiao shichang lilun—jianlun zongjiao guanzhi de jingji jichu" 论亚当·斯密的宗教市场理论—兼论宗教管制的经济基础. *Shijie zongjiao yanjiu* 世界宗教研究. 2012.5: 1–7.

Long Wende 龙文德. "Yuanfang piao lai de caiyun" 远方飘来的彩云. *Zhongguo zongjiao* 中国宗教. 2008.3: 56–57.

Lu Wei 吕微. *Yinyu shijie de laifangzhe: Zhongguo minjian caishen xinyang* 隐喻世界的来访者：中国民间财神信仰. Beijing: Xueyuan chubanshe, 2001.

Lu Yao 路遥 et al. *Zhongguo minjian xinyang yanjiu shuping* 中国民间信仰研究述评. Shanghai: Shanghai renmin chubanshe, 2012.

Lu, Yunfeng. *The Transformation of Yiguan Dao in Taiwan: Adapting to a Changing Religious Economy*. Plymouth, UK: Lexington Books, 2008.

Lu Yunfeng 卢云峰. "Chaoyue jiduzongjiao shehuixue—jianlun zongjiao shichang lilun zai huaren shehui de shiyongxing wenti" 超越基督宗教社会学—兼论宗教市场理论在华人社会的适用性问题. *Shehuixue yanjiu* 社会学研究. 2008.5: 81–97.

Lu Yunfeng 卢云峰. "Kunan yu zongjiao zengzhang: guanzhi de feiyuqi houguo" 苦难与宗教增长：管制的非预期后果. *Shehui* 社会. 2010.4: 200–216.

Lu Yunfeng 卢云峰. "Weihe shi 'zongjiao meiguo, shisu ouzhou'?" 为何是'宗教美国, 世俗欧洲'? *Dushu* 读书. 2016.3: 150–159.

Madsen, Richard. *China's Catholics: Tragedy and Hope in an Emerging Civil Society*. Berkeley: University of California Press, 1998.

Madsen, Richard. Review of *Religion in China: Survival and Revival under Communist Rule*, by Fenggang Yang. *Journal of Asian Studies* 71.4 (2012): 1126–1127.

Madsen, Richard. "The Upsurge of Religion in China." *Journal of Democracy* 21.4 (2010): 58–71.

Mansfield, Katie. "China Launches 'Religious Winter' in Bid to Destroy Christianity in Fierce Crackdown." Express.com.uk. Sept 30, 2017. http://www.express.co.uk/news/world/715834/China-Christians-launches-religious-winter-bid-destroy-Christianity (accessed August 20, 2019).

Marsh, Christopher. *Religion and the State in Russia and China: Suppression, Survival, and Revival*. New York: Continuum, 2011.

McLeister, Mark. "A Three-Self Protestant Church, the Local State and Religious Policy Implementation in a Coastal Chinese City." In *Christianity in Contemporary China: Socio-Cultural Perspectives*, edited by Francis Khek Gee Lim, 234–246. London: Routledge, 2013.

McQuillan, Kevin. "When Does Religion Influence Fertility?" *Population and Development Review* 30.1 (2004): 25–56.

Mingcheng difangzhi bianzuan weiyuanhui 明城地方志编纂委员会, ed. *Mingcheng shizhi* 明城市志. Beijing: Zhonghua shuju, 1994.

Mitchell, Timothy. "Society, Economy, and the State Effect." In *The Anthropology of the State: A Reader*, edited by Aradhana Sharma and Akhil Gupta, 169–180. Oxford: Blackwell, 2006.

Monsen, Marie. *The Awakening: Revival in China, a Work of the Holy Spirit*. Translated by Joy Guinness. London: China Inland Mission, 1961.

Morgan, S. P. "Is Low Fertility a Twenty-First-Century Demographic Crisis?" *Demography* 40.4 (2003): 589–603.

Mou Zhongjian. "Zongjiao shengtai lun" 宗教生态论. *Shijie zongjiao wenhua* 世界宗教文化. 2012.1: 1–10.

Nichols, Brian J. Review of *Religion in China: Survival and Revival under Communist Rule*, by Fenggang Yang. *Religious Studies Review* 39.3 (2013): 198.

Overmyer, Daniel. *Folk Buddhist Religion: Dissenting Sects in Late Traditional China*. Cambridge, MA: Harvard University Press, 1976. Translated by Liu Xinyong 刘心勇 et al. as *Zhongguo minjian zongjiao jiaopai yanjiu* 中国民间宗教教派研究. Shanghai: Shanghai guji chubanshe, 1993.

Parsons, Talcott. *The Social System*. Abingdon, UK: Routledge, 1991.

Pew Research Center. *The Future of World Religions: Population Growth Projections, 2010–2050*. April 2, 2015. https://www.pewforum.org/2015/04/02/religious-projections-2010-2050/.

Philips, Tom. "China on Course to Become the 'World's Most Christian Nation' within 15 Years." *The Telegraph*, April 19, 2014. https://www.telegraph.co.uk/news/worldnews/asia/china/10776023/China-on-course-to-become-worlds-most-Christian-nation-within-15-years.html (accessed August 20, 2019).

Potter, Pitman B. "Belief in Control: Regulation of Religion in China." *China Quarterly* 174 (2003): 317–337.

Putnam, Robert. *Making Democracy Work: Civic Tradition in Modern Italy*. Princeton: Princeton University Press, 1993.

Qian Ning 钱宁, ed. *Jidujiao yu shaoshu minzu shehui wenhua bianqian* 基督教与少数民族社会文化变迁. Kunming: Yunnan daixue chubanshe, 1998.

Qin Heping 秦和平. *Jiduzongjiao zai xinan minzu diqu de chuanbo shi* 基督宗教在西南民族地区的传播史. Chengdu: Sichuan minzu chubanshe, 2004.

Qiao Long 乔龙. "Reyi kasiteluo zhi si duibi xianxing tizhi duoge zhongguo weixin qun zao guanbi," 热议卡斯特罗之死对比现行体制 多个中国微信群遭关闭. *Radio Free Asia*, November 29, 2016. http://www.rfa.org/mandarin/yataibaodao/meiti/ql1-11292016104848.html (accessed August 20, 2019).

Qiu Yue 秋月. "Zongjiao shichang, dui shei kaifang?" 宗教市场，对谁开放? *Kexue yu wushenlun* 科学与无神论. 2011.2: 14–18.

Qu, Hong. "Religious Policy in the People's Republic of China: An Alternative Perspective." *Journal of Contemporary China* 20.70 (2011): 433–448.

Qu Jingdong 渠敬东, Lu Yunfeng 卢云峰, Liang Yongjia 梁永佳 et al. "You guan 'zongjiao shichang lilun' de yici yuanzhuo taolun" 有关'宗教市场理论'的一次圆桌讨论. *Zhongguo yanjiu* 中国研究 19.1 (2014): 208–227.

Ren Weidong 任维东. "Hongdong shengcheng de miaozu shanmin hechangtuan" 轰动省城的苗族山民合唱团. *Guangming ribao* 光明日报. September 20, 2005.

Reny, Mari-Eve. *Authoritarian Containment: Public Security Bureaus and Protestant House Churches in Urban China*. New York: Oxford University Press, 2018.

Robbins, Thomas, Dick Anthony, and James Richardson. "Theory and Research on Today's 'New Religions.'" *Sociological Analysis* 39.2 (1978): 95–122.

Robertson, Roland. "The Economization of Religion? Reflections on the Promise and Limitations of the Economic Approach." *Social Compass* 39 (1992): 147–157.

Ruan Rongping 阮荣平, Zheng Fengtian 郑风田, and Liu Li 刘力. "Zongjiao xinyang xuanze—yige xifang zongjiao jingjixue de wenxian shuli" 宗教信仰选择——一个西方宗教经济学的文献梳理. *Shehui* 社会. 2013.4: 193–224.

Russell, Jeffrey Burton, and Douglas W. Lumsden. *A History of Medieval Christianity: Prophecy and Order*. New York: Peter Lang, 2000.

Said, Edward W. *Orientalism*. New York: Vintage Books, 1979.

Schein, Louisa. "Gender and Internal Orientalism in China." *Modern China* 23 (1997): 69–98.

Schein, Louisa. *Minority Rules: The Miao and the Feminine in China's Cultural Politics*. Durham, NC: Duke University Press, 2000.

Shahar, Meir, and Robert Weller. *Unruly Gods: Divinity and Society in China*. Honolulu: University of Hawaii Press, 1996.

Sharot, Stephen. "Beyond Christianity: A Critique of the Rational Choice Theory of Religion from a Weberian and Comparative Religions Perspective." *Sociology of Religion* 63.4 (2002): 427–454.

Shen Zhang 沈璋. "Ye tan 'zongjiao shichanglun' jiqi zai zhongguo dalu 'zongjiao wenhua' zhong de maidian" 也谈'宗教市场论'及其在中国大陆'宗教文化'中的卖点. *Kexue yu wushenlun* 科学与无神论. 2011.3: 5–13.

Smith, Adam. *An Inquiry into the Nature and Causes of the Wealth of Nations*. Edited by Edwin Cannan. London: Methuen, 1904. Repr., Chicago: University of Chicago Press, 1977. Translated by Guo Dali 郭大力 and Wang Yanan 王亚楠 as *Guomin caifu de xingzhi he yuanyi de yanjiu* 国民财富的形制和原因的研究. Beijing: The Commercial Press, 1997.

Smith, Christian. *American Evangelicalism: Embattled and Thriving*. Chicago: University of Chicago Press, 1998.

Spickard, James V. Review of *Religion in China: Survival and Revival under Communist Rule*, by Fenggang Yang. *Journal of Contemporary Religion* 29.1 (2014): 162–164.

Stark, Rodney. "From Church-Sect to Religious Economies." In *The Sacred in a Post-Secular Age*, edited by Phillip E. Hammond, 139–149. Berkeley: University of California Press, 1985.

Stark, Rodney. *The Rise of Christianity: A Sociologist Reconsiders History*. Princeton: Princeton University Press, 1996. Translated by Huang Jianbo 黄剑波 and Gao Mingui 高民贵 as *Jidujiao de xingqi: yige shehuixuejia dui lishi de zaisi* 基督教的兴起：一个社会学家对历史的再思. Shanghai: Shanghai guji chubanshe, 2005.

Stark, Rodney. *The Triumph of Christianity: How the Jesus Movement Became the World's Largest Religion*. New York: HarperOne, 2011.

Stark, Rodney, and William Sims Bainbridge. *The Future of Religion: Secularization, Revival, and Cult Formation.* Berkeley: University of California Press, 1985. Translated by Gao Shining 高师宁, Zhang Xiaomei 张晓梅, and Liu Dianli 刘殿利 as *Zongjiao de weilai* 宗教的未来. Beijing: Renmin University of China, 2006.

Stark, Rodney, and Roger Finke. *Acts of Faith: Explaining the Human Side of Religion.* Berkeley: University of California Press, 2000. Translated by Yang Fenggang 杨凤岗 as *Xinyang de faze—jieshi zongjiao zhi ren de fangmian* 信仰的法则—解释宗教之人的方面. Beijing: Zhongguo renmin daxue chubanshe, 2004.

Stark, Rodney, and Laurence R. Iannaccone. "A Supply-Side Reinterpretation of the 'Secularization' of Europe." *Journal for the Scientific Study of Religion* 33.3 (1994): 230–252.

State Council of PRC 中华人民共和国国务院. "The Revised Regulations on Religious Affairs" 宗教事务条例. August 26, 2017. http://www.gov.cn/zhengce/content/2017-09/07/content_5223282.htm (accessed August 20, 2019).

Sun Mingyi 孙明义. "Renshi Zhongguo chengshi jiating jiaohui" 认识中国城市家庭教会. *Jumu* 举目 (*Behold*), no. 26 (2007): 12–17.

Tang, Edmond, and Jean-Paul Wiest, eds. *The Catholic Church in Modern China.* New York: Orbis, 1993.

Tang Xiaofeng 唐晓峰. *Gaige kaifang yilai de Zhongguo jidujiao ji yanjiu* 改革开放以来的中国基督教及研究. Beijing: Zongjiao wenhua chubanshe, 2013.

Tapp, Nicholas. "In Defence of the Archaic: A Reconsideration of the 1950s Ethnic Classification Project in China." *Asian Ethnicity* 3.1 (2002): 63–84.

Taylor, Charles. *Modern Social Imaginaries.* Durham, NC: Duke University Press, 2003. Translated by Lin Manhong 林曼红 as *Xiandai shehui xiangxiang* 现代社会想象. Shanghai: Yilin chubanshe, 2014.

Tencent Research Institute. "The 2015 Annual Report on the Economic and Social Influence of WeChat" 2015 年微信社会经济影响力研究报. March 2016. http://www.199it.com/archives/452179.html (accessed August 20, 2019).

Tönnies, Ferdinand. *Community and Civil Society.* Edited by Jose Harris. Translated by Margaret Hollis. Cambridge: Cambridge University Press, 2001.

Turner, Bryan S. Review of *Religion in China: Survival and Revival under Communist Rule*, by Fenggang Yang. *European Journal of Sociology / Archives Européennes de Sociologie / Europäisches Archiv für Soziologie* 53.3 (2012): 338–342.

Vala, Carsten T. *The Politics of Protestant Churches and the Party-State in China: God above Party?* Abingdon, Oxon: Routledge, 2018.

Vala, Carsten T. Review of *Religion in China: Survival and Revival under Communist Rule*, by Fenggang Yang. *Social Forces* 93.2 (2014): e54.

Wang Guangzhou 王广州. "Zhongguo laonianren qinzi shuliang yu jiegou jisuanji fangzhen fenxi" 中国老年人亲子数量与结构计算机仿真分析. *Zhongguo renkou kexue* 中国人口科学 34.3 (2014): 2–16.

Wang Xiaobo and Gu Xiaotong. "The Communication Design of WeChat: Ideological as Well as Technical Aspects of Social Media." *Communication Design Quarterly Review* 4.1 (2016): 23–35.

Wang Yi 王怡. "Jidutu shi yige quntixing shijian" 基督徒是一个群体性事件. *Xinghua* 杏花 (Fall 2010): 80–88.

Wang Ying 王莹. *Shenfen jiangou yu wenhua ronghe—zhongyuan diqu jidujiaohui gean yanjiu* 身份建构与文化融合—中原地区基督教会个案研究. Shanghai: Shanghai renmin chubanshe, 2011.

Wang, Yuting, and Fenggang Yang. "More Than Evangelical and Ethnic: The Ecological Factor in Chinese Conversion to Christianity in the United States." *Sociology of Religion* 67.2 (2006): 179–192.

Warner, R. Stephen. "Work in Progress toward a New Paradigm for the Sociological Study of Religion in the United States." *American Journal of Sociology* 98.5 (1993): 1044–1095.

Warner, R. Stephen, and Judith G. Wittner, eds. *Gatherings in Diaspora: Religious Communities and the New Immigration*. Philadelphia: Temple University Press, 1998.

Weber, Max. *Sociology of Religion*. Translated by Ephraim Fischoff. Boston: Beacon Press, 1963. Translated by Kang Le 康乐 as *Zongjiao shehuixue* 宗教社会学. Guilin: Guangxi shifan daxue chubanshe, 2011.

Weber, Peter. "China Has an Amazing Smartphone Super-app. You May Not Want the West to Replicate It." *The Week*, August 10, 2016. http://theweek.com/speedreads/642014/china-amazing-smartphone-superapp-may-not-want-west-replicate (accessed August 20, 2019).

Wei Dedong 魏德东. "Zongjiao shehuixue de fanshi zhuanhuan jiqi yingxiang" 宗教社会学的范式转换及其影响. *Renmin daxue xuebao* 人民大学学报, 2010.3: 61–69.

Wei Dedong 魏德东 and Liu Yang 刘洋. "Zongjiao yanjiu de renti lilun: Fang zongjiao shehuixuejia luodeni sidake" 宗教研究的人本理论：访宗教社会学家罗德尼·斯达克. *Zhongguo minzubao* 中国民族报, October 7, 2008.

Wenger, Jacqueline. "Official vs. Underground Protestant Churches in China: Challenges for Reconciliation and Social Influence." *Review of Religious Research* 46.2 (2004): 169–182.

White, Chris. "The Haicang Voice: Modernity, Cultural Continuity, and the Spirit World in a 1920s Church." In *Protestantism in Xiamen, Then and Now*, edited by Chris White, 103–139. London: Palgrave, 2019.

Whyte, Martin King. Review of *Religion in China: Survival and Revival under Communist Rule*, by Fenggang Yang. *American Journal of Sociology* 118.1 (2012): 240–242.

Wielander, Gerda. "Protestant and Online: The Case of Aiyan." *China Quarterly* 197 (2009): 165–182.

Woo, Franklin J. Review of *Religion in China: Survival and Revival under Communist Rule*, by Fenggang Yang. *China Review International* 18.4 (2011): 549–554.

Wu Changqing 吴长青. "Cong 'celüe' dao 'lunli' dui 'yifa kangzheng' de pipingxing taolun" 从"策略"到"伦理"对"依法抗争"的批评性讨论. *Shehui* 社会, 2010.2: 198–214.

Wuthnow, Robert. "New Directions in the Study of Religion and Economic Life." In *The Handbook of Economic Sociology*, 2nd ed., edited by Neil Smelser and Richard Swedberg, 603–626. Princeton: Princeton University Press, 2010. Translated by Luo Jiaojiang 罗教讲 and Zhang Yonghong 张永宏 as "Zongjiao yu jingji shenghuo yanjiu de xin fangxiang" 宗教与经济生活研究的新方向, in *Jingji shehuixue shouce* 经济社会学手册. 674–700. Beijing: Huaxia chubanshe, 2009.

Xiao Hong 肖虹. "Ruhe zhengque kandai Zhongguo de zongjiao zhengce" 如何正确看待中国的宗教政策. *Zhongguo zongjiao* 中国宗教. 2004.5: 57–59.

Xie Xiaheng. "Religion and Modernity in China: Who Is Joining the Three-Self Church and Why." *Journal of Church and State* 52.1 (2010): 74–93.

Yan Ling 严玲. "Weixin: meijiahua shengcun de xin wuzhong" 微信：媒介化生存的新物种. *Xiandai chuanbo* 现代传播. 2016.2: 140–143.

Yang, C. K. (杨庆堃). *Religion in Chinese Society: A Study of Contemporary Social Functions of Religion and Some of Their Historical Factors*. Berkeley: University of California Press, 1961. Translated by Fan Lizhu 范丽珠 as *Zhongguo shehui zhong de zongjiao* 中国社会中的宗教. Shanghai: Shanghai renmin chubanshe, 2007.

Yang, Fenggang. *Atlas of Religion in China: Social and Geographical Contexts*. Leiden: Brill Academic Publishers, 2018.

Yang, Fenggang. "Between Secularist Ideology and Desecularizing Reality: The Birth and Growth of Religious Research in Communist China." *Sociology of Religion* 65.2 (2004): 101–119.

Yang, Fenggang. "The Definition of Religion for the Social Scientific Study of Religion in China and Beyond." In *Concepts and Methods for the Study of Chinese Religions I: State of the Field and Disciplinary Approaches*, edited by André Laliberté and Stefania Travagnin, 23–44. Berlin: De Gruyter, 2019.

Yang, Fenggang. "Exceptionalism or Chinamerica: Measuring Religious Change in the Globalizing World Today." *Journal for the Scientific Study of Religion* 55.1 (2016): 7–22.

Yang, Fenggang. "The Failure of the Campaign to Demolish Church Crosses in Zhejiang Province, 2013–2016." *Review of Religion and Chinese Society* 5.1 (2018): 5–25.

Yang Fenggang 杨凤岗. "The Final Version and Draft Version of the 'Religious Affairs Regulations'" 《宗教事务条例》颁布版和送审稿文本对照. CareerEngine, September 10, 2017. https://posts.careerengine.us/p/59b4a5e5a6a1de190ea0368e (accessed August 20, 2019).

Yang, Fenggang. "Oligopoly Dynamics: Consequences of Religious Regulation." *Social Compass* 57.2 (2010): 194–205.

Yang, Fenggang. "The Red, Black, and Gray Markets of Religion in China." *Sociological Quarterly* 47.1 (2006): 93–122. Translated and abridged by Yang Fenggang 杨凤岗 as "Zhongguo zongjiao de sanse shichang" 中国宗教的三色市场, *Zhongguo renmin daxue xuebao (shehui kexue ban)* 中国人民大学学报（社会科学版）, 2006.6: 41–47. Also translated by Yang Jianghua 杨江华 as "Zhongguo zongjiao de sanse shichang" 中国宗教的三色市场, *Zhongguo nongye daxue xuebao (shehui kexue ban)* 中国农业大学学报（社会科学版）, 2008.4: 93–112.

Yang, Fenggang. *Religion in China: Survival and Revival under Communist Rule.* New York: Oxford University Press, 2012. Korean edition: 중국의 종교: 공산 통치하에서의 생존과 부흥. Translated by Song Jae-ryong and Yoo Kwang-suk. Seoul: Dasan Publishing Co., 2017. Italian edition: *La religione nella Cina comunista: Dalla sopravvivenza al risveglio.* Translated by Emanuela Claudia Del Re. Milan: Franco Angeli, 2020. Chinese edition: 宗教在中國：黨治下的存活與復興. Forthcoming.

Yang, Fenggang. "Religion in China under Communism: A Shortage Economy Explanation." *Journal of Church and State* 51.1 (2010): 3–33.

Yang, Fenggang. "Sinicization or Chinafication? Cultural Assimilation vs. Political Domestication of Christianity in China and Beyond." In *The Sinicization of Chinese Religions: From Above and Below*, edited by Richard Madsen. Leiden: Brill, forthcoming.

Yang, Fenggang. "Studying Religions in Time and Space." *Asian Journal of Religion and Society* 4.2 (2016): 19–35.

Yang, Fenggang. "What about China? Religious Vitality in the Most Secular and Rapidly Modernizing Society." *Sociology of Religion* 75.4 (2014): 564–578.

Yang Fenggang 杨凤岗 "Zongjiao meiguo, shisu ouzhou de zhuti yu bianzou" 宗教美国、世俗欧洲的主题与变奏. *Dushu* 读书. 2016.4: 159–168.

Yang, Fenggang, and Anning Hu. "Mapping Chinese Folk Religion in Mainland China and Taiwan." *Journal of the Scientific Study of Religion* 51.3 (2012): 506–522.

Yang Juhua 杨菊华. "Yiyuan yu xingwei de beili: fada guojia shengyu yiyuan yu shengyu xingwei yanjiu shuping ji dui Zhongguo de qishi" 意愿与行为的背离：发达国家生育意愿与生育行为研究述评及对中国的启示. *Xuehai* 学海. 2008.1: 16–22.

Yang, Xiaozhao Y., and Fenggang Yang. "Estimating Religious Populations with the Network Scale-Up Method: A Practical Alternative to Self-Report." *Journal for the Scientific Study of Religion* 56.4 (2017): 703–719.

Yao Meixiong 姚美雄. "Ba quanmian guli shengyu dingwei xin jiben guoce henyou biyao" 把全面鼓励生育定为新基本国策很有必要. *China Reform (Zhongguo gaige luntan* 中国改革论坛). February 28, 2017.

Yao, Xinzhong. Review of *Religion in China: Survival and Revival under Communist Rule*, by Fenggang Yang. *Journal of Chinese Religions* 40 (2012): 155–157.

Yao Xiyi 姚西伊. *Wei zhendao zhengbian: zaihua jiduxinjiao chuanjiaoshi jiyaozhuyi yundong (1920–1937)* 为真道争辩：在华基督教新教传教士基要主义运动 (1920–1937). Hong Kong: China Alliance Press, 2008.

Ying Fuk-tsang 邢福增. *Dangdai Zhongguo zhengjiao guanxi* 当代中国政教关系. Hong Kong: The Alliance Bible Seminary, 1999. Repr., Hong Kong: China Alliance Press, 2005.

Ying, Fuk-tsang. "The Politics of Cross Demolition: A Religio-Political Analysis of the 'Three Rectifications and One Demolition' Campaign in Zhejiang Province." *Review of Religion and Chinese Society* 5.1 (2018): 43–75.

Ying Xing 应星. "Caogen dongyuan yu nongmin qunti liyi de biaoda jizhi—sige gean de bijiao yanjiu" 草根动员与农民群体利益的表达机制—四个个案的比较研究. *Shehuixue yanjiu* 社会学研究. 2007.2: 1–23.

Yu, Anthony C. Review of *Religion in China: Survival and Revival under Communist Rule*, by Fenggang Yang. *Journal of Church and State* 54.3 (2012): 459–462.

Yu, Anthony C. *State and Religion in China: Historical and Textual Perspectives*. Chicago: Open Court, 2005.

Yu Jianrong 于建嵘. "Dangdai Zhongguo nongmin de 'yifa kangzheng'—guanyu nongmin weiquan huodong de yige jieshi kuangjia" 当代中国农民的"以法抗争"——关于农民维权活动的一个解释框架. *Wenshi bolan (lilun)* 文史博览（理论）. 2008.12: 60–63.

Yu Jianrong 于建嵘. "Zhongguo jidujiao jiating jiaohui hefahua yanjiu" 中国基督教家庭教会合法化研究. *Zhanlüe yu guanli* 战略与管理, 2010.3–4. Featured on Aisixiang 爱思想. http://www.aisixiang.com/data/70584.html.

Yuan Hao 袁浩. "Tingbujian de shengyin: Guanyu Zhongguo jidujiao chengshi mingong jiaohui de yanjiu" 听不见的声音：关于中国基督教城市民工教会的研究. *Daofeng* 道风. no. 39 (2013): 337–353.

Yuan Hao 袁浩. "Zhongguo jidujiao yu bufucong de chuantong: yi Wang Mingdao, Tanghe jiaohui yu Shouwang jiaohui weili" 中国基督教与不服从的传统：以王明道、唐河教会与守望教会为例. *Daofeng* 道风. no. 44 (2016): 87–122.

Yunnan Chuxiong Prefecture Ethnic Affairs Commission 云南楚雄州民委. "Miaozu daxing yanchanghui zai Yunnan Chuxiong yanyi 'Xianghe zhiye'" 苗族大型演唱会在云南楚雄演绎"祥和之夜." August 4, 2005.

Zhan Zhongle 湛中乐. *Gongmin shengyu quan yu shehui fuyangfei zhidu yanjiu* 公民生育权与社会抚养费制度研究. Beijing: Falü chubanshe, 2011.

Zhang Hua 张华 and Xue Heng 薛恒. "Zai shehui zhuanxing zhong chuangxing zongjiao shiwu guanli Jiangsu xin nongcun jianshe zhong de zongjiao hexie guanxi yanjiu" 在社会转型中创新宗教事务管理 江苏新农村建设中的宗教和谐关系研究. *Zhongguo zongjiao* 中国宗教. 2013.8: 66–67.

Zhang Wenjie 张文杰. "Zhongguo zongjiao yanjiu de 'zhengzhi jingjixue' changshi: ping *Zhongguo de zongjiao*" 中国宗教研究的 "政治经济学" 尝试评《中国的宗教》. *Shehui* 社会 34.3 (2014): 205–229.

Zhang Yinan 张义南. *Zhongguo jiating jiaohui liushi nian* 中国家庭教会六十年. Hong Kong: Revival Chinese Ministries International (HK) Ltd., 2010.

Zhang Zhigang 张志刚. "Dangdai zhongguo zongjiao guanxi yanjiu chuyi" 当代中国宗教关系研究刍议. *Beijing daxue xuebao (zhexue shehui kexue ban)* 北京大学学报（哲学社会学版）48.2 (2011): 33–41.

Zhao Dianhua 赵殿桦. "Miaozhai feichu jinfenghuang—ji Fuminxian Xiaoshuijing miaozu nongmin hechangtuan" 苗寨飞出金凤凰—记富民县小水井村苗族农民合唱团. *Jinri minzu* 今日民族. 2008.5: 21–24.

Zhao Tianen (Jonathan Chao) 赵天恩 and Zhuang Wanfang (Rosanna Chong) 庄婉芳. *Dangdai zhongguo jidujiao fazhanshi* 当代中国基督教发展史. 1949–1997. Taipei: Zhongguo fuyin hui, 1997.

Zhao Yi 赵亿. "Cong weixin gongzhonghao kan chuantong meiti de xin fazhan: Yi *Yangzi wanbao* weixin gongzhonghao wei li" 从微信公众号看传统媒体的新发展——以《扬子晚报》微信公众号为例. *Chuanmei* 传媒. 2014.5: 36–39.

"Zhejiang Church Demolitions: Timeline of Events." CSW website, https://www.csw.org.uk/zhejiangtimeline (accessed August 20, 2019).

Zheng Xiaochun 郑晓春. *Zheng ye Henan, xie ye Henan?—tantao Henan heyi chengwei jidujiao ji "xiejiao" dasheng* 正也河南，邪也河南？—探讨河南何以成为基督教及"邪教"大省. Hong Kong: The Alliance Bible Seminary, 2006.

Zhong, Zhifeng. "Multiple Modernizations, Religious Regulations and Church Responses: The Rise and Fall of Three 'Jerusalems' in Communist China." Ph.D. diss., Baylor University, 2013.

Zhonghua quanguo funu lianhe hui 中华全国妇女联合会. *Shishi quanmian lianghai zhengce dui jiating jiaoyu de yingxiang* 实施全面两孩政策对家庭教育的影响. December 22, 2016.

Zhou Xueguang 周雪光. "Weiquan tizhi yu youxiao guanli: dangdai Zhongguo guojia zhili de zhidu luoji" 权威体制与有效治理：当代中国国家治理的制度逻辑. *Kaifang shidai* 开放时代. 2011.10: 67–85.

Zhou Xueguang 周雪光. *Zuzhi shehuixue shijiang* 组织社会学十讲. Beijing: Shehui kexue wenxian chubanshe, 2003.

Zhou Yue 周越 (Adam Chau). "Zhongguo minjian zongjiao fuwu de jiahu zhidu" 中国民间宗教服务的家户制度. Translated by Zhang Xixiang 张细香. *Xuehai* 学海. 2010.3: 44–56.

Zhu Haibin 朱海滨. "Minjian xinyang—Zhongguo zui zhongyao de zongjiao chuantong" 民间信仰—中国最重要的宗教传统. *Jianghan luntan* 江汉论坛, 2009.3: 68–74.

Zimmerman-Liu, Tereza, and Teresa Wright. "What Is in a Name? A Comparison of Being Branded a Religious Cult in the United States and the People's Republic of China: Witness Lee and the Local Churches." *Journal of Church and State* 60.2 (2018): 187–207.

Zrinščak, Siniša. Review of *Religion in China: Survival and Revival under Communist Rule*, by Fenggang Yang. *Religion and Society in Central and Eastern Europe* 6.1 (2013): 75–77.

Index

Abortion 10, 281, 289–97
Acts of Faith 36, 60, 208, 216, 323–24, 328–29, 331, 334, 339–41
America, American (US) 1, 12, 37, 93, 142–43, 150–51, 200, 219, 239, 243, 282, 295, 305–6, 315, 323–25, 330, 332, 336–37, 339, 347
ancestors 178, 198, 224, 228
Anhui 30, 140, 149, 239, 242, 244, 296
Assembly Hall Church(es). *See* Local Church
atheism/atheist 19, 21, 24, 61, 80–81, 157, 214, 216, 230, 232–33, 326, 333, 335, 338, 340–41

Bai 197
baptize/baptism 29, 39, 142, 148, 166–68, 170, 172–73, 177, 179, 264, 271–72, 282, 284
Beijing 9–10, 64, 66, 82, 89, 93, 113, 156–57, 238–57, 260, 262, 265, 276, 281–84, 286, 289–90, 292, 295–97, 338, 343
Bible 19, 22, 28, 42, 44–45, 47–48, 52–53, 56, 144, 155, 165, 167, 169, 170–72, 176–77, 193, 198, 202, 267, 286, 290, 294, 297, 305, 307–8, 314–15
black (market) 1, 3–8, 11, 35, 37–38, 41–42, 47, 50, 54–55, 57–58, 61–62, 67–69, 75–77, 183–86, 190–91, 193, 196–98, 211, 308–9, 317, 325, 329–31, 342, 344–45. *See also* gray (market); red (market); religious market(s); tricolor market
Black Dragon King 80, 99, 104, 107–8
Bodhisattva 101, 102, 104–5, 108
Buddhism 2, 7, 12, 19, 90, 101–2, 108–9, 114, 120, 145, 147, 164, 164n1, 176, 184, 197, 324n8, 343

Caishen (God of Wealth) 7, 100–6, 108–9, 112–113, 343
  Caishen Ya 100–114
Catholicism 2, 11–12, 25, 41, 63n9, 80, 112, 197, 323, 341
Chen Yun 25
China Christian Council (CCC) 7, 21, 62, 64, 69, 71–74, 147, 193, 196
China Inland Mission (CIM) 63, 69

Chinese Communist Party (CCP) 2, 4, 11, 12, 17, 20–26, 31, 39, 61, 80, 86–7, 93, 102, 114, 340. *See also* party-state
Christianity 2, 3, 6–8, 11–12, 17, 25, 27–28, 30–31, 35, 38–39, 48, 62n9, 80–82, 84–87, 91–92, 94, 96, 119–21, 124, 136–43, 145, 145n27, 152, 155, 160, 170, 173, 183–88, 190–203, 238, 244, 253–54, 264–66, 275, 278, 299–300, 307, 315, 332, 335, 338–42, 347
Christmas 31, 69, 120, 154, 178, 188, 265
Church of Almighty God (*Quanneng shen*; CAG, Eastern Lightning) 6, 19, 41–42, 50–51, 54–58, 66, 70, 113, 342
church-state (relations) 8, 21–22, 25, 32, 35, 49–50, 56–57, 62, 80–81, 86, 158–59, 177, 185–86, 190, 238, 342
civil society 35, 110–11, 113–14, 151, 301, 312, 319–20
Confucianism 19, 176
cross(es) 31, 44, 52, 122, 128, 146, 165, 262, 292, 307, 341
cults 4, 6, 35–36, 38–41, 49–51, 53–58, 69, 76, 155, 186, 198–99, 202, 232, 340, 342, 344. *See also* sects
Cultural Revolution 2, 21, 24, 64, 69, 71, 102, 138, 143, 167, 220, 232, 244, 341

Dai 184
Daoism/Daoist 2, 7, 9, 12, 99, 101–102, 103n8, 108–9, 114, 120, 122, 145, 207, 207n2, 213–14, 220–21, 226–28, 230, 343
Daoshi. *See* Daoist
deacon(s)/deaconess(es) 22–23, 43, 52–53, 240
Deng Xiaoping 23, 23n14, 25
Derung 84
Document No. 19 2, 22
Donations 23, 50, 52–53, 56–57, 65, 73, 102–6, 113, 167, 169–172, 177, 190, 196, 209, 239, 305–7, 312–13

Early Rain Church 180, 295, 305, 308
Easter 154, 188
Eastern Lightning. *See* Church of Almighty God

elder(s)   20–21, 23, 27–29, 144, 188, 190, 196
Established King   38
Europe   12, 25, 139n7, 324, 332, 336–37

Falun Gong   4, 19, 55, 58, 113, 335–336, 340
fengshui   8, 100, 112, 122–26, 128–30
fertility   8, 10, 280–291, 294, 296–97
Finke, Roger   1, 36–38, 60, 174, 209–11, 213–18, 323, 324n8, 334–35
folk religion   3, 7, 12, 38, 85, 90, 94, 99–104, 106–114, 119–131, 133–37, 147, 164n1, 214, 218, 227, 229, 232–33, 238, 280, 296, 333, 343, 345–46
Fujian   23, 141n10
funeral   190, 192, 194–95, 207, 222–23, 223n34, 226

God   10, 23, 28, 39–40, 43–49, 51–54, 65, 123, 144, 153, 157, 168–70, 169n6, 178–80, 185, 197–98, 286–87, 290, 292–94, 307–8, 315, 338
God of Wealth. *See* Caishen
"Grace to the City"   147–48, 150
gray (market)   1, 3–8, 10–11, 17, 35, 37–38, 47, 50, 55, 57–58, 61–62, 64–65, 67–68, 70, 72, 74–77, 107–8, 112–13, 184, 186, 191, 197–98, 211, 220, 244, 300, 308–9, 317, 319–20, 325, 329–31, 333, 341, 342–46. *See also* black (market); red (market); religious market(s); tricolor market
Gu, Pastor Joseph   31
Guangdong   9, 91–92, 207, 219–220, 224, 227, 241
Guanyin   101–2, 104–6, 109
Guizhou   84–85, 296

Han   80–82, 183–84
Hangzhou   31
Hani   8, 183–85, 189, 191–92, 195, 197–98, 200, 342
Henan   6, 22, 28, 39, 69–70, 140, 149, 177, 242, 244, 246–47, 256, 264–65
Holy Spirit   29, 47
Hong Kong   5, 144, 150–51, 154–55
house church(es) (unregistered churches)   2–4, 6–10, 17, 19–20, 24, 28, 55, 62–65, 67–69, 72, 74–77, 95, 138–41, 143, 145, 147–48, 150–51, 153–61, 166, 172, 176, 180, 243, 281–82, 289, 291, 295, 297, 300, 309, 316, 338, 341, 343–44
Hu Jintao   62
Hubei   29, 39
Huhan pai. See Shouters
Hunan   41, 42n, 46, 53, 84–85

Inner Mongolia   41n11, 265
Islam/Muslim   2, 12, 287, 340–41, 347

Jesus   41n11, 45, 138, 146, 149, 153, 161, 170, 178, 187–88, 244, 275, 286, 292, 307, 314, 335
Jesus Family   142
Ji Sanbao   38–40, 48
Jiang Zemin   25–26, 86
Jiangsu   8, 29, 138, 140–43, 145, 145n27, 147, 160, 164, 244, 343

Korea/Korean   5, 201, 265, 275–76, 328, 346
kowtow   178, 195
Kunming   80, 82n5, 83, 83n8, 85n13, 89, 91–93, 188

Lahu   84
Laozi   48, 313
Leizu   101–2, 109, 113
Li Xianting   262–63, 271
Lingling Sect   38
Lisu   84, 87, 199
Local Church (*Zhaohui*, also called Assembly Hall)   4, 39, 142, 144
Lord God Sect   38

mainland China   5, 38, 150, 154, 302, 311, 315, 339
Marxism/Marxist   336, 338
megagroup   10, 299, 301, 309–16, 318–19
Miao   7, 80–96, 199, 343
Miao choir. *See* Mountain-Dweller Chorus
miracle(s)   28, 38, 40, 45–47, 56, 101, 103–4, 113, 121, 123, 139, 184
Mentuhui (Society of Disciples)   6, 11, 35, 38–45, 47–58, 342
Mountain-Dweller Chorus   88–91, 95

Nanjing   8, 71, 144n21, 164–67, 171, 178, 181n, 343
Nanjing Theological Seminary   71

New Year (Spring Festival)   42, 93, 105, 177–78
Nu   197

oligopoly   325, 327, 345
orientalism   80, 96, 338
overseas Chinese   27, 149, 315

party secretary   86, 132, 134, 263
party-state   2, 6, 9, 11, 17, 21–22, 25–26, 31, 63, 330, 333, 342–44, 347
pastor   23, 27, 29, 31, 47, 52, 64, 67, 70–71, 74–75, 139, 143–45, 148–51, 158, 165, 167, 169–70, 172, 179, 181, 198, 202, 240, 247, 250, 254–55, 256n25, 257, 267, 273, 278, 282, 295, 297, 305, 309, 311
patriotic association   2, 4, 18, 24, 27, 61, 64, 77
Pentecostal   74–75, 177, 253–54, 257
People's Republic of China (PRC)   2, 67, 80, 88, 224, 229, 232, 288, 303
Political Consultative Conference   81, 88–90, 94
pray/prayer   23, 40, 43–47, 49–50, 53–54, 86, 123, 158, 165, 167–70, 176–77, 223, 244, 282, 292, 316
Presbyterian   142–43, 150–51
priest. *See* Daoist priest
Protestant   2, 4, 6, 8–12, 20–21, 24, 30, 35, 38, 45, 50, 62n9, 69, 80, 120, 142, 151, 164, 164n1, 197, 199, 238, 243–44, 253, 253n18, 260, 264–65, 267, 271, 300, 323, 341–42
Public Security Bureau   21, 25, 144, 149

Qing (dynasty)   19, 102, 112
qigong   3–4, 61

rational choice   60, 209–10, 213, 323, 332, 334
red (market)   1–6, 8, 11, 17, 37, 55, 61–62, 65, 68–69, 72, 74–76, 107–8, 114, 183–84, 186, 191, 193–97, 211, 308–9, 325, 329–30, 342–45. *See also* black (market); gray (market); religious market(s); tricolor market
reform (and opening policies/era)   2, 17, 23–27, 35, 37, 63–64, 69–70, 80, 87, 138, 151, 160, 216, 218, 220–21, 227, 229, 238, 240, 242–43, 255, 327, 341
Reformed (theology)   149–51

Regulations on Religious Affairs   2, 11, 47, 134, 180, 299, 308–9, 316
Religious Affairs Bureau (RAB)   11–12, 21–23, 25, 29–30, 54, 68, 73, 75–77, 85n12, 149, 156, 188, 330, 343
religious economy/market   1–7, 9–11, 35–38, 41, 50, 55, 60–63, 68, 75–76, 80, 107, 113, 174, 183, 191, 197, 201–2, 207–20, 233–34, 244, 300, 308, 317, 322, 325, 327, 329–30, 332–39, 341, 343–47. *See also* black (market); gray (market); red (market); tricolor market
Republic of China   80
Republican era   19
ritual(s)   9, 42, 44, 56, 81, 102, 108, 121, 166, 189, 195, 207–8, 213–18, 219n, 220–33, 240, 344
rule of law   132, 136, 140, 156–57, 173, 201

sect   2, 4, 6, 11, 19, 35–39, 41, 45, 50, 56, 58, 69, 174, 176, 178, 208n2, 342, 344. *See also* cults
secularization   6, 19, 212, 215, 217, 219, 226, 229–30, 233, 326, 336
Shaanxi   39, 48, 81, 108, 289, 296
Shandong   242, 244
Shanxi   6, 63, 67
shortage economy   323–25, 332, 343
Shouters (*Huhan pai*)   4, 39, 69
Shouwang Church   113, 250, 256n25
Sichuan   7, 46, 85, 100, 103–4, 108, 144n21, 196, 296, 324n7, 343
Smith, Adam   208–9, 213
social scientific study of religion   12, 324, 328–29, 340, 345, 347
Society of Disciples. *See* Mentuhui
sociology of religion   36, 323–24, 326–28, 332–33, 336
Songzhuang (artist village)   260–72, 274–78
Spring Festival. *See* New Year
Stark, Rodney   1, 36–38, 60, 139, 139n7, 174, 209–11, 213–18, 323, 328, 330, 332, 334–35, 337
State Administration of Religious Affairs (SARA)   26, 91
State Council   2, 26, 39, 309, 316
Sunday school   148, 156, 165, 167–69, 171
Sung, John (Song Shangjie)   139, 167

superstition   7, 40, 102, 107, 109, 129, 178, 185, 188, 198, 227, 232–33

Taiwan   37, 43, 58, 149, 151, 335
temples   3–4, 7, 61, 90, 99–109, 111–14, 120, 129–30, 133–34, 145, 147, 168, 207, 209, 212, 223–224, 227–28, 323, 343–45
    temple fair   99, 101, 103–8, 111, 113
Three Grades of Servant   38
"Three Rectifications and One Demolition" campaign   31
Three-Self Patriotic Movement (TSPM)/ Three-Self church(es)   6–7, 17–18, 20–21, 24, 28–30, 32, 42, 45, 47, 50, 52–53, 55–57, 62, 64, 68–76, 138–39, 139n4, 141n14, 143–45, 147, 154, 156–7, 159, 167, 169, 177, 186, 193, 196, 198, 201, 243–44, 265–66, 271, 295, 297, 342
Thrice Redeemed Christ (*Sanshu jidu*)   42, 44, 48
Tiananmen Square (massacre, incident)   12, 25, 166
Tibetan   19, 197
Torch Festival   88
Tricolor market (theory)   1–3, 5, 7, 10, 35, 38, 41, 55, 61–63, 68, 75–76, 80, 107, 183, 300, 308, 325–26, 330–34, 340–41, 344–46. *See also* black (market); gray (market); red (market); religious market(s)
True Jesus Church (TJC)   6, 11, 20–22, 28–30, 39, 342
Tudigong   99, 101, 104

United Front Work Department   12, 21, 25, 26n19, 86
United States (US). *See* America
unregistered church(es). *See* house church(es)
urbanization   8–9, 74, 220, 238–45, 251, 253, 255–57, 260, 278, 343

Wang Yi   160, 303–8
WeChat   10, 281, 299–320, 343
wedding   190, 194, 223
West/Western   9, 21, 30–31, 48, 111, 138–39, 142, 151, 199–200, 212, 219, 233, 243, 314, 322, 324n8, 327, 329, 331, 335–36, 338

Xi Jinping   11–12, 30, 87, 299, 331, 340, 344
xiejiao (evil cult)   4, 6, 342

Yang, Fenggang   1–3, 10, 35, 38, 60–61, 80, 107, 183, 186, 197, 201, 308, 317, 330–31, 333, 336–37, 339–41
Yanjing Theological Seminary   64
Yao   184
Yi   82, 88, 90–91, 184
Yiguandao   37–38, 43, 58, 335, 344
Yuanmingyuan   262, 270, 277
Yunnan   7–8, 80–89, 91–94, 148, 183–84, 194, 197, 199, 201, 342–43
Yunnan Ethnic Theme Park   7, 80–81, 83–86, 343
Yunnan Theological Seminary   83

Zhaohui. *See* Local Church
Zhejiang   7, 31, 119, 136–37, 141n11, 242, 343

Printed in the United States
by Baker & Taylor Publisher Services